SMILING DOWN THE LINE:
INFO-SERVICE WORK IN THE GLOBAL ECONOMY

Just as textile mills and automotive assembly plants have symbolized previous economic eras, the call centre stands as a potent reminder of the importance of information in contemporary economies. Bob Russell's *Smiling Down the Line* theorizes call-centre work as info-service employment and looks at the effects of ever-changing technologies on service work, its associated skills, and the ways in which it is managed. Russell also considers globalization and contemporary managerial practices as centres are outsourced to poorer countries such as India and as new forms of management are introduced, refined, or discarded.

Invoking extensive labour force surveys and interviews from Australia and India, Russell examines employee representation, work intensity, stress, emotional labour, and job skills in the call-centre work environment. The cross-national approach of *Smiling Down the Line* highlights the effects of globalization and scrutinizes the similarities and differences that exist in info-service work between different industries and in different countries.

BOB RUSSELL is an associate professor in the Department of Employment Relations at Griffith Business School, Griffith University.

Studies in Comparative Political Economy and Public Policy

Editors: MICHAEL HOWLETT, DAVID LAYCOCK, STEPHEN MCBRIDE, Simon Fraser University

Studies in Comparative Political Economy and Public Policy is designed to showcase innovative approaches to political economy and public policy from a comparative perspective. While originating in Canada, the series will provide attractive offerings to a wide international audience, featuring studies with local, subnational, cross-national, and international empirical bases and theoretical frameworks.

Editorial Advisory Board

For a list of books published in the series, see page 327.

BOB RUSSELL

Smiling Down the Line

Info-Service Work in the Global Economy

UNIVERSITY OF TORONTO PRESS
Toronto Buffalo London

© University of Toronto Press Incorporated 2009
Toronto Buffalo London
www.utppublishing.com
Printed in Canada

ISBN 978-1-4426-3994-2 (cloth)
ISBN 978-1-4426-0981-5 (paper)

∞

Printed on acid-free, 100% post-consumer recycled paper with
vegetable-based inks.

Library and Archives Canada Cataloguing in Publication

Russell, Bob, 1950–
Smiling down the line : info-service work in the global economy /
Bob Russell.

(Studies in comparative political economy and public policy)
Includes bibliographical references and index.
ISBN 978-1-4426-3994-2 (bound). – ISBN 978-1-4426-0981-5 (pbk.)

1. Call center agents – Employment.   2. Call center agents – Social
conditions.   3. Call centers – Management.   I. Title.   II. Series: Studies
in comparative political economy and public policy

HE 8788.R87 2009   331.2′041658812   C2009-902400-4

This book has been published with the help of a grant from the Canadian
Federation for the Humanities and Social Sciences, through the Aid to
Scholarly Publications Program, using funds provided by the Social
Sciences and Humanities Research Council of Canada.

University of Toronto Press acknowledges the financial assistance to its
publishing program of the Canada Council for the Arts and the Ontario
Arts Council.

University of Toronto Press acknowledges the financial support for its
publishing activities of the Government of Canada through the Book
Publishing Industry Development Program (BPIDP).

For Ariana and Kendra

Contents

Tables and Figures

Figures

Abbreviations

ACD	automated call distribution technology
ACTU	Australian Council of Trade Unions
ATA	Australian Teleservices Association
AWA	Australian Workplace Agreement (individual employment contract)
BPO	business process outsourcing (India)
CMS	customer management system (software)
CSR	customer service representative
HPWS	high-performance work system
HRD	human resource development
HRM	human resource management
ICTs	information and communication technologies
IVR	integrated voice-recognition technology
IT	information technology
ITeS	information technology–enabled services (India)
KPI	key performance indicator
KPO	knowledge process outsourcing (India)
LDC	less developed country
MNC	multinational corporation
QCU	Queensland Council of Unions

Acknowledgments

In many ways this book is a trinational effort, perhaps befitting the age of globalization. Funding for the research it is based on was provided by the Australian Research Council, the Queensland Council of Unions, the Australian Services Union (Clerical and Administrative Branch), the Community and Public Sector Union, the Finance Sector Union of Australia, and the Queensland Public Sector Union. Behind these organizations and making the decisions to support the research on call centres that eventuated in the book were Grace Grace, Chris Barrett, Julie Bignell, Michael Clifford, Bill Marklew, and Alex Scott. The backing of these organizations allowed me to employ three wonderful research assistants over the course of the project: Chris Houghton, Karin Behrens, and Liz Todhunter. Their commitment, assistance, and good humour in lining up case study organizations, inputting data, and helping prepare the bibliography is gratefully acknowledged. The faculty at the Griffith Business School generously granted a teaching load reduction, which allowed me to finish writing this book, which has already taken too long to finish. Lastly, a research grant from Griffith University's Service Industry Research Centre was instrumental in supporting field research and data collection in India, the second country involved in the project.

Research in India would not have been possible without the assistance and collaboration of my colleague Dr Mohan Thite. Mohan generously provided access to his extensive network in India, which included managers of outsourcing firms and HR practitioners who were ultimately responsible for granting access to the Indian case-study companies that are reported on in chapter 7 of the book.

The book most likely would not have been a book without the support of colleagues and funding bodies in Canada. This book has been published with the help of a grant from the Canadian Federation for the Humanities and Social Sciences, through the Aid to Scholarly Publications Program, using funds provided by the Social Sciences and Humanities Research Council of Canada. Ron Carlson of the Communications, Energy, and Paperworkers Union of Canada provided me with my very first introduction to call centres. As always, it has been a positive experience working with Virgil Duff of the University of Toronto Press and with Daniel Quinlan of the Press. I would also like to thank the two anonymous external readers who vetted the original manuscript and made numerous helpful suggestions, as did the reader for UTP's manuscript review committee. Such support often goes unacknowledged in academic life as 'invisible work,' so let me take the opportunity here to thank these three readers. On the production side, I want to acknowledge the thorough and good-natured assistance of Wayne Herrington and Matthew Kudelka. This is a better book owing to the time and effort that each of these individuals has put into it.

The book is dedicated to my daughters, Ariana and Kendra, both of whom are now young adults. Together they and my partner, Vija, have shown a willingness to accompany me and fully participate in life's journeys no matter where they have quite literally taken us. My deepest hopes rest with the ability of my generation to leave these wonderful people with at least as decent a world as Jessie and Stewart and George and Betty bequeathed to me.

SMILING DOWN THE LINE:
INFO-SERVICE WORK IN THE GLOBAL ECONOMY

1 New Workplaces: The Call Centre

1.1 Introduction

Sociological interest in the unsolicited telephone call of the telemarketer begins not with the fact of the call or the volume of such calls in today's world, but with the observation that our usual indifference to the product or service being offered is matched by curiosity, unease, concern, or even anger with the origins of the interaction itself. How was my name selected? Where was information about me obtained? Has it been sold without my knowledge? Where is the caller calling from: another city, state, country, or perhaps continent?

Reversing the situation does not necessarily reduce the social actor's uncertainty. The author can recall the first time he tried to book a local reservation and had his call answered in another country – a mere cross-border Canadian–American experience. The futility of trying to make polite 'small talk' during the transaction or to get basic information on the nearby hotel and city that I would be visiting quickly became apparent. The transaction eventually worked, the reservation made, but the process was vaguely unsatisfactory. In such situations one is left wondering: Will my inquiry be responded to by someone who works for the organization I am calling and dealing with? Will they be knowledgeable with the products or services I am trying to access or with my needs? Will they be familiar with my culture?

In this book I want to problematize these everyday events from the perspective of their production. Thirty years ago such interactions were not possible. Today, using information and communication technologies (basically telephones, personal computers, fibre-optic lines, and digital switching devices that link everything together), we now connect with others through a variety of media with amazing ease, practically anywhere, anytime. Mostly these encounters occur between individual social actors – citizens, consumers, beneficiaries – and organizations – businesses, governments, charities, and so on. We take them for granted, yet despite their inexpensiveness and efficiency we are still troubled by them. Why is this the case? Throughout this book I will attempt to answer this question.

The title I have selected for the book is intended to convey some of these ambiguities. In strictly literal terms the notion of smiling down a telephone line has no meaning whatsoever. Yet this is what people who work in customer contact centres are exhorted to do every day. The idea of smiling down a line in this sense refers not only to producing and maintaining an acceptable level of service – a problematic concept if ever there was one – but also to taking up a labour that produces feelings in others across distance and in the absence of physical co-presence, conditions that are quite dissimilar to those that formed the basis of the theory of emotional labour (Hochschild 1983).[1] These expectations are nicely captured by what two other observers refer to as the creation of 'quality time' through the production of the 'beautiful call' (Alferoff and Knights 2002). Distance and the non-materiality of such work render its management by others problematical and uncertain, and it is precisely these ambiguities that are explored in this book.

Another reading of our title could lay greater emphasis on 'the line,' as in a production line. Indeed, one of the first published pieces of academic research on the new labour process of the call centre referred to 'an assembly line in the head' (Taylor and Bain 1999) to characterize its object of analysis. We will have ample opportunity to return to this discussion in later chapters, but for now we can ask how it might be possible to conceptualize non-material interactive service labour as if it were being conducted on an assembly line. How could such work be subject to the dictates of scientific management or what is widely known as Taylorism? If it *were* subject to those dictates, what would workers have to smile about? What possible aesthetic qualities could be left in such work?

The second part of the book's title, with its reference to info-service labour, extends these questions further. It alludes both to the informational aspects of contact-centre work and to the servicing function that workers in call centres perform. The informational aspects suggest skill: working with information, analysing data, and resolving problems for people. The servicing function suggests servitude: servicing the needs of others as part of making a living. Moreover, as indicated in the title, this work is now done everywhere. It is performed by workers in rich and poor countries alike, mainly for the citizens and customers of the wealthiest economies. This lends aspects of such work a servitude relationship, but it is also altering the old international division of labour in which different kinds of economic activity are undertaken in different ways in different zones of the world economy. In short, the title is intended to problematize these different aspects of long-distance service production in an increasingly globalized information economy. How is it possible to manage the different elements that enter into info-service work? How is control exercised over such work when it is conducted from greater and greater distances after it has been outsourced and offshored? Is the work that is done in different places in the global economy converging? Or is a new 'international' division of labour for the information age taking shape? How are workers responding to these changes?

In the first instance, then, this book is about the growing legions of workers who are employed in what, throughout the remainder of the text, I will term info-service jobs. This refers to employment that uses information to create information and that is undertaken as a service for a 'public' from a centralized worksite such as a contact centre. There are several reasons for undertaking a project of this sort. Call, contact, and 'customer care' centres have become the most important means of providing information services to publics in the developed economies. The clearest evidence of this is the sheer numbers of people employed in such workplaces and the volume of commerce thereby transacted. To give only one indication, more people are now employed in Australian call centres than in each of the following industries: mining; textiles, apparel, and footwear manufacturing; printing, publishing, and media production; food and beverage manufacturing; and, finally, metal fabrication, including automotive production (Russell 2006b).

National estimates of employment in contact centres vary; they are rough and thus only indicative rather than definitive. Nevertheless, available approximations do provide some idea of the sheer numerical importance that info-service employment has come to assume. It has been estimated that around 2005, four million Americans were working as customer service representatives (CSRs) (Holman, Batt, and Holtgrewe 2007, App. B; see also Bain and Taylor 2002a), while in Canada, call centres employ more than half a million workers (Van Jaarsveld, Frost, and Walker 2007; see also Buchanan and Koch-Schulte 2000 for earlier estimates). In the United Kingdom it is thought that around 800,000 workers staff contact centres (Bain and Taylor 2002a; Holman, Batt, and Holtgrewe 2007, App. B); it is estimated that at least 276,000 Germans, and perhaps more than 400,000, work in call centres (Arzbacher et al. 2002; Bittner et al. 2002; Holman, Batt, and Holtgrewe 2007, App. B). Australian estimates are in keeping with these figures: it has been estimated that in 2003 some 220,000 Australians were employed as CSRs (Budde 2004), and that currently just over 250,000 are (Callcentres.net 2008b). Meanwhile, the same type of employment is expanding very rapidly in several less developed economies (LDCs), the prime example being India, where remote service provision has encouraged the rise of an export-services-led model of development (Thite and Russell 2007). On the Subcontinent, info-service employment has catapulted from around 171,000 jobs in 2002 to an estimated 545,000 in 2007, in the process rivalling the number of jobs provided by the IT sector (Nasscom 2007b; Government of India 2003, Fig. 3.4; KPMG 2004).[2] Growth in info-service employment has also been rapid in other LDCs, where competition to service overseas markets has become fierce. For example, there were an estimated 112,000 workers in the Philippines in 2005; that number has since grown to 167,000 (Ofreneo, Ng, and Marasigan-Pasumbal 2007; callcentres.net 2008a). Also, call centres employ 100,000 workers in South Africa (Benner 2005; Holman, Batt, and Holtgrewe 2007) and about 42,500 in Malaysia (callcentres.net 2008a).

Employment levels are only one indicator of the growing significance of info-service work. Computer-mediated voice-to-voice interaction is now the dominant form of information generation and distribution in the developed market economies. For example, it is estimated that in 2003 in Australia, 75 per cent of all customer contacts occurred through call centres (Budde 2004). Mirroring these trends is one large urban government centre that is included in this study. This facility is the public face for a large metropolitan government and is equipped to respond to inquiries through a variety of media. In this instance, 76.6 per cent of all contacts with the public are conducted through its customer-contact centre (1.7 million calls per year), 22.5 per cent take place through face-to-face encounters at suburban 'storefront' locations, and a mere 0.8 per cent are handled through e-mail exchanges. Staying in Australia, industry-based research finds that direct voice-to-voice interactions between CSRs in call centres and members of the public have declined from 79 to 70 per cent of all exchanges conducted through call centres in the two-year period between 2001 and 2003, though partially and fully automated interactions through integrated voice- and speech-recognition technologies have increased. Other familiar forms of communication are also declining in their utilization rates: faxes are down by 40 per cent, to 3.2 per cent of total communication transactions, and letters are down by 27 per cent, to a mere 1.6 per cent of all communications processed through contact centres. On the other hand, e-mail has increased by 83 per cent to 7.7 per cent of all communications, and Web inquiries have increased by 175 per cent to 4.4 per cent of all contact centre activity (ibid.).

Such figures vary from sector to sector of the economy. In some instances, call-centre traffic, and consequently employment, has already reached its peak and is now trending downward as self-service through the Internet gains in popularity. This is particularly the case in relatively straightforward transactions such as the booking of online reservations. Whether by offering discounts for self-service or by applying a service charge for using a live agent, firms may encourage Internet self-service. In other fields, such as certain areas of the public service, the establishment of a call centre may increase familiarity with and uptake of the service. In these instances, call-centre employment is still expanding. Overall, the growth of employment in customer-service centres has been spectacular, and this provides one justification for studying these new workplaces. Here, we can consider the call centre an object of analysis sui generis, treating it as a new socio-technical system for the production and delivery of information – a system that is worth studying on its own account.

The sheer numerical significance of call-centre info-service employment is impressive in its own right, but apart from the statistics on job creation, the call centre presents a site from which to study a host of other matters pertaining to the contemporary world of work. In this sense we can also treat the call centre as a *metaphor* for changes in the type of work that is performed and the ways in which it is done. In other words, the call centre can be used as a lens through which to explore larger theoretical issues in much the same way that textile mills and (later) automotive plants were used to analyse changes in the ways work was organized in previous economic eras (see, for example, Silver 2003). As an organizational design for the production and delivery of information, the contact centre stands as a useful platform from which to study recent developments in work and employment, and it is with this purpose in mind that this volume has been undertaken.

Three issues in particular merit our attention: the effects of information and communication technologies (ICTs) on work; the seeming ease with which info-service work is being globalized; and the use of new managerial paradigms, including human resource management (HRM), that focus more strongly on organizational culture and non-union forms of representation as the preferred approach to managing workers in an information-oriented economy. Changes in how work is done, where it is performed, and how it is managed are having an immense impact on economies and on workers. Call centres are work-sites where the developments outlined above have come together very quickly. These centres serve as opportune research sites from which to study the singular and interdependent effects of these shifts. Figure 1.1 provides a focus for the relationships of interest. The diagram gives a synopsis of the route that is taken in the remainder of the book. The analysis to follow unfolds against changes in the technical and social divisions of labour that are enabled by changing modes of managerial practice. In the remainder of this chapter we take a first cut at explicating these trends, drawing attention to the ways in which a study of work in info-service centres can help us understand what is involved. Subsequent chapters of the book strive to ferret out the effects of these changes on employment in greater detail.

1.2 The Three Changes

1.2.1 ICTs and the Technical Division of Labour

Clearly, part of the fascination with call centres lies in the battery of new technologies they employ and in the effects these new tools are imputed to have on work and workers. Call-centre work has been iden-tified with the centrality of ICTs in the work process – that is, with a technological marriage of modern digital switching equipment, fibre-optic cable, software development, and the personal computer that allows requests for information to be sorted, queued, delivered, and acted on by waiting workers (Russell 2007; Taylor and Bain 1999). In addition to the automated call-distribution systems, which are taken as the hallmark identifying feature of call centres, 'drop down' call tech-nology that obviates the need to 'pick the phone up' to receive calls is now commonplace. Newer-generation technologies such as integrated voice-recognition systems provide callers with computer-generated op-tions to progress their inquiries, while natural-speech-recognition soft-ware whereby callers communicate directly with computers without

Figure 1.1: Contact centres: Influences and intersections

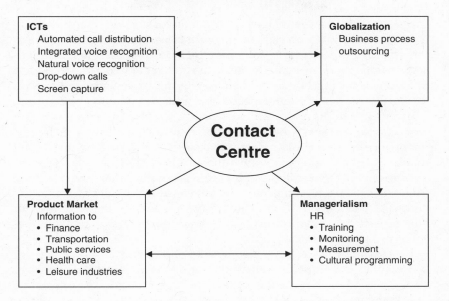

the intermediation of workers is making an appearance in some work flows.[3] Also of note is the adoption of 'screen capture' systems in some workplaces. This technology provides supervisors with the power to review the navigational processes workers enact on their computers either in real time or as part of performance reviews.

A study of contact-centre workers also provides an opportunity to advance the analysis of ICT use and its effects on work design, management controls, and skill levels. The workers who constitute the subjects of this study rely on ICTs every step of the way in their jobs. Automated call-distribution systems route incoming calls to available workers; 'drop down' technologies can be used to automatically select the next available worker. Integrated voice-recognition technologies may further stream calls into designated queues destined for specific functional teams, thereby allowing for myriad work configurations. Outbound calls may make use of predictive dialling technologies that interact with 'pop-up' screen displays, bringing the potential customer's details to light as the number is being connected. Digital switching may be used to seamlessly blend calls and transfer workers back and forth between inbound customer service and outbound telemarketing functions as determined by overall incoming call volumes at each particular moment.

In each instance, digital telephony is networked with computer systems that store data on people and processes. Workers utilize one or more software packages, which may include customer- and relationship-management systems as well as information on the products and services being offered and the operating procedures to be used. In short, ICTs constitute the means of production in info-service work, and contact centres are saturated with such tools. The ways in which workers use and serve these technologies and the ability of such tools to enhance or limit choices over the design of work will be the subject matter of later chapters, in which the effects of ICTs on responsibility, job variety, required skills, and the exercise of discretion are examined in detail. This exercise has obvious relevance for the debates over the emerging economy and whether we are witnessing the formation of new semi-professional cadres of information workers or a new white-collar proletariat.

Though the call centre is a comparatively new example of a work process that is completely reliant on the use of ICTs, researchers have struggled with analysing the impacts of such tools on work since the personal computer became a common workplace artefact some thirty years ago. For the purpose of entertaining a more general discussion on this topic and what it might have to offer the study of info-service work, it is instructive to begin our considerations with two ethnographies that describe the effects of ICT utilization. Both studies are anchored in continuous-process operations in manufacturing industries, where ICTs were first adopted. As we will see, it makes little difference that these descriptions come from a pulp-and-paper mill and a bakery respectively. Indeed, the main point that Shosana Zuboff (1988) is making in her study of paper-mill workers is that such work has been informationalized: ICTs have the power to 'informate' was well as automate work, and in many respects it is the former effect that is most significant. What are the implications of this?

According to Zuboff and a host of other researchers working out of a post-industrial theoretical paradigm (Castells 1996; Hirschhorn 1984), work processes that rely on ICTs as the principal means of production issue forth with not one but two joint outputs: the intended physical product, and information about the processes that occurred during its manufacture. Inspection and study of the latter can lead to ongoing process improvements, superior quality, and cost savings in a virtuous iterative cycle of diagnosis, action, and improvement. Should these latter functions also be incorporated into the operator's job, computerization opens up the possibility of moving beyond the automation of work with its associated deskilling tendencies (also see Kenney and Florida 1993). Working with ICTs makes possible the development of what Zuboff terms intellective skills, should managers wish to pursue this option. This refers to the ability to extract value from information – in this case, production-related data – and to connect it to the real, sensual world in novel ways. In the labour processes that Zuboff describes, the distinction between mental and manual labour is undone; 'mental imaging' becomes a critical component of even the manual operator's job. Physical effort and non-discursive tactile skills are displaced in favour of the development of new diagnostic and intellective skills such as familiarity with the principals of statistical process control (also see Smith 2001). Moreover, management appears ready to pay workers handsomely to use the new technologies (Adler 1986) – further evidence that jobs are being reskilled in the aforementioned manner.

These tendencies are often best described by the people who are living through them. According to one of Zuboff's process-operator informants: 'You need a new learning capability, because when you operate with the computer, you can't see what is happening. There is a difference in the mental and conceptual capabilities you need – you have to do things in your mind ... You have to know what is happening when something is wrong by being able to relate the data you see to the actual process as you can envision it' (Zuboff 1988, 71, 86).

It would be difficult to find a better lay definition of mental labour than the one contained in the above quote. Moreover, at least in some settings, the introduction of ICTs provides the user with a broader overview of the organization and what it does. ICTs permit intra-networking and offer workers portals through which they can oversee wider expanses of the operation. Employees are encouraged not only to focus on the firm's external relations with its buyers, but also to treat in-house relations as market relations – that is, peers are to be viewed as internal customers and accorded requisite levels of service (Hill 1991; Tuckman 1995). This can serve as the pretext for inviting the worker to identify with the needs of the business. In these scenarios, managerial control is traded off against the more efficient exploitation of the new technologies by those who use them. This may actually attenuate the distinction between managing and being managed as workers use ICTs to assume decision-making powers on behalf of the employing organization and as managers ascertain what the learning needs of the workforce aré in order to make optimum use of the new technology (Zuboff 1988, 301–2, 393, 401; see also Grey 1999). This vision could have profound implications for self-identity among workers and the political alignments that follow from it. In chapter 6, when we consider the question of identity in greater detail, we will examine the extent to which such organizational identities have been realized. In the meantime, 'while it is true that computer-based automation continues to displace the human body and its know-how … the informating power of the technology simultaneously creates pressure for a profound *reskilling'* (Zuboff 1988, 57).

Certainly many of these observations would appear apt with regard to the info-service work that forms the subject matter of this book. Often in such work there is no material output whatsoever. The CSR uses technology to interface with unseen clients. Information in the form of verbal cues and archived data is used to provide informational services to a variety of publics. Incoming requests cannot be completely foreseen in advance; there is an element of uncertainty around each job/interaction. Despite the use of standard operating procedures, info-service workers are often required to engage in 'repair work,' fixing things that have gone wrong between organizations and their publics. There is often little if any division of labour between the jobs that different workers do. Rather, CSRs are responsible for whole jobs from the beginning interaction of an inbound or outbound call to final resolutions. This means that workers must necessarily have an overview of the whole operation and are urged to identify with it, often in the guise of providing the levels of customer service they would expect if they themselves had placed the call (Korczynski 2002a).

Richard Sennett (1998) studied a similar group of continuous-process operators. However, he pushed the analysis back one step and reached starkly different conclusions. Conducting fieldwork in a highly automated bakery, he described what happened when one of the computerized baking machines broke down: 'Though simple to use, the dough-kneading machine was complex in design; its computer operating system was opaque … We sat for two hours waiting for the service saviors to arrive from the firm which had designed the machines … The waiting workers were morose and upset … The bakers felt this impulse to cope but were flummoxed by the technology' (1998, 72–3).

In this narrative, the workers are utterly dependent on the technology they *serve*. As with Zuboff's mill operators, physical contact with the production process has been displaced by the attentive monitoring of computer screens. But Sennett draws very different conclusions from those reached by Zuboff: 'Bread had become a screen representation. As a result of working in this way, the bakers now no longer actually know how to bake bread' (ibid., 68).

In Sennett's account, these dynamics have flow-on effects that are again just about the mirror opposite to those depicted by Zuboff. Owing to changes in the work process, occupational and organizational identification has become weak and tenuous. Role occupants no longer identify with an occupational community – they no longer define themselves as bakers. Turnover is high, seniority is low, and solidarity, be it directed towards fellow workers, the business, or the workers' union, is largely absent. In Sennett's words, 'identity as a worker is light' because intrinsic understanding of the work is low. In this world, even though opportunities for engaging in informational problem solving are present – 'the workers can fool with the screen to correct somewhat for … defects' – skills have become superficial, as has the whole experience of work (ibid.). Commitment to anything related to the world of work does not flow easily out of this scenario, but then neither does resistance. Indifference to all but personal satisficing behaviour is the operant motif in this analysis. Instead of continuous improvement, we are left with an overarching apathy, testified to by the enormous levels of wasted product that Sennett observes in the bakery's trash bins.

Again, the scenario painted by Sennett has possible relevance to the work situations described in this book. Staff turnover, absenteeism, and burnout have been identified as major challenges in call-centre work environments (Deery, Iverson, and Walsh 2002). Some researchers trace these problems back to rigidly structured target-driven operations in which workers are expected to adhere to highly standardized operating procedures, including sanctioned scripts and computer-generated algorithms. Like Sennett's bakers, CSRs may be depicted as serving the technologies they employ in a rote manner. Understanding of the technology, its capabilities, and its possible problem-solving uses remains superficial as workers are prevented from deviating from or experimenting with prescribed procedures.

The reason for juxtaposing the work of Sennett and Zuboff is not to come to some conclusion as to which analysis provides the more accurate portrayal of the effects of using ICTs in work. Each author has provided us with detailed and painstaking research. In each case the interpretations placed on the fieldwork are entirely believable. It would also be specious to suggest that something called *the truth* lies somewhere down the middle of the two analyses. Clearly both authors have presented accurate representations of what they saw and heard.

To the extent that important insights are contained in each of the above studies, it is possible to hypothesize the emergence of divergent and contradictory tendencies associated with ICTs. Zuboff and other post-industrial theorists point towards the *potential* of the new technologies to improve the experience of work by reintroducing problem-solving and decision-making attributes to it. Yet there is also the frequent admission that perennial hopes fail to materialize. In Zuboff's framework, work may be automated rather than informated: 'For many managers sharing information and maximizing opportunities for all members to become more knowledgeable is felt to be a kind of treason' (1988, 238 and passim).

Sennett for his part recognizes that work is being 'delayered' in what amounts to a reversal of the technical division of labour that Adam Smith first identified in the opening pages of the *Wealth of Nations:* 'The managerial overburdening of small work groups with many diverse tasks is a frequent feature of corporate reorganization – and contrary to the ever finer divisions of labor Adam Smith imagined in the pin factory. To make such experiments … requires immense powers of command' (1998, 55).

These opposing tendencies – bigger jobs imbibing more responsibility and greater managerial scrutiny or accountability to management – can be theorized as a *dual movement* that is exhibited in much contemporary work. The notion of a dual movement refers, on the one hand, to a fundamental reversal in the directions assumed by the division of labour in work, and on the other, to the growth of managerialism as a response to these very same shifts. Both these tendencies are manifested in the organization of info-service work in call centres. Changes in the movement of the technical division of labour and in the compensating growth of managerialism are depicted in Figure 1.1 by the two-way relationship portrayed between ICT use and managerial practice. The restructuring of work around ICTs provides a pretext for new forms of managerial oversight, which are partly made possible through the very same ICTs. In the remainder of this section we examine the modern technical division of labour in greater detail. Later in the chapter we return to the theme of contemporary managerialism.

Acknowledging the common distinction between the technical and the social division of labour, it has been commonplace from Adam Smith onward to depict finer subdivisions in both divisions of labour as industrialization progresses. In this representation the division of labour is subject to ongoing change, but always in a one direction. As far as the social division of labour goes, this entails the chopping up of occupational categories into finer and finer subcategories. As will be shown in chapter 3, occupational proliferation and gradation is a common feature of the social division of labour. Standard occupational-classification systems that have been devised and revised by national governments for the purpose of charting labour-market changes now list thousands of occupations as the social division of labour becomes ever more intricate. The social division of labour also includes a spatial element – that is, certain kinds of work have, in the past, been conducted in specific locales. The issues associated with this aspect of the social division of labour are taken up in the next section of this chapter.

Changes in the technical division of labour, which are of concern here, touch on the ways in which specific transformative labours are organized into jobs. Any given job is composed of different task elements, which, when taken together, determine the size, scope, complexity, and other characteristics of assigned work. From the dawn of management as a discursive practice, control has been equated with task simplification, a point formalized in the principles of scientific management as first laid out by Fredrick Taylor (1967; see also Braverman 1974). The significant point here is that the movement into informational labour is beginning to place into question at least some of the features associated with this depiction of the technical division of labour.

First, with respect to specific jobs, as both Sennett and Zuboff point out, working with ICTs has made possible the recombination of tasks into larger job bundles. In info-service work ICTs are deployed by labour to create and distribute information, which is the main output of the work process. Information is typically a joint product: it is produced on behalf of a public and provided as a commodity or public good as the case may be. But in the process of creating information *for* users, information *about* users is also often produced and is captured by the organizations that generate it for future reference. Commonly in such work, elements of both front- and back-office activity are combined into one job role. The incumbent both interacts with a public to produce and provide required information and also creates data as organizational archives for possible future analysis and use. In this case, instead of subdivision – where, for example, a receptionist might take the initial inquiry, pass it along to an investigator or software navigator for actioning, and then to a file clerk for archiving – we see recombination, where a CSR is responsible for each of the above actions. Other examples of the tendency to increase job span are found when workers are cross-trained to provide service in what were formerly distinct product markets. In the financial services sector this occurs when CSRs assume responsibility for service and sales in discrete areas such as insurance and home and car loans or when workers in government call centres respond to queries that were formerly resolved through separate departments and programs (see also Baran and Teegarden 1987). Again, when info-service work is outsourced to specialized firms, frequently CSRs take on duties that are associated with different clients and work flows simultaneously as part of the one job.

Superficially at least, larger jobs might be thought to require skill upgrading, but this assumes that all else is being held constant. Equally important are the counteracting tendencies to which task recombination gives rise. The perceived need for managing becomes ever greater as work becomes more complex. This is the other side of the *dual movement*, and it is expressed in the ethos of managerialism, which pervades so much of contemporary social life. Managerialism may have different emphases, depending on the nature of the work process at hand, but at bottom it represents an effort to render transparent the work methods that constitute the object of its practice. This may be done by prescribing in ever greater detail how work should be conducted and establishing ways of measuring conformance to such standards. Greater specification does not necessarily mean simplifying work, though it may; and as previously suggested, it tends no longer to occur through task fragmentation. Of course, as work becomes more involved – for example, when it contains an aesthetic element or requires 'smiling down the line,' as much info-service work does – such prescription is made more challenging. Moreover, insisting on conformity to an ideal may undermine those elements of the work that are especially valued by management (see Knights and McCabe 1997 and 2000 for an instructive example).

Alternatively, if work processes are more opaque and defy standardization, the managerialist impulse will be directed towards establishing systems of *documented accountability*. In this case, increasing amounts of time are taken up in documenting just what has been accomplished. In any case, as informational work becomes more complex, so does the practice of trying to manage it. The contemporary popularity and mystique of knowledge management is a discursive expression of this dynamic and perhaps of its futility. In short, as work is put back together again, or defragmented, concerns about the adequacy of documented processes and adherence to them are magnified. The nature of work moves in one direction of potential empowerment, while managerialism, as a statement on contemporary employment relations, moves in another. This is the contradiction that is summed up in the notion of a dual movement in current workplaces. It has helped spawn an interest in new managerial paradigms, including HRM, the last of the three changes introduced in this chapter. A study of contact centres and the work that CSRs do will provide a first-hand opportunity to put these arguments and their implications to the test.

Another manifestation of the current trend towards expanding the scope of work through the call centre can be detected when the product markets that workers are responsible for are examined. As indicated in Figure 1.1, info-service work is associated with a plethora of economic sectors and a multitude of products/services within each sector, and this brings us to a final point in this section. In essence, info-service work, the object of the analysis, is a common labour process that is now being applied to the production and delivery of informational services in a host of different industries. As indicated in the product market box, info-service work is a means of producing and distributing information utilized by a host of separate industries in different sectors of the economy. These activities are now undertaken using common technologies. Only when such work is outsourced to separate firms, as in the case of the Indian business process outsourcing (BPO) companies described in chapter 7, can an information industry *tout court* be accurately referred to. In the economies that first spawned the call centre, info-service activities are still usually supplied by in-house corporate departments across a variety of industries. The popularity of the call centre in a range of industry sectors suggests that an analysis of this labour process with its similarities and differences from one context to another is worthy of further attention.

1.2.2 Globalization and the Social Division of Labour

Not that long ago, a CEO from a large Indian company that specializes in providing information technology (IT) and info-service work to Western companies is reputed to have observed that any work that can be digitized and communicated via fibre-optic cable is capable of being outsourced. Overlooking the hyperbole, it is possible to agree that info-service work of the kind analysed in this book is a prime candidate for globalization. The movement of work around the globe to locations of convenience refers to another one of the large changes identified in Figure 1.1. Such spatial mobility entails shifts in the social division of labour – in particular, in what kinds of work are undertaken in which specific locations. Led by the outsourcing of production in standard commodities such as branded clothing and footwear in buyer-driven production chains (Dicken 2007; Gereffi 1994; Harvey 1989; Lipietz 1985, 1987), no matter of manufacturing process has proven to be immune from the opportunities presented by the exportation of production to locales that are very far away from intended markets. However, whereas the globalization of manufacturing has been an ongoing project first associated with tariff reduction and the deregulatory regimes that came to power in the 1980s (McBride 2005; Strange 1998; Weiss 1998), the globalization of info-service work is a more recent phenomenon that, as the employment numbers cited above indicate, has been proceeding at a very rapid pace.

For a long time the service sector was thought to be immune to the type of productivity gains witnessed in twentieth-century agricultural and manufacturing production (Brenner 2003; Greenbaum 1995). Limits to the mechanization of interactive information provision placed constraints on productivity increases as such undertakings often remained face to face or localized in facilities that were in close proximity to the markets they served. However, the centralization of info-service work in operations such as customer-contact centres has gone hand in hand with the adoption of new technologies that bring with them possibilities for tighter control over the queuing, distribution, and allotment of time dedicated to each job. In addition, the centralization of such work means that it can be undertaken at greater and greater distances from the markets being served. In other words, the centralization of info-service work has also opened up the possibility for its radical spatial dispersal. This spatial divorce between the production of services and the markets they are directed towards offers additional potential advantages to organizations that have spearheaded such developments. Remote info-service provision was first tried out in the financial-services sector (Bain and Taylor 2002b), with banks replacing local branch outlets with centralized customer-contact centres; other information-based providers have quickly followed suit.

Initially a spatial divorce between the production of info-services and the markets provided for was manifested in the locational decisions that were made when new call centres were established. This relative spatial freedom provided a powerful stimulus to further the economizing logic that underpinned the advent of call centres in the first place (Burgess and Connell 2004). Locational decisions could be taken on the basis of the savings that particular *national* locations had to offer in terms of rents, taxes, and (above all) wage norms (Arzbacher, Holtgrewe, and Kerst 2002; Bain and Taylor 2002b; Bittner et al. 2002; Bristow, Munday, and Gripaios 2000; Good and McFarland 2005; Richardson, Belt, and Marshall 2000; Richardson and Belt, 2001). Calculations of this sort accounted for the clustering of info-service providers, often in regional areas (northeastern England, Scotland, Ireland, New Brunswick, the U.S. Midwest) of above-average unemployment. The more recent sending of such work offshore to even more distant locations is simply an extension of the same cost-saving fundamentals (Friedman 2006; Srivastava and Theodore 2006) when naturally occurring comparative advantages are overtaken by managerially constructed competitive advantages.

The displacement of comparative advantage by strategies of competitive advantage lies at the heart of what is being termed globalization in this book. The former concept is central to the classical theory of trade as first advanced by Ricardo. According to this theory it is advantageous for all concerned if national economies exchange those goods and services in the production of which they enjoy the greatest comparative advantage over their neighbours. Such advantages come in the form of natural endowments, such as more fertile soils, mineral wealth, longer growing seasons, and so forth. This is a world of bilateral trading relationships in which the gifts of nature are leveraged into mutually advantageous trading relationships. Commodities circulate among national economies, but productive factors – including capital – are immobile on an international level.

This world is a far cry from the densely interlocked and networked global economic system of today, in which money capital is the most mobile of all elements and where advantages are neither accidental nor enjoyed – however unequally – by all. Competitive advantage refers to the practice of establishing units of production in those locations, wherever they may happen to be, that offer the greatest cost savings to producers. When it is relatively easy and cheap to move capital around the world, firms have the option of locating their operations in distant locations. In a globalized world the principal rationale for undertaking such moves is not to serve overseas markets but rather to diminish the costs of production on the world stage by bringing wages back into competition. Establishing production facilities in offshore locations in so-called captive units, or outsourcing work to overseas domestic producers for re-export, is the distinguishing feature of economic globalization. In the theory of comparative advantage, various national economies exchange various commodities with one another in a loose form of economic integration. According to the theory of competitive advantage that is being advanced here, different countries compete mainly on labour costs to produce the same commodities for a small number of large firms to be sold on the world market. Economic relationships involving firms producing the same goods and services in a number of different national locations for re-export represents a far thicker form of integration.

An analysis of info-service work and its conduct in globalized markets through the establishment of offshore contact centres sheds additional light on these dynamics. Such centres are the epitome of mobile installations – 'plug and pull' operations, as they are sometimes referred to. Even if this designation and the words of the Indian CEO with which we began this section are an exaggeration, the amazing mobility of info-service work as captured in its take-off in countries such as India, the Philippines, and other LDCs is beyond doubt. In the case of the labour processes being discussed here, the automated delivery of work to employees spread out across the world, and the continuous quantification of real-time results, equate to greater numbers of transactions at greatly reduced cost. Theoretically at least, productivity levels can be made invariant across different sites, while organizations can take advantage of huge wage differentials. As detailed in chapter 7, outsourcing is an activity that has increasing relevance for the production of such info-service products as customer-contact service, data mining, telemarketing, and health-care diagnostics, all of which are now subject to distant provision through the establishment of BPO facilities. In turn the globalization of such work has led to the promulgation of new fields of management, including quality assurance and risk and cross-cultural management, as well as to the rapid growth in an accreditation/certification industry (e.g., Six Sigma protocols).

If we know why and how globalization has come about, there are still huge debates about the consequences. Info-service work provides an excellent platform from which to study the emerging global division of labour further. Of particular interest here are the contours of the global division of labour that is being brought forward by the outsourcing of work to overseas locations and the economic and social repercussions that such activities are likely to have. Traditionalists suggest that current patterns are a repeat of well-worn cyclical trends. As labour in the most developed economies becomes comparatively more expensive, less-skilled work will be exported abroad, while more highly skilled and remunerated work will be retained 'onshore.' Alternatively it could be suggested that the developments being considered here have rendered this division of labour passé. Instead, similar kinds of work remunerated at vastly different levels are being done in a variety of locations around the globe. The study of info-service work provides a window through which we can study competing prognoses about the globalization of work and its effects on workers and the places they call home.

Apart from debates about the social division of labour, globalization, as it is commonly understood, has additional implications that are relevant to this study. Few analysts would dispute that globalization has added immeasurably to the contingency of modern employment (Bauman 1998; Beck 2000) while making commitment a seemingly unquestioned sine qua non of competitive performance (Boltanski and Chiapello 2007). As Guy Standing (1999) has observed, protection and security in the labour market were treated as reasonable costs in closed economies or when trading partners maintained similar standards of social welfare. However, once all types of employment from semi-skilled manufacturing to info-service work become subject to outsourcing, such presumptions no longer hold. When productivity is more or less standardized through the use of common technological suites across global space, relative labour costs become very decisive indeed. Under such conditions new competitive pressures are placed squarely on labour as national systems of regulation are expected to adapt to new global benchmarks of performance. Under these circumstances, jobs may come under the perennial threat of global relocation, and businesses may face bankruptcy in deregulated national markets if producers located elsewhere can supply at lower costs while still meeting their required margins.

The insecurity associated with globalization may contribute to a sense of dispossession in employment, as well as to greater vulnerability and contingency, as a number of ethnographies on deindustrialization have demonstrated (Dudley 1994; Milkman 1997; Nelson and Smith 1999). The sceptic may well wonder how a regime driven by employment arbitrage is expected to produce the enthusiastic and committed workforce that global competition is said to require. What do workers have to smile about when their jobs may be exported abroad with very short notice? Alternatively, what do workers in employment-receiving LDCs have to smile about knowing that their positions may be re-exported to even less expensive locations in the future or, indeed, re-established in the developed home countries from which they were sent should performance not be deemed satisfactory or should consumer resistance be greater than expected? This question brings us to the third item on our theoretical itinerary – namely, to changes in the way workers are managed in contemporary, information-driven workplaces.

1.2.3 Beyond Consent? Managerialism and Human Resource Management

The final component of the new employment relations to be considered in Figure 1.1 is the rise of human resource management (HRM) as a distinct discourse and discursive practice in employee management. Like the term globalization, HRM is a concept of recent vintage. Storey (2001) dates the rise of HRM from the early 1980s, when it began to displace the older notion of personnel administration. In its broadest sense, HRM is claimed to portray the employment relationship in a different light and in a different relationship to the other dimensions of successful business practice. That is, HRM is theorized as a more thoroughgoing, holistic set of discursive practices than the personnel-management function, which in its day was viewed as little more than a necessary bureaucratic feature of corporate life (Drucker 1954; Legge 1995; Storey 1992; Torrington 1989). In the parlance of HRM, given the mobility of capital and the possibilities for technological transfer in a rapidly globalizing world, employees ought to be viewed as the most important competitive asset the organization possesses. Technologies can be copied, leased, or otherwise appropriated, and capital can be raised on global financial markets; by contrast, commitment on the part of employees is an input that cannot be superficially replicated. Performance is best viewed as a strategic organizational issue rather than the concern of a specialized department/function. With these as starting assumptions, HRM casts itself in the role of a driver rather than a passive attribute of contemporary business strategy.

High and sustainable employee performance can only come about through the sort of commitment that constitutes the goal of successful HRM practice. Commitment in turn presumes goal alignment between the parties to the employment relation and integration with an overarching business strategy (Guest 1987). A thoughtfully constructed HRM system should be capable of fulfilling both the business needs of the organization and the personal aspirations of job holders, at least according to proponents of the paradigm (Peters and Waterman 1988; also for criticisms see Guest 1990; Legge 1995, 3). It has been suggested that efforts to instil internal coherence among various HRM programs and policies, and to align those programs and policies to the needs of other units in the organization, lent HRM a strategic quality that earlier management paradigms lacked. As conveyed in the images of 'best practice' and the currently fashionable 'high-performance work systems' approach (Appelbaum et al. 2000), HRM aims – in theory at least – at a holism that is directed at the worker and her performance.

For a number of reasons, call centres present an ideal terrain from which to launch a critical study of HRM and its impact on work. The advent of the call centre, and its technologies and work designs, coincide with the rise of HRM as an influential paradigm in the 1990s. As new workplaces, call centres afforded something of a blank slate on which the imprimatur of HRM could be stamped from the commencement of operations. Many if not most of the hallmarks of contemporary HRM will be found in the call centre, perhaps to a greater extent than is customary in older workplaces. It is unlikely that this is coincidental. Rather, HRM is advanced as a system of documented accountability that is well suited for managing workers in the context of intangible outputs and the absence of a highly detailed division of labour. In an era when customer service has become a mantra for the realization of competitive advantage, managers want to leave as little as possible to chance, and HRM presents itself as a means for managing people who are themselves responsible for managing organizational customers, clients, and publics. In other words, the project of HRM is about the construction of accountable selves who commit to organizational means and ends. Ideally, self-control or accountability on the part of workers supplants managerial control through other means and translates into high levels of organizational commitment, though HRM certainly retains an interest in ensuring the accountability of its charges.

Figure 1.1 displays the main practices associated with HRM. Contemporary managerialism is very much a cultural project; and the various elements of HRM are intended to lend support to the mission of the call centre, while simultaneously being constitutive of organizational culture – that is, those elements are meant to be a system of documented accountability in their own right. Common components of a strategic HRM system, which are analysed in greater detail later in the book, begin with recruitment, where multistage interviewing processes are advocated that may include telephone and in-person interviews, psychometric testing, and role-playing exercises (Iles 2001; Nankervis, Compton, and Baird 2005) and that are certainly widespread in the call-centre work environment (Callaghan and Thompson 2002; Thompson, Callaghan, and van den Broek 2004). This is followed by systematic induction and training, which typically lasts for weeks rather than days and which includes both classroom and on-the-job components with designated trainers (Houlihan 2000). Also typical is ongoing, continuous training, which is provided by dedicated training budgets and staff. This training is intended to develop generic skills, ranging from knowledge of Erlang queuing theory to cooperative working practices; these and other modules are incorporated into organizational curricula and are meant to foster a culture of lifelong learning. As detailed below, many call-centre managers view training budgets as a source of pride rather than angst.

The adoption of work teams as part of the organizational design of info-service work is frequently encountered (van den Broek 2002; van den Broek, Callaghan, and Thompson 2004). The availability of time for teams to involve themselves in problem solving and decision making over matters that directly affect them is also taken to be part of HRM best practice in call centres (Batt 2000). In theory, team involvement corresponds nicely with the existence of larger and more complex jobs and with the organizational belonging and commitment that HRM seeks to promote.[4] Work teams are also claimed to be more conducive for a style of management that is more effective in the context of info-service work – namely, one that emphasizes coaching, the setting of personal and group goals, and the provision of frequent feedback on performance (Frenkel et al. 1998, 1999) as part of the emphasis on creating accountable selves. Compensation systems that support the foregoing by recognizing and rewarding individual contributions to team and organizational goals are also considered part of enlightened HRM management generally (Sisson and Storey 2000, Table 2.1; Appelbaum et al. 2000; Pfeffer 1998; Pfeffer and Veiga 1999)[5] and in call centres specifically (Batt 2002).

It would be easy to treat contemporary HRM as something akin to a policy toolbox that blankets the employment relationship from recruitment through to reward and retention, and that holds out the promise of greater employee involvement and commitment to work. However, this would miss a key aspect of the new managerialism – the cultural one, which is displayed through specific aspects of HRM such as selection, training, recognition, and indeed cultural programming itself, and which is embedded in the underlying assumptions that inform HRM as a theoretical discourse. In this sense HRM is an intrinsic cultural practice as well as one that works explicitly on culture through the values and policies it enunciates and puts into place (Ezzamel and Willmott 1998; Willmott 1993). Besides grouping together a set of practices or social techniques that supposedly embody what the organization stands for, HRM is a belief system, a culture in its own right, one that targets organizational culture as of primary importance in the realization of its mission. Thus, besides *administering* the employment relationship through recruitment, training, remuneration, and so on, HRM is very much about operating on workplace culture in order to achieve the competitive alignments that are sought (Legge 1995, ch. 6). As such, HRM is not driven simply by the search for competitive advantage that underpins globalization. In undertaking such activities as the benchmarking of best practices, HRM also contributes actively to the phenomenon of globalization and to the diffusion of its culture and standards across worksites.

As a conscious cultural practice, HRM has a strong impact on hiring and selection (who gets hired, for what reasons, etc.) as well as on training/development and recognition/reward. Each of these activities emits signals as to which kinds of behaviours are valued by the organization. Additionally, as others have documented (Kinnie, Hutchinson, and Purcell 2000; Russell 2002b), call centres are rich in managerially sponsored cultural activities. Organized cultural events are a common feature of call-centre life (Alferoff and Knights 2001). These events range from activities that are immediately directed towards supporting performance, such as interteam competitions within the worksite, to more general morale-sustaining efforts, such as sponsored games, events, and theme days, to activities that include aspects of both, such as entry into state- and national-level contact-centre competitions. In Australia the ATA, and the national contact centre association and its state branches, sponsor annual events that hand out awards to, for example, the best new contact centre of the year, the best centre (by various size categories), and Agent of the Year. Entry into these 'black tie' galas is voluntary and is undertaken by individual call-centre managers. As chapter 6 details, info-service work is 'thick' with cultural initiatives, and contact-centre managers spend a good part of their time 'working on culture.'

At a more general level, in moving from compliance or even consent to working arrangements to organizational commitment, shared beliefs about the fairness and commonsense nature of means, including HRM, and overall objectives are a requirement. For this reason work practices need to be situated in a broader field of subjective understandings or meanings about working for a specific organization that make the requirements of a system of documented accountability seem normal and fair. The object here is to provide an interpretive framework, a lens, through which organizational history, working relationships, and organizational choices may be decoded by group members in ways that make ethno-methodological sense, simply as 'the way "we" do things around here.' As Schoenberger (1997) reminds us, culture is very much about the exercise of power, about the ability to have specific ways of defining and seeing accepted as legitimate (see also Kunda 1992). In turn, culture is a background datum for strategy formation.

Officially sanctioned cultures will try to influence commitment by operating on identity. HRM practices attempt to establish strong identity ties with the meanings, codes, norms, rituals, and values that constitute the official face of the organization (Bolman and Deal 2003; Schein 1985). This is particularly important in customer-focused info-service work, where identification with organizational goals ideally feeds into quality service experiences (Korczynski 2002a, 2002b). Given the sometimes indeterminate nature of such work (e.g., what exactly differentiates a satisfactory from an exceptional experience?), call-centre HRM focuses on the creation of accountability in work. Workers are asked to identify with their jobs and with the publics they serve. As previously suggested, there has been something of an undoing of the classical division of labour as a result of the ways ICTs are used, and this has led to the production of larger jobs. Broader jobs were once associated with systems of responsible autonomy (Friedman 1977) and perhaps with stronger identity ties with one's work. In info-service work, job design seems to have gone hand in hand with new forms of managerial regulation that place a greater onus on ensuring employee accountability. Usually, though, greater accountability does not translate into high levels of autonomy or trust being bestowed on workers. Rather, in addition to fostering the development of accountable workers, HRM is also responsible for creating mechanisms to ensure its documentation, as well as a culture that normalizes such activity. Monitoring and ongoing performance reviews are two of the principal techniques used to ensure that CSRs are carrying out organizational intentions, and this leads to the paradox of more complex work being subject to greater levels of managerial oversight as opposed to enhanced degrees of self-determination (see also Boltanski and Chiapello 2007, 430–2 and passim).

To highlight the differences that HRM as the principal manifestation of managerialism has made to work, it is again instructive to engage in a brief sketch, one that compares the call centre to a more traditional work environment. Consider for a moment Burawoy's (1979) analysis of machine-shop workers and the significance of the mental games they construct around the execution of their work as compared to the practices of cultural management that one might encounter in a contemporary call centre. Burawoy locates the meaning of such activity beginning with the point that games are constructed by workers for their own individual edification. Such alternative mental constructs help people get through the working day, by producing satisfactions from the travails of bending and shaping metal. But just as important are some of the unintended consequences that emerge from such activity. Getting tacit agreement over the legitimacy of the game garners a broader consent to the social structures (i.e., employment relations) in which they are housed: 'The game does not reflect an underlying harmony of interests; on the contrary, it is responsible for and generates that harmony … The game becomes an end in itself' (1979, 82).

The game being referred to is known as 'making out' among the social actors who construct it. Workers decide whether or not they will strive for the bonuses that are attached to producing above specific levels on individual jobs. Burawoy argues that the main incentive for 'making out' is not monetary, but the challenge, interest, wiles, and camaraderie that such activity lends to labour. Deciding whether or not to pick up the challenge of making out on any particular job constitutes an act of autonomy in its own right. Playing the game leads to acceptance into the informal work groups and status circles that populate the shop floor. Post-mortem narratives of making out dominate discussions among workers during meal breaks. Risk, uncertainty, and ultimately victory over recalcitrant materials add new layers of meaning to the lived experience of work, and in the process the self is validated as a competent worker. One can imagine that this comes to represent an important facet of individual identity as compared to the situation Sennett describes among the bakers. In the process Burawoy describes, even if production is not maximized – there are well understood ceilings to the amount of work that will be turned in at the end of every shift – it is enhanced. For this reason, shop-floor managers collude in the practices that workers initiate. This lends itself to the production of a pluralistic culture that, though outwardly adversarial, also contains important elements of normative understanding around the rules of making out. This in turn contributes to the creation of consent in a private for-profit establishment.

Though this scenario of manufactured consent has several prerequisites (e.g., piece-rate wages paid to skilled metal workers producing in small batch lots), fast-forward thirty years and what changes might we detect? First, even if production outcomes are more indefinite in info-service work (a quality call/interaction), less seems to be left to chance. Burawoy in his account of consent describes the production of an *organic* culture that percolates up from the shop floor. In the workplaces that concern us in this book, it is no longer the case that workers informally agree among themselves on an acceptable range of output, or negotiate this with line management, nor do unions do it on their behalf. Rather, it is far more likely that workers will receive targets or benchmark key-performance indicators (kpi's) to which adherence is expected following a period of induction and training. Nor are workers likely to have the option of choosing to meet such targets. Again, failure to attain kpi's may quickly escalate into a 'performance management issue' for the worker. It is also the case that today's workforce will be interacting directly with other human beings to provide a service, which may be fully or partially consumed in the act of its production. This scenario adds an immediacy to work that is often absent in other forms of labour. People are expected to be accountable for their actions in producing and delivering the service, and the tolerance for games on the part of the public is much less obvious. The ethic of customer service is constantly being emphasized in team meetings and training sessions. To the extent that fun and games are part of the job, they will be authored and led by management, with workers expected to join in.

Whether or not HRM has the desired outcomes of producing accountable workers who never tire of having their actions documented for the purpose of ascertaining commitment to specified means and ends is a matter of considerable interest. A key issue relates to how widely a common belief in organizationally ordained cultures extends and how deeply organizational identities have sunk roots and resonate with today's workforces. To what degree are organizationally defined frames shared, and to what extent do they serve as an organizing force among an establishment's labour force? This question ultimately reflects back on the success of the managerialism project. Whether organizationally given cultures are still subject to reinterpretation or contestation and whether the social space exists within call centres to permit the development of other cultures and identities are points that are explored later in the book, as are the means by which alternatives to official culture transcripts may be expressed in the call centre.[6] In the end, these are empirical questions, but they have important theoretical implications, for which we have conflicting evidence from call centres (Houlihan 2002) and more generally (see, for example, Grenier 1988; Scott 1994). These topics will be taken up in later chapters, which analyse HRM practice specifically as it relates to identity regulation in call centres as well as the issue of voice and representation in info-service work.

1.3 The Rest of the Book

This book is concerned with understanding info-service labour such as that which is conducted in customer-contact centres. What changes has this new labour process brought to the world of work? To unpack this rather ungainly question, this chapter has advanced an orienting structure with the intent of imposing some theoretical order on our inquiry. It has been suggested that the analysis be guided by a study of how CSRs work, and where they work, and what the implications of both questions are for the management of such work. The first question refers to how workers use tools to produce outputs. In this case the tools, ICTs, are of fairly recent vintage and the products that are produced – information and related services – have unique characteristics, including intangibility and immediacy. These traits pose special challenges for the design of such work. How workers are organized to use such technologies is a fundamental issue that is not determined simply by the technologies in use. The argument here is that info-service work brings about changes in the ways that jobs have been designed – that is, in the technical division of labour. This point is documented throughout the text and leads inexorably to other questions. How does a different technical division of labour affect working life, job quality, and the expectations that are attached to work? Does info-service work, in the ways it has been designed, enhance expectations with regard to work effort or skill levels? Is it providing more challenging or satisfying forms of employment?

Regarding *where* work is done – more specifically, which kinds of jobs are undertaken where – this question refers to the social division of labour. The globalization of work is practically a received fact. However, further weighty questions are attached to the boom in overseas outsourcing. A particular concern of this book is to clarify the contours of the emerging globalized division of labour in info-service work. Does globalization entail the establishment of different technical divisions of labour in info-service work in different parts of the world, or is such work being homogenized around the world wherever it is undertaken? Insights into this issue will also be instructive with regard to tackling an even larger question: What are the effects of globalization on job-exporting and job-importing economies?

Finally, there is the question as to how people who staff the information economy are managed. Again, it has been suggested that the advent of info-service work poses new challenges and new practices with regard to the management of labour. Possible contradictions associated with managerialism in the form of HRM and the type of work that is undertaken in workplaces such as call centres have been hinted at. The question of whether management differs by location – for example, in call centres located in the developed world as opposed to offshore destinations – also requires attention. The remaining chapters of the book explore these three interrelated issues – the technical division of labour, the social/spatial division of labour, and the management of info-service work – in greater detail.

This chapter has advanced three themes: the changing technical division of labour, globalization, and managerialism as a way of making sense of new forms of work – specifically, the info-service work that is conducted in call centres. It is also the case that a study of info-service labour provides a valuable opportunity to advance our understanding of what working with ICTs, globalization, and managerialism means. Thus the call centre constitutes the focus for this study both as an object of analysis in its own right and as a metaphor for those larger processes that are altering how we work, where work is done, and how it is managed.

The rest of the book poses some familiar questions albeit in the relatively new context of info-service work, as well as some new questions that are thrown up by the study of call centres and that consequently do not have as much of an intellectual heritage attached to them. For this reason, readers may find the book to be theoretically eclectic. Far from constituting a weakness, I would suggest that given our subject matter and a desire to treat it in as thorough a manner as possible, a degree of theoretical pluralism is necessary. Those sections of the book that analyse the design and organization of info-service work are undertaken mainly from a labour-process perspective, or what in chapter 5 is referred to as an extended materialist analysis. Labour process theory casts the study towards such issues as control, work intensity, and job skill. The importance of these points to an examination of new occupations and jobs should be self-evident. As critics have pointed out, though, labour process theory has been less successful in accounting for workers' perceptions of and responses to the situations they encounter (Knights 1990). Responses to questions pertaining to how workers interpret and make use of the new technologies or cultural programs they are confronted with as part of working in an info-service environment are of vital importance for arriving at a more complete understanding of the labour process. For this reason, various sections of the book make use of organizational theory (as part of an extended material analysis of ICT utilization), of critical management theory (in the discussion of HRM and culture and identity in call centres), and of social mobilization theory (in the examination of union organizing in info-service work). While these approaches most certainly have different emphases, they share a critical approach to the study of work, and it is this analytical slant that provides coherence to the work that follows.

It is also my intent that a study of how workers 'smile down the line' should add to our theoretical understanding of the ways in which labour processes are changing, and how the management of them is undertaken, and of the repertoires that workers develop for meeting the novel circumstances they confront. In other words, this book does not simply appropriate certain strands of theory and apply them to the subject at hand. Rather, the questions that the advent of info-service work call forth suggest certain theoretical approaches, and the answers that turn up in this book will indicate where some revision to existing theory may be in order.

Subsequent chapters tease out the complex relations among technology, globalization, and managerialism in the info-service work that is enacted in contact centres. The chief aim is to come to a better understanding of the nature of this work, the ways in which it is managed, the skills it requires, the demands it places on those who do it, and their perceptions and responses to the process. The similarities and differences among info-service labour processes in different product markets and global locations constitute another important theme of the book. Chapter 2 begins by describing the three empirical studies on which the book is based. Background information that pertains to the study and its genesis is provided, and the methodological choices that have been made are explained. Brief precis of the Australian organizations that participated in the main labour-force survey are provided as contextual background for readers. Chapter 3 is concerned with who does info-service work – that is, with the creation of a labour market for this type of work and the nature of that labour market. Though this chapter broaches questions that pertain to the HRM function, such as recruitment and selection, it does so from the macroscopic perspective of creating a new occupation, the CSR.

Chapter 4 presents results from a large-scale employee survey, supplemented by qualitative interviews with call-centre managers that deal with questions about work intensity, job discretion, responsibility and variety, and the associated skills of info-service work. The inquiry in this chapter is guided by two central questions. First, is skill principally a function of the product/service market that is being tended, or is a common labour process across contact centres creating similar skill sets within a distinct occupational category – the CSR? Following on from this, is skill variation, to the extent it exists, greater between commercial sectors such as health-care and communications industries, or greater among individual study sites within the same sector? The latter would indicate that job-design options can affect the nature of work in these environments and that high-performance work systems are possible even with common ICT-support platforms. In other words, how much organizational choice is allowed for in contemporary info-service work? How much variation exists among call centres regarding skill levels, and what factors account for the heterogeneities or homogeneities that are observed among the organizations represented in this study? Such an analysis entails examining how CSRs assess the skills they utilize in their work. Chapter 4 focuses on the labour process of the contact centre and the levels of skill that are required for the work. This chapter tackles the question of what kinds of jobs are being created in the labour processes we catalogue. As such, the chapter has considerable relevance for contemporary labour process theory.

A different slant on the same question is taken up in chapter 5. Here the focus is on the design of the means of information production and the implications of this for how the work is done. In chapter 5 the logics of ICT design and selection are examined using a qualitative case-study analysis of technological change in one call centre. By arguing that technology is purpose built to be used in certain ways and not in others, we extend the analysis of labour process theory into the field of management decision making. By investigating the ways in which workers actually do use the tools they are supplied with – including the unintended consequences of managerial decisions – labour-process analysis is extended in fruitful ways. The study of ICT design, choice, and actual utilization provides yet another window through which to view the question of skill in info-service work. While chapter 4 provides a quantitative snapshot of how workers evaluate the labour processes to which they are subject, chapter 5 brings management squarely into the picture while affording a longitudinal analysis of call-centre development.

Chapter 6 further widens the analysis of info-service work by turning to HRM in call centres. Concerns here revolve around the importance of cultural management and its importance in shaping work-related identities. To what extent do workers identify with the organizations that employ them, and how important is such identity regulation in supplanting other forms of managerial control? This also has some relevance for debates over whether the basis of social organization has shifted from work-based to extra–work-based identities (Bauman 1998) or to work identities that are more in line with employer ideals (du Gay 1996; Scott 1994), including acceptance of the documented accountability that has been associated with our use of the concept of managerialism. Besides examining the current state of employee identity in the call-centre case studies, this chapter assesses the importance of HRM in influencing identity in the workplace. The focus here is on how workers in the case study organizations respond to HRM and whether it is having an impact on employee identity or whether it is mainly a means by which management engages in self-legitimation.

Chapter 7 considers global extensions of info-service work – specifically, the outsourcing of such work to offshore destinations. This chapter is particularly concerned with India, the largest recipient of outsourced info-service work. Chapter 7 has both a longitudinal and a cross-national component to it. With respect to the former, the chapter provides a synopsis of the export-service–led model of growth that is being enacted through the encouragement of outsourcing as a development strategy and the impacts this is having on India. While this discussion proceeds at a macroscopic level, it is important to recognize that what is occurring on the ground, in the workplace, is important for the larger social changes we can detect. The second part of chapter 7 gets closer to the ground by reporting on findings from an investigation into four of India's largest BPO providers. A modified version of the survey instrument that is used in the Australian contact-centre worksites is administered in the four Indian organizations. Chapter 7 reports on similarities and differences in info-service work in the two locales, focusing on the respective labour processes, including work intensity and job skills associated with in-house info-service work conducted in Australia and outsourced BPO work that is exported to India as well as on HR practices and their effects at the Indian and Australian research sites.

Chapter 8 rejoins the analysis of chapter 6, examining the other side of the HRM coin by extending the research into the realms of employee misbehaviour and resistance to the work environments they are presented with in call centres. In the current political context, the argument is made that union organizing is a form of resistance. Factors that can contribute to successful union organizing in call centres, including the connections between organizing and servicing strategies, are considered. The relationships between HRM and unionism in call centres are also considered. Finally, the possibilities for a significant trade-union presence in Indian operations are brought to the reader's attention.

Chapter 9 summarizes the principal findings of the book. As the spread of info-service work to new realms of social life and to new global locations is very much an ongoing project, possible future inquiries are mapped out in what the author hopes will be ongoing collaborative work with researchers from other places.

2 The Call-Centre Case Studies

2.1 Studying Call Centres: Methodological Matters

The call-centre phenomenon has generated a good deal of interest apart from the broader theoretical issues raised in the last chapter concerning the way services are being reorganized and the effects this has on the staff who provide them and the publics who receive them. Concerns over working conditions in call centres, expressed somewhat differently by trade unions in Canada and Australia, yielded my introduction to the work of customer service representatives (CSRs). Below, I describe the genesis of this project, to provide the reader with an account of how the case-study organizations that form the heart of this study were selected. This will also afford insights into the methodological choices that have been made for this study. First, though, a very brief history of the call centre is presented.

It is important to recognize at the outset that employment growth in contact centres has not been restricted to any particular industry. Rather, as depicted in the last chapter, the contact centre is best viewed as a form of service delivery, *a labour process* for producing, treating, and distributing information that is widely applied across a range of business and social activities. This labour process was pioneered in the financial and telecommunications sectors, partly for the economizing reasons that were examined in chapter 1 (see also Bain and Taylor 2002b; Ellis and Taylor 2006). For financial services, centralized customer-contact centres offered greater economies of scale (e.g., more transactions per hour) and progressively replaced walk-in branches as the main way of receiving and delivering information. In the case of the telecommunications sector, telcos were early users of call centres as well as providers to other industries, supplying communications and routing technologies that form the backbone of any contact centre. We can see this dynamic at work in an early forerunner of the contemporary call centre that the author came across in the course of this research.

One of the first call centres to be established in Australia was in the gaming industry. It took telephone bets from punters on all manner of sporting events. Even before the mid-1970s a local, phone-based facility was equipped with a primitive ACD (automatic call distribution) system, comprised of a meter on the wall indicating whether any calls were waiting. In 1976 this 'call centre' obtained an early Erikson system, 'probably 25 years ahead of its time … it was a true ACD [automated call distribution – BR] system and the calls dropped in, the operators never had to accept the call, the calls arrived automatically and even in those days they went to the operator who's been waiting the longest.'[1]

What is interesting about this vignette is not just the dates that are supplied, which are considerably earlier than what we are used to supposing for the advent of call centres, but also how info-service work in this sector developed in partnership with the national telephone provider at the time. As the manager quoted above proceeded to observe, 'her' industry has evolved with its telecommunications supplier. Initially, telephone betting systems grew up in every city and town to service the local region. But with the neutralization of distance as a major cost factor in telephony from the 1990s onward, small regional exchanges gave way to the large national call centres that exist today. Nowadays, calls originating anywhere in Australia are automatically routed to the next available agent whether that worker is sitting at a workstation in Adelaide, Brisbane, Darwin, or Perth. As this example illustrates, in work that requires the transmission of information, the cost of distance has largely been eliminated.

The creation of customer-contact centres also coincided with the opening up of new product markets in financial services and telecommunications; this included a much wider array of superannuation and investment-fund products in the former and mobile telephony and inexpensive long-distance calling cards in the latter. These types of products, both in their own right and in comparison with competing services, often embodied a greater informational content, while the volumes in which they were marketed and sold could be more effectively managed through the new work design of contact centres. As a means of undertaking work, call and contact centres now account for more than half of all banking and financial operations that are undertaken with the public as well as close to half of all telecommunications and IT-provider customer contacts in Australia (Budde 2004). While initiated by the banks and telcos – often in tandem with providing business services to other enterprises – customer-contact centres have been widely adopted in public as well as private services and by manufacturing entities as the chief means of communicating with their customers. Utilities, health-care providers, transportation and freight companies, social-service agencies, travel and entertainment providers, and marketers now conduct significant amounts of their core activities via inbound, outbound and blended customer-contact centres.

The genesis of this book reflects these developments. In 1999 I was approached by the Communications, Energy, and Paper Workers Union of Canada (CEP). The CEP represents workers in the telecommunications sector. Union leaders were troubled to find that their members were bidding out of comparatively well-paying jobs in the call centres of a large provincial telco in order to accept lower-paying work elsewhere in the organization. In the world of job-control unionism, seniority-based job ladders, and job bidding, things like this were not supposed to happen; as a general rule, workers do not bid on lower-paying jobs further down the ladder! Clearly, workers were using the customer-contact centres as points of entry into what was regarded as employment with a 'good company' and then bolting at the first opportunity to accept alternative, lower-paying jobs in other departments. The union wanted to know why its call-centre members were willing to bid downwards in such a unique pattern. My research journey began with this apparent anomaly.[2]

These were still only vaue concerns that followed me to Australia. My interest was still unfocused, but my curiosity about these new workplaces had been whetted. For one thing, the issues that CEP had raised and my preliminary research seemed to dovetail with ongoing debates over the nature of work in post-industrial economies – debates that have proven both fruitful to explore and difficult to resolve. Ever since the initial publication of Daniel Bell's *The Coming of Post-Industrial Society* (1973) and Harry Braverman's *Labor and Monopoly Capital* (1974), debate over the future parameters of work has been raging (Clement and Myles 1994). Increasingly, we in the West live in information- and service-oriented economies (Castells 1996). Clearly, these jobs are different from the employment that was taken up in the Fordist factories of mass production, which raises interesting questions. For example, *how* are these jobs different? And how *different* are they? The study of what this book refers to as info-service work provides one platform from which these questions can usefully be tackled.

In Australia the same level of interest was evident, coinciding with an explosion of employment in call centres. I was working at a large, multicampus, urban university where many students – contingent workers par excellence – were funding their education by employment in call centres. Invariably, they were keen to share their experiences of this work with me, and they didn't seem to mind my theorizing about their workplaces in the lecture hall. A small start-up research grant was instrumental in gaining focus. These resources funded the design and administration of an initial survey in four customer-contact centres, the results of which I have reported on elsewhere (Russell 2002a, 2002b, 2004, 2006b). This preliminary work provided an entry into new, less obvious issues associated with employment growth in info-service work, such as how customer-service software is designed and how as-sumptions about the work are embedded in the technology by software developers. One piece of this exploratory research is directly relevant to the themes explored in this book and reappears as chapter 5.

Higher education is one of Australia's largest 'exports,' and India is one of several key sources sending students to study in Australia. My growing engagement with the study of info-service work coincided with the take-off in contact-services employment outsourcing on the Indian Subcontinent. Owing to the rapid expansion of job opportunities in MNC operations in India and in newly created Indian companies that were providing front- and back-office outsourcing support, reciprocal interests began to flower. Students and colleagues from India encour-aged me to look farther afield as I pursued my research interests in info-service work. Meanwhile, the sudden growth in the offshoring of such work was becoming a source of concern in Australia, as well as in the United States and Britain, where job losses in customer-service work through outsourcing by some prominent firms were making headlines. The globalization of info-service work was suddenly a hot topic.

As curiosity spawned by the growth of employment in info-service work in both developed and less developed countries intensified, I was approached several times by a variety of organizations that one way or another had an interest in call centres. I was invited to work as a con-sultant in establishing training programs for overseas call-centre agents in India as part of a foreign-aid initiative and to help establish special-ized management-training programs for call-centre staff in Australia; I declined these invitations. An approach that I found more engaging was made by a union, which asked me to present to a conference of call-centre shop stewards some insights into employment and working conditions in these settings.

The concerns raised by the Clerical and Administrative Division of the Australian Service Union (ASU) differed somewhat from those of CEP. In a country where trade-union membership has been placed on an entirely individual voluntaristic basis, overall union membership has more than halved over the past twenty-five years, from almost one in two workers at the beginning of the 1980s to less than one in five today. In this context, unions were seriously interested in the potential organizing opportunity that rapid employment growth in call centres might offer. Chapter 8 of this book discusses in detail the shifts in Australian industrial relations that are at least partially responsible for the dramatic deunionization of the workplace and the organizing possibilities that are held out by call centres. Suffice it to note here that given an ever more hostile legal environment, the ASU was keen to know what factors might encourage union membership growth in the call centres they nominally represented. So, apparently, were other unions. What features, if any, do call centres present that unions might get a handle on? Out of these concerns, a research project was born.

The project that was to develop and that constitutes the major part of this book has been coordinated with the Queensland Council of Unions (QCU), the peak labour body in the state. In addition to the ASU, other unions with representation rights that cover workers in customer-contact centres were invited to and did participate, including the Financial Sector Union, the Community and Public Sector Union, and the Queensland Public Services Union. The QCU played a vital coordinating role in gaining both the financial support and the cooperation of the four unions involved in this project. My brief was a generous one: simply to continue with the research on working conditions and employment regulation in call centres.[3]

Subsequent joint meetings with the research partners resulted in the formulation of a novel study protocol. Each union nominated five case-study sites from its representational field. The sites were selected on the basis of being typical of the workplaces each union confronted in its respective industry. In some cases, the sites were highly unionized; in others, union densities were low or non-existent. Generally, union density was not a criterion in research-site selection, as this would have defeated one of the initial research objectives, which was to explain why call-centre workers joined unions or refrained from doing so. Additional nominations were made by each union in case access proved impossible with any of the first group of 'short-listed' organizations. The goal was to include twenty call centres in the study, from which valuable comparisons could be made relating to job design, work flows and job skills, HRM practices, and trade-union membership.

Once the lists of nominated study sites had been obtained and agreed on, the call-centre manager at each location was contacted and inquiries were made as to whether the centre would be interested in participating in a research project that was anchored on a labour-force survey of CSRs. When the proposal was positively received, the employee survey that was designed for the project (see below) was turned over to management at the site, with instructions to distribute it to all employees who spent 80 per cent or more of their time on the phones. Potential respondents were required to have a minimum of three months' job service at the site and were excluded from participation if they exercised any supervisory responsibilities such as a team leadership role. In some cases, at management's discretion, employees were provided with rostered time off the phones to complete the thirty-minute questionnaire; in other cases, workers were requested to do it on their own time, during or after working hours. At one site that prided itself on being a 'paperless' work environment, the manager requested and was furnished with an online version of the survey, which employees completed when they weren't servicing the public. In all cases, though, the surveys were self-completed by the respondents.

Another set of scenarios was set in motion if the manager declined to participate in the study, as happened in a number of instances. If the nominating union had a strong presence on the call-centre floor, as was the case at some sites, the study went ahead under union auspices. In these situations, shop stewards (or 'delegates,' as they are known in Australia) took 'ownership' of the study and received the same instructions as noted above as to who should receive the survey. Special care was taken to not simply distribute the questionnaire among union members, but rather to get a representative sample by distributing it to all employees who were occupied mainly with telephone-voice–based work and who had at least three months of job seniority. In a number of instances, management indicated that it would not support the study but added that it would not block the union from conducting it. In some cases, after surveys were completed, managers agreed to let the author conduct field visits and participated in a post-survey qualitative managerial interview.

In three instances, managers indicated that they would not participate in the research and would not condone employee participation. In
one case, thanks to the determination of the call-centre union delegates
and their close relationship with the union organizer, administration of
the survey proceeded and a reasonable response rate (43 per cent) was
garnered. In the other two occurrences of non-cooperation, it was determined by the union that proceeding with the survey could result in
disciplinary actions, including having union organizers' rights of entry
to the workplace terminated![4] On these occasions the particular worksites had to be abandoned and alternative case-study sites substituted.

The first two of the above scenarios potentially omitted an important
category of sites – namely, those where there is no union presence at all.
To overcome this problem, additional study sites were nominated for
sectors that would otherwise have been underrepresented in the study,
including the telecommunications and banking industries, which currently have low levels of union representation in the call-centre field. In
these cases, different centres were approached for permission to carry
out the study. Numerous organizations declined, but just as important,
some decided to participate, including one large multisite bank and one
medium-sized telco, neither of which had any recent history of union-
certified collective agreements. Overall, seven of the case studies came
under the first scenario (union nominated and administered with the
cooperation of management), nine of the case studies were conducted
solely by the unions without active management involvement, and four
were nominated by the researcher and conducted under management
auspices without union participation. This protocol resulted in a wide
range of call centres in different industries and with varying degrees of
collective employee organization being included in the study.

Meanwhile, partially overlapping with this work, research opportunities were starting to beckon offshore, in India. The political sensitivity of outsourcing, and the universal practice of concluding principal/
agent confidentiality agreements between businesses that outsource
and the service providers, are undoubtedly factors that have hindered
access to case-study sites and empirical work in India and other Third
World economies that are competing for a share of the business-process
outsourcing (BPO) market. These obstacles to conducting research in
India were partially overcome through networks that my colleague
(the co-author of chapter 7) and a PhD student had developed from
past work experience. These connections were generously made available and resulted in an opportunity to enter four of the largest Indian-

owned BPO providers. Two of these businesses are headquartered in the IT capital of Bangalore, one is located in Hyderabad, and the final site is found in the capital, New Delhi. Chapter 7 is given over to a comparative analysis of these sites alongside the Australian case studies.

The sheer size of this comparative study had implications for the methodologies that were selected for it. The need for systematic and rigorous comparisons across a multitude of research sites favoured the adoption of a survey approach, with the individual CSR as the ultimate unit of analysis and the employing organization one of many independent variables. The research partners concurred, so a second objective of obtaining 1,000 useable responses was set for the Australian segment of the study. Again, with these numbers and the available budget we had to work with, a self-administered survey design was selected as the most appropriate way forward.

The QCU and a number of the participating unions took an interest in, and made use of, the opportunity to shape the survey while it was being constructed. The design of a unique questionnaire for call-centre workers was an integral part of the project. The obvious advantage of a special-purpose survey is that it can be developed in a way that highlights the specificities and nuances found in a new occupation (info-service work), as it is conducted across a range of industries. A potential issue relates to the proven reliability of indexes that are built up from the survey questions and used later in the study. All of the index measures constructed for this study have been subjected to and meet appropriate reliability levels. The final interview schedule had five sections: training and learning experiences and the career intentions of CSRs; working in the labour process of a call centre; perceptions of HRM, including occupational health and safety; and the state of employment relations, which encompassed the role, if any, of trade unions. A final section of the survey collected basic demographic data on the backgrounds of respondents. Note that queries included not only workers' perceptions of their jobs but also questions that garnered details about their actions and responses with regard to their working conditions. The survey document consisted of a combination of fact-gathering questions – predominantly nominal or interval in measurement level (e.g., the number of software programs used) – and banks of Likert scale questions on thematic issues such as perceptions concerning the pace of work over the course of the job cycle, the appropriateness of specific organizational cultures, the reasonableness of performance targets, and the effectiveness of unions in the workplace.

Overall, the survey contained 96 questions, but if we include the question banks, which contained multiple queries, there were 197 questions (114 scale questions + 83 other questions).

The Indian research, though theoretically and methodologically allied with the Australian study, was formally independent of the QCU-sponsored project. Thus the Indian research evolved into a project within a project. The main Australian call-centre survey provided a template for the questionnaire that was used in India. This research had two objectives. The first was mainly descriptive in nature: to map out the parameters of info-service work in Indian BPO/call centres and in the process further our understanding of the dynamics of this form of globalization. The second objective was more specific: to conduct a comparative analysis that brought the responses of Indian and Australian CSRs into the frame of analysis. For example, how do work targets and benchmarks in India compare with those in Australia? And how do workers in the respective locations perceive and respond to these expectations? For the comparative side of the analysis, many of the questions on the Australian survey were imported into the Indian questionnaire.

As it turned out, India threw up unique issues that warranted further exploration. For example, Indian workers typically provide information services that are not part of their own personal lives to overseas customers. Few of these workers consume cable television or hold a personal credit card, yet they are expected to provide the same level of product information and service as workers in the West, who are intimately familiar with such products as part of 'everyday lived experience.' Does this make a difference in terms of the challenges that workers face in their jobs, or in the amounts of labour they have to invest in their work? Also, overseas workers may be subject to greater levels of abuse, including overt racism, despite being required to undergo training in 'accent neutralization' as well as to assume a false identity (e.g., a Christianized name). Do these aspects of work occasion greater levels of job stress or higher attrition rates? To accommodate these concerns, the Indian survey included some queries that were simply not relevant to the Australian scene. Other questions that were on the Australian survey – for example, those dealing in detail with trade-union representation – were judged to be wide of the mark in Indian circumstances and were omitted from that version of the survey. Overall, about 90 per cent of the questions were shared between the Australian and Indian versions of the questionnaire, which made possible direct comparisons on a host of issues.

Two other precautions were taken prior to releasing the Indian surveys for completion. One of our students had extensive experience working in an Indian call centre. She suggested some minor changes in the wording of a few questions. This precaution was taken before any further pretesting was conducted, with an eye towards ensuring that the questions were appropriate and that terminology would be understandable to the respondents. Following this, the survey was sent off to one of the firms that had agreed to participate in the study, where a pretest was conducted. On the basis of the satisfactory results obtained from this exercise, the survey was released for general distribution at this firm and over time at three other companies as access was negotiated. At the time of the survey, in late 2005, the Indian case studies were union-free organizations, as was the whole of the BPO sector. As outlined in chapter 8, this situation is now being challenged. However, owing to the circumstances as encountered, distribution of the survey was, of necessity, conducted by the call-centre managers and their staff at the respective locations.

A survey such as the one employed in this book allows the researcher to collect a wide array of data on numerous themes and from large numbers of people. The strength of such an approach is to be found in the ability to generalize from the results. One criticism of this strategy is that depth of understanding is sacrificed in the process. As previously mentioned, respondents took about thirty minutes on average to complete the interview schedule. How much thought and reflection can social actors put into answering questions in this format? This is an impossible question to answer. The survey was entirely voluntary, so presumably those who were not interested in the topics it dealt with would not participate, or would withdraw and not submit a completed return. The Australian questionnaire went through several iterations and one pretest. In addition, important lessons had been learned from the earlier pilot study and the survey instrument that had been designed for it. This earlier survey was revised and reworked in significant ways, the main problems being that it was overly exploratory in nature and was not conducive to multivariate analysis. In other words, the pilot study provided a much clearer picture of info-service work and in the process allowed for more precise specification of the research questions and refinement in the data collection.

Notwithstanding any of the above, the reflective researcher may still have nagging doubts pertaining to survey methodologies, especially if the phenomenon under study is both novel and complex. To assuage these concerns and to gain a thorough acquaintance with the organizations and people being studied, I undertook a number of complementary pursuits over the course of the work. Methodological triangulation (Denzin 1970; Neuman 2006) consisted of two additional research activities. First, a structured open-ended interview protocol was created to carry out managerial interviews at each organization to which access had been granted. In each case an interview with the call-centre manager was requested and permission was sought to tape-record the session. These interviews provided, among other things, a history of each research site, an overview of its structure – including the place of the call centre within the larger organization for the mostly intraorganizational ('in-house') operations – and a managerial perspective on such functions as recruitment, future business plans, and relations with trade unions. This work also served as a check and validation for information that had been collected from the surveys on such topics as work targets and key performance indicators (kpi's). Interviews with the call-centre manager at each of the twenty Australian sites were conducted by the author. Following each interview, I produced a partial transcription of the session. Each of these interviews lasted at least an hour; often they went considerably longer.

In each organization where access was obtained, a request to spend time 'on the floor' to engage in observational study was also made. In these work environments such observational fieldwork was aided by technology that enabled me as the researcher to 'double-jack' alongside the CSRs. This allowed direct access to interactions between workers and their publics. In other words, I was privy to all that was said and done to complete the job cycle from the moment the call was answered to its final disposition (i.e., any necessary follow-up work). Where different work teams had different functions (e.g., different call queues), I would request time with workers from each team to get a feel for the type of work being conducted and its comparative complexity. In those centres where team members did the same work, I would spend time with a few workers, who were sometimes selected on the basis of job seniority – for example, I would observe a long-serving employee, then a less experienced one.

During each call/job cycle, extensive field notes were kept. In these I recorded the nature of the inquiry, how it was responded to, and any associated (e.g., post-call) work generated by the interaction. These observations allowed for an evaluation of such factors as the amount of variety in the work and the typical amounts of time devoted to calls.

Of course, there was much that I did not understand, particularly in the realm of integrating talk with computer navigation and data-file management in the seamless manner that is used to produce the informational outputs callers require. So, after many of the interactions, I would debrief the CSR in order to see if my understanding of what had transpired – the nature of the call and the actions taken – was correct. Such impromptu sessions added to the richness of the field data. These interviews, which were structured around the job cycle that had just been completed, provided another form of validity check for the survey data that were being collected on the labour process; they also provided a deeper level of meaning to those data. By this I mean that it is sometimes difficult to understand why people respond to a survey question in a certain, perhaps unexpected manner. Quantitative data do not always 'speak for themselves,' and it is often necessary for the researcher to provide further interpretation of what the statistics are 'saying.' Though we might be able to 'explain' responses to a question by reference to a statistical association with other variables, this may not provide a totally satisfying solution. Fieldwork sometimes enables an intuitive understanding of inherently complex and alien social situations. In short, it yields a complementary dimension of understanding. This observational field research was carried out at fourteen of the twenty sites included in the study. At the other sites, caller confidentiality was often raised as a concern and permission for direct observation was denied.

In most cases, observational fieldwork involved spending from half to a full working day at the call centre. Further understanding of the work being conducted was enhanced by previous qualitative work reported on elsewhere (Russell 2002a, 2002b, 2004, 2006b), and in particular by the unique opportunity to undertake participant observation as part of a new group of trainees at one centre that participated in the earlier pilot study. This experience, which ran over a two-week period, provided a rich qualitative window onto call-centre work. Following this sojourn, extensive focus-group interviews were conducted at this centre in order to delve more deeply into how workers used the information technologies at their disposal. Once again these interviews were tape-recorded; partial transcripts were subsequently produced by the author. Though this work formed part of the 'prehistory' of the main survey project presented in the following chapters, it was highly influential in shaping the research that followed. Results from these focus-group interviews inform chapter 5 in this book on ICT utilization and job skill.

In India it was not possible to engage in direct field observation. All four Indian companies included in the study were strictly outsourcing providers for overseas (mainly American) clients. Concerns about principal/provider confidentiality – especially in the wake of damaging international press stories concerning the sale of confidential financial information from India – proved to be too large a hurdle to overcome. However, the author and co-author of chapter 7 were able to conduct more extensive managerial interviews at the Indian centres than had been possible in Australia. For the Indian cases, two interview protocols were created, one for the human-relations manager and one for the operations manager at each site. In some cases these individuals brought other members of their management team along with them, and these staff members also participated in the discussions. These management interviews in India covered the same terrain as in Australia, but they also sought more detailed information on the unique business profiles and organizational structures of the Indian operations. Given the nature of BPO, which tends to be unfamiliar and in some ways more complex than what is encountered in typical in-house contact-centre operations in Australia, these intensive qualitative interviews were deemed necessary. These interviews, which generally took up one full day at each establishment, helped compensate for the absence of direct fieldwork at the Indian sites. During these sessions additional data were sought on wage and non-wage employee costs, recruitment challenges, work design, and the problems posed by high attrition rates. Given that BPO is an industry in its own right, generally more time was devoted to discussing future strategies on the part of the Indian firms.

Standard open-ended interview schedules were used in the meetings with Indian managers, and notes were entered directly onto the schedules. Once again, to allay concerns on the part of the interviewees and to minimize the possibility of self-censorship, a decision was taken beforehand not to request permission to tape-record these meetings. Instead, at the end of each day the researchers placed the contents of the notes they had kept into common computer files created for each site. Schedules were then exchanged, and any information that had been missed by one of the interviewers but captured by the other was added to the file on each company in a form of observer triangulation. In total, eight management interviews were conducted in India. At one company these interviews were conducted after the survey had been distributed and collected from the workforce. At the remaining three organizations the management interviews preceded the workforce sur-

Table 2.1
Participating Australian organizations by industry sector and ownership

Sector	# of call centres in study	Private/public ownership
Banking, insurance, finance	4	All private sector
Health care	2	Public/private
Leisure/hospitality	1	Private
Telecommunications	2	Private
Transportation	2	Private
Public and Social Services	9	8 Public
		1 Private tender/outsourcer
Total	20	

vey.[5] Throughout the remainder of the book and in keeping with my previous comments on the need to interpret statistical data, every effort has been made to integrate the qualitative and quantitative data that inform the analysis. Leaving aside the Indian organizations until chapter 7, we now turn to a brief descriptive discussion of the Australian organizations that participated in the study.

It is important that the sites selected for inclusion in a comparative study of this type be broadly representative of the distribution of call centres and info-service workers across the field. As noted earlier, this objective was achieved with the help of the principal unions with representational rights in call centres. Recalling that the fundamental units of analysis in the study are individual workers and their experiences, perceptions, actions, and reflections, it would have been inappropriate to draw a sample of respondents from only one or two industries that make use of customer-contact centre modes of service delivery.

An industry breakdown for the twenty Australian organizations on which this book is centred is provided in Table 2.1. As can be seen, the study reflects the important place of banks and financial institutions as pioneers in the use of customer-contact centres. This mode of information and service delivery has also been wholeheartedly adopted by various levels of the public sector in the provision of social and quasi-social goods.

Our categorization of call centres by industry sector raises an important definitional issue. Though one frequently hears references to the contact-centre 'industry,' and though call centres do exhibit certain *industry traits*, such as common technological platforms and their own peak managerial associations in countries such as Australia,[6] it is more accurate to look on the call centre as a specific way of organizing work – that is, as a labour process for producing and distributing information. This labour process is utilized by a broad array of private- and public-sector organizations. Only under special circumstances – for example, when info-services are outsourced to other businesses – can it be considered an industry in its own right.

There are strong theoretical and empirical reasons for adopting this position – that is, for considering info-service employment to be a new occupational category rather than an industry per se. As will become clearer in chapter 4, one important problem concerns the heterogeneity/homogeneity that is found across call centres and the jobs they offer. Looking at contact centres as an industry already makes certain assumptions in this regard – namely, that there is something that we can call 'an industry' and that as such, certain attributes are shared in common by members of it. Normally, an industry produces specified outputs that set it apart from other sectors. The outputs or products created, whether these are auto parts, microchips, or whatever else, differentiate a given industry from others that produce other things. In info-service work it is not possible to categorize outputs in this way. Each centre produces unique and quite often *joint outputs* that bear little if any resemblance to the products of other, even neighbouring centres. All one can say is that the technological platforms used in call centres are very similar across worksites and that this may have important implications for the organization of work (this topic will be held back for discussion in later chapters). Here it is better to begin by assuming heterogeneity across centres in different industries and then to see whether, and to what degree, this actually is the situation.

A second consideration refers back to the unit of analysis that has been adopted for this study. In the first instance our concern lies with the worker and the work she does. Surveys were completed by individual workers. Likewise, time in the field was spent one on one with people doing their jobs. Our subject matter concerns a particular type of work – info-service labour – and the people who do it. Obviously, this will be influenced by the structures in which the work is 'housed,' which are organizations with specific histories and cultures, as well as by managers and the decisions they make. Fundamentally though, our referent in this study is an occupational one – the CSR.

It is also the case that in the countries where they first arose, most contact centres have retained their status as in-house departments to existing businesses (Budde 2004; Holman, Batt, and Holtgrewe 2007, Fig. 1.3). Our sample reflects this. Only one of the twenty participating Australian organizations in this study provided outsourcing services to another party; it had been contracted to supply a social service on behalf of the federal government to a designated group of users. The other nineteen centres were part of existing organizations in a variety of industries, including finance, telecommunications, health care, leisure services, and the public sector.

Having distinguished between the new occupational category of info-service worker and the manifold industries in which these workers are found, it is also necessary to note the modifications that occur when info-service work is outsourced. This practice is increasingly associated with sending work offshore to Third World sites such as India and the Philippines. As we will see in chapter 7, in these cases a new industry is indeed springing up. This industry has been termed information technology–enabled services (ITeS), and it is an important component of the business-process outsourcing (BPO) sector. Many of the comments made above are still germane, especially those relating to the diffuseness of outputs; what distinguishes these developments is the extension in the social division of labour they represent. In these cases, stand-alone firms are being established to provide long-distance customer service, telemarketing, and back-office work to business clients and their customers located abroad. In these circumstances the outsourcing of info-service provision is evolving into a specialized industry, albeit one with highly unique characteristics, which are explored later in this book.

Table 2.2 provides further information on the Australian study sites and sample. Fictitious names are used for each of the case-study sites. A total of 1,232 surveys were returned from the Australian workplaces, marking an approximate overall response rate of 36 per cent. The raw number of responses exceeded the target initially set of 1,000 completed returns, though as readers will see, response rates varied considerably on a site-by-site basis. The recorded response rates are, in my view, mainly a product of whether or not someone took 'ownership' of the distribution and collection of the surveys at the worksite. This factor is largely a matter of luck and chance. If a manager or team leader rostered workers off the phone to complete the survey, or if an influential union organizer or shop steward happened to take a special interest in the project, response rates were invariably good. Unfortunately, we could not always count on this happening. Brief descriptive overviews of the research sites enumerated in Table 2.2 are provided to round this chapter out.

Table 2.2
Organizational employment and survey response rates for the Australian sample

Site	# of CSRs	# of responses	Response rate (%)
Banking, finance, and insurance			
Insurer1	165	45	27
Insurer2	42	35	83
Bank1	31	17	55
Bank2	735	228	31
Health care			
Health Premium	40	5	13
Health Authority	93	79	85
Leisure/hospitality			
Telebet	380	145	38
Telecommunications			
Telco1 (T1)	110	84	76
Telco2 (T2)	177	100	56
Transportation			
Bus company	98	64	65
Airline	370	116	31
Public and social services			
Urban Space	250	71	28
Advisory Services	50	15	30
Licensing	80	34	43
Gov't Pensions (GP)	50	9	18
Statewide	40	10	25
Collections	45	22	49
Delivery Services	145	23	16
Social Services	250	80	32
Third-party outsourcer			
Tender	74	50	68
Total	3,352	1,232	36

2.2 The Centres

Given that banks were among the first systematic users of call centres, the financial sector invokes a special interest in a study of info-service work. Among the financial-services firms included in the study are a small, member-based credit union (*Bank1*) and a large national organization (*Bank2*). Both these organizations offer a full range of banking and insurance services; the other two companies are insurers only. On the surface at least, work flows and team organization appear to be idiosyncratic, with each centre presenting different ways of dividing up work among different product clusters. *Bank1*, perhaps on account of its small size, takes the approach of grouping different product segments into one job, with workers providing both standard banking services – such as account information and transfers, term-deposit investments, and the setting up of telebanking facilities for customers – with either loan and/or insurance provision. Initially the *Bank2* centre also dealt with a full range of products (banking, loans, insurance, and wealth management) from its head office, but with rapid expansion it has since located product divisions at its different call centres. While CSRs from across the company participated in the study, fieldwork was conducted at one centre with responsibility for the insurance sales, service (product information and quotes), and claims side of the business. Workers are allocated to teams that conduct one of these three activities.

Insurer1 provides further variation on the structuring of work. Here, work is divided among sales, service, and complex resolutions teams. Service at this centre includes product information as at *Bank2*, as well as claims; the resolutions teams take questions and problems as they are escalated up from the sales and service teams. The other dedicated insurance centre, *Insurer2*, is solely a claims-processing operation; no other service or marketing activities are carried out from this site. Teams at *Insurer2* are divided between those that take inbound calls regarding home-insurance claims and those that receive motor-vehicle claims. Workers are responsible for inputting information into the system before separate, non-voice fulfilment teams write up the claims.

Two telco customer-contact centres are included in the study: *Telco1* (*T1*), a relatively new niche-market player specializing in the sale and servicing of phone cards, discounted landlines, and mobile and Internet services; and *Telco2* (*T2*), a well-established national carrier. Research at *T2* dealt specifically with one centre that specialized in mobile-phone sales and service. In line with the explosion in mobile-phone telephony and Internet use, both centres have witnessed dramatic growth in recent years. *T1*, for example, employed 8 CSRs five years ago and 25 two years ago; presently, 120 CSRs work at its new greenfield site. The product markets these centres deal with are highly dynamic, as are the business arrangements that oversee the production and distribution of the products they offer. New products, new alliances, partnerships, and corporate mergers characterize the industry. Reflecting this dynamism, both telco centres are among the few operations in the study that operate on a 24/7 basis. Even though *T1* and *T2* are both inbound call centres, marketing and sales constitute major aspects of the work that is conducted at both sites, and this tends to dictate the organization of work. Thus, unlike in some of the financial centres, there is no division between service and sales work in the telcos.

Work teams at *T2* are organized simply on the basis of market segment, with teams providing services to the 'Select' customer base (<$50 per month) and the 'Preferred' customer base of higher-spending households and small-business clients.[7] This type of work organization based on market segmentation has also been observed in other studies of the telco sector (Batt 2002). Unsurprisingly, except for the greater levels of product knowledge associated with the high-value teams, jobs throughout the centre are similar, though workers on the 'Preferred' teams do have enhanced earning possibilities with the availability of both higher incentive bonuses (a fraction of the revenues brought in by the agent) and greater access to overtime rates on account of the longer hours of business service that are allocated to these market segments. At *T1* the workforce is divided between prepaid and postpaid services. The former deal exclusively with phone cards, between 300 and 400 of which are on offer to different call destinations with varying connection fees and per-minute charges attached to them. Postpaid services represent a larger share of employment, and this is clearly the end of the business where growth is occurring. These teams deal with all forms of billed communication services, including discounted landline access and Internet and mobile-phone services. At the time of our fieldwork there were plans afoot to create a new designated corporate team that would specialize in servicing the higher-value business traffic, as was the case at *T2*. Members of this team will be placed on a higher salary than CSRs on the prepaid and postpaid teams, who currently are on the same payment grid.

Compared to the growth trajectory associated with the take-off in mobile-phone and Internet use that characterizes telecommunications, the transportation sector offers a different picture – one of a mature industry that has to make significant adjustments in uncertain times. The companies included in this study include a national/international air carrier and a national bus company. Airlines have been capturing news headlines in recent years with the bankruptcy and collapse of major carriers around the world, the arrival of upstart discount companies, the formation of new global strategic alliances, and a generally volatile market. Much the same pattern characterizes the economics of domestic surface transportation. In the case of the surface carrier included here, the company had recently acquired a larger competitor, which had its own call centres. The acquisition led to the closing of the competitor's existing two centres and centralization in the one remaining site.

Though they are in different subsectors, info-service work at *Bus Company* and *Airline* consists of similar general functions – inbound sales and booking, timetable information, and in the case of *Airline*, administration of the frequent-flyer program. These functions are more complex in the airline industry, where international travel and connections are part of the job and where frequent-flyer itineraries are complicated by the limited number of seats that are available for passengers seeking to take advantage of the program. Neither of the transportation call centres differentiates between service and sales in the assignment of work. At *Bus Company*, agents are expected to convert inquiries for timetable information into sales revenue. Not only is each job the same, but at this centre work teams have been done away with. Again, at *Airline* there is no division of labour between the teams; nor are there specialized call queues.

Reflecting the two-tier (public/user pay) system of health insurance and care in Australia, the two health-care centres in our study serve different markets and often operate in different ways. The *Health Premium* call centre is part of a nationally networked system that takes calls from individual private health-care subscribers. Typical calls relate to the policy details of holders, the services insured, the proportionate costs of specific procedures that *Health Premium* will defer, the availability of specific medical practitioners, and the status of submitted claims. Apart from a split between customer service and a corporate-service team that deals with employers who provide private health-care coverage to their employees, there is little division of labour at *Health Premium*, though difficult or more complex inquiries can be referred to a help desk at the centre, which is staffed on a rotating basis by more experienced employees. Contact centres in each state pick up regional traffic, but inquiries can also be networked nationally if queues become too long at any one site. *Health Authority*, the other centre in this industry sector, is part of the public system and a chain of call centres. Workers at this centre collect information from medical providers such as general practitioners and supply them with authorization numbers that allow their patients access to subsidized medicines under a national pharmaceutical-benefit scheme. Callers to the *Health Authority* centre included in this study consist only of medical personnel (physicians and pharmacists). Only *some* drugs used to treat *some* conditions are eligible for subsidization under the program, and it is up to the CSR to determine whether a given request meets the criteria. Typically, in these interactions the physician calls in with details of the drug, the patient's condition, dosage levels, and the need (if any) for repeat prescriptions; the CSR then uses pharmaceutical schedules to decide whether an authorization number will be issued.

At the beginning of this chapter, readers were introduced to the one leisure-services company included in the study. It owns four call centres across Australia, which receive and process telebets on horse races and other sporting events. Much about this centre is determined by the singular specificity of the service it provides, which is premised on economies of speed and accuracy. Gone are the days when work was divided up among operators – who took and manually wrote up bets – as well as account managers, bet collators, ledger machinists, and ledger keepers. Today the 380 staff employed at the *Telebet* centre that participated in this study conduct all of the work associated with this aspect of the gaming industry, taking up to 200,000 calls per day, with average call lengths that last no longer than 45 seconds! Hypothetically, work teams at *Telebet* could be organized along different dimensions: by revenue stream, or by type of bet. Some of these structures were tried out in the past, but this created problems of unequal workloads among the teams. As a result, 'the whole centre is [now] doing the same thing,' though there are still agents who are trained in different product groups (e.g., sports betting and horse betting) and others who are familiar with only one product.

The remaining Australian call centres are located at various levels of the public sector (federal, state, municipal), though in one case the centre provides services to the public sector on a tendered basis. Diversity is the watchword when it comes to summarizing the activities of these workplaces. Some centres offer fairly specific info-service products to the public, state employees, or other branches of government. *Licensing*, *Delivery*, and *Tender* are examples of centres that provide discrete outputs, which include answering questions and providing follow-up in relation to inquiries about vehicle registration and driver's licences in the first case; postal services in the second case; and relaying communications for hearing-impaired individuals in the third case. *Tender* is the sole outsourced centre among the Australian organizations in this study, operating under contract to the federal government. The main role of *Tender* is to enable communication to take place between its clients and other members of the public. Hearing-impaired clients or the public at large may use the call centre, which functions as an intermediary communications-relay service between the two groups.

Government Pensions is an example of a centre that provides information and services to a specific clientele: state employees who are or have been contributors to public superannuation schemes. Most calls involve providing information on the following: account balances and earnings, options for accessing accounts, the effects of changing circumstances (e.g., marriage dissolution) on pension benefits, and advice on retirement planning seminars that the organization runs for its members. This centre bears some of the hallmarks of the other financial-services operations included in the study – in particular, it utilizes generalist work teams that respond to a broad range of incoming inquiries. Meanwhile, *Collections* is a public-sector contact centre that works on behalf of other government departments, serving as an intermediary between those units and the public. Its role is to arrange for the payment of fines that have been levied by the police and the courts by providing inbound call-centre services. Two teams, which will soon be expanded to three, do exactly the same work of establishing payment schedules for back fines owed by members of the public. The work does not require any specialized legal knowledge; it does, however, require conflict resolution and communication skills as well as knowledge of the centre's software system. Knowledge of the State Penalties Enforcement Act, a 126-page piece of legislation, is also called for.

Other centres in the public sphere deliver a more diverse range of informational products. *Social Services* is one of twenty-six national call centres responsible for taking up inquiries and disbursing payments under federal social-welfare programs for families, youth, and the unemployed. Each 'payment stream' has various program entitlements attached to it – for example, job-search services and unemployment benefits in the employment-services queue. Agents may be skilled to work in up to two different payment streams. Workers at *Advisory Services* respond to legal questions from the public and, if necessary, arrange referrals to lawyers or other advocacy services. Callers may have a question in law that they want answered – for example, 'What does the defamation law say and am I liable under it?' or 'What rights of access do I have to my children?'[8] Client Information Officers, as they are called at this centre, provide basic information as to what the law says with regard to the client's particular concern. If legal advice or an opinion is sought, the CSR will arrange an appointment with the appropriate professional and establish a file on the case. About 50 per cent of the calls to the centre relate to family law, 40 per cent to civil law, and the remainder to criminal law, but there is no division of this work into separate call queues for designated work teams.

A third category of public-sector centre consists of two large facilities that are organized along a different model. *Urban Space* and *Statewide* each aim to provide whole-of-government services through a single centralized establishment. In both these cases, various government departments at the level of a local municipality (*Urban Space*) and a state jurisdiction (*Statewide*) have progressively been incorporated into the respective call centres. These two centres are exemplars of a further application of the call-centre labour process to a much wider scope of info-service activities than has hitherto been trialled. We can think of these two contact sites as 'supercentres' within their respective domains. Before the start of *Urban Space*'s operations in 1996, the local government directory listed 650 different phone numbers for the various departments and services offered. A member of the public would have to search through this directory and hope to hit upon the correct number. This process led to high rates of call transfer before 'ownership' of the call was taken and to correspondingly high rates of call abandonment and public dissatisfaction with the functioning of local government. Commencing in 1996, all 650 local government phone numbers were, within a short space of time, replaced by the same one number of the new call centre. Furthermore, except for a very limited range of inquiry (zoning and planning applications), all calls are dealt with in one general queue. *Statewide* later offered the same template for the broad range of government services offered by the state government, with work teams divided between two call queues: human services and business/customer services. This centre continues to take more government services under its ambit, with corresponding growth in employment levels.

2.3 Summary

The aim of this chapter has been to provide a brief overview of the organizational contexts in which this study of info-service workers has been carried out. The methodological decisions that have gone into the design and data collection for the research have also been laid out. Other researchers working out of both labour process paradigms (Bain and Taylor 2002a; Taylor, Hyman, et al. 2002) and HRM paradigms (Batt 1999, 2000) have drawn attention to the fact that every contact centre is in some sense different, while recognizing that like any truism, this may be only part of a more complex reality. At one level of understanding, no two centres are the same (Russell 2004); nor, in industries characterized by continuous 'chop and change' in the products they offer and the processes they invoke, does any one centre maintain a steady state over any length of time.

Yet an objective of any social-scientific inquiry is not only to document specificities but also to remain cognizant of overarching patterns, while trying to make sense out of both. Work in contact centres can be organized in different ways. Workers may be placed in broad general queues or aligned with specific products, services, or market segments. As suggested in chapter 1, jobs are becoming broader; the trend is towards replacing narrower specialization with wider capabilities. As this introduction to the research sites illustrates, in numerous instances workers have moved from responsibility for the delivery of one product, service, policy, or function to charge of a more diverse range of outcomes. This trend is most visible in the creation of the public-sector 'supercentres' discussed above (*Urban Space* and *Statewide*) but is also occurring in centres in banking and financial services as well as in telecommunications, transportation, and gaming. In at least some of these cases, wider job responsibilities coincide with greater variability in amalgamated work processes. This makes the measurement and control of such work more difficult for management. Just how management deals with this conundrum, and the consequences of such efforts, will be discussed in forthcoming chapters.

3 Making a New Occupation

3.1 Introduction

One can comb through various national occupational classification guides from the early 1990s and search in vain for any mention of call or customer-contact centres or for customer-service representatives/ agents or for any other reference to our subject matter. The 1997 *Australian Standard Classification of Occupations* (ABS 1997) contains many familiar occupational titles under 'Advanced Clerical and Service Workers' and 'Intermediate Clerical, Sales and Service Worker,' but 'CSR' is not among them. 'Call or Contact Centre Workers' first make their appearance in the 2006 edition of the *Australian and New Zealand Standard Classification of Occupations* (ANZSCO) (ABS 2006). Call-centre workers are given their own separate entry under this latest version of the ANZSCO system. Here they are said to fall within skill band #4, meaning that within the Australian Qualifications Framework they require a Certificate II/III (high school or community college completion) and/or at least one year of relevant experience. Supervisors of these workers are pegged at Certificate III or IV level, which equates to community-college graduation and/or three years of associated work experience (Australian Qualifications Framework Advisory Board 1996).

The latest occupational grid (2006) from Human Resources Canada includes call-centre agents under the category of 'customer service, information and related clerks.' This designation includes workers 'who answer enquiries and provide information regarding an establishment's goods, services and policies and who provide customer services such as receiving payments and processing requests for services' (Human Resources and Skills Development Canada 2006). In this schema, call-centre and customer-service agents are lumped together with such other occupational titles as 'bus information clerk' and 'tourist information clerk' and are said to require a high-school diploma and perhaps some tertiary education.

In addition to the above entry, call-centre/customer-service agents reappear under the categories 'User Support Technicians' (item #2282) and 'Supervisors, Library, Correspondence and Related Information Clerks' (item #1213) in the Canadian occupational matrix. Under the former item, 'call centre agents-technical support' employees provide 'first-line technical support to computer users experiencing difficulties with computer hardware and with computer applications and communications software.' These are the workers who staff the IT help desks on which computer users rely. They may be employed by computer companies (manufacturers and retailers) or software developers or in IT units in both the private and the public sector. According to the classificatory scheme, such workers will generally require college courses in computer programming or network administration. Meanwhile, supervisors of call-centre agents are included among a group of occupations that also cover supervisors of library clerks and survey interviewers. Their positions entail work planning and assignment as well as training and may require college completion according to this particular matrix.

In the earlier Canadian occupational index (Department of Human Resources and Social Development Canada 1992), the 'customer service, information and related clerks' category exists, but there is no mention of 'call centre agent-customer service' or 'customer service representative-call centre' in the earlier edition. Interestingly, these are the *only* new additions to this job category in the 2006 edition. Nor is there any reference to post-secondary educational requirements in the earlier 1992 entry for the occupations that are mentioned under the customer-service/information entry. The same holds for supervisory positions within this stream. Call-centre supervisors are the only new item to be added to the 1992 titles at the information/clerk supervisory level in the 2006 index. Finally, in 1992, the category of user support technician did not exist in the Canadian guide.

The latest U.S. Bureau of Labor Statistics *Occupational Outlook Handbook*, which appears to have replaced its *Dictionary of Occupational Titles* (DOT), continues past practice by referring to customer-service representatives. In the final 1991 edition of DOT, these jobs include relatively few specific entries. CSRs in financial institutions and workers who take customer complaints in the telecommunications and power/utility sectors are mentioned, though the only occupation specifically connected with long-distance over-the-phone service relates to IT help desks. By 2006, CSRs are a generic job title, 'employed by many different types of companies,' with the assumption made that 'many [will] work in call or customer contact centers' using multiline phone systems (U.S. Department of Labor 2006). Indeed, by 2006 contact centres provide the benchmark for customer-service employment in the U.S. occupational guide. CSRs, we are told, are expected to be capable of providing all information necessary to satisfy the needs of the caller; in other words, they are more than telephonists or exchange operators. Furthermore, the requirements for such jobs are likely to increase, according to the U.S. Department of Labor. While such jobs have been associated with high-school graduation in the past, 'due to employers demanding a higher skilled workforce, many customer service jobs now require an associate or bachelor's degree.' Bilingualism and, in certain fields (e.g., insurance), licensing are becoming more common, while overall employment in this category is expected to grow at an above-average rate despite the effects of automation and the sending of work offshore.

I quote the contents of these various occupational classifications to make a simple but important point. Before 1990 or thereabouts, informational work conducted in contact centres was the exception rather than the norm. Between 1990 and 2000 this form of information/service delivery exploded, as was recognized by the various national statistical agencies sometime after 2000, when the contact-centre CSR made her 'official debut.' The extent of this development in terms of numbers of jobs created was reviewed briefly in chapter 1. But numbers are easily glossed over. More significantly, what we need to discuss in this chapter is the making of an occupational labour market for the conduct of info-service work.

As a considerable pedigree of social-scientific (Marx 1971; Polanyi 1965) and historical (Thompson 1966) literature has been at pains to emphasize, labour markets do not just appear. Rather, they are the product of social and political agency, which in turn has significant economic consequences.[1] Emerging occupations are often associated with new technologies that have to be developed and adopted. Workers must be trained in their utilization, often through a combination of formal public education, accreditation, and work-based training; the latter may include on-the-job training and – albeit less often than in the past – apprenticeships, as well as computer-assisted, self-paced, modularized learning in contemporary settings. Employers may eventually come to agree on occupation-wide training standards, which then become a requirement for employment; the state may also assume a vital role in these processes by establishing specific training programs and institutes in consultation with industry. These dynamics often lend the evolving labour market a particular spatial quality (Bristow, Munday, and Gripaios 2000; Good and McFarland 2005; Richardson, Belt, and Marshall 2000; Richardson and Belt 2001). Industries that employ members of the occupation in large numbers as well as supporting human infrastructure (e.g., relevant educational and training facilities) cluster in specific places that establish a 'reputation' for specialization in the particular field (Arzbacher, Holtgrewe, and Kerst 2002).

In practice, training and accreditation overlap with the recruitment and selection of workforces. The latter may occur in a variety of ways but often involves social networks of employees, employers, and perhaps third-party intermediaries such as public and private employment agencies and recruitment firms, which bring large numbers of workers into contact with employers (Benner 2002). Networks may operate to bring ascribed as well as achieved elements into hiring (Castilla 2005), as when certain groups (genders, age ranges, etc.) are identified as possessing 'characteristics' that are particularly well suited for the work that is being offered (Belt, Richardson, and Webster 2000, 2002; Belt 2002a, 2002b; Durbin 2006; Mulholland 2002).

Embedded in this process and constituting the formation of a 'labour market' is the establishment of the terms and conditions of employment that are part of the offer of employment. Positions will be designated by job titles and descriptions and will be offered as full- or part-time, permanent or casual. Levels of remuneration will be defined as appropriate for the occupation; and the various job bands that have been created within it and may come packaged as hourly wages, yearly salaries, commissions, and bonuses, and with other fixed and variable elements (Fernie and Metcalf 1998). Particular populations or communities may be targeted as ideal potential candidates for filling emergent positions; examples are mothers with school-age children, university students, and workers over the age of fifty (Arzbacher, Holtgrewe and Kerst 2002; Bittner et al. 2002; Buchanan and Koch-Schulte 2000).

Responding to these dynamics, workers will find such arrangements to be more or less satisfactory in terms of meeting expectations, even as these are subject to alteration and revision. This in turn will create patterns of retention and attrition that are associated with the occupation. Such patterns will lend the labour market either stable or fluid qualities that may see it reproduced in its current form or altered. For example, the changing educational requirements associated with the call-centre agent occupational title noted above are indicative of a changing labour market. Retention and attrition will also be related to available opportunities, which may be enhanced through spatial clustering. The conditions that give rise to employment networks and common systems of accreditation and training may also provide conditions that are conducive to the 'poaching' of workers – or perhaps the blacklisting of unsatisfactory employees on the part of employers – as well as to job-hopping behaviour on the part of workers.

This chapter examines the formation of a labour market for info-service workers. This subsumes the main points raised above – recruitment, selection, and hiring, as well as formal contractual conditions, learning and training, and retention and attrition. These are relational processes that enter into the constitution of a 'labour market' that is spatially bounded. For example, ongoing experience with recruitment and selection may necessitate the revision of contractual conditions. There may be shifts towards greater amounts of part-time or permanent employment. Favourable terms of employment and the perceived availability of suitable, employable workers may lead other employers to seriously consider moving into the area to set up their operations. The attractiveness of certain areas may be influenced by the presence of publicly funded training and accreditation facilities and so on.

The journey commences in the next section with the hiring of labour. This chapter is macro-oriented and begins to make use of the survey data that were collected at the case-study sites. The aim is to examine the formation of a new occupational labour market in one particular locale – a large urban centre in Australia. We will return to some of the same themes in chapter 6, where the effects of HRM practices on employee identity are examined in greater detail. Chapters 3 and 6 can therefore be read in conjunction with each other, though they approach some of the same topics (e.g., employment status and training and development) from different angles and with different analytical purposes in mind.

3.2 The Recruitment and Selection of Call-Centre Labour

Two distinctive paths have been traversed in the creation of info-service labour markets, each leading to somewhat different outcomes. In some instances organizations have restructured their information, customer-service, and sales processes to take advantage of the new technologies and work designs associated with running a call centre. Existing departments have been collapsed, branch offices and over-the-counter services have been cut back or terminated altogether, and work has been reorganized into new, multifunctional contact centres, while workers have been transferred en masse and *remade* as CSRs. Essentially these are 'brownfield' call-centre sites, which have inherited workforces and often pre-existing cultures from other sections of the organization as in-house call centres have been established. In such circumstances it is often an open question as to how long existing employees will stay in the new work environment of the call centre. This pattern has been common not only in banking and the financial-services sector but also in the provision of public and social goods, where government services are increasingly accessed through information centres.

Alternatively, call centres may be staffed with new employees, who have been hired specifically to work in recently established call-centre operations. These operations can be depicted as 'greenfield' sites – that is, instead of *remaking* an existing workforce, the employer seeks out a new one. Greenfield sites allow the hiring organization much more discretion as to where the work will be located, who will be hired, and what the terms of employment will be. In most of the cases included in this study, greenfield conditions prevail. Regarding the fifteen organizations for which we have some detailed historical information, only three can be classified definitively as brownfield operations. In those three, the call centres developed out of existing organizational structures. The other twelve cases were greenfield start-ups. Note, however, that greenfield status should not be equated with a regional or rural presence. While commencing operations afresh does entail considerably more locational freedom, call centres may be established in either urban or regional settings, contiguous with or apart from the organizations they serve (see also Bristow, Munday, and Gripaios 2000).

Previous research on call-centre labour markets has drawn attention to two key features. New contact centres and the labour markets associated with them have exhibited a tendency to cluster, both in regional locations (Buchanan and Koch-Schulte 2000; Good and McFarland 2005; Rainnie and Drummond 2006; Richardson, Belt, and Marshall 2000; Richardson and Belt 2001) and within larger urban systems (Arzbacher, Holtgrewe, and Kerst 2002; Bain and Taylor 2002a; Thite and Russell 2007). Spatial clustering has to do with economies of agglomeration in labour-market formation, specifically with regard to training, skill-pool formation, and employment networking. State subsidies and development policies may also be implicated in the regionalization of call centres. However, in both Australia and India, call centres are chiefly urban phenomena.

Of the twenty Australian centres considered in this book, only one operates exclusively from a regional location, and it is a brownfield centre located where the company was founded. Another seven centres have regional branches in addition to their metropolitan operations. National companies often have centres located in more than one major city, while public and former public-sector operations often maintain a regional presence. In the case of the public sector, two different locational logics can be observed. In some instances, pressures to centralize – usually to an urban location – prevail as branch offices are closed. In other instances, regional development and employment policies promote the establishment of non-metropolitan call centres. A more inclusive census of Australian centres, based on self-reporting, suggests that just under 10 per cent of all centres are located in regional Australia, with the largest cities dividing the lion's share of info-service employment among themselves (Budde 2004).

The second notable feature of call-centre employment, at least in the developed information economies, is its gendered texture: female employees predominate on the floor (Belt 2002a, 2002b; Belt, Richardson, and Webster 2000, 2002; Buchanan and Koch-Schulte 2000; Durbin 2006; Mulholland 2002). Most commonly, the gendering of info-service employment has been related to the skills associated with the work and to the characteristics ascribed to female agents. Active listening, empathy, a 'customer focus,' the ability to engage in emotional labour, and team participation are privileged in many centres (Belt 2002b; Callaghan and Thompson 2002), and this has gone hand in hand with the feminization of the occupation – though as developments in India will show (see chapter 7; see also Cohen, El-Sawad, and Arnold 2009), not in all places. Female workers comprise more than three-quarters of our Australian sample (76.2 per cent) and no fewer than 56 per cent of the respondents in the least gendered workplaces, which include a telco and one of the public-sector call centres. Males compose 61 per cent of the Indian sample, while female workers range from 26 to 49 per cent of the respondents at the four BPO providers included in the Indian component of the study. For clarity of presentation, the remainder of this chapter will refer only to the Australian call-centre labour market and the conditions encountered there. We will return to the very different labour-market conditions of India and the outsourcing of info-service work in chapter 7.

The most common means by which employment is obtained in the Australian call centres is via responses to newspaper and Internet ads. The weekend careers section of the local metropolitan newspaper now contains a separate section dedicated solely to call centres and tele-marketing jobs. Overall, 35 per cent of the respondents acquired their current position by responding to a job advertisement. Recruiting in this manner may be conducted directly by the employer or may be partially or totally outsourced to a third-party employment agency. The latter scenario has spurred the development of a 'professional' re-cruitment industry, of which call centres are major users. Some hiring agencies have developed a reputation of expertise and reliability in the call-centre field, maintaining specific units to service this labour mar-ket. Decisions whether to retain recruitment in-house or to use an ex-ternal provider are usually left in the hands of the call-centre manager. The decision depends on the manager's resources – chiefly, the cen-tre's budget and time constraints and the associated opportunity costs. It seems that recruitment policy is one area where the contact-centre manager has considerable autonomy.[2]

Among the study sites for which we were able to collect informa-tion, seven indicated a preference for managing their own hiring, seven outsourced this function, three used a mixed approach, and one relied solely on 'walk-in' applications. Furthermore, the decision to outsource or retain recruitment activity is not fixed for all time. Some managers indicated that they had experimented with different practices. As well, managers come and go. Thus, one set of recruitment preferences may have been exercised in the past; then a new manager brings different priorities and deliberately alters past practices. Many instances of shift-ing from in-house to outsourced recruitment or vice versa were encoun-tered during this study; in one case we documented, the organization moved from in-house to outsourced and back again to in-house. The means by which workers are recruited seems to have next to nothing to do with the industry in which the centre operates. Thus, centres that go about sourcing recruitment in completely different ways were encoun-tered in the same sectors, an example being the insurance industry.

In interviews, managers advanced various reasons for preferring one strategy over another. The costs of externalization and outsiders' lack of familiarity with the needs of the business provided some managers with grounds for retaining recruitment processes. At *Airline*, the manager estimated that internal recruitment saved the company in the order of AU$800 to 900 per agent. For a centre that employed close to four hundred CSRs such as this one, this amounted to sizeable savings. Recruitment at this centre has been conducted completely in-house for more than a decade. Jobs are posted solely on the company's website and through a telephone hotline rather than in outside media. The same organization looks favourably on voluntary applications, as managers consider that through these processes they are getting applications only 'from people who want to work here.' Culling is conducted through a four-stage process that encompasses previous customer-service experience, telephone interviews, psychometric testing, and face-to-face interviews with team leaders.

One manager in the financial sector (*Insurer1*) did not consider it good business strategy to hand recruitment over to people who don't know the core business. This individual was simply more comfortable with the assurances provided by overseeing recruitment, believing that his involvement led to a more rigorous process. Job candidates who got through the company's internal process would 'tend to be a very high quality person.' This manager made a point of identifying direct involvement in recruitment and selection with 'best in practice' processes.[3] Additionally, defining recruitment as part of management's role was viewed as a means of keeping managers motivated and of producing better-rounded and higher-quality managers. Needless to say, internal recruitment also saved the company money, though the point was made that to avoid 'amateurism,' managers have to be trained in recruitment techniques. Under the previous manager, recruitment at *Insurer1* had been outsourced; the current regime has brought it back in-house as a core managerial function.

Similar motives were expressed in a public-sector centre (*Advisory Services*), where concerns had arisen that external agencies were not providing the centre with enough candidates of the calibre expected and required. As with *Insurer1*, recruitment and selection have switched back and forth between in-house and third-party over the course of this centre's history. At present, hiring is the preserve of the centre's management-coordination team. Though the centre is a provider of legal information, the main criterion for selection is said to be possession of a customer focus. Tellingly, the manager of *Advisory Services* rates such an orientation above any specialized paralegal training the agents may bring with them to the job.

In one of the larger firms (*Bank2*) it was suggested that the organization's size played an important role in determining recruitment and selection practices. With more than seven hundred CSRs spread across two states and multiple sites, the company had reached dimensions that justified operating its own careers department. Here the resources were available to develop an advanced careers website; it was implied that the company had become more sophisticated in its recruitment practices than many external providers. Responsibility for recruitment and selection was handed over to this unit in 2004. In this case the shift to in-house capability coincided with the growth of e-recruitment and the construction of a designated website for applicants.

Yet another reason for retaining the recruitment function was provided by the manager of *Delivery Services*, who was interested in moving towards more autonomous work teams in the call centre. In his view, recruitment provided an opportunity for greater levels of team involvement. In that organization, two external agencies are used to source applications. In tandem with management, those agencies construct shortlists. Then in-house interview panels consisting of team members from units that have vacancies make the final selections. A similar rationale was provided from a rather more unlikely source – the greenfield *Telco1* centre, which mainly employed young people. The manager at this site explained: 'Because we work on ... very much on a team environment, I think the only way we can actually ensure that we are employing people that are going to fit into our team environment is for us to do it [recruitment – BR] ourselves' (*T1*, call-centre manager).

Other managers found persuasive reasons for *outsourcing* the recruitment function. The manager at *Insurer2* had made the opposite journey as her counterpart at *Insurer1* – that is, she had gone from treating recruitment as an internal function to outsourcing it to a single specialized agency that is part of this manager's professional network. This manager cited the huge drain on her time that hiring could become. She had found one agency that she had a history of positive experiences with, and she now relied on her relationship with it. The argument we encountered here in favour of outsourcing was that it saved the manager time. This manager estimated that her centre's staff spent only half an hour recruiting each new CSR.

A number of other managers indicated that they had good experiences with particular recruitment agencies in the past, or knew of other managers who had, and this was given as a rationale for employing an external provider. One health-care centre relied on an agency that had developed a special expertise in this particular service area. The public-service manager at *Social Services* observed that her organization had switched from in-house to outsourced recruitment at a national level five years earlier in order to address its 10 per cent annual attrition rate. Prior to that, the centre had conducted its own recruitment, but current management views the outsourcing of the first stages of recruitment as a savings on organizational resources. The managers also argue that as the call-centre network has matured, external recruiters have become much better at what they do.

The manager of *Social Services* linked the maturation of the recruitment industry to the development of expertise specifically targeting the call-centre labour market. This had led to the growth of an occupational hiring network spearheaded by specialized firms.

Time constraints and the presence of employer/industry job networks were referred to in other instances as well. These factors become more pertinent when centres are expanding quickly, as is the case with *Statewide*, a government centre that is taking over responsibility for representing a host of departments and programs, and with *Government Pensions*. At the latter centre, an aging population has translated into larger numbers of calls per year, and more complex queries have resulted in increased call-handling times. Employment growth, combined with 'fairly high' turnover (much of which is internal to the organization), has resulted in a reliance on external recruitment agencies to maintain a steady flow of workers into *Government Pensions*. Normally, external agencies are involved right up to the shortlisting phase of the recruitment process. Team leaders usually take part in the final selections, alongside recruitment-agency personnel. In these cases a continuous demand for labour is associated with the outsourcing of employment recruitment.

Several sites utilized what can best be referred to as a mixed-methods approach to acquiring labour. This usually entails contracting out the early stages of the recruitment process, such as sourcing applications; then at a later stage, the principal employer enters the picture to make the final selections. Again, this procedure has different rationales. The manager at *Health Authority*, for example, found that a recruitment agency she was using had instilled unrealistic expectations in new recruits. Having confronted several misunderstandings about employment terms and conditions with new hires, *Health Authority* now supplies the recruitment agency with HRM material, which is provided to all applicants. Also, the centre's managers now conduct the final interviews and render the final hiring decisions. Under a mixed-model strategy, call-centre management works more closely with the employment agency in preparing information kits and in other stages of the process. Similar protocols are used at *Telco2*, where recruitment and selection processes are split between the external provider and in-house managers. An external agency is responsible for pooling applicants through advertisements and initial shortlisting; after that, managers test for interpersonal and computer skills at the call centre. Overall, and across the sample of CSRs as a whole, 20 per cent of the respondents indicated that they had obtained their position through an employment agency.

Managers are not the only social actors to use networks in the recruitment process. More than one-fifth of the sample (22.5 per cent) indicated that contacts such as friends or family members were the most important factor in securing their job. At some centres, such as the social-services provider *Tender* and the *Telebet* centre, this figure was considerably higher (56 and 72 per cent respectively), which reflects the importance of informal networks, especially among older women. For centres that have been operating for some time, and especially at brownfield sites that are not in the public sector, informal job networks among wage seekers may be important. Organizations/companies that have a brand name or an iconic status in the local labour market, or that are otherwise well known in a particular community (such as on a university campus), often rely on these informal means of securing workers. In these situations, pools of applicants are assembled mainly through employee referrals or 'walk-ins' (i.e., voluntary job applications); these are especially significant in centres such as *Telebet*, *Airline*, the not-for-profit centre, *Tender*, and the regional *Bus Company* centre. Start-ups that receive favourable publicity at the time of their inauguration, such as *Statewide*, can also take advantage of large numbers of voluntary applications.

Educational placements or traineeships are not important for placing workers in jobs even though a local community college offers a certificate program in customer-contact services. Nor are intra-organizational transfers to contact centres a common means of acquiring labour. Overall, only 8.8 per cent of the sample indicated that their current job was the result of a transfer; note, however, that this form of recruitment is more common in the public sector, where internal labour markets still exist, and among workers over fifty. The youngest group, meanwhile (the under-twenties), relied much more heavily than any other group on friendship networks to secure work.

At most call centres the selection process has a number of stages, regardless of whether recruitment is outsourced, in-house, or mixed-model. Commonly, three steps are mentioned: an initial telephone interview, abilities testing, and a final interview, which is often with a team leader or (as mentioned earlier) with representative CSRs from teams that have vacancies. At some centres the point was made that the first interview/cull was used to screen for previous customer experience. Such is the importance attached to the customer-service ethos (Korczynski 2002a, 2002b) that even at the centre that dispenses legal aid, the manager reported that customer service 'is one of the things that a lot of call centres talk about, but our customer focus is about people who want to deal with other people ... We find our most successful applicants come from hospitality and retail industries because they have been there, done that and they've seen it all and they know what it's like to deal with a range of people' (*Advisory Services*, call-centre manager).

So-called 'abilities testing' involves different things at different centres. Psychological profiling, testing for 'emotional intelligence,' 'scenario testing,' and computer navigational and keyboard testing are some of the items that were discussed in interviews with managers. Very often an emphasis is placed on social skills in the enactment of emotional labour (see also Callaghan and Thompson 2002; Thompson, Callaghan, and van den Broek 2004). As the same legal-aid manager recounted, one of the things she looks for is 'ability to separate themselves from the issues that they're dealing with ... It's a case of pulling out the pieces of information you need and looking for the rest, a lot of which is sometimes quite graphic in detail, just goes straight over you and not take, not absorb that and hang on to it, because it's the sort of job that if you do that type of thing, it will probably kill you.'

Two significant observations follow from the above. First, the selection process is used to screen for the presence of such things as a customer-focused approach and the appropriate demeanour – in other words, applicant qualities that are associated with the possession of social skills. As will be reinforced below, these are skills that are not so much trained for as *sought after* in recruitment. Second, the overall investment that is put into call-centre recruitment is notable. By this, I am referring to the systematic multistage selection process that is engaged in. Many of the centres in this study receive huge numbers of applications for limited numbers of intake positions. Ratios in the order of 6:150 – that is, 6 positions filled from 150 applicants, as was mentioned during an interview at one of the financial centres – are not unheard of. The competition for available positions and the vital importance attached to recruitment and selection processes are significant, especially when put up against the turnover and impermanency associated with much info-service work (also see below). In light of the above, the recruitment, selection, and attrition dynamic in many call centres presents the analyst with an intriguing puzzle.[4]

Who is recruited for call-centre info-service work? As noted earlier, the work is heavily gendered. This is particularly the case in the health-care, leisure, and social-services sectors of our sample, where women compose over 80 per cent of the respondents. In the telecommunications and finance-sector call centres, female respondents ranged from 60 to 70 per cent of the sample. Newer or rapidly expanding industries that use call centres as the main means of information and service distribution employ younger workforces, and these tend to be less gendered. This workforce demographic is especially evident in the telcos, where workers at a site such as *T1* offer relatively new products (e.g., mobile-phone packages and international calling cards) to the public. Similar age and gender patterns characterize the organizations dealing in financial products. In this sector, an astonishing 60 per cent of the sample was under thirty; the telcos did not trail by much, with 50 per cent of responding CSRs indicating that they were under thirty. Male workers are more likely to be found in these age brackets and in these call centres.

A degree of workforce blending is also observable when the educational qualifications of job holders are considered. The largest proportion of our sample of CSRs (21.4 per cent) had completed some high school, followed closely by university graduates (19 per cent), community college graduates (18.3 per cent), those who had completed some university (17 per cent), and, finally, those who had graduated from high school (16 per cent). Again, this conveys a picture of greater heterogeneity than may be found in other occupations. For example, the highest proportion of respondents in the financial centres had at least some university education, while university graduates in this group were almost as numerous as high-school graduates. Given that those with some university education or university graduates were as likely to be working in a permanent full-time capacity as others in the sample, we cannot assume that call-centre employment is only a stopgap measure that students use to fund their education.

To return to the question of who gets hired as CSRs, we can say primarily – but certainly not exclusively – women, as well as individuals from a wide range of ages and educational backgrounds. Though all of the call centres in the Australian component of the study employed more women than men, the centres that dealt with new products and services were more likely to employ significant numbers of male agents. Overall, six centres in the survey were 30+ per cent male, and five of these were in the telecommunications or financial-service sectors. Other centres, especially in health care, social services, and other arenas of the public sector, displayed higher levels of gendered employment.

3.3 Employment Status

The call centres in this study by and large do not approximate the model of contingent insecure work that is sometimes thought to characterize the information economy (Smith 2001). Less than one-fifth (18 per cent) of the workers who participated in the study were employed as casuals or temps, which is considerably below the national Australian average of 27.6 per cent (Campbell 2004). To the extent that it does exist, casualization is a gendered phenomenon, with just under 10 per cent of the male CSRs on a casual contract and just over 20 per cent of the female workers in this category. In the Australian context, casual status refers to workers who are not entitled to standard legislated benefits such as annual leave and employer contributions to superannuation. Almost all the casual workers who participated in the study were employed at two of the larger case-study sites: *Telebet*, which is 100 per cent casualized, and *Tender*, the outsourced social-services provider. Apart from these two centres, temporary workers are used mainly to fill short-term gaps in recruitment, often in the public sector. In other sectors such as finance, the use of casual workers is extremely low – less than 1 per cent of the respondents. Besides women, those with lower levels of educational attainment (i.e., less than high-school graduation), teenage workers, and those over fifty are more likely to be within the ranks of the temporary call-centre workforce than other CSRs in our sample.

Comparatively low levels of casualization may reflect different things, including the nature, demands, and expectations associated with info-service work and/or the state of the labour market in which the research is being carried out. With respect to the latter, CSRs were asked several questions about how they perceived the labour market and their position in it. The sample was divided regarding how much competition interviewees thought there was for the jobs they succeeded in filling: 49.8 per cent suggested that the competition was considerable, 20 per cent disagreed, and 30 per cent were uncertain. A slim majority (52 per cent) considered the likelihood of downsizing in their current employment to be remote (with another 25 per cent uncertain), and 55 per cent stated that they would not find it difficult to replace their current job with an equivalent position if they had to (24 per cent uncertain). These perceptions all point towards a buoyant market for info-service labour – a perception borne out by the thirty-year unemployment lows that prevailed as the study was being conducted. This may be one factor militating against greater casualization.

Additional statistical tests demonstrate a weak correlation between casualization and the perceived likelihood of downsizing (r = .218), and between permanent employment conditions and the perceived ease of job replacement (r = .109). In other words, a greater perceived probability of job loss on the part of employees does not *automatically* translate into a greater use of casual labour by employers, while strong labour markets are no assurance of permanent employment in today's world. More important than such macroeconomic conditions in accounting for rates of casualization are the specific labour-market requirements of employers. In numerous centres, casuals were used only to plug holes – in the case of unexpected quits, for leaves, and to cover staffing requirements in between intakes of new permanent agents. A few managers noted that the flexibility associated with casualization can work in more than one direction and that moving away from the use of casuals can provide greater staffing flexibility. According to one manager, given the training requirements at the centre, it did not make sense to use casual labour: 'Here, four weeks of intake training and a further eight weeks of development [and] familiarization is necessary before they're at a level where they're competent, so to me it doesn't make any sense to invest three months of your time in a casual employee' (*Insurer2*, call-centre manager).

Part-time work, defined as fewer than thirty-five hours per week in our survey, is a more common experience than the use of casual labour. Survey respondents were split into an approximately 60:40 ratio of full-time to part-time work. Apart from the *Telebet* centre, where all workers are both casual and part-time, this form of employment is more prevalent in the public/social services sector, where over 40 per cent of employees work on a part-time basis. Most of the part-time work appears to be by employee choice. That is, workers either use flexible work/

life balance policies that their employers offer to take up the option of part-time work, or they seek out employers who are known for offering part-time options. Part-time work applies mainly to female CSRs, 44 per cent of whom are in this employment category as compared to 23 per cent of the male workers. Among the men working part-time, one-quarter would prefer full-time employment, while involuntary part-time work affects less than 15 per cent of the female CSRs in the sample. Early school leavers, teens, and those over forty are also more likely to be among the part-time workforce in our sample.

There are reasons why some managers restrict the amount of part-time work that is available. The manager of the insurance centre who was quoted as arguing against the utility of casual work at her centre also reflected on her experiences of using part-time workers:

> In theory it sounded really good, but what it actually created for us was more inflexibility with our rostering because even though essentially that's our core pattern things can shift to the left or right a few hours each day. Particularly with changing winter to summer we still require flexibility from staff to work weekends and public holidays, and the part-time staff just weren't prepared to do weekends, weren't prepared to do public holidays. It just became a battle for us, so we decided to keep the part-timers at a sort of minimal level and keep the full-timers up, but it has a lot to do with our demographic as well, down in this area ... It's sort of, part-time staff we attract are working mums, okay, so there's mums wanting to come into work, do a few hours. And they want to do school hours, they don't want to come to work on the weekends, they don't want to and they don't want to work public holidays. (ibid)

In this case it was a problem of obtaining staff to work unpopular hours – an issue that was minimized by building such hours into the regular rosters of permanent full-time staff and by offering attractive overtime rates of pay. Where acquiring staff to work specific rosters is less problematic, or where the work is especially stressful, part-time employment may be favoured by management and more conventional arguments may come to the fore. For example, in the public-sector centre *Advisory Services* the manager tied part-time employment with both the enabling features of call-centre measurement and rostering tools that permitted maximum staffing flexibility and with consequent improvements in agent productivity: 'The proportion of, the high proportion of part-time and casual staff allows us to match the workforce to the demand, so we do a lot of measurement of when the clients are actually calling, how long it takes, all being supposedly scientific stuff in behind running a call centre, we do that and then plan how we can best use our staff' (*Advisory Services*, call-centre manager).

In this example, management had actually plotted an inverse correlation between hours worked and productivity. According to this manager, when agents went from part-time to full-time work their productivity declined. Moreover, part-time work suited the law students, who at any given time constituted between one-fifth and one-third of the workforce at *Advisory Services*.

In our sample, one-third of workers came to their jobs with previous call-centre work experience and two-thirds were novices. This means that once hired, the second aspect of making a new workforce commences in earnest. The next section considers training in greater detail.

3.4 Training

Training in call centres is usually divided into an initial period of full-time instruction, followed by ongoing updating and continued learning. Most centres have their own dedicated training staff; larger centres normally have a manager in charge of training and development as well as a training team. Training is often defined as part of the HRM function – specifically, as human-resource development (HRD).

Investments in training are often taken as an indicator of other things, including the skill demands of the work and the type of employment regime in effect. More training presumably equates with higher skill levels. Organizations that pour resources into training are also thought to epitomize what have been termed 'high-performance work systems' (HPWSs) (Appelbaum et al. 2000; Batt 2000, 2002; Hutchinson, Purcell, and Kinnie 2000). For a variety of direct and indirect reasons, HPWS practices are theorized as leading to greater organizational productivity as well as to improved working conditions. Investments in training and skill upgrading are central to the HPWS construct.

Across our sample the mean number of weeks of initial training was 4.2. A month of training was also the most frequently cited amount. A comparatively small fraction of the workforce (16 per cent) received a week or less of initial instruction, while 20 per cent obtained a month of intake training. Inspecting the results by organization fails to produce any outstanding industry patterns. For example, one of the two telcos in our study provided substantial numbers of workers with two months of training, while the other conducted virtually all of its initial training in less than a month. Similar variation in amounts of training can be observed across the insurance companies in the sample, which lends weight to the notion that investments in training are – to a degree at least – a matter of organizational choice. In other words, training is one aspect of strategy as it relates to market specialization and job design (Batt 2002; Kinnie, Purcell, and Hutchinson 2000).

Call-centre work, which we will go into in more detail in the following two chapters, entails the use of computers and software programs in structured interactions with a public. By definition, such interactions do not entail physical co-presence; rather, they are conducted through and across distance in real time. In such work environments, training covers a variety of subjects, including process knowledge (by which we mean software and systems utilization, information retrieval, data-file management, and archiving); product and policy knowledge; social and interactional competence;[5] and (in some cases) marketing savvy. A good deal of ink has been spilt on the relative weights of these aspects of info-service work and their overall relationship to required occupational skill.

In terms of time spent on different training activities, the acquisition of specific product knowledge was nominated as the most important aspect of training by the largest proportion of the sample (60 per cent), followed by software and systems training, which was accorded 'most important' status by 28 per cent of CSRs. Only 8 per cent regarded the acquisition of social skills as the most important component of their initial training. Software/systems training is also most frequently advanced as the second-most-important matter covered in intake training. By examining results across the different industry groups and for the individual organizations, we can control for the unweighted nature of our sample (i.e., different numbers of responses in different organizations). Similar results still hold when this statistical control is introduced into the analysis. Out of the twenty call centres, CSRs in three ranked something other than product knowledge – in all three instances, software and systems training – as of greater importance in terms of time devoted to subject matter during initial intake training. At two of these centres, *Tender* and *Collections*, there *was* no product knowledge per se. At *Tender*, workers provided a communications-relay service to hearing-impaired clients in their telephone communications with other members of the community; at *Collections*, CSRs were in charge of compiling fines that had been levied through the criminal-justice system.

At the third centre, *Telebet*, where agents nominated systems training as most important, customer interactions were extremely short and instrumental and the speed and accuracy with which work was conducted was all-important.

These results are all the more interesting when put up against employee perceptions of job demands and employer priorities in recruitment and selection. When asked what they consider to be the most important skill used in their work, 48 per cent of respondents nominated social skills – that is, an ability to carry out effective interactions with members of the public; 39 per cent specified product knowledge; and 14 per cent stated computer skills. With some qualifications, these evaluations also applied at the individual centres. When we inspect the findings at the individual case-study sites, we find that product knowledge is even with or surpasses social skills in the estimation of CSRs in two of the financial centres (*Bank2* and *Insurer2*) and two of the public-sector/social-services centres (*Social Services* and *Licensing*) and at one of the health-sector contact centres (*Health Premium*). Computer skills are designated as the most important skill set at only one centre, *Telebet*. Elsewhere, social skills are lent much more importance than is reflected in training agendas.

This disjuncture between training content and job content carries forward when we consider ongoing training, where once again, in terms of the time invested, the acquisition of context-specific product and service knowledge is rated as the most important aspect in continuing learning by the largest proportion (53 per cent) of the sample. As in the case of induction training, software and systems instruction is more frequently listed as the most important component of ongoing learning (23 per cent) than is time given over to the acquisition of social skills (16 per cent). These results are reproduced across the various industries and individual organizations. In fact, at nine out of the twenty research sites, greater proportions nominated product knowledge as a more important component of ongoing learning than of initial training. The tying of training and learning to product and service information does not seem to abate at any time in the working history of the CSR.

CSRs' perceptions of training priorities are largely reinforced by managerial comments on the issue. The manager of a large public-sector centre recognized that new products, services, and policies are continually being introduced by government, noting that most ongoing training is taken up with creating worker proficiency in these offerings and the processes used to deliver them. She also lamented that much more could be done – especially in the realms of development training and team building – if the budget were available.[6] The head of one of the financial contact centres made similar observations. Though systems and product training absorbed most of the training budget – 'release training around new systems' as he defined it – ideally more time could have been given over to what he described as training in the 'soft skills.'[7]

The manager at the largest bank in our study confirmed that the most challenging aspect of inductee training was the complex financial-systems software, followed (again) by product knowledge. Communications training at this operation was provided only after the first three months of employment and was incorporated into the sales-training modules. This was similar to the situation encountered at the *Delivery Services* centre. In this case, initial training periods at the centre were conducted for four weeks, with the emphasis on product and services instruction. Thereafter, about 5 per cent of an agent's time was taken up with continuous training; thus about 100 hours per agent per year were devoted to topics such as changes to privacy legislation and occupational health and safety instruction. Professional-services training was available only for CSRs who had been identified as potential future team leaders. It could be accessed only by those who had been in the job from six to twelve months and who were performing at an above-average standard. This training was clearly integrated into front-line leadership succession planning at the centre to compensate for attrition at this level to other parts of the organization. At another financial centre (*Bank1*) an impressive 30 per cent of agent time had been given over to training in the preceding months; however, this was completely consumed with the introduction of new financial systems and with providing to agents the details of new government legislation relating to product disclosure and compliance requirements.

Comparable conditions pertained at one of the public health-insurance centres, *Health Authority*, where training was largely taken up by remaining current with changes to the government's authorization schedules for the subsidized pharmaceutical-benefits scheme. Building on induction training, agents at this centre were provided with one hour per week of 'self-learning time' in order to remain current with the subsidy schedule and were rostered for an additional half-hour per fortnight with team-program advisers for updates on monthly changes to the benefit program.

When asked about ongoing learning at his centre, the manager at

Airline replied: 'We do heaps of it.' Then he checked his figures and confirmed that the centre had undertaken 56,000 hours in the preceding year – which, according to my calculations, equates to about three weeks a year for each CSR at this one centre – impressive by any standard. Most of this, though, was taken up with moving from a commission-based to a fee-for-service transactional model in interactions with the public and with learning the ins and outs of a new passenger-booking system. In this industry the upgrading of operational processes is non-stop, as is the need for constant (re)training on the revised systems.

One gets a similar impression not only in the other transportation-sector call centre that was included in the study but also in the two telecommunications centres. The immediacy and hype surrounding new-product releases – 'campaigns' as they are called in call-centre argot – along with very limited product life cycles, places considerable demands on a call centre's training regime, as was drawn to our attention in both of the transportation and telecommunications companies studied. New products, variations in the options available, continuous price alterations, and accompanying changes in the software systems that support them featured in these training regimes. As the manager of *Bus Company* observed: 'Because a lot of changes happen immediately, it's too hard to get formalized training, so we have a lot of online. It's all online, everybody has access to Reservation Internet, and this is what we're selling today – this is the time frame, this is how you do it' (*Bus Company*, call-centre manager).

A similar sense of training priorities in relation to what the work entails was relayed by the manager at *Telco1*, a long-distance phone-care business. In her mind, 'the job out there is not difficult at all ... It's not brain surgery, we're not asking anyone to be a brain surgeon, but there is a lot to learn, and we are continually putting new cards out to the market. We're continually forming alliances with other groups of people, we've just branched out into New Zealand, we sell cards, New Zealand cards, we're actually going to Fiji ... There's a lot for them to know' (*T1*, call-centre manager).

Training in call-centre work has largely been professionalized. Overall, 47 per cent of the sample indicated that the greatest proportion of their *initial* training had been classroom-based, while 38 per cent stated that it was evenly divided between classroom and on-the-job training. Only 15 per cent said that on-the-job training was the largest component. The same results pertained to the greatest number of individual organizations. In twelve of the call centres the largest proportion of respondents specified that more time was given over to classroom-based training than to any other modality, while the largest percentage at seven other sites indicated a roughly even split between classroom and on-the-job training. As expected, the greatest amount of introductory training was delivered by formal instructors. Co-worker/buddy instruction was viewed as important by significant numbers of respondents (≥ 20 per cent) at only four centres, while at another two sites the largest proportion suggested that their training was evenly divided between designated instructors and co-worker peers. Online training remains comparatively unimportant in the estimation of CSRs at this stage.

Similar practices characterized recurrent training. Once again, the greatest proportion of the sample (54 per cent) stated that classroom-based learning constituted the most important venue for ongoing training, and this result held across every organization save one: the public-services provider *Urban Space*, where two-thirds of the respondents said that e-learning was the most important form of delivery.[8] Following from this, designated trainers were estimated to be the most important component of ongoing training and learning, again at all centres except for one (*Licensing*), where peer-based learning was assessed as more important by a greater number of respondents.

That a more professional approach is taken towards training and learning in the info-service work environment of today than in the staples or manufacturing jobs of yesteryear seems beyond debate. Yet how much of this effort goes towards the training of professionals? Without wishing to prejudge later chapters, which take up the question of job skill, it is the case that occasional glimpses of the professionalization of info-service work were captured over the course of the research. Five weeks of initial training are conducted at *Social Services*, but this is followed by a lengthy six-month probationary period – considerably longer than what is encountered elsewhere. Following on from this, all CSRs are allocated ten hours of learning and development time per month. This time may be given over to further training as well as to self-guided Web-based learning. It is expected that all workers at *Social Services* will attain a Certificate IV, the highest level of contact-centre accreditation available. While the CSRs at *Social Services* are not qualified social workers, there is an element of professional service delivery in knowing how to match social-benefit programs with a diverse client base. Similarly, workers at the *Government Pensions* centre receive six weeks of classroom instruction followed by another stint of up to six weeks of on-the-job training. During this latter period, CSRs receive accreditation to provide general advice, though they are prohibited from providing specific recommendations with respect to products, investment options, or financial planning more generally. An average of one hour per week in continuous training that combines self-instruction with trainer-led seminars then becomes a regular feature of employment at *Government Pensions*.

Overall, these results raise a number of important issues. First, unlike some other research findings that have devoted attention to training in post-industrial work environments (Smith 2001) and found a new emphasis being placed on the acquisition of social and team-building skills, our investigation finds greater prominence being given to product and process training. Ironically, in more information-intensive environments than Smith analyses, less formal training time is devoted to proficiency in communication and other social skills. At one level, the emphasis that is placed on training in the presentation of products is completely understandable. Post-industrial societies are often equated with consumption and the risks that accompany it (Beck 1992; Du Gay 1996). Business strategy in a globalizing world is increasingly associated with product differentiation, market segmentation, choice, and the glorification of the sovereign consumer (Batt 2002; Porter 1985; Korczinski 2002a, 2002b). Whether we consider mobile-phone packages, health-care benefits, airline mileage plans, superannuation options, or qualifying conditions for the receipt of welfare benefits (all products/services encountered in the course of this research), the array of options, plans, and conditions attached to such services can quickly become overwhelming. It is little wonder, then, that so much customer-service training is taken up with familiarization as to what is or can be offered. It could therefore be argued that product and process training is a necessary precursor for the demonstration of social competence in info-service work.

But it is also significant that the social skills associated with info-service work remain something of a black box, especially when it comes to training and development in this area. According to employee *and* managerial respondents, training and development in communication and related social competencies take up relatively little time in call centres. Workers attribute considerable importance to this aspect of their occupation, yet this is not reflected in the considerable amounts of training that are undertaken in contact centres. The whole issue of skill is examined in the following two chapters. Here we can say that such skills tend to be the focus of recruitment practices rather than developmental ones that occur after hiring. Social skills are viewed as an attribute to be sought out during the selection process. As recounted by the manager of the *Advisory Services* centre (see Section 3.2), though in the 'business' of providing legal assistance, the most successful agents are those who come not with a legal-studies background but with one in hospitality or retail. New employees are expected to offer up social skills as a 'gift' or perhaps a 'quid pro quo' at the behest of HR management and on behalf of an expectant public. To the extent that such skills are an object of training and development programs, they are largely reserved for team leaders under the rubric of 'people management skills.' The importance of social skills is accentuated in the call-centre/customer-service literature, yet so far, little is known about them.

3.5 'Shall I Stay or Shall I Go?': Attrition and Retention in Call Centres

When customer-contact centres first entered the scene, publicity around the issues of turnover, attrition, and employee 'churn' was not far behind. It was less clear whether this was part and parcel of a new labour market in formation or whether it pointed towards more systemic issues such as problematic job design. Our data indicate that in the interim, things have only partly settled down. Overall, a minority of the employee respondents (47 per cent) intend to remain in their current position for the next three years. Almost one-third (31 per cent) indicate a desire to quit, which is very close to the average call-centre attrition rates that managers quoted as pertaining to the local labour market for CSRs. The remaining 22 per cent of interviewees are undecided. Thus the potential attrition rate is in excess of 50 per cent over a three-year period. Naturally, these estimates vary by call centre. Financial centres in particular exhibit greater employee intentions to exit; perhaps this is because they tend to recruit younger workers. Retention rates appear to be higher in the public-sector centres. These trends were confirmed during our interviews with management.

All else being equal, men in our sample are about 10 per cent more likely to quit their jobs than women, with more than one-third of male workers (38.4 per cent) and just over one-quarter of female employees (28.4 per cent) having definite intentions to exit. These results hold across all employment categories – that is, men in either full-time or part-time positions as well as in permanent or casual job arrangements are less likely to indicate an intention to remain in the call centre. The same gender differential holds for most age groups. Thus the percentage of women saying they will stay is higher for all age groups, except for the twenty- to twenty-nine-year-old bracket, where it is identical to the male rate, and in the forty- to forty-nine-year-old and sixty-plus deciles, where a higher proportion of the male respondents say they have no intention of quitting. Overall, and as expected, younger workers are less settled. From age thirty onward, greater proportions of both genders indicate an intention to remain in their jobs than to leave.

What lies back of these patterns? At this stage we can answer this question only in its most immediate sense. Most frequently cited as the number-one reason for remaining in a particular centre is the money – satisfaction with the wages on offer – which is nominated by 28 per cent of those who intend to stay put. This is followed by those who mention an intrinsic enjoyment of the work as the most important consideration (20 per cent). Employment security is the next most frequently referenced rationale. Job security is more often connected with public-sector employment and especially with health services, while intrinsic job satisfaction is frequently mentioned by those in financial services. Again, this may have something to do with the average age of the workforce in that sector. Overall, men are more likely to nominate wages as the most important inducement for remaining in their current job, by a 10 per cent margin over women (36 versus 26 per cent). Men are also more likely to rate opportunities for advancement as the most important reason for staying (12 versus 4 per cent), while women are more likely to prioritize flexible working hours (18 per cent of women versus 4 per cent of men) and workplace friendships in their decisions to continue (4 per cent versus < 1 per cent). Part of the attraction of call centres would appear to be the flexible working hours they offer female workers, who combine info-service work with domestic labour in a double working day (Armstrong and Armstrong 1994). Almost as many women indicate that working-time flexibility is the most important reason for working in their current job as cite enjoyment of the work or satisfaction with the wages (18, 20, and 26 per cent respectively).

Of the almost one-third of respondents who definitely intend to quit their jobs, dissatisfaction with the work looms as the most important point. One-third of foreseeable attrition is attributable to this factor. The second most frequently provided reason is related to this point as well. The absence of opportunity structures in call-centre work is given by 14 per cent of those who intend to exit as the most important factor

Table 3.1
Most important factor in deciding to quit, Australian sample
(% of those intending to leave employment)

Reason for quitting	%
Dissatisfaction with wages	11.0
Routine/boring nature of work	32.5
Lack of opportunity to advance	13.7
Job stress	9.7
Unfair treatment by mgt	9.0
Lack of employment security	3.1
Call-centre work viewed as only temporary	8.2
Unfriendly social environment	1.3
Unsafe working conditions	0.5
Other	11.0

lying back of their decision. While dissatisfaction with wages is the third most frequently stated reason, this is closely followed by other job-related considerations, including work-related stress. Overall, work-related factors account for more than half (56 per cent) of planned quits (see Table 3.1). Moreover, as revealed in the table, most of the workers who intend to quit did not enter employment with the expectation that it would be a short-term commitment. Fewer than 10 per cent of the sample had entered call-centre work with the assumption that it would only be a temporary placement.

In fifteen of the twenty centres included in this portion of the study, the nature of the work is cited as the most important reason for wanting to quit. This factor seems particularly salient in the telecommunications centres. Ironically, job-related stress stands out in the health sector as a principal reason for leaving. The routinization of work and its ensuing consequences are, singularly, the most important reason for voluntary attrition in telecommunication, transportation, finance, and public services. Only in the one leisure-services centre, *Telebet*, where casual employment is the norm, is the temporary nature of the work given as the main reason for intentions to leave. Women and men in equal proportions cite boredom as the most important reason for intentions to quit, though a greater proportion of women indicate that job stress is the most important factor in their choice to leave (11 per cent of women versus 6 per cent of men). Men are somewhat more likely to refer to the absence of opportunities for advancement than are women (18 versus 12 per cent).

A few call-centre managers were prepared to be blunt when discussing the attrition challenge and what they thought lay back of it. According to a manager in a financial centre that specialized in superannuation accounts and that lay at the high end of annual attrition numbers:

> At the end of the day, what we find is that people are happy to be on the phones probably a maximum of two years. Once they come to eighteen months to two years, they really are burned out, they don't want to be on the phones anymore ... I guess we've come to the point where we expect that we will have turnover, it's only natural, it's not the kind of job that people can and want to do forever, so I guess we're now trying to manage around that in terms of the way we recruit. (*Gov't Pensions*, call-centre manager)

In other financial institutions the call centre was referred to as the 'breeding ground' for the rest of the organization. As explained, at *Insurer2*:

> It is inevitable that after twelve months, eighteen months, people will look for other opportunities in the organization ... We tend to find people with opportunities after twelve months. If they haven't gone to other parts of the business they tend to hang around for a while longer. (*Insurer2*, call-centre manager)

These managers are suggesting that they have learned to live with high rates of staff turnover as a 'fact of life.' However, the manager of another public-sector contact centre explained a 16 per cent drop in attrition rates (from 25 to 9 per cent) as follows:

> There's a theory that says only 5 per cent of the workforce is actually suitable to work in call centres, I am probably looking for somewhere less than 1 per cent of that 5 per cent to be the sort of people we are really needing here. (*Advisory Services*, call-centre manager)

This individual offered two reasons for the decline in attrition rates. First, as implied in her statement, a more rigorous selection process had been brought into play in which final recruitment decisions were made by a management coordination team that included the call-centre trainer and the work-team coordinator, among others. This coincided with the centre bringing recruitment and selection back in-house as a core managerial responsibility and with the undertaking of detailed entrance and exit interviews with shortlisted job applicants and staff who were quitting. Second, this centre now promotes the use of part-time labour as a deliberate strategy for dealing with the stresses associated with the job. As this manager was prepared to admit: 'This is a really tough job to do for eight hours a day. I think it's a tough job to do for *five* hours a day. Eight hours for me is a bit mind-boggling' (ibid.).

One feature of the preceding quotations is the role assumed by recruitment and selection as a response to high attrition. Managers acknowledge that stress and burnout seem to be part and parcel of info-service work and have responded by recruiting more carefully. The adequacy of this 'solution' is far from apparent. Indeed, it could be suggested that the discussion leads us inexorably into the labour process of info-service work – a theme that is taken up in the next two chapters of the book.

In this chapter I have alluded to the high degree of ambiguity regarding how to conceptualize the work of CSRs. At first, official statistical agencies subsumed this work under clerical/clerk designations. But even within this classification there seemed to be important outliers, such as IT help-desk consultants and bilingual workforces, that did not fit comfortably into such a narrow pigeonhole. Adding further to the confusion is agreement over the importance of certain skills for the performance of the work, skills that no one can define clearly – namely, the social skills required for info-service work. The following chapters focus on the call-centre labour process, the technologies it utilizes, and the implications for skill and employee development. Here we can conclude by stating that the call centre is *a labour process*, the nature of which remains to be specified.

4 The Call-Centre Labour Process (1): The Division of Labour, Work Effort, and Job Skill

4.1 Introduction

As suggested at the beginning of the book, the call centre has become something of a metaphor for the way in which work is organized in the global service economy. This follows directly from the point that besides being integral to many organizations – or in certain situations such as outsourcing, an industry in its own right – call centres represent a new way of organizing a broad spectrum of work. A central claim of this book is that the call centre is a labour process for the production and distribution of information, a site for the performance of what we have termed info-service work. As a labour process, the organization of info-service work in contact centres has proven to be far more efficient than past ways of accomplishing such work. For this reason the call centre format has quickly displaced earlier ways of working, becoming the most common means by which service users and supplier organizations communicate. But what are the implications of this? Does all info-service work that is conducted through the call centre share an underlying logic of organization, a common socio-technical paradigm? What are the consequences of this for the skills that the work requires and develops? How much variation is introduced by call-centre work occurring across different industries and sectors of the economy? How mutable is this labour process to organizational choice?

In this chapter we go onto the floor of the contact centre with the CSRs and managers who work there. It is the first of two chapters devoted to an analysis of this new labour process. In this chapter the focus is on scrutinizing the commonalities and differences that exist among the contact centres included in the Australian component of the study as reported by those who daily inhabit such workplaces. We enter the floor of production as the 'guests' of those who work there in order to gain a perspective on the type of work they do. In the next chapter we drill deeper and look at the construction of the floor itself and what it means for conducting work. The specific concerns of this chapter are with the work and the ways it is accomplished. This includes an analysis of how info-service work is structured and of workers' and managers' expectations regarding what constitutes 'reasonable' efforts and outcomes. The skill demands that are attached to call-centre work are also evaluated. Owing to the growth of employment in contact centres worldwide, this has larger implications for labour-force skill trends – implications that warrant attention. Do work expectations and skill levels vary much from centre to centre, industry to industry? Or is there a tendency towards standardization – and if so, at what level? These are the issues that are posed in this chapter, and they have immediate implications for the theoretical concerns enunciated in chapter 1 with respect to changes in the technical division of labour associated in particular with info-service work.

These questions are by no means new. They are reminiscent of debates that have arisen in the sociology of work at other research sites in the past. At the height of the industrial era the automotive industry was regarded as leaving its imprint on a much larger swath of society than that industry alone (Gramsci 1971). It exemplified a particular form of manufacturing that became known for its efficiency as well as for the alienating affects it had on those who laboured under its methods (Blauner 1964; Beynon 1973; Chinoy 1992; Milkman 1997). The fast-food industry enjoyed a similar iconic status among sociologists in the latter twentieth century, for in that location Fordist manufacturing techniques met a service economy of youthful workers (Leidner 1993; Reiter 1991) in a socio-technical paradigm that has been dubbed 'McDonaldization' after the corporation that pioneered the new approach (Ritzer 2004). As in the case of its predecessor concepts such as Fordism, the McDonaldization designation is intended to point towards the far-reaching economic and cultural implications that are hypothesized as extending well beyond the immediate sites of work.

There have also been debates over the saliency of such stylizations and the value of 'epochalist' theorizing (Du Gay 2007). For example, the extent to which the techniques of the automotive industry have been adopted by other manufacturers in other places, or have been responsible for the successes attributed to them, has been hotly contested (Hirst and Zeitlin 1991; Littler 1982; Williams, Haslam, and Williams 1992). The question of whether there are genuine (more humanistic?) alternatives to a dominant paradigm such as Japanese 'toyotism' or Scandinavian 'volvoism,' or whether at the end of the day these are simply variations on a common template of work organization has also generated much heat among social scientists (Rinehart, Huxley, and Robertson 1997; Berggren 1992; Womach, Jones, and Roos 1990). Analogously, in the service economy the question of whether workers view the techniques of routinization as onerous social controls or as aids to accomplishing their work has been posed effectively (Leidner 1993, 1996).

The advent of contact centres and info-service labour processes enhances the complexity of these questions by virtue of the fact that the outputs of such operations are a good deal more amorphous than the products of the automotive or fast-food industries. Outcomes associated with info-service work are diffuse – they stretch across a plethora of industries and also take in the public and increasingly the not-for-profit sectors. For example, in addition to the call centres introduced in chapter 2, it is common now for manufacturers to operate their own customer-contact centres, which supply a variety of services – including product information and repair scheduling – related to the commodities they manufacture.[1] In the not-for-profit sector, charities in particular have adopted the outbound call-centre format, sometimes outsourcing their fund-raising activities to third-party provider centres that specialize in such work and sometimes developing their own in-house capabilities. In such cases, how similar or dissimilar are call centres from one another in terms of the work processes they unleash? If commonality turns out to be the dominant motif, around what structures and norms is the central tendency grouped? If conditions are wider ranging, what factors give rise to dispersion, and is it possible to identify and account for more preferable work practices?

The sizeable existing literature on call centres, depending on its theoretical lineage, attaches greater significance to the similarities among call centres – or alternatively, to the possibilities for substantial variation among centres based on the choices managers make. In a series of articles, Taylor and Bain emphasize the common features that constitute a call-centre labour process. Their argument rests on a number of key points. First, similar means of production/communication are found in all call centres. As Taylor and Bain (1999) observe in one of the first pieces published on the subject, 'a call centre [is] a dedicated operation in which computer-utilising employees receive inbound – or make outbound – telephone calls with those calls processed and controlled either by an Automatic Call Distribution (ACD) or predictive dialling system. The call centre is thus characterised by the *integration* of telephone and VDU technologies.' Digital technologies, including personal computers networked with digital telephone systems, have made possible the automated call distribution systems that are at the core of every call centre. These integrated technological ensembles are the 'transmission belt,' delivering work in a lineal fashion to waiting workers.

In order to avoid a narrow technological determinism (see also chapter 5), Taylor and Bain also situate the call centre within a specific political-economic context that includes the deregulation of national communication systems and the concomitant rise of global capitalism (Taylor and Bain 2007; Ellis and Taylor 2006; see also Glyn 2007). Customer-contact centres promote the rationalization of white-collar service delivery while economizing on the transactional costs associated with the communication of information. They are one important response to the continuous pressures to realize efficiencies in the ways in which work is conducted in a global-service–based economy (Taylor and Bain 2005). The use of ICTs to automatically deliver work to waiting agents and the employment of standardized 'call structures' in the form of scripts or common call-management techniques equate to a greater number of transactions per worker per hour and per day than is possible in walk-in, face-to-face encounters. In fact, contact centres do away altogether with the need for spatial proximity between 'senders' and 'receivers' in the production and consumption of information. For these reasons the call centre has quickly become the new face of business and public-service delivery in the information economy.

As suggested by the above comments, call centres render info-service work more transparent. Having reduced the importance of proximity in the relationships between producers and consumers of information, the call-centre labour process has been able to tackle the challenges of managing working time to great effect in work that was once thought to be impervious to productivity improvement. In this sense, call centres may accurately be portrayed as 'time conscious' organizations. The technologies that stack, queue, and sort calls are also capable of offering a host of measurements pertaining to organizational and individual performance (Bain, Watson, et al. 2002; Taylor, Hyman, et al. 2002). Individual workers can be appraised according to their availability for work (i.e., to take calls), their strict adherence to rosters (e.g., punctuality, observance of allotted time for breaks), the amount of time they spend interacting with clients, and their non-call work time. In many centres it is common to divide the job cycle – one complete interaction – into various segments for which prescribed durations are laid down in agent key-performance indicators (kpi's). The division of work into preparation time – especially common in outbound work, where the CSR familiarizes herself with details pertaining to the recipient of the call before an interaction commences – talk time spent in person-to-person communication, and wrap-up work in which post-call activities such as data-file management and pending actions to be taken are completed, is a recognizable feature of work flows in many centres.

This division of the job cycle into separate, measurable components is suggestive of a Tayloristic approach to the design and organization of the CRS's role – a point that has not been lost in earlier research conducted from a labour-process perspective (Bain and Taylor 2000; Bain, Watson, et al. 2002; Callaghan and Thompson 2001). As put forward by Taylor and Bain (2001), 'notwithstanding organizational and functional difference and variety, management has sought to define new "frontiers of control," which in the majority of call centres, means repetitive, routinized and Taylorized work' (2001, 42). Images of 'an assembly line in the head' (Taylor and Bain 1999), as well as references to 'team Taylorism' (Baldry, Bain, and Taylor 1998; see also van den Broek 2002; van den Broek, Callaghan, and Thompson 2004) and 'sacrificial' HRM strategies (Wallace, Eagleson, and Waldersee 2000), are common features of this analysis, and these designations are deemed applicable to the majority of call centres (Taylor and Bain 2005).

The Taylorization of info-service work is a consistent theme in studies of the call-centre labour process. As described by Callaghan and Thompson (2001), it is inscribed in the technologies that define contact-centre work. Relative to previous ways of enacting customer-service work, CSRs exert less control over their tasks and consequently are subjected to higher levels of work intensification and associated levels of job stress (Ellis and Taylor 2006; Taylor, Baldry, et al. 2003). Cost containment, delivered through the specific socio-technical paradigm that characterizes the call centre, is a feature that goes hand in hand with the intensification of info-service work.

On this reading, the Taylorization of the labour process and attendant levels of work pressure are features that circumscribe the amount of variation that is possible in info-service work. While most analysts would readily acknowledge that no two call centres are the same (Glucksmann 2004), from a labour-process perspective, variation occurs within limits (Russell 2004; Taylor, Hyman, et al. 2002; Taylor and Bain 2007). Accordingly, even the much vaunted distinction between mass-production systems that emphasize call throughput and more customized approaches that focus on quality or relationship management (Gutek 1995) can be overblown. While many centres struggle with the trade-offs between quantity and quality, and while emphases in particular sites are likely to 'wax and wane' over time, very few centres can afford to ignore the costs associated with the level of service offered (Houlihan 2000). These costs form an absolute limit to possible variation away from Tayloristic norms and the associated work patterns that have been observed in a number of different national settings in spite of unique national regimes of employment regulation (Bain and Taylor 2002b; Benner 2005; Bittner et al. 2002; D'Alessio and Oberbeck, 2002; Lee and Kang 2006; Raz and Blank 2007; Zapf et al. 2003).

A final feature of this genre of research is worth reflecting on, and that is the responses of workers to the conditions of the labour process with which they are confronted. The adoption of Tayloristic work practices leads to familiar managerial challenges, including eliciting co-operation – or better yet, commitment and discretionary effort – while minimizing resistance. In contradistinction to analyses of the call centre that are based on Foucauldian premises (Fernie and Metcalf 1998; Winiecki 2004), labour-process analysis is at pains to emphasize that the technologies of control are far from foolproof and that contestation over the work–effort bargain in the call-centre work environment remains as relevant as ever. Existing studies contain rich examples of non-sanctioned behaviours, including 'fiddles,' scams, and employee whistle-blowing occurring in the midst of the call centre (Bain and Taylor 2000; Mulholland 2004; see also chapter 8).

Other research, in part appearing out of an emerging critical-management paradigm, has taken a different direction, suggesting that Tayloristic work systems are fundamentally incompatible with the demands of the information economy (Castells 1996). With respect to the call centre, two points are of relevance. First, info-service work involves working *with* and working *on* other human subjects (Macdonald and Sirianni 1996). The customer/client or member of the public becomes part of the labour process. Second, this introduces elements of variability and uncertainty into work that do not exist to anywhere near the same degree in the manufacturing pursuits that formed the mainstay for forays into scientific management (Frenkel, Korczynski, et al. 1999). The potential uniqueness of each job cycle creates indeterminacies that can only be handled by extending workers more rather than less discretion over how their work is accomplished (Korczynski 2002a). To provide the services they are called on to deliver, front-line CSRs require greater levels of autonomy than Tayloristic work designs are capable of permitting. Bureaucracy, which has long been identified with scientific management (Bendix 1974), gives way to what has variously been identified as mass-customized bureaucracy (Frenkel et al. 1998, 1999), customer-oriented bureaucracy (Korczynski, Shire, et al. 2000), or flexible bureaucracy (Dose 2002). As suggested by these designations, while info-service work retains some features of 'the old economy,' these are modified by new aspects of work that have been introduced by 'informationalism.'

Specifically, customer-oriented work flows are said to make use of 'info-normative' systems of managerial control. This refers to the hybrid nature of control in workplaces such as call centres, where rules-bound compliance/enforcement is modified by an ethos of professional service as well as by normative systems of self-control/responsibility that inform organizational cultures (Alferoff and Knights 2002; Knights and Odhi 2002; Korczynski 2002b; Wray-Bliss 2001).[2] Even while information technologies supply data on employee performance, workplace norms foster identification with the public that is being served. This latter factor lends management a 'soft touch,' with 'corrections' issued to workers legitimated through references to a customer-service ethos (du Gay 1996; Fuller and Smith 1996) in which workers are urged to identify with the caller. This sort of management regime is equated with facilitative styles, in which supervision is replaced by leadership and coaching and training and performance management replaces discipline (Frenkel, Tam, et al. 1998).

A basic premise of the research that emphasizes info-normative controls relates to the growing requirement to customize the outputs of work flows for members of the public. First observed in departures from Fordist systems of mass production in manufacturing industries (Piore and Sabel 1984), such tendencies are reinforced in info-service work, where, as some call-centre case-study research has documented (Knights and McCabe, 1997, 1998), rigid adherence to pre-defined engineered processes may well be suboptimal in terms of the goal of obtaining and retaining user loyalty. In other words, strict adherence to Tayloristic protocols may undermine the very objectives that management is seeking. This thesis, which derives from a critical-management approach, also suggests the limited usefulness of rigid quantitative benchmarks to measure worker performance (Korczynski 2002a) – a further departure from Taylorist prescriptions. Significantly, in these accounts relations between workers and management are displaced in favour of exploring the Janus face of managements divided over the means and ends that are employed in call-centre work, especially as it relates to relations with clients. This shifting emphasis marks one of the main differences between labour-process and critical-management approaches to the subject matter (Russell 2008b).

Intellectually allied to the research that has identified and defined the need for post-Taylorist work designs in info-service work are typologies of call-centre operations that (again) stress the potential for variety. Alongside mass-production operations, professional-service and mass-customization or hybrid forms are referred to in the literature (Batt and Moynihan 2002; Kinnie, Purcell, and Hutchinson 2000; Hutchinson, Purcell, and Kinnie 2000). Mass-production systems tend to retain the essential elements of Taylorism, whereas customized operations are associated with the adoption of so-called high-performance work practices, which have the potential to 'enhance or "quasi-professionalize" the work behaviour and attitudes of production level workers' (Batt 2000, 541). The work-design choices that are made may be part of a wider business strategy. For example, Taylorist systems of mass production may be used to service low-value customers, while socio-technical teams may be used for higher-value market streams in evolving patterns of market stratification (Batt 2000, 2002; Kinnie, Purcell, and Hutchinson 2000). Other empirical evidence purports to show relationships between call-centre job design and employee behaviour (Holman 2002; Deery, Iverson, and Walsh 2002; Rose and Wright 2005), which again are premised on the argument that considerable variation may exist among centres regarding the working conditions they offer.

Having sketched out a preliminary picture of info-service work and the debates swirling around it, the remainder of this chapter inspects how two of the fundamental features associated with any job – the intensity of work (or work–effort bargain), and the skills required to carry it off – relate to the different theoretical positions that have been taken with regard to call centres.

4.2 Experiencing the Labour Process: Work Intensity and the Effort Bargain

The ability to set encompassing work targets and to measure worker conformance to them has been related to the rationale for establishing call centres – namely, as part of an effort to increase productivity in an important realm of service work (Bain, Watson, et al. 2002; Burgess and Connell, 2006; Ellis and Taylor 2006; Russell 2006b). As suggested in the last section, research that portrays the info-service work conducted in call centres as an application of the principals of scientific management to the information field, suggests a demanding set of work expectations, which are reflected in both quantitative and qualitative measures of performance. Calls received and/or made, conformity with recommended call and operational protocols, and fulfilment of call-handling targets are commonly incorporated into personal 'developmental plans.' Time targets are measured automatically by the same technologies that workers use to produce informational outputs; quality, which is defined as adherence to process procedures, is observed through covert call monitoring and (more recently) through 'screen capture' technologies that allow employee use of software to be reviewed. The image that emerges from all of this is of intense work expectations/ norms, promoted by a regime of continuous measurement and feedback on CSR performance. As Bain, Watson, and colleagues (2002) conclude: 'The daily experience of most workers still appears likely to be framed by Taylorist practice and continuing managerial efforts to impose target-setting.' As previously suggested, the division of the job cycle into discrete parts or 'moments' – 'prep, talk, and wrap time' – strengthens this sort of focus.

A considerable portion of our survey of call-centre work is taken up with the issue of work intensity. This includes questions that pertain to workers' perceptions of the amount of time prescribed to accomplish the various items associated with their jobs, as well as their perceptions of overall expectations regarding work targets and kpi's. Readers will not be provided with the results of individual questions or from individual organizations, for this would be overly cumbersome. The results can be conveyed more effectively by providing an overall index of work intensity and then comparing all twenty centres along this measurement. This will allow us to examine levels of work intensity through the evaluations of info-service workers and then to examine whether organizations differ in significant ways from one another on work-effort expectations.

Sixteen questions have been selected for inclusion, in what can be referred to as a work-manageability index (see Table 4.1). Work manageability can be defined as the opposite of work intensity: as the term

Table 4.1
Work manageability index ($\alpha = .873$)

a)   The work targets that we are set are reasonable.
b)   It is difficult for me to consistently meet my key performance indicators. (reverse coded)
c)   Management's expectations of workloads at this call centre are reasonable.
d)   I feel as though I am under a great deal of pressure in my job. (reverse coded)
e)   Since I have worked here expectations regarding the number of calls handled have increased. (reverse coded)
f)   Management is too focused on call handling statistics at this call centre. (reverse coded)
g)   We have found just about the right balance between talk time and quality customer service at this call centre.
h)   I have an adequate amount of time to meet the expectations of the caller.
i)   I have sufficient time to read e-mails from my team leaders and managers.
j)   I have an adequate number of breaks over the course of my working day.
k)   I have an adequate amount of time between calls to compose myself.
l)   I take as much time as required to complete a call.
m)   For me personally, I feel the pace of work here is reasonable.
n)   It is possible for me to vary the pace that I work at – more quickly or less quickly when I feel like it.
o)   I have to work very fast to deal with the call volumes that we receive. (reverse coded)
p)   We don't seem to have enough employees given the levels of call demand. (reverse coded)

suggests, more manageable expectations are easier for workers to accommodate. They are less intense. The reason for selecting this concept is pragmatic: it minimizes the amount of reverse coding of individual survey questions that is required for the creation of the overall index. Each question in the index has five response categories ranging from 'strongly disagree' to 'strongly agree'; and each question is given equal weight in the construction of the index. The scale shows a high degree of internal consistency among the items that make it up, with an alpha (α) coefficient of .873.[3] Each question in the index refers to an aspect of work intensity – for example, the difficulty of meeting management targets, the ability to fulfil the public's expectations without undue stress, and the ability to work at a reasonable pace while enjoying adequate break time.

To compare perceived work-effort norms at the different contact centres, a one-way analysis of variance or ANOVA procedure – which looks for statistically significant differences among groups – would normally be used. Unfortunately, our data violate one of the assumptions of this test.[4] To overcome this limitation we must use a non-parametric test (Kruskal-Wallis one-way analysis of variance), as is done in Table 4.2. This table provides us with the mean rank score of reported work intensity at each centre. Recall that the index comprises sixteen items with possible scores ranging from one to five on each question. Thus, respondents' scores on the workload-manageability index can range from a low of 16 (indicating very intense workload) to a high of 80 (indicating a very manageable load). The mean rank score is simply the sum of ranks for each organization divided by the number of responses obtained from the organization. If we arbitrarily divide the range of mean rank scores into thirds and call them low, medium, and high workload manageability, this will aid in reading Table 4.2. The first column in the table provides this division for each of the twenty call centres identified in column two; while the third column of Table 4.2 presents the mean rank for each site.

The lower the score in Table 4.2, the more intense the workload. Less manageable, more intense workloads are reported by CSRs in both the health-insurance centres, one centre in property insurance, and two public-sector centres. Interestingly, both of the latter are in the federal government, which has borne the brunt of the changes in new employment-relations legislation (see chapter 8). Overall, the largest number of centres (ten) fall within the medium tier of work intensity, with five each grouped in the high and lower workload-manageability categories. The greatest numbers of significant differences in pair-wise comparisons using the Mann-Whitney test for two independent samples (not shown in Table 4.2) tend to be found at the low end of the index. That is, those centres that report lower workload-manageability scores/ higher work-intensity are significantly different from greater numbers of other centres in the study. Overall, the centres at the bottom of the table seem to be the ones that stand out from the other organizations on account of their high levels of workload intensity.

The public sector, especially those centres associated with service delivery at the state level, presents as having the most reasonable workloads. Four of the five centres that are judged to have the fairest work expectations fall within this category. Explanations for this may include the following. In several public-sector centres many of the common, individually measured targets either made little sense or were intentionally downplayed by management. For example, at *Government Pensions* we were informed that

Table 4.2
Work intensity at the Australian call centres*

Workload Management	Organization	Mean rank
High workload manageability (low intensity)		
Above 600	Statewide	633.75
	Gov Pensions	604.06
	Bus Company	601.57
551 to 600	Advisory Services	584.77
	Collections	561.90
Medium workload manageability		
501 to 550	Urban Space	528.25
	Tender	510.42
451 to 500	Telebet	496.40
	Telco2	493.51
	Licensing	484.25
	Bank1	481.25
	Insurer2	480.69
	Bank2	457.45
401 to 450	Telco1	448.98
	Airline	406.43
Low workload Manageability (high intensity)		
351 to 400	Delivery Services	352.00
301 to 350	Insurer1	320.25
	Health authority	310.01
Below 300	Social services	299.93
	Health Premium	222.60

*Kruskal-Wallis test
Chi-square = 104.854, df = 19, p = .000

we're not aiming for a certain handling time, we've gone away from that. That might have been a focus a few years ago, but really what we are try- ing to aim for now is that every phone call is a quality phone call, so it has a certain number of elements to it which we sort of, I guess, mark people on. One of the elements might be handling time, but it's not something that people are judged on. However, each month each person would be ... we sort of report back to their team as to the average handling time so the individuals in the team and the team as a whole and we talk about where we're trying to get to there, but it's not an active measure. (*Government Pensions*, call-centre manager)

The emphasis at *Government Pensions* now lies on group or whole-of- centre 'production' targets, though as we can see from the manager's remarks, there are ambiguities in what is expected from the workforce. Just as important as call-handling time is adherence to the structure of the ideal call, which is how 'quality' is measured. At the time of the study, call-handling times averaged around 6.5 minutes. If anything, though, as superannuation rules and regulations become more com- plex and as clients are required to become more sophisticated in the face of more options, calls have tended to become longer. Meanwhile, the ICTs associated with the work have reduced the amounts of time dedicated to related activities such as document delivery, which can now often be done online with members during conversations. A simi- lar emphasis on collective metrics was observed at other government contact centres as well, including *Licensing*, where CSRs are required to adhere to their work schedules, which means availability to take calls for 85 per cent of their rostered hours. This, however, is about as pre- scriptive as the targets are. Adequate staffing ratios to ensure an accept- able grade of service in terms of queue lengths and call waiting times are ultimately a managerial responsibility that does not fall entirely on labour's shoulders.

Other managers recognized the inevitable variability of human com- munication even with regard to transactional matters. For example, at another centre that was at the low end of work intensity and that was by no means a transactional operation, the manager confided:

There are people who can handle the call and cover everything they need to in three minutes and there are other people who can cover exactly the same information but it will take them six minutes to do it. We accept that happens. We're not so worried about the people who are under the four-and-a-half minute mark, provided we do a bit of testing to make sure they're not underservicing.

   The people who are over the six-and-a-half-minute mark, we work with them to see how we can … help with their skills to reduce their talk time … We have people that when we worked with them, in fact we've ended up saying … we got you down to seven minutes, seven minutes is fine, we can't think of what else you can do. [Much] of the variation that occurs, because our clients are varied … we really want the people to be people as opposed just to answering machines. (*Advisory Services*, call-centre manager)

This particular centre, which provides legal advice to callers, falls at the top end of having what CSRs deem to be reasonable work expectations. Elaborating on the variation in calls that CSRs face at this particular centre and tying it back up to the queuing theory that generally informs operations management in call centres, the same manager observed with some irony:

   Random call delivery is a really lovely theory, [but] I'll tell you it does not work in practice because I can have an operator sit out there and I can sit there for an afternoon and hear every call that they take and every call will be a family law call that will take ten to fifteen minutes whereas everyone else is belting through their calls … It's average call-handling time [that] is not reliable … So those sorts of measures for us are really a hard thing to say who's performing and who's not. (ibid.)

As suggested in these interviews, a certain amount of ambiguity enters managerial discourse on the subject of targets and kpi's. The performance management of info-service workers is viewed as vital to the management project in call centres, and as part of this, call-handling time is important. Attention is certainly paid to organizational and individual statistics, but it is not the whole story. It is tempered by other considerations, including avoidance of the perception that CSRs are simply 'answering machines.'

   The centre that ranked highest according to our measure of workload manageability is one of the public-sector 'supercentres' that handle inquiries for a wide range of government departments. This centre reflects a growing preference among various levels of government to route all calls through one central number, with agents trained to resolve most queries that come through at the first point of contact. Though call-handling times can easily be measured, they are not used as a benchmark kpi at *Statewide*, again owing to the great diversity in call types. As in other instances, averages don't mean much in these cases. Queue lengths, first-point-of-contact resolutions, and customer-satisfaction ratings are the main variables used in rating performance at centres such as *Statewide* and *Urban Space*. As previously noted, the first is a function of managerial staffing decisions, while the second and third are more related to training and 'multiskilling' than to work intensity.

The antinomies of managing call handling are again exemplified at *Urban Space*, where targets reflect a moving average, which stood at 4½ minutes when the research was undertaken. Agents are expected to keep within a band of +5 per cent to –10 per cent of this average. Once again, something of a mixed message comes through in the manager's observations, which express the ambiguities that other researchers have characterized as the quantity/quality conundrum in call-centre work:

> We don't expect that every call will be three minutes … or five minutes or whatever, recognizing that every call is different and some calls are two seconds, some calls are two hours, if you satisfy the customer and you know, handle it really professionally. But by the same token we know that we can't have people just having a nice chat, and so you have to have some measures in there to coach … to control the calls, to ask appropriate questions – you know, empathize appropriately, resolve it appropriately, as quickly as possible without harassing, hassling, rushing the customer. (*Urban Space*, call-centre manager)

Similarly, at *Statewide* the averaging of call-handling times into definitive kpi's can be problematical, given the diversity of calls associated with such an operation. Team leaders do receive data on individual agents, and this can be used for 'coaching and development' purposes if call-handling problems are identified. Additionally, both *Statewide* and *Urban Space* employ a state-of-the-art screen-capture technology that not only allows team leaders and senior consultants to remotely tap into calls but also permits the monitoring of individual computer screens in order to verify that correct information is being provided in the prescribed manner. In these cases the assumption seems to be that if workers are following the procedures that they have been instructed in, call-handling times should not be an issue. This characterization turns our attention towards the problem of standardization and its counterpart – the routinization of work, which is taken up in greater detail in the next chapter.

Similar expectations regarding employee performance and metrics are evident at *Collections*, where workers arrange for the payment of fines and on average are expected to handle eight calls per hour, consisting of five-minute conversations and two-and-a-half minutes of wrap-up work per call. And if they don't? The call-centre manager at *Collections* explains: 'We have staff who … still don't meet our benchmarks, but they are very thorough and have excellent customer service skills and they do offer one-call solutions … But as I said, that's just who they are … It's not an issue, it doesn't affect … their ability to an increment or anything like that' (*Collections*, call-centre manager).

As suggested by this remark, an important criterion for success at *Collections* is the provision of single-call resolutions and the avoidance of callbacks. The same manager went on to elaborate: 'We can give you quantity, but we can't give you quality at this point and we don't want you to have … skyrocketing stats if you're not doing well, because it just makes it worse for us in the long run.'

A number of these themes, including the inherent ambiguity of measures and the quantity/quality trade-offs, are not restricted to public-sector information providers alone. Variations in the nature of calls and a tendency for information requests to become more complex over time has led some centres to move away from 'hard' kpi's towards 'soft' targets, or to pay greater attention to organizational rather than individual performance. A manager in the airline business reflects this shift, as does a counterpart in a financial-contact centre. Both centres fall into the medium-workload group. As the manager of *Airline* explains: 'We have gone … from hard kpi's … because we can have a call that takes thirty seconds or a call that takes an hour and a half, so it's really difficult to compare those sorts of and to say to someone that's had an hour-and-a-half frequent-flyer call that you've exceeded your kpi's of three minutes by 500 per cent … So our industry [finds it] difficult to measure those sorts of things, because the calls don't have a consistency about them in terms of length.'

In recognition of this problem, *Airline* has redefined the business strategy of its contact centre, moving from a cost-focused strategy to a profit-focused one. In practice this has meant instituting customer-service user charges. To receive help in booking a flight, the customer must either pay a user fee or self-service using the company's online booking facilities. This has changed the metrics by which performance is measured, shifting it from call-handling times – which have become largely irrelevant – to revenue targets that are set for the agents.

The manager at *Insurer2* admits that when she took up her position, 'I went berserk with trying to measure everything,' which included not only call-abandonment rates and grades of service (proportion of calls responded to within a given number of seconds), but also average call-handling time, talk time, and work time, as well as various productivity measures such as claims lodged per hour. She also set targets for call monitoring and for the quality audits.[5] If nothing else, this was testimony to the potential surveilling power of the new technologies. However, as indicated in the touch of implied naivety in the manager's remarks, a regime of intensive measurement did not necessarily achieve what was intended. Realizing that there were limits to managing by measurement, she came to place greater emphasis on call monitoring as opposed to quantitative measures: 'If you focus lots on coaching a person on how to manage a claim effectively and how to service the customer correctly, kinda the rest just follows' (*Insurer2*, call-centre manager).

Again, two familiar themes emerge from this individual's recollections: first, the *tempering* of purely quantitative measurements of work outcomes, in that the centre continues to measure average call-handling times, which are expected to converge with preset targets of between 350 and 470 seconds (!), depending on the type of insurance claim being lodged; and second, the notion that there is one basic way to 'effectively' and 'correctly' do the work, which is now the focus of management at the centre. Similar themes emerge from an interview conducted at *Bank2*: 'The key focus .... is about customer service so if it takes a bit longer then that's what it needs to take in order to get the result or the customer satisfied at the end of it. So whilst we say that obviously there's still gotta be some control over what the average handling time and the other metrics are doing – and that's something that the leader will help … in terms of developing their questioning skills or what not – but being able to reach [call handling time], it's not really one of the key drivers' (*Bank2*, implementation-strategy specialist).

Other factors can be related to the higher-than-average work intensity that is revealed in the centres that fall to the bottom quarter of Table 4.2. These include the number of calls taken per hour and the distinction between servicing and selling. Two of the more intensive centres exhibit one of these factors each. In the case of *Health Authority*, CSRs receive calls from medical doctors seeking permission to have drugs they are prescribing to their patients included under a pharmaceutical subsidization scheme. These calls can be fraught with tension. For one thing, they reverse the usual patterns of social status, with doctors having to provide 'explanations' in order to acquire authorizations from CSRs, who in turn have to ensure that the account provided fits the criteria for issuing a subsidy number. As elaborated on by the call-centre manager at *Health Authority*: 'They [doctors] do not want to be kept waiting. They do not want to have to ring, they don't think it is appropriate for a government or for a clerk to tell them what they can prescribe and not prescribe, but we are not actually doing that, we're saying you can prescribe whatever you like, but if you want government to subsidize the price then you need to get a subsidy number.'

On average, the 130 CSRs at this centre field more than eight thousand calls per day. These calls are very short and pointed; they also have the potential to be very intense if a disagreement arises between the CSR and the physician. This scenario suggests why agents at this centre view their workloads as less manageable. Short calls typically involve less work than longer calls. But when they are unrelenting, as in this case, and when they have high responsibilities and expectations attached to them, work is experienced as more intense.

As suggested by Table 4.2, workers at *Health Premium* also feel under pressure. As the manager at this centre explains: 'What our CEO has said is that he wants our members to feel valued and that he doesn't want to be like setting a time … It's quite emotive, the information that they may be dealing with. Having said that, as a manager, I manage my team leaders so there's not a lot of variance between the staff, so we do set, like calls per hour, so we expect a minimum of calls per hour per consultant per day' (*Health Premium*, call-centre manager).

In this case, as in the others, CSRs are expected to deliver a satisfactory service 'experience' and to do so in volumes that have been established by the centre's management. Adherence to the process protocols that workers have been instructed in is presented as the means for meeting the multiple objectives established by the manager, but that same adherence can have unintended consequences that challenge management's goals. A managerialism that consists of continuous measurement and monitoring to ensure conformity with prescribed operating procedures (e.g., length and structure of calls) is being brought to bear on work that by its very nature resists regimentation.

Another factor that may be associated with workloads being experienced as intense is the remuneration structure. At *Insurer1*, CSRs working in the sales division of the call centre are on a commission plan. Prior to our study, the variable component of agent's salaries was quite sizeable. Commissions could equate to an additional $7,000 per month (!) – a fact that might explain why agents pushed themselves and accordingly reported comparatively intense workloads at this centre.

Overall, the data presented in this section permit a comparison of the research sites with one another and thereby afford a relative perspective on workloads. It is not possible on the basis of these results to come to absolute findings. While there can be little doubt that the routines of info-service work are exacting given the battery of measures and monitoring practices employed, the image of advanced 'electronic sweatshops' does not appear to be the norm. This conclusion leads to a question: Why have the informational capabilities of call-centre technologies not been pressed further to intensify work effort? A closer examination of the labour process may reveal part of the answer. On this point, one could argue that too much of a burden has been placed on the assembly-line metaphor in analyses of call-centre work. To the extent that work is automatically delivered to waiting agents via routing and distribution systems, it is an apt analogy. But in true assembly-line work, every aspect of what the worker does is *not only timed but also paced* by the operant technology (Edwards 1979, 113). The worker has no choice but to keep up with the speed of the line. Failure to do so means that work tasks go uncompleted, with immediate implications for the work of those who are located 'downstream' in the production process. The pace of the line is not a *guideline or a target, it is a fact* – albeit a contestable one that regulates the labour process (Aronowitz 1973; Blauner 1964).

The situation the CSR faces modifies the assembly-line metaphor. In the first place, though workers do not control the volume of calls (nobody does) or the length of call queues – which is ultimately a rostering (i.e., managerial) responsibility – they do control the amount of time invested in completing each job cycle. Work is not delivered autonomously at a set pace, but only when the CSR is available to take the next call; ultimately it is the agent who controls this dimension of the labour process. Additionally, as the evidence presented above suggests, there can be considerable variation in the amount of work required for each 'job.' The uniqueness of human interaction renders machinelike pacing all but impossible in most of the call centres considered here, which is not to say that management does not attempt to introduce greater levels of control through the standardization of the labour process and its call-handling protocols (see chapter 5). Reflecting this, the metrics that are employed to measure performance – such as average call-handling times – are no more than averages. That is, they operate as *targets* rather than as firm and fast *determinants* of work pace. Note that at the centres included in this study, when call times are generally exceeding the target ranges that have been established, it is the latter – that is, the handling-time targets – that are subject to adjustment. This is why a number of sites have reverted to the use of rolling-average call-time targets in recognition of the fact that the length and complexity of calls are subject to change when new products and processes are introduced. In some cases, targets are adjusted even to the day of the week or time of the year.

Finally, one must bear in mind that there is little if any technical division of labour in call-centre work. Though the job cycle of the CSR is subdivided into different elements (talk time, wrap time, etc.), these aspects of the job are not performed by different people. Call-centre work does not entail task fragmentation, and it is on this point that strict analogies with classical Taylorism break down. Instead, CSRs are responsible for whole jobs, for completing entire interactions with their respective publics from start to finish. This is one half of the dual movement in the labour process that was theorized in chapter 1, where info-service work was portrayed as a reassemblage of tasks into whole jobs. This means that the work of one agent is rarely dependent in any immediate sense on the prior work of another for its completion. This absence of interdependency among workers in a collective labour process removes considerable pressure. As we will see, it also has implications for the ways in which work teams function in this type of labour process. Meanwhile, work is conducted in a comparatively individualistic fashion. But if there is less interdependence among workers, there is also greater managerial dependence on the goodwill of labour. This reliance is manifested in the considerable efforts managers make to develop a cooperative work culture – a theme taken up more systematically in chapter 6.

In concluding this section, we can say that what impresses the observer most is not so much the intensity of call-centre work but rather its *relentlessness*. This distinction becomes clearer if we distinguish between control over the job cycle – that is, over individual calls – and control over work flows – that is, control *from* call to call or *over* whole blocks of time. In most interactional encounters, workers exercise some control over individual calls, including their duration and content, through the interpretative work they perform and the creation of negotiated understandings with callers. But at the same time, CSRs do not have the autonomy to vary the pace of their work over the course of a working day. Info-service workers do not generally have the ability to not be available once they are rostered onto the phones. They cannot choose to 'bank' their work or otherwise vary their effort by working with greater or less diligence over the course of the shift. These are not negotiable aspects of their work. In other words, while the pace of work may be reasonable, the inability to vary work intensity is an unnatural feature of this labour process. Recognition of the main features of info-service work means that in analysing call centres, analytical priority must still be given to relations between managers and workers as opposed to relations between clients and workers, as is suggested in critical-management theory. Control over job cycles and work flows is still – and will continue to be – a contested feature of info-service work. These points will become more obvious when we move on to a discussion of the skills associated with this labour process.

4.3 Call Centres and Job Skills

The skills demanded by a new occupational category – especially one that is providing scope for significant employment growth – are an important issue, for ultimately those skills bear on the question as to what types of positions are being created in the labour markets of the 'new economy.' This has obvious implications for the 'good jobs–bad jobs' debate (Betcherman 1991; Duffy, Pupo, and Glenday 1997; Picot, Myles, and Wannell 1990; OECD 2001). With respect to info-service work and call centres, there has been no lack of controversy on these matters.

Picking up from the discussion in the first section of this chapter, three theoretical positions on the question of skills and info-service work can be identified. For those researchers who identify the call-centre labour process with a Taylorization of white-collar work, it is hardly surprising that a control-oriented managerial paradigm that leads to highly routinized and standardized jobs will be unlikely to place a premium on skills or their development (Baldry, Bain and Taylor 1998; Taylor and Bain 1999; Warhurst and Thompson 1998). The thesis that the call centre represents a Taylorization of informational work flows is strongly suggestive of a low-skill or work-simplification strategy being applied to info-service labour. However, having said that, we should note that Bain and Taylor do not specifically focus on the question of job skill (Bain and Taylor 2000; Bain, Watson, et al. 2002; Taylor and Bain 1999, 2001; Taylor, Hyman, et al. 2002). Other labour-process theorists have urged caution when it comes to deducing skill requirements from operating procedures. For instance, Thompson and Callaghan (2002, 118) argue that any notion of deskilling 'underestimates the extent to which interactive service work is distinct from rather than a debased version of previous white-collar occupations ... it fails to recognise that emotional labour does not fit neatly into the classic manual/ mental divide.'

Other researchers have drawn more explicit links between the call-centre labour process and associated job skills. Richardson, Belt, and Marshall (2000) observe that except for IT help-desk workers, call-centre staff do not require specialized technical knowledge or qualifications. The skills associated with the work (communication, customer service) do not carry high social validation with them and have tended to be gendered as a result (Belt, Richardson, and Webster 2002; Mulholland 2002). Meanwhile, there seem to be limited opportunities for either skill enhancement in call-centre employment (Belt 2002a; Durbin 2006) or for full utilization of the skills workers bring with them to the job (Belt 2002b; Knights and McCabe 1997). However, again it must be said that while Belt and Richardson downplay the technical aspects of the CRS's job, they also recognize the importance of a variety of other skill sets, including communication, customer-service, database, and keyboard skills. To this one might add that such skills are deployed synchronically rather than diachronically in the work CSRs do.

Ambiguities with regard to the skill question reflect larger problems with making *unmediated* connections between Taylorism and info-service work. In this regard, the 'whole' nature of the job (as opposed to task fragmentation) is one important job aspect that analyses of call-centre work need to consider. Historically (Nelson 1980; Burawoy 1979), Taylorism has also had a very uneasy relationship with the quality concerns that – as we saw in the previous section – are espoused at many of the centres in this study. Finally, existing research seems to suggest that the call-centre labour process entails some new wrinkles that may not be fully captured by references to Taylorism or such amended constructs as 'team Taylorism' (Bain and Taylor 2000; Baldry, Bain, and Taylor 1998), given that team structures are not a feature usually associated with scientific management.

In conclusion, there is some tension between the ideal typification of Taylorism and the actual labour process of the call centre, and it is necessary to recognize this and to account for its effects. But at the same time, there is no denying the repetitive, routine, and highly rationalized work process of the call centre. As Taylor and Bain and their co-authors

correctly point out, in the final instance, the rationalization of information work is the raison d'être of the call centre (Ellis and Taylor 2006;
Taylor and Bain 2007). The labour process of info-service work shares
many of the traits that have been identified with scientific management
– routinization, rationalization – but at the same time it departs from
Taylorism in other important aspects that need to inform our analysis.
In short, even if call-centre labour is most accurately depicted through
the lens of labour process theory and the critique of scientific management, the question of skills and skill trends is still left open. Elements
of Taylorism, to the extent that they are present, no longer equate with
simplified, deskilled labour in any immediate fashion (D'Alessio and
Oberbeck 2002; Thompson, Callaghan, and van den Broek 2004).

As we might expect, a different note is struck by those who position
info-service work not in terms of the reproduction of Taylorism in new
workplaces but as a forerunner to the emergence of a knowledge-based
economy. Mass customization is hypothesized as requiring new work
skills such as increased self-management and flexibility in the ongoing acquisition and application of information- and knowledge-man-
agement systems. In line with these developments, this thesis holds
that the work of the CSR is likely to become more complex with the
introduction of a wider variety of products, options, and policies and
with the tendency to combine sales and customer-service functions
into one job. Consequently, info-service work is 'becoming more like
that of professional employees' (Frenkel, Tam, et al. 1998), and CSRs
are better classified among the new breed of 'semi-autonomous' job
holders (Herzenberg, Alic, and Wial 1998) than as part of a Fordist service
proletariat.[6] Overall, and regardless of the market stream being served,
research in this genre is in general agreement that the advent of the
call centre is associated with skill enhancement, brought about by
the ways in which information is produced, handled, and distributed
(Arzbacher, Holtgrewe, and Kerst 2002; Bittner et al. 2002). Intentional
deskilling strategies are likely to be counterproductive, given the demands of the work. Call centres tend not to fragment work into discrete
jobs in a typical Taylorist fashion; indeed, they are better represented as
work-integrating organizations (Dose 2002).

These projections also have to confront some difficult points. First,
arguments of improved job quality through the availability of more
highly skilled jobs sit uncomfortably alongside the high attrition rates
associated with call-centre work (see chapters 3 and 7). Many managers in our study noted that 24 months was just about the maximum

working lifespan of a CSR. This is a 'fact of life' in this type of work that managers have come to take for granted.

Second, info-service work needs to be distinguished from knowledge work, especially since the two concepts are often used interchangeably, which in my view is a mistake (see also Alvesson 2004). Unlike knowledge work, info-service labour typically does not involve the use of theory to interpret information as part of the creation of new knowledge, nor does it *explicitly* set out to generate or revise theories about the way things work. Theory is the outcome of a dedicated constructivist practice that systematically ties a coherent body of ideas to the interpretation of something and that is subject to evaluation. While a central component of info-service work involves what we can call interpretative labour, this is done in comparatively short interactions with many others. Such labour does not entail the systematic testing or extension of theoretical knowledge. Rather, the CSR works as an intermediary between the wishes of a public and bodies of information, but she usually does so without the explicit or knowledgeable intervention of theory. Interpretative effort is deployed to ascertain and clarify client needs and to bring these into relation with existing organizational policies, services, and practices.

Tellingly, some advocates of the customer-oriented-bureaucracy thesis are now less optimistic about the job-skill potential of info-service work. In a significant autocritique of his earlier writing on the subject of call-centre job skills, Korczynski writes that '[we] make a huge and unsupported leap ... by claiming that front-line workers will need access to more *information* which they will then need to convert to *knowledge*' (2002a, 202; emphasis in the original; Russell 2008b). CSRs are now better viewed as information receivers than as knowledge workers. The discretion that accompanies such work is usually highly constrained, often involving recovery from mistakes that have arisen as a result of adherence to standard process routines.

A third body of literature seeks to emphasize the role of organizational choice in job design. This one has the practical effect of merging aspects of the 'info-service work as Taylorism' position with post-Taylorist analysis. From this perspective, different work designs – mass-production, professional-service, and hybrid paradigms – exhibit different levels of job skill. Mass-production approaches can be expected to exhibit the characteristics of low-skilled, Taylorized work; hybrid and professional-service models will likely show greater evidence of job traits associated with high-performance work systems. For Batt

(2000), HPWSs include the use of more highly skilled labour, opportunities to use those skills in team-based problem-solving work, and incentive structures – such as performance-based payment systems – that encourage people to use their skills on the job (see also Kinnie, Purcell, and Hutchinson 2000; and Hutchinson, Purcell, and Kinnie 2000). Once again, these approaches make for a quasi-professionalization of non-managerial work. While HPWSs are associated mainly with high-value market segments (e.g., business-to-business services), note that for Batt, such practices offer advantages that could also be profitably exploited by call-centre providers in less lucrative markets (Batt 2000, 2002).[7] In this 'social varieties of work' approach there are plenty of opportunities to up-skill information work if managers see fit to do so.

The foregoing review brings two counterpoising forces to bear on work design in info-service provision. Economizing pressures, which stand behind the advent of the call centre, point towards a model of tight labour control, a model that is advanced through job simplification and the deskilling that accompanies it. Here the focus is squarely on the management/employee dyad. Meanwhile, placing the spotlight on the worker/customer relationship highlights quality issues and the employee discretion and job empowerment that are essential components of a quality strategy. This focus provides an argument for skill accretion in info-service work. In short, we are in possession of compelling arguments that also have definite limitations that have been alluded to. Each argument has quite different implications for how we look upon call centre employment.

To advance the discussion further we can inspect the results of the survey data, which contain a number of questions pertaining to job skill. As with the examination of work intensity, it is expedient to create an overall index of job skill from the individual questions contained in the survey. Table 4.3 itemizes the questions in the survey that relate to the concept of skill. Besides applying standard measures such as discretion, responsibility, variety, and full employment of human capital (Blauner 1964; Burchell et al. 1994; Cappelli 1993; Clement and Myles 1994; Felstead, Gallie, and Green 2004; Gallie 1991; Livingstone 1999; Rose, Penn, and Rubery 1994; M. Rose 1994; Spenner 1983, 1990), the index that has been created contains items that are specific to call-centre work and examines different aspects of opportunity, such as the skill enhancement associated with participation in process improvement and career advancement.

Using the nine-item skill index summarized in Table 4.3, scores that

Table 4.3
CSR skill index (α = .793)

a) I have a great deal of responsibility to carry in my job.
b) This job makes full use of my education and experience.
c) I am satisfied with the opportunities that this job gives me to make use of my skills.
d) I have a lot of discretion in responding to customer's questions.
e) My work has a lot of variety in it.
f) Management treats me like a professional in this job.
g) We are encouraged to come up with new and better ways to do our job.
h) I feel that my conversations with customers are too closely scripted. (reverse coded)
i) There are opportunities for me to advance myself in this call centre.

range from nine to forty-five are logically possible, with lower scores indicating a lower evaluation of the skills involved in the work and higher scores indicating the opposite. For argument's sake we can divide the possible range of scores into three parts and call them low-, semi-, and high-skill bands. The low-skill category consists of scores in the 9 to 20 range, semi-skilled work falls within the 21 to 32 group band, and highly skilled work consists of scores above 32. It is important (a) to acknowledge that a different index composed of a different number of items would alter our operational definitions of 'low,' 'semi,' and highly skilled work, and, for that reason, (b) to use the results that are generated in the analysis in a heuristic as opposed to an absolutist fashion. That said, the index is statistically reliable and exhibits a reasonable level of content validity. In other words, when taken together the components of the index are measuring something we can reasonably call skill.

This time the data conform to the requirements that are needed to perform a one-way analysis of variance (Anova) test. This procedure allows for the simultaneous comparison of intra- and inter-organizational differences in evaluations of work skills. The results are set out Table 4.4. As can been seen, the organizations in our study all tend to fall towards the middle – that is, within the semiskilled band. The average score across the twenty centres is 27.33. In fact, all of the centres fall within our operational definition of semiskilled work, albeit at various levels. Seven of the twenty organizations are below the mean, including one of the two transportation companies, one of the two telcos, one of the four banking/insurance companies, and the one call centre in the leisure sector. Two of the public-service providers and the one outsource provider of social services also fall below the mean (see Table 4.4). Another three

Table 4.4
Skill rankings of participating Australian call centres (mean score on scale from 9 to 45)

Skill level	Organization	Mean score on skill index	Significantly different (.05) from N other organizations*
High skill			
33+	No entries		
Semiskilled			
32	No entries		
31	*Delivery Services*	31.7	4
	Government Pensions	31.0	–
30	*Urban Space*	30.8	4
	Bank1	30.1	1
	Statewide	30.0	–
29	*Telco2*	29.3	3
28	*Insurer2*	28.3	1
	Health Authority	28.0	–
27	*Social Services*	27.9	1
	Health Premium	27.9	1
	Collections	27.9	–
	Bank2	27.8	1
	Telco1	27.6	1
	Bus Company	27.1	1
26	*Advisory Services*	26.7	–
25	*Insurer1*	25.9	1
	Airline	25.8	3
24	*Tender*	24.7	2
23	*Licensing*	23.7	3
	Telebet	23.1	10
22			
21			
Low skill			
9–20	No entries		
Average		27.33	

*Tukey's HSD

centres, including a financial-sector company, a transportation company, and a public-service provider, are sitting right on the mean.

The Anova procedure also allows us to compare the differences within centres to the differences among sites across all twenty organizations simultaneously. The information in the last column of Table 4.4 on the right-hand side shows how many other centres differ in a statistically significant fashion on the variable of skill from the organization being considered. As can be seen, only four organizations are significantly different from three or more of the other centres included in the study.[8] The gaming services provider, *Telebet*, significantly differs on the skill index from ten of the other call centres in the study. It is at the low end of the index, and in all ten cases of significant difference it falls below its matched comparison. A public-sector contact centre is at the high end of the scale and is significantly different from four other centres. The differences that the other centres display are for the most part variations away from the skill levels represented by these two sites. Other differences are not statistically significant. For example, differences in the skill perceptions of workers at the two transportation centres, *Bus Company* and *Airline*, are not significantly different from each other, nor are the variations between *Insurer1* and *Insurer2*. Additional insights into the skills associated with info-service work can be had by examining the centres that do display the greatest amount of difference in greater detail.

At *Telebet*, CSRs take the wagers that callers place on sporting competitions. The work is transactional in the extreme. Though it entails timely accuracy, the job cycle is shorter than in any other call centre in the study, with an average call-handling time of only 45 seconds. Additionally, there is no pre- or post-call work associated with providing the service, nor does any data management accompany the work. Owing to these job features, training periods at the centre are modest, with only sixteen hours of computer-simulated training, followed by twelve hours of 'buddying'/on-the-job training before agents 'go live.' In all, this is less than the equivalent of one full working week of instruction, which immediately casts this centre as an outlier. Additionally, there is no functional differentiation between the twelve teams at the centre. As the call-centre manager relayed during an interview: 'The whole centre is doing the same thing.' And notably, the 'same thing' is done with a workforce that is 100 per cent casual.[9] The main – some would say the only – focus of the work is on accuracy – taking information from the client and placing the money where requested. In terms of an information/service dichotomy, work here is clearly at the service end of the spectrum. The flow of information is almost completely one way, from the customer to the CSR, who in turn is expected to *repeat rather than interpret* the details the client has provided and then action them.

The emphasis on procedure and accuracy at *Telebet* is emphasized by the manager at this centre and recounted in her narrative about an incentive scheme that was intended to focus CSRs on developing and rewarding accuracy in the performance of work:

> They [staff] interpreted good customer service as to get the customer's bet on, it didn't matter if it was right, just get it on. So, cutting corners – they saw that as good customer service, and we had to *reprogram* them to think, but if you get it on and it's wrong, the customer's not happy, we have an error loss. So I introduced an incentive scheme that said, 'Well, okay folks, this is the amount of money I budget to pay out on errors when people haven't followed procedure and I have to pay the customers, and this is the amount of money I allocate as an incentive. For every dollar that I save, that I don't pay out, I'll go you half' … Well, it was the most unpopular thing I have ever done in my life. (*Telebet*, call-centre manager; my emphasis)

In this description of the labour process, decisions are taken by the client and actioned by the CSR. However, as the manager implies, CSRs do have some leeway as to how they enact the requests of their clients in terms of what they prioritize as being more important (e.g., speed versus accuracy), and this is something that management desperately wants to control. As a result, accuracy and adherence to schedule constitute the main kpi's that agents are measured against. Again, as put to us: 'If you're following procedure, you're meeting your kpi's' (ibid.).

As shown in the previous quotation, management's view is that accuracy is best achieved through strict conformity to rigid operating procedures; indeed, it openly refers to training and coaching as the 'reprogramming' of CSRs, the goal of which is to avoid error losses, which are payable by the business to its customers. Management focuses on enforcing adherence to operational procedures by, for example, stamping out the practice of 'cutting corners'; the result is that agents lose what little autonomy they possess. Interestingly, though management is willing to pay for greater work accuracy through the 'purchase of autonomy' (as the manager's narrative hints at), workers have resisted the new operating protocols. Still, agents at this centre are responsible for large sums of money, which must be moved around with accuracy and alacrity. In the terminology of the centre, workers are 'multiskilled,' meaning that they can take calls from any of six different income streams (low- to high-value bets); indeed, some teams have been trained to provide coverage for every type of gaming event the centre handles. The work requires both speed and attention to detail. It can involve considerable amounts of pressure. It also entails training in social skills and emotional management. Tact in dispute resolution features in this labour process. As the manager explained: 'Coaching people the difference that if a customer swears at you, or yells at you, he's yelling at the organization, he's not yelling at you. You're job is not to make him happy [and] not to make him a nice person, it's to give him what he rang for' (ibid.).

This message captures the dual aspects of work at this call centre. It is mainly about providing a service in conformity with strict operating procedures rather than interpreting and producing information. But it also involves the execution of emotional control. Thus, though less skilled than the work encountered in the other call centres, the CSRs at *Telebet* cannot be called unskilled.

Two other *visible* outliers on the skill index, each of which differs significantly from four other centres, are government providers. The first, *Delivery*, supplies logistical services to the public. It provides an example of how job and team design may contribute to skill acquisition in customer-service work. First, work teams at *Delivery* are graduated in terms of the complexity of the work. CSRs start off on a complaint-and-investigation team. This provides an overview of both the diverse product market that the organization serves and the organizational network that makes it possible. From this entry point, teams are divided into customer-management and business-service functions. The latter is further subdivided into separate teams for high-value customers, international clients, business marketing, and general business bookings. These teams conduct a mix of inbound and outbound work. In effect, something of an internal labour market has been created at *Delivery*, and this presents agents with prospects of job mobility. Agents may move into jobs of greater complexity as they gain experience. They may also stay within the larger organization but bid for jobs outside the call centre as they become available. All of this offers a sense of progression. Unlike in *Telebet*, everyone at this centre is clearly not doing the same thing.

To this organizational design the manager at *Delivery* has introduced elements of what he describes as team self-management. This includes such initiatives as opening up the rostering software to all staff to allow them to swap shifts with one another without referring such changes to team leaders. The manager hopes that eventually this change will extend to team-managed holiday leave. Teams also nominate a different representative each month to attend problem-solving meetings with management. These sessions normally run from one to one-and-a-half hours and have an open agenda. Typically at these meetings, issues are aired relating to training and development, and operations and products. Though the point should not be overstated, these sorts of initiatives do expand workers' involvement in the centre; to that extent they can be viewed as skill enhancing as compared to the situation that would exist in their absence.

Of the other centres that beckon our attention, *Urban Space* and *Statewide* are representative of the 'supercentres' to which reference has been made. Especially in the public sector, such centres provide another emerging model of info-service work, one that has implications for the skill levels workers require. These centres are responsible for all government offices that fall within their respective political domains. Instead of the hundreds of individual department numbers that used to exist, the public now has access to just one contact number for any form of inquiry. The manager of *Urban Space* recounts the thinking that lay behind the creation of this centre: 'They didn't just want to set up a call centre that was basically a switchboard, where it was still phone in to a number that then got fed out. They wanted to have the information and the skilled staff available whereby 90 per cent of everything that confronted them at the front end was resolved as a result of that one phone call' (*Urban Space*, call-centre manager).

In this case, the call centre is defined as the 'professional face' of government and workers are expected to handle all manner of items that fall within its ambit. Inbound calls involve everything from simply transferring inquiries to particular politicians or their mailboxes (i.e., basically telephone-operator functions) to responding to questions about tax assessments, eligibility and conditions pertaining to government grants, and protocols for bidding on public tenders.

At *Statewide* a similar design logic has been brought to bear on the organization of workflows. Operations are divided into two general queues: human services and business/customer services. Within these broad areas, CSRs are expected to be able to handle up to forty-five different subject-inquiry areas, including information on senior citizens', recreational, and social-service/housing programs. At both these centres the initial training lasts between seven and ten weeks. The skills that workers associate with these jobs relate to the breadth of information they have to know across a range of policy areas. For the call-centre managers, the work is highly representative of 'multiskilling.'

Another interesting case of work extension – one that may explain this centre's location in Table 4.4 – is found at *Government Pensions*. At this centre the four teams rotated among inbound call reception, e-mail response, front-counter service, written correspondence, seminar-program delivery, and personal interviews with superannuation holders. This translated into approximately 30 per cent of an employee's working time being spent off the phones. These types of arrangements are, however, mutable, as this case demonstrates. Between the time the survey was administered and the interview with the centre's manager, this job design had been altered in favour of more specialized team assignments that resulted in an increase in telephone time for most workers. The manager explained:

> The reason we've gone down that path, even though we didn't want to because we felt we really wanted to hang on to something we thought was a bit unique in that people had job variety, it just wasn't that efficient. At the end of the day what we find is that ... the great majority of work is phone work and people rotating through the general business work ... If there [was] anything difficult or hard amongst it, it never got done because people could say, 'I am only here in this job for a day so I just want to get done the easy stuff,' so it just really wasn't working, it wasn't working in terms of getting the work done, so we [sic] decided to go with the specialist model. (*Government Pensions*, call-centre manager)

The manager at *Government Pensions* equated specialization with efficiency. Yet she was also cognizant of the implications of this change, conceding on her own and without prompting that less interesting jobs might force up turnover rates. Reflecting on this further, she concluded that 'at the end of the day that could be a balancing act and at the end of the day it mightn't be more efficient' (ibid.). Though a bow had been made in the direction of greater specialization in the labour process, the manager was clearly having some second thoughts about this and its suitability for work in this call centre.

Developments at *Government Pensions* have a parallel at *Insurer1*, where previously the centre made use of only general teams and queues, which assumed total responsibility for the three specialized areas (service, sales, and complex resolutions) that now exist. Some view the movement to more specialized teams as illustrative of a greater concern with quality at the company; others associate the changes with narrower and more mundane jobs. Significantly, though, at both *Insurer1* and *Bank1*, CSRs now underwrite standard insurance policies up to quite high values. In this respect the jobs have grown significantly and can no longer be viewed as simply clerical-support functions.

The same general point can be registered with respect to the much larger *Bank2*, which also exhibits a three-tier division of labour, with service, sales, and claims teams as well as a dedicated back-office team and a separate team responsible for customer retention. Within the three main divisions, there is no further division of labour. For example, each agent in each of the six customer-service teams has the same responsibilities and is expected to be able to respond to the same variety of calls that would be received in a normal working day. Management acknowledges that the three functional areas have different skill sets attached to them; unlike at *Insurer1*, however, base salary levels are the same across all teams, though bonuses are awarded on the basis of different metrics.

Another factor associated with the results in Table 4.4 is the level of responsibility associated with certain info-service jobs. We can see this element at work in *Social Services* and *Health Authority*, both of which are also ranked above the average level of skill exhibited. At the former, agents administer a range of social benefits and service entitlements for those who qualify. Teams at this centre are broadly dedicated to specific programs/clienteles (e.g., job searchers, family-benefit recipients), but again, agents may be multiskilled to work in two of the three broad program/policy areas offered by this centre. Work here is rich in interpretive effort. The call-centre manager explains: 'They have to question to get the right information … All those sorts of things, they have to be quite skilled at questioning people to get the information. It's not black and white – nothing here is black and white' (*Social Services*, call-centre manager).

Many of the calls to *Social Services* present unique circumstances. CSRs are required to probe and interpret the particular situation of the client and then link that person to the program policies that are relevant. This entails working within a complex policy environment – a condition that is attached to several other contact centres that score more highly on the skill index. As the manager at *Social Services* explains, the implications of arriving at the wrong decision can be serious, and the labour involved in reaching a defensible outcome can be extensive:

There's some judgement calls. That's why they're saying the work is more difficult. There are points in their calls where they have to make a judgment, a decision that's not so scripted ... They actually have to go into a live record ... So there are times on the information provided [that] they have to make a judgment decision, and that's why they're saying it's so complex ... And particularly the payment you make ... it varies depending on the age of the children, how many children you've got, and all this sort of thing ... We're talking about a lot of money, some of these payments that are made could be thousands of dollars and over a period of a year could be ten, twenty, thirty thousand dollars, whatever, and so ... in relation to making a decision it's got to be the correct decision. (ibid.)

At this centre, CSRs must, on the basis of the information they receive, make decisions as to the eligibility of clients and the disbursement of benefits – decisions that conform to existing legislative and program policies. Once again, there is an emphasis on accuracy and consistency; in this case, however, CSRs create 'transactional trails' that are used as input data for future interactions. Personal and family situations are often unique and must be framed by the CSR in a manner that 'makes sense' and that can be defended to both clients and managers. At the same time, social policies are fluid, so the job also requires the CSR to keep abreast of the continual changes in priorities and emphases. As the manager of *Social Services* points out, the complex and ever-changing policy environment in which CSRs work has an impact on efforts to multiskill across policy areas: 'Because again, it's so complex we found we had a number of people training up across two different streams, say, in the last couple of years, but we found that it's very, very hard to keep up to date in both of them' (ibid.).

Health Authority presents a somewhat different situation with regard to assuming responsibility. At this centre, physicians call in to obtain authorization numbers that permit their patients access to the pharmaceutical-benefits scheme. CSRs must ascertain whether the patient's condition, as described by the doctor, fits the criteria for issuing a subsidy code as contained in the plan's benefit schedule. In other words, the centre's agents mediate between the government's benefits scheme and the medical profession. Responsibility for administering the plan in accordance with the law is very much a part of the job at this centre. On top of this, though all workers are equipped to handle the most common inquiries, they may also apply to upgrade to be able to provide additional services besides administering the pharmaceutical-benefits plan. In total, a CSR at *Health Authority* may acquire up to fifteen skill sets, though this would not be common. Nevertheless, the fact that there is job progression at this centre may have something to do with the skills that workers attribute to the positions. Both *Social Services* and *Health Authority* offer examples of exercising what we can call 'interpretive labour.' Workers are responsible for making sense of the verbal and textual accounts they are given and, on that basis, reaching decisions that conform with existing laws.

Responsibility for policy interpretation and application in arriving at decisions is a feature of other centres that rank higher in terms of the skill evaluations in Table 4.4. In the financial sector, for example, the agents at *Bank1* (a credit union) are skilled in two of the three service areas the organization provides: banking (general inquiries), loans (including mortgages), and insurance. Workers commence their training in banking and then move on to specialize in either loans or insurance. Further training allows CSRs to become adept at handling mortgage applications or at writing up commercial-insurance policies. Specialists and team leaders move on to be multiskilled in both sides of the business – loans and insurance. Work processes here provide a good example of the general streamlining that has occurred in the financial sector. Though approval for loans can only come from managers at individual bank branches, mortgage applications are completed over the phone, submitted electronically to the customer's closest bank branch, and accepted or rejected by the bank manager at that level. Meanwhile, CSRs make all decisions on the issuance of standard insurance policies, including payment schedules.[10] The extent of multiskilling at *Bank1*, which goes beyond product diversification within a single area to take in different functional areas and levels of authorization that CSRs have, may explain why workers at this centre rate their skills more highly than agents in the other financial centres, which exhibit greater levels of product specialization. Also noteworthy is the negative connotations that are attached to scripting at *Bank1*. As outlined by the manager:

If you're confident and you understand how to flow a call based on what's a good interaction, you know, how to build rapport, how to ask questions, how to probe … and you know your product well then you don't need scripting, you just need to … adopt your own style within that framework, it's much more effective. It's all about identifying, you know, options, solutions, adding value in every interaction … Any type of call can be a sales opportunity and that's an area that we are actually working on now. [It's] an awareness thing [as opposed to] 'do you want fries with that.' (*Bank1*, call-centre manager)

In the above quotation the manager inadvertently, and with some disdain, compares the work that CSRs do with work in a fast-food establishment to point out the differences between highly routinized, ritualistic service encounters and what she hopes occurs at the call centre. This suggests that strict adherence to scripts of the sort Leidner (1993) observed in industries such as fast food and door-to-door insurance sales may be less suitable for the type of work being discussed here.

A final example of discretionary responsibility is found at one of the telcos (*Telco2*), which also ranks comparatively high on our measure of skill. At this centre, agents have budgets ranging from $500 to $1,000 – depending on the customer stream they serve – to 'fix' problems that may arise in disputes with mobile-phone subscribers. The use of these funds is not subject to immediate managerial authorization. Rather, agents use their discretion as intermediaries between the company and its customers in deciding whether a disbursement is in order.

Many of the interactions subsumed under the concept of info-service work, whether they involve making and processing insurance claims, distributing welfare funds, or offering legal aid, may be fraught with emotion. As we have already seen, even in the highly transactional telebetting centre, emotionally charged encounters are an aspect of the CSRs' work – one that must be negotiated at the same time as information is being received and acted on. A further examination of the emotional labour enacted in info-service work will extend our understanding of skill – in particular, the social skills that are so important in this labour process. Emotional labour is discussed briefly in the next section.

4.4 Emotional Labour in Call Centres

In a review of the literature on info-service work, references to the importance of 'social skills' are often encountered (Belt, Richardson and Webster 2000; Belt, Richardson and Webster 2002; Callaghan and Thompson 2002; Mulholland 2002). Also, the problematic nature of the concept of social skill was signalled in chapter 3. Both workers and managers emphasize the importance of social skill in info-service work, but this is seldom reflected in the training programs that organizations offer their employees. One aspect of what is taken to be social skill is the exercise of emotional labour; another is what I have been calling 'interpretive' work.

The term 'emotional labour' as a theoretical construct was first coined by Hochschild (1983) in her study of airline flight attendants. Drawing from and extending dramaturgical approaches (Goffman 1959), Hochschild defines emotional labour as the work that 'requires one to induce or suppress feeling in order to sustain the outward countenance that produces the proper state of mind in others' (1983, 7). This presentation of self combines 'surface acting' – the standard subject matter of interactionist and role-playing models as found in modernist sociology – with a practice Hochschild refers to as 'deep acting.' Surface acting is all about the presentation of officially sanctioned selves; deep acting involves such things as the suppression and substitution of existing feelings (e.g., anger with pleasantness to a rude customer) in order to sustain organizationally given definitions of the situation as well as expectations regarding appropriate service levels.

A perfect example of this is found in the quotation from the *Telebet* manager cited in the previous section, when she explains the importance of coaching workers in the arts of personally deflecting customer anger away from the self and back onto the organization. Success in this exercise requires a degree of 'deep acting' – a labour that requires the actor to work on modifying existing feelings and substituting them with organizationally prescribed emotions. Actors in service roles are expected to go beyond a presentation of self for the public, which may appear phoney, and to wholeheartedly adopt job-related identities as part of the self. Deep acting is an exercise in self-deception. We are told not only *what* to display (surface acting) but also *how* to feel (deep acting), and we are trained in the techniques for accomplishing it. This involves the (re)training of the imagination so that interactions with the public can be interpreted in ways that meet the goals of the employer. Korczynski (2002a, 2002b) provides examples of coaching in deep acting within the contact-centre setting, including it under his rubric of info-normative control. During training, workers are prompted to imagine 'the self as customer' and to base their interactions with the public on this ideal. Such deep acting is said to require another layer of work apart from that which is required in surface acting.

In some places, Hochschild's argument seems quite deterministic. Organizations train workers in the arts of deep acting and expect them to take on their parts with all of the commitment that method acting requires. 'As a farmer puts blinders on his workhorse to guide its vision forward, institutions manage how we feel' (Hochschild 1983, 49; see also Bolton and Boyd's 2003 critique). However, Hochschild also allows for the possibility of rejection, especially under conditions of routinization and work intensification. Workers may refuse to play their parts with the sincerity that is demanded of them. Their acting may be annoyingly transparent. They may engage in self-mockery and deviate from the ways they are supposed to 'feel.' Unfortunately, Hochschild does not elaborate on the relationship between deep acting and identity construction/regulation in the contemporary service organization. The extent to which workers assume organizationally authored identities and the determinants of this may provide a better theoretical handle on the subject of deep acting. We will reserve this problem until chapter 6 on HRM in info-service work.

Empirical examinations of Hochschild's theory have provided, at best, mixed findings. Wharton's (1996) attempt to operationalize the theory finds that factors such as job autonomy and control are more important than emotional labour in accounting for burnout – a finding echoed in the call-centre environment by Deery, Iverson, and Walsh (2002, 2004). The expenditure of emotional labour may be a source of fulfilment or of pain, depending on the conditions under which it is enacted and the reception it elicits from clients (Korczynski 2002a). Other researchers have unearthed little evidence for the deep acting that Hochschild hypothesizes in a variety of service settings, including those of flight attendants (Bolton and Boyd 2003) and call-centre agents (Mulholland 2002). In another study of airline call-centre agents and flight attendants, Taylor and Tyler (2000) argue that workers are trained in the arts of deep acting and are expected to engage in it. However, final results are underdetermined: workers may or may not practise deep acting. Once again, linking this issue to identity formation would seem to be a promising way forward.

Three questions in our survey relate to the topic of emotional labour, and they turn up a mixed pattern. First, CSRs were asked whether they found it necessary to become emotionally detached from their publics; affirmative responses were taken as an indication of deep acting. Overall, the largest proportion of the sample (43 per cent) said that this was the case; slightly fewer than one-third disagreed with the statement. Interestingly, differences by gender are slight and statistically insignificant. Second, in a stronger version of the first question, workers were asked whether they had to 'mask true feelings' in their interactions with the public. Here, a bare majority admitted that this was the case (53 per cent), while 22 per cent denied having to disguise their emotions. Female CSRs were marginally more likely to agree with this proposition than their male counterparts (54 versus 51 per cent), with the difference being statistically significant but the correlation being quite weak ($r = .092$, $p < .05$). Finally, in response to a question that asked whether workers could be 'their true self' while on the phone with clients, the largest proportion of the sample, 45 per cent, answered in the affirmative, whereas just over one-third (34 per cent) said this was not possible. On this question there was virtually no difference between women and men. For the most part, then, both women and men consider emotional self-management to be part of info-service work. This, however, is a different point than the gendered attributions that employers make regarding emotional labour and their preference for assigning work that demands these skills to women.

Interestingly, the one organization that stands out across these measures is *Tender*, the non-profit call centre that provides a communications relay service for hearing-impaired clients. Here workers are more likely to agree that they have to emotionally disengage from callers, camouflage their emotions, and conceal their selves. More than likely this has to do with the personal nature of communications that workers at this centre are sometimes called on to convey.

Taking the three questions that deal with emotional labour, it is possible to generate a reliable composite measure for the concept.[11] Using this index, emotional labour is correlated with work-related depression ($r = .314***$) and with job pressure ($r = .240***$).[12] Emotional labour is also negatively correlated with the workload-manageability index ($r = -.287***$) – in other words, more manageable loads are associated with less emotional labour, while more intensive efforts are associated with greater levels of emotion expenditure. However, emotional labour is also inversely related with skill ($r = -.287***$).[13] The former results are in line with Hochschild's theory and with our expectations that the expenditure of emotional labour is a source of tension for workers; the latter finding is more of a surprise. Perhaps it indicates that workers relate emotional labour with servitude and consequently denigrate its association with skill.

Ultimately, emotional labour and especially deep acting are about assuming definitions of self and others that are congruent with organizational goals. Both entail subscribing to definitions and meanings supplied by the employer. Here it is important only to recognize that engaging in deep acting as defined by Hochschild has manifest implications for the construction and regulation of identities – implications that may be problematic both for organizations and for individuals who are the objects of such regulation.

4.5 Conclusions

To conclude this chapter, it might be useful to briefly examine recent changes at one of the contact centres included in the foregoing analysis, for those changes seem to encapsulate the main themes. While employment growth is a feature of many of the case-study organizations, especially in the public sector, *Airline* is what might be described as a 'mature' call centre. Indeed, over the past two years the demand for telephone booking has fallen by almost 90 per cent, while online bookings have risen considerably.[14] What used to be a separate, specialized call queue – Web-based inquiries and help – has now been merged with the general duties of all CSRs. In keeping with the argument of chapter 1, this has entailed an expansion of the job as well as the acquisition and application of new skills. The manager of *Airline* helps us put these changes in perspective. When queried about their effects, he qualifies that this work is 'only helping people navigate through the website. It's not technical, computer-type help ... It's really only helping customers navigate through the Website when they get a booking, checking if it's in the system and stuff like that' (*Airline*, call-centre manager).

This description adds some substance to one of the main findings of this chapter – namely, that info-service work can for the most part be viewed as semiskilled. This designation must be used advisedly, however – that is, we should not immediately jump to the conclusion that info-service labour is the twenty-first century's equivalent of twentieth-century semiskilled manufacturing work. Braverman (1974) has reminded us that the concept of semiskilled work was itself largely a statistical creation heralding from the early years of the last century and used to classify machine-operator positions in factories. This work required more skill than non-mechanized labouring jobs, but far less skill than the craftwork it was replacing. In Braverman's view this semiskilled work was much more closely aligned with unskilled labour than with craft artisanship. He associated the growth in 'semiskilled' operative positions with general deskilling tendencies in society at large, using the craft worker as his benchmark for measuring social change. When it is stated that the work observed in this study is semiskilled, this should not be conflated with the work of Braverman's machine operator, nor should it be taken to imply a deskilling process. Rather, the call-centre labour process creates and uses semiskilled labour in terms of contemporary standards.

The semiskilled designation is appropriate in two senses. First, in a narrow statistical fashion we have seen that the centres examined in this study fall within the midranges of the skill index employed here. While I do not think this is an artefactual result, it hardly clinches the debate in its own right. Also, there are substantial theoretical reasons lying back of our judgment. The job of the CSR is clearly different from that which is performed on a real assembly line. The jobs generally entail longer training periods (weeks/months as opposed to days), involve broader spans of process understanding (e.g., often a number of software utilizations), and require a more holistic familiarity with final outcomes/products. Additionally, since the work combines simultaneous computer applications with live social interaction, considerable ethno-methodological tact is required. Accompanying these features are greater levels of responsibility and discretion within the job cycle than is customary in machine-paced semiskilled manufacturing labour. Taken together, these factors lend the work unique skill sets, which I have summarized under the rubric of interpretative labour, and which are constantly exercised in its accomplishment. By this I am referring to the negotiation of meaning around the production and use of information. When we take the term 'info-service' labour literally, we are presented with the essential components of the work. A CSR's job is part informational work and part service delivery. The skill demands of the job depend on how these two elements are positioned with respect to each other and with how they are combined into one function.

These aspects of info-service work require deviation from the strictures of Taylorism, especially in the form that the technical division of labour assumes. The movement witnessed in a variety of our case studies, towards the use of general queues in which each agent and each team is responsible for the host of functions and services represented by the call centre, provides the most tangible expression of half of the dual movement that was theorized in chapter 1 – namely, the creation of less fragmented jobs. Even in those cases where work is not designed around general queues, it is common for workers to now possess cross-team skills that allow them to work with different products and processes in their industry.

At the same time, we should be careful not to overstate the case. CSRs may exercise limited discretion *within* the job cycle, but this does not extend to the structure of the cycle itself or to broader control over the rhythm of the working day. Simply put, workers have little or no ability whatsoever to decide to do the job in a different manner from that which has been prescribed by management. Discretion is limited by standardized operating procedures and does not leverage into real autonomy over the selection of the order in which to do jobs or a choice over what tools or technologies to use in their completion. As a result, call-centre work can display a deadening routine that quickly becomes bereft of challenge, let alone stimulation. This is why workers through their actions and managers through their words tend to agree that two years is an upper limit for retention in many such positions. As the quotation from the manager of *Airline* alludes to, info-service work is to be distinguished from professional work in any strict sense of the term.

The second main finding of this chapter relates to our ability to generalize. Overall, the picture that takes shape is one of general homogeneity with respect to the job-skill levels that adhere to the work of a CSR. Most of the centres examined in this study do not differ in a statistically significant fashion from their counterparts in terms of the skill index that has been used. All of the sites fall within the operational notion of semiskilled work that we have been using – albeit at different levels within this band. These findings do little to support the theoretical bifurcation of call centres into low-standard mass-production operations and higher-order professional socio-technical systems. For the most part, the situation lies somewhere between these poles. Apart from a couple of obvious outliers at the bottom of our scale such as *Telebet*, the centres tend to be more alike than different in terms of how CSRs evaluate the skill demands associated with the work. This is not to say that a professional model of call-centre service delivery cannot be found. Having visited call centres that employ town planners, nurses, and trade-union organizers/researchers, I can attest to their existence. Indeed, it is a fascinating sign of our times that more and more professional services in areas such as health care are adopting the call-centre labour process as a mode of delivery. The effects of displacing traditional work designs with the call centre on professional skills and identities are only just beginning to be investigated (Smith, Valsecchi, et al. 2008; Van den Broek 2008; Wise et al. 2007) and extend beyond the remit of this book. Even so, in terms of the overall number of contact centres, those that employ certified professional workers are still very much the exception.

This chapter suggests the need for a more nuanced analysis – one that moves beyond the juxtaposition of Taylorism and knowledge work, recognizing that one of the contradictions of info-service work is that it contains contemporary traces of both. These dynamics can only be glimpsed at through the use of a labour-force survey. As is the case with any one-off survey, what has been presented in this chapter is a snapshot of employee perceptions of work effort and skill evaluations at single points in time. This provides us with some first-hand approximations of conditions at the time workers are surveyed. However, even in comparatively new organizational settings such as call centres, the labour process both has a history and is subject to change. Such features can, at best, be captured only indirectly through survey-based research. The next chapter provides a different take on some of the same questions vetted in this chapter, while extending the analysis. Using a longitudinal case-study approach, chapter 5 examines the design, adoption, and utilization of IT software in one case-study call centre. Chapter 5 also shifts our gaze from the first half of the dual movement – that is, changes in the technical division of labour at work – to the second half – namely, the response of managerialism, its growth and contradictions.

5 The Call-Centre Labour Process (2): Technological Selection and the Means of Communication in Info-Service Work[1]

5.1 Introduction

Power is a customer-contact centre in the consumer-energy sector dealing in electricity and natural-gas distribution to households and businesses.[2] It exemplifies many of the features covered in the previous chapter and more than likely would fit comfortably among the other call centres in terms of the workload expectations and job skills we have already reviewed. Fifteen electricity teams, along with one gas, one multiskilled, (electricity and gas), and one emergency loss-of-supply team, field inbound calls that mainly deal with connections, final readings/disconnections, consumption, billing, payment inquiries, and complaints. Pam, the CSR whose calls I am listening in on, is a former Pizza Hut manager. She finds that her job as a call-centre agent at *Power* requires greater concentration and leaves her feeling more tired at the end of the day than her previous position in the food-service sector. She has talk-time targets of between three and four minutes plus one-and-a-half minutes for wrap-up work, making for a prescribed job cycle of approximately five minutes per call. She does not complain about this, though she does find the targets she is given for trying to persuade customers to take up automatic debit accounts difficult to make.

Power's contact centre was created shortly after major changes were introduced regarding how utilities are regulated and power is distributed. Previously a single public corporation, in 1994 the existing state energy provider was split into two separate public entities with coverage for different parts of the state. These new entities were to run along much more commercial lines, in anticipation of eventual privatization. Following the division, *Power* remained one of the largest energy distribution companies in Australia, with a $2.3 billion infrastructural network and more than a million customers. The call centre was established in 1997 as an alternative to the twenty-seven existing suburban walk-in depots. Many of the original sixty CSRs came from these local centres, where they had provided over-the-counter and local telephone service to the company's customers. Most did not stay for long in their new settings. Within the first six months of operation over 80 per cent of the original staff had quit their new call-centre jobs.

By the time I arrive at *Power* in mid-2001, things have settled down somewhat. The centre now has 150 CSRs working in eighteen inbound customer-service teams. Together they field an average of 7,600 inquiries per day. There is still an annual attrition rate of about 26 per cent (10 per cent internal transfers and 14 to 16 per cent exits from the organization), but this is down significantly from the previous 49 per cent and, just as important, is less than the current local call-centre labour-market average of 38 per cent.[3] The centre has a popular new manager who is energetic, hip, and very much into building a unique culture around the centre. Some of the things that catch my attention on initial visits to the centre include the bowls of fruit scattered around the open-office setting, the disused overhanging grade-of-service display boards, and the background FM radio programming that is audible from all sections of the operations floor. In one corner of the main floor area sits a large TV that is available for members of the specialized emergency loss-of-supply team during slack periods.[4] The mission of the new centre as coined by the manager is nothing less than to provide 'wicked service' to the public. Kpi's, reward and recognition programs, induction and training, and communication all revolve around embedding the new culture of 'wicked service' levels at the centre. 'Wicked service' is to be excellent, remarkable, and without compromise. It is even given a persona in the form of a mascot who goes under the name of 'Wicked Willy.'

In sessions with the manager, I find that a particular emphasis is placed on the opportunities for communication and the role this plays in developing the new culture of *Power*. I am shown copies of the centre's in-house newsletter, which contain very specific information on budgets, resourcing issues, and new developments. The manager has also rostered in 'bash the boss' sessions for the teams and occasionally runs focus-group sessions to keep check on the pulse of the centre. Recently the centre has won some important accolades. *Power* has become the first registered call-centre training organization in the state, which means it is eligible to receive federal and state subsidies for training new workers. A comparatively high percentage of staff (over 20 per cent) have attained training certificates, so in this respect *Power* is becoming something of a model centre. Perhaps in recognition of these accomplishments, the centre has also won a coveted Best New Call Centre of the Year award from the Australian Teleservices Association at the state level. This has been a huge morale and confidence booster for the centre according to the manager, who has overseen preparation of the entry bid and is now planning to enter the national call-centre competitions.

Communication is where culture building begins, according to the manager, and it is possibly this belief that accounts for the open reception I receive when approaching the centre to conduct an earlier set of exploratory workforce interviews on employee perceptions of call-centre work.[5] Without much hesitation, a decision is made to participate in the survey and to allow observational work to be carried out around the centre. Free rein is also extended to conduct interviews with other management personnel and, most important, to attend and participate in an induction training program for new employees.

Though the cultural attributes of *Power* are what first make an impression, at the top of everyone else's agenda is the new customer-management software system (CMS) that is about to be rolled out. While CSRs dutifully complete my survey, what quickly becomes apparent is the depth of concern over the technological changes that are about to beset them. There are practically no questions on the topic of technology in the survey. As we have seen, call centres are largely defined by the technologies they employ (Taylor and Bain 1999), and these tend to be taken as a given. Thus it takes a while before I begin to hear and recognize the voices that are pointing towards exploring further the issue of technology in info-service work. As it turns out, it is the main order of business at *Power* before, during and after my residence there.

In hindsight, the clues were there from the very first visits to the centre. In an initial interview with the call-centre manager, the resources devoted to training were emphasized. This was something of a double-edged sword: a source of pride, but also a huge call on time and budgets – something like 'biting off an elephant,' to use the colourful turn of phrase the manager employed to describe *Power*'s training regime.[6] Much of this investment is consumed by the eight weeks of initial training for new hires. Managers do not attribute this to the innate complexity of the call centre's business, but rather to the outmoded software system that drives operations at the call centre. The new system that had just been introduced at the time of my approach to *Power* offers to improve this situation. Training will be reduced to four weeks, and a better level of service (i.e., greater standardization in service-quality levels) is promised as part of the change project. Work will be made easier and more customer focused for reasons that will be detailed below. Meanwhile, though, this is not what I am observing on the floor of the centre.

Pam, the agent introduced at the beginning of the chapter, expects that the new software will limit the flexibility she currently has to arrange repayment schedules with customers who have fallen into arrears on their accounts with *Power*. This will lead to more disputes, which will make her job more difficult rather than easier. Later, though, she confides that more standardization around the treatment of arrears may be a good thing: it will stop customers from 'shopping around,' trying to seek out more lenient CSRs with whom to negotiate repayment schedules for their utility bills.[7] Standardized responses for dealing with routine matters, including customer debt, will reduce the number of repeat calls and thus help get the call queues under control. A worker on the emergency loss-of-supply team expects that the new system will involve the generation of more prompts and reminders for agents, which this person doesn't necessarily see as a good thing. Meanwhile, a trainer I speak with hopes that the new system will be a closer approximation to her ideal of a 'sausage factory' (her term), in which each new CSR emerges from induction training at the same level. The new system will make her job easier and the turnaround time for qualifying new CSRs much shorter. The trainer thinks that the new system will also save CSR talk time. Customer-management software is also projected to make the CSR's job easier – a point that is reiterated by *Power*'s manager, who does not consider the existing system to be at all user-friendly.

Five months later I return to *Power* to begin my own induction along with eleven other new hires. The new CMS is up and running, while the old system has been consigned to a legacy position. It is used only when the new software calls it up for archived information or when the new system is 'down.' I am surprised when I discover that the training period is still eight weeks. In response to a question about this, my training 'buddy' explains that the new system has not made everything easier. Rather, there have been mixed effects regarding training and job simplification – a result at odds with one of the rationales for introducing CMS in the first place. It comes as an even greater surprise to learn that the switch over to the new system has created unending call queues – something that is witnessed in stints of on-the-job training where queues blow out into a backlog of up to one hundred calls waiting to be answered at any given time. It turns out that the overhanging display boards that produce the continuous streams of information on operational performance have been deliberately turned off owing to the dismal state of the measured grade of service. These developments constitute a paradox. Wasn't the $30 million investment in the new system that took more than two years to develop and adopt supposed, as its name suggests, to improve service levels? As it now stands, there are simply no lulls in the wall of waiting calls confronting the agents.

Each additional day I spend at *Power*, I witness conversations with trainers and permanent employees that keep returning to the mounting problems associated with the new technology. A trainer discloses that the new system has 'lots of bugs.' The integration of CMS with existing work structures and expectations is having unanticipated effects. CSRs are no longer 'making decisions that they have been trained to take,' and this has implications for the work roles of team leaders.[8] Agents that I buddy with complain about the navigational inflexibilities that have been designed into the new software algorithms – a practical example of how the new system has not made work easier or, for that matter, more efficient. A problem within a problem has emerged. The 'black box' of technology must be deconstructed in order to better understand the labour processes and skills associated with call-centre work, connections that the sojourn at *Power* are making increasingly evident. In recognition of this, I request interviews with people such as the technology-integration manager, who can provide more information about the old system and its replacement. I also decide that my 'problem within a problem' demands further methodological revision.

To delve deeper into the effects the new technology is having on the agents and the work they do, I obtain permission to conduct focus-group interviews at the centre. In discussions with the manager, it is agreed that three focus groups, consisting of eight participants each, will be held during regular working time. Members from the centre's different teams are randomly selected to participate in the sessions, which last from sixty to ninety minutes and are tape-recorded. The sessions are structured around a set protocol-of-discussion questions, which are used across the groups. The following topics are taken up by each group: the effects of the new CMS system on training requirements; the adequacy of current training and support systems; and the consequences of the new technology on various dimensions of over-the-phone customer-service work, including the effects on decision-making autonomy, job-cycle time, workloads, and job stress. Each group is also probed with regard to whether the new technology is being used as efficiently as possible and whether there might be more effective ways to employ it. At the suggestion of one of the groups, I convene a fourth focus group, composed entirely of team leaders. This group is queried on the same issues as the previous employee groups and provides a view from the lowest ranks of front-line management. Partial transcripts of these sessions are produced, and they provide the key component of the data used in this chapter.

At bottom, the research is guided by two central questions. First, what factors influence the design of the technologies that are used by info-service providers, and in this specific case, what motivated management to adopt a new technology, especially when service levels under the previous platform appeared to be satisfactory? Second, how do the workers who are assigned to the new technology actually make use of it? In other words, what effects does call-centre technology have on the labour process and the skills the work requires? Utilizing what I will term an 'extended materialist approach,' I will advance an account of the incongruities between plans and outcomes that have been outlined above. This theoretical approach is developed in the next section, which reviews and critiques some of the influential theoretical approaches previously used to study the relationships between technology and organizational structure. Following that, the extended materialist approach that I am advocating is placed in the service of studying the technology of the call centre. This will provide a valuable window through which to build on the results of the last chapter by re-evaluating the labour process, the skill demands associated with info-service work, and how management attempts to influence both.

5.2 Theoretical Issues

As we have already seen, call centres are defined by the integrated information and communication technologies they use rather than by particular product markets or outputs (Frenkel, Tam, et al. 1998; Taylor and Bain 1999). Technologies such as automated call distribution are taken as received fact. When 'technologies' are assumed as a given or are lent the status of an independent variable, it is all too easy to *inscribe* specific effects or outcomes to their use. With some notable exceptions,[9] the tendency to take ICTs as a received fact has been quite common in the research on call centres. For example, it has been argued that the technology of the call centre constitutes a version of technical control (Edwards 1979), where the 'technology … tends to control speed … through ensuring CSRs know queue numbers and average waiting times' (Callaghan and Thompson 2001).

Managerial control through technology is the logical ramification of this scenario. Other readings impute different effects. Thus, the informationalizing capacities of ICTs in call centres (Fernie and Metcalfe 1998; Winiecki 2004), as well as in other work settings (Menzies 1996; Sewell 1998), render workflows amenable to extreme levels of measurement, monitoring, and ultimately 'panoptic' control. Alternatively, the potential that inheres in ICTs can be construed as favouring the creation of a skilled and enabled workforce (Frenkel, Tam, et al. 1998; Kinnie, Purcell, and Hutchinson 2000; Korczynski 2001). In this case, enhanced employee autonomy may come about through the use of technology to produce more sophisticated outputs (Batt 1999; Batt and Moynihan 2004), with dynamics of empowerment displacing the reality of control.

It would be overly simplistic and a disservice to cast the debate on call-centre work in terms of technological determinism. Rather, the point I wish to draw attention to concerns the inadequate treatment of technology in the analysis of call centres. The purpose of this chapter is to open up the discussion on call-centre technologies and their effects on work and workers by using the opportunities provided at *Power* to explore managerial intentions, design specifications, and implementation and utilization of a new software system in the daily work of CSRs. Having studied these different phases in detail, it will be possible to move beyond simply inscribing effects of operant technologies on employee autonomy, job control, and requisite skill levels. A more nuanced understanding of technology in the call centre will aid in our comprehension of info-service work and the skills required to conduct it. A qualitative investigation of technological change and its effects will provide a useful validity check for the arguments and findings of the previous chapter, while allowing us to extend the analysis to the other half of the dual movement in contemporary work – managerialism.

A number of different theoretical approaches have been utilized in analyses of technological choice and change. The focus of labour process theory is cast on the interests that shape the design of technologies. Here it is hypothesized that technologies that have the potential for enhancing managerial control are favoured in the design and selection phases (Braverman 1974; Cooley 1980; Noble 1984; Shaiken 1984). As put forth by Shaiken (1984, 268), the components of technology can be combined in a variety of ways, but 'once these building blocks are assembled into more complex designs, the bias of the designer is built in. The machines ... embody the relations of power in the workplace.' Adopting technologies that render the labour process more transparent to oversight may enhance managerial control. Building superintendence into technology has, as one of its outcomes, the deskilling of work. Simply put, when the use of a given technology prescribes the exact manner in which the work will be accomplished, control is removed from the person deploying the technology.

Labour process theory has made an important contribution in drawing our attention to the social influences affecting the design of given technologies. However, there is also an element of teleology associated with some of the positions that theory puts forward. The spotlight is trained on the design phase of new technology and on the conscious intentions of the engineers who build it and the managers who adopt it. The implementation and utilization of new tools and techniques are often treated as foregone conclusions, with the denouement of the overall story being the realization of management's aims. When such a position is adopted, it is not possible to do full justice to the repertoire of possible responses to new technologies on the part of users. Consequently, a mechanistic control/resistance model to the introduction of new technology, whereby management acts and labour reacts to the introduction of new technologies, has often been associated with labour process theory (Ehrlich and Russell 2003). However, to cast the narrative in this mould is often to miss much of the richness associated with technological innovation.

As applied to call centres, ICTs are portrayed as the embodiment of what Edwards (1979) classified as technological control. In one of the clearest formulations of this thesis, Callaghan and Thompson (2000, 20) argue that 'management deliberately choose a technology that has been designed to limit worker autonomy ... The workers are almost seen as part of the machine – of a technology which continuously "fires" calls at them.' This is the 'assembly line in the head' metaphor (Taylor and Bain 1999), where technology supports the formulation of specific production targets, to which workers are then held accountable (Taylor and Bain 2001).

Since the appearance of the first labour-process analyses, attention paid to the social element of technology has broadened considerably.

Particular attention has been paid to the politics of technological development; this often highlights the intensely political nature of such decision making (Bloomfield and Danieli 1995; Brown 1995; Dawson 2000; Laurila 1997; McLoughlin, Badham, and Couchman 2000; Noon 1994). The politics of technological adoption are rightly portrayed as far more complex than a simple juxtaposition of managerial control versus worker resistance will allow. Power plays among managers for recognition, status, and resources (Knights and Murray 1994; Schoenberger 1997) are also often part of the story associated with the adoption and completion of particular technology projects. Managerial politics may involve different departments or divisions competing with one another to have 'pet' projects funded. Unintended consequences such as significant cost overruns, employee burnout, and unmet deadlines, while a reality of many technology-change projects, are seldom ever part of official narratives (Thomas 1994). This research has bequeathed us a much richer picture of management; however, as with labour process theory, the emphasis in the politics-of-technology and critical-management literature lies on the design and development phases. Occasionally the working conditions of IT employees are discussed (Knights and Murray 1994), but these seldom feature as a central concern. Interactions among designers, adopted technologies, and final users are often missing from the picture.

Research in the organizational-behaviour tradition does not suffer from these limitations. Here the researcher's gaze is fixed on the effects that (new) technologies have on the (re)organization of work. Barley (1986, 1990), for example, insists that researchers need to concentrate on precisely how new technologies are incorporated into the everyday working lives of organizational members. He demonstrates how the introduction of exactly the same technologies can have quite different effects on the division of labour, job status, work autonomy, and opportunity, depending on the organizational environment into which the new technology is received. On being introduced into organizations, new technologies undergo processes of social negotiation as part of their acceptance. How the technologies are eventually used, and their impacts on employees' jobs and skill levels, are the result of organizational structures, histories, and cultures that need to be studied in their own right. Orlikowski (1996) extends this approach further with her 'situated change perspective.' This analysis pays heed to the accommodations, experiments, and deviations in the use of newly adopted technologies; all of these have to be treated seriously if outcomes – including effects on work effort and job skill – are to be properly understood. Inevitably, new technologies will have outcomes that are unforeseen and certainly not intended by the engineers and system analysts who design them. Furthermore, such practical outcomes may or may not be contested by various stakeholders in the change process.

This last point regarding what will be contested and with what intensity is important, but it is also difficult to specify further, because organizational-behaviour approaches ignore precisely what labour process theory takes as its starting point – the originating intentions that inform technological design (Badham 2005). In both Barley's structuring approach and the situated-change perspective of Orlikowski, new technologies simply arrive on the scene to be put into practice in ways that are contingent on the outcomes of interactions among the actors involved. However, without some analysis of why the new innovations have been adopted, of what has been promised by designers and vendors, and of what is hoped for on the part of purchasers, it is difficult to account for the negotiation, contestation, and unintended consequences that often accompany their introduction. In other words, technology is still implicitly regarded as an exogenous variable that 'impacts' the organization rather than as a manifestation of managerial prerogative. Though managerial rights extend to decisions of whether to invest in new technologies, as the case study analysis in this chapter show, this decision-making prerogative cannot ensure successful outcomes.

The issue of outcomes and unintended consequences after new technologies are adopted has also been raised by radical deconstructionists (Grint and Woolgar 1997; Willmott and Bridgman 2006), who urge us to drop the very dichotomy between the 'technological' and the 'social.' From this perspective, what matters is how individuals interpret technology and which interpretations gain 'most favoured status.' According to this approach, technologies cannot be imbued a priori with specific politics, nor can they be gendered or socially imprinted in any other manner. Instead, gendered discourses and other discourses develop around the interpretation of the technology, and this results in the assignment of capabilities, constraints, and other characteristics that may entail social exclusions in the use of the technology and in other decisions pertaining to it.

Like the organizational-behaviour approaches, 'anti-essentialist' arguments emphasize the consumption of technology by users rather than the design and production of technology. In this analysis the privileged moment is the interpretation of technology by users. However,

unlike the organizational analysis of Barley or the situated-practice perspective of Orlikowski, anti-essentialism denies any efficacy to the material artefact. We can agree that design does not uniquely determine
deployment outcomes; nevertheless, it is a good place to begin analysis.
Technologies are designed to allow for certain possibilities and to rule
out others – in other words, with certain intentions in mind. To ignore
these realities is to dissolve the social power that is part of the employment relationship into an epistemological relativism. It is preferable,
instead, to consider the ways in which the materiality of technology
limits the scope of possible 'interpretations' even as those 'interpretations' are developed through reflexive practice and negotiation on the
part of users. This leaves open the question of whether design intentions are ultimately realized in the use of the new technology, but it at
least recognizes the importance of intention on the part of designers,
engineers, and managers, while allowing for the possibility of contested intentions among these power holders as well as between them and
final users.

   In the analysis of technology change at the *Power* call centre, it will
be argued that one must apply the strengths of labour process theory
and organization theory respectively in order to provide an extended
materialist account of technological change. Labour process theory focuses our attention on intentions, especially as they relate to the design
of technological artefacts. This is its strength. It need not – nor should it
– deny the possibility of contested intentionality through the selection
and design phases of technological development. As critical management theory suggests, there may well be divisions over how best to
allocate limited budgets on new technologies and on what features to
prioritize. Organizational theory, for its part, draws our attention to the
actions of users and how they 'feel' their way through the employment
of new technologies to establish patterns of use that may conform to or
significantly deviate from the intentions of designers. Such action may
be constituted as knowledge in practice. It may remain only partially
discursive, and only when other actors solicit specific knowledge of the
practice from users. As we shall see, such knowledge may become the
object of managerial forays into the arena of 'knowledge management,'
or it may congeal at the informal level to become part of the 'customs
and practices' of the workforce that applies it.

   An extended materialist analysis, such as the one being advocated
here, joins the production of operant technologies (with all their intentionality) to an analysis of consumption on the part of users (with all its

contingency). It provides a bridge by which to cross the gap between originating intentions, which remain important, and ultimate user outcomes, which remain decisive. An extended materialist approach also takes us beyond mechanistic models of control/resistance and allows us to consider other repertoires of action that workers evoke as they encounter new production systems. While practices such as 'repair work' and 'work-arounds' have been identified in previous research that studies the utilization of ICTs (Gasser 1986; Harley et al. 2006; Suchman 1996; Petrides, McClelland, and Nodine 2004; Wagner and Newell 2006), they have not been adequately theorized. An objective of this chapter is to reach greater clarity on the meanings that social actors attach to what Orlikowski and Yates (2006) problematize as 'workability in practice.' While call-centre work has been subjected both to labour process theory (Bain, Watson, et al. 2002; Callaghan and Thompson 2001; Taylor and Bain 1999, 2001; Taylor, Hyman, et al. 2002) and to approaches influenced by socio-technical theory with its emphasis on 'choice' (Batt 1999, 2000, 2002; Batt and Moynihan, 2004), it has not been studied from the extended materialist analysis I am proposing here.

The analysis that follows is materialist to the extent that the adoption of specific technological artefacts is postulated as having real outcomes that may be both planned and unintended, which is to say that such outcomes ultimately depend on more than how individuals interpret the technology. While a given technology is both enabling and constraining, the ways in which it will be used cannot be entirely predicted in advance, nor can they be deduced from an ascribed objective class position that workers are said to occupy. An example of this is when technologies are used in non-sanctioned ways to increase efficiency and thereby productivity. The analysis is extended insofar as it examines all aspects of the technology issue in organizations, from the origin of the tools through to their utilization by workers. An extended materialist analysis, such as the one I am advocating here, exposes new features of call-centre work that have hitherto been overlooked. Specifically, such an approach encourages a deeper inquiry into the dynamics of actual work practices and their relationship with the aims of management control in the determination of job skill.

5.3 The Case Study: What Did Management Want?

An extended materialist analysis begins with the originating issue around any new technology. Given that such decisions are a managerial prerogative in a capitalist economy, a start can be made by asking what management hoped to gain by investing in a new software technology. This question is best answered by examining the situation that existed before the new technology was adopted.

Both before the creation of the call centre at *Power* and then more recently, workers used a DOS-based software package called Facom in their transactions with the public. The main function of this system was accounts management. Management liked to refer to Facom as a 'billing engine' for creating and maintaining the accounts of the company's customers. Readers of a certain age will recognize this as the sort of 'green screen,' code-driven system that pre-dated Windows software. Facom was the call centre's principal 'tool,' and our analysis focuses on its replacement by a new software technology known as the Customer Management System (CMS).

As an accounts-based software system, Facom allowed jobs to be logged and accounts maintained for residential and business addresses alike. Addresses provided the identifiers on which the system operated. Like other 'green screen' systems, Facom was code based – that is, any query or operating function required the input of a specific code to accomplish a given task. Training largely involved familiarizing CSRs with the almost four hundred codes that drove the system. As previously indicated, this meant an eight-week induction period, much of it dedicated to the development of keyboard and navigational skills.

Workers typically used the Facom system both to access data to satisfy customer queries and as the means for inputting new data into customer files. This required an ability to take information and enter it into the program in order to produce information and, ultimately, results in the field. Queries were often unexpected or involved complex forms of search, navigation, and negotiation. By CSRs' own estimates, up to half of all calls entailed customer requests to defer payments or to establish special repayment schedules. Minimally, the job involved exercising information-gathering and computer navigational skills. It also required product knowledge and a capacity for empathy. All of the above needed to be conducted in a manner that conformed to the centre's call-handling targets.[10] Agents were adept at using the existing software system to accomplish these tasks, which quite often could not be accomplished in a neat, preset, or scripted order.

This was the scene into which management introduced the CMS in late 2001. The technology was attractive on a number of levels, and management's actions were guided by mixed albeit complementary motives. Fundamentally, these motives were cost reduction, commercialization, and increased managerial control.

The justification for introducing CMS was that it would provide better customer service in line with the change in the company's status from a public utility to a corporate service provider. Improved customer service' was, in fact, a euphemism for the new emphasis that was about to be placed on commercialization. As implied by its name, CMS was to focus on the customer rather than the residence. As *Power* began to redefine itself as a business rather than a public utility, this was a key consideration. CMS permitted better data-tracking and data-mining opportunities because its trigger was the customer rather than the individual residential address. This opened up new opportunities for holistic customer management, for highlighting customer profiles, and for maximizing sales opportunities, in that users could now be configured as consumers of a potentially broad basket of goods and options that *Power* would be allowed to offer. CMS could be used for 'product and service promotion' and 'customer education' – euphemisms for 'soft' forms of marketing – in ways that had not been identified with the old technology. For example, CMS would easily be able to corral account holders into special market segments. This had not been possible with the Facom system.

CMS's capabilities had a number of implications for CSRs. For example, managers would be able to build 'product promotion' into the work expectations, in effect turning customer-service jobs into something more akin to sales-consultant jobs. Sales could be added to the list of employee-performance targets, and indeed, there were now expectations that CSRs would suggest product purchases on 3 per cent of the calls they took and direct debit billing on 5 per cent. There is little doubt that workers viewed these new targets as an additional imposition that increased workloads – 'more buttons to click on, more products to sell to the customer even when they are not relevant,' as one member of a focus group explained the effects of adding more screens and scripts to the job cycle (Focus Group 2, hereafter FG2). At the same time, the new system might open opportunities for employees to acquire skills such as data analysis.[11] Thus, greater work expectations and revised skill levels could both be associated with the commercialization potential of the new technology.

A second attraction of the new system was the promised halving of training time. This hearkens back to the cost advantage associated with adopting CMS. As we have already previewed, given the size of the call centre and the turnover rates, training represented a large resource commitment for *Power*. Time taken up with training provides a metric of its significance; so does resources dedicated to the training function. Though 6 per cent of total rostered hours had been planned for training, at the time of our study this was averaging closer to 8 per cent.[12] The centre employed four full-time trainers to manage its training program. Management was anxious to see a reduction in the amounts of time dedicated to training, and the discourse established around CMS promised to make this happen. Managers fully expected that once the code-based system was replaced with 'point and click' technology, training times for new recruits would be halved from eight weeks to somewhere between three and four. As described by the participants in one of the focus groups, the old system required extensive knowledge before the CSR could start using it, whereas CMS

> does flow. It's going to show you a pathway and you choose the options and from selecting an option on this side it's going to give you a list of options on this side and you sort of know where you're going ... With Facom it's 'What do I do now?' ... You have to have that knowledge before you start working on it so you have to be trained, whereas [with] CMS ... the questions are at the top ... You just click on the options and there you go. I'd say [CMS] probably [requires] less [skill] because it's all there in front of you and you can just follow it. It's logical whereas Facom is more, you got to know things ... the codes and things like that. CMS is fairly basic to follow. (Focus Group 1, hereafter FG1)

Because it came with self-paced training modules and online scripts, CMS was expected to require considerably less training time than was currently being expended on Facom. In an organization the size of *Power* with its ongoing intake of new employees, this represented a considerable future savings on training costs.

In addition to the *time* devoted to training, there was the issue of its *content*. Before CMS the greater portion of training time at *Power* was taken up with acquiring code-based navigational finesse. This did not accord with the new commercial focus, which placed greater emphasis on 'customer education' and the ability to generate interest in the company's new products, such as air conditioners and security systems. Adoption of CMS meant that training could be reconfigured and aligned with emerging business priorities. Eight weeks of mainly code-based navigational and keyboard training would be replaced with three to four weeks of instruction that emphasized relationship management and 'soft' marketing techniques. The new technology promised to enable a new business strategy, one that would combine elements of growing market share through product and service diversification with customer targeting, then marrying all of this to a strategy of cost reduction.

The third and final objective associated with the adoption of CMS was enhanced managerial control as reflected in greater levels of process standardization. Facom presented a comparatively open system for its users. In responding to customers, the CSR had to know where to go into the system as well as which codes to enter in order to retrieve the required information. Knowledgeable CSRs could generate much better call-handling statistics than less experienced agents by applying the tacit knowledge that comes with the experience of using a complex system. This included employing abbreviations and other shortcuts that were permissible under the existing platform. To a significant degree, customer-service levels depended on the de facto 'ownership' that CSRs took of their own call-handling processes. The skills involved in taking, entering, and retrieving information, all the while maintaining a sociable comportment, should not be underestimated; nor should the discretion that the system extended CSRs when it came to providing satisfactory levels of customer service.

CSRs exercised discretion in the work they performed and in their use of the existing technology in different ways. Nowhere is this better illustrated than in the gestation of operating procedures at the centre. In the early days of the call centre, processes were informal and worked as follows. After fielding an inquiry, the agent would jot down notes for herself for future reference. These could be amended as greater familiarity with the system and its flexibilities was acquired; just as important, those notes could be shared with co-workers in informal knowledge networks. The absence of standard operating processes worried the centre's managers, who, after the contact centre was created, set about compiling a formal process manual as a way to manage existent knowledge. This exercise took a considerable amount of time to complete, but the key point is that the final outcome was based largely on the specific processes that had been developed, refined, and shared among CSRs. Management relied on the CSRs when writing the original process manual, which basically was a compilation of the informal 'notebooks' and jottings that agents had been compiling in the course of their work.

Generating standard operating procedures in this fashion gave the agents some latitude over what was entered into the system and over how subsequent job orders were executed. Expressions of agent autonomy were found in the setting of required security deposits for new customers, the treatment of overdue accounts, and decisions to disconnect, reconnect, and reschedule payments. While there were guidelines in these matters, ultimately it was up to the CSR to establish terms that met the needs of the company and the 'duty of care' to customers, as the following comments detail: 'One thing I find that I still have to go back to the old system is when it comes to the waiving of security deposits. That just isn't captured readily for our eyes on CMS, which is something I think is fairly important, especially when we're taking a new application for a customer because we don't want that customer to pay any more than they need to and I don't want to charge a customer any more than I need to' (FG1).

Such interactions often entailed both negotiation and mediation on the part of the worker – that is, precisely the kinds of interpretive labour discussed in the previous chapter. But instead of defining this type of flexibility as an asset, managers viewed it as a source of angst that required a technological 'fix.' Consistency of information and standardization of actions were key managerial objectives in the CMS project; both were viewed as too dependent on the individual knowledge of CSRs.

A related aspect of the control issue that came out in the course of the fieldwork was the 'problem' of the informal knowledge and status hierarchy associated with old ways of working. Managers were well aware that longer-serving employees served as unofficial mentors and enjoyed increased status on the call-centre floor for that reason. These employees knew short cuts that made little sense to a novice but made working life much easier. The ability not just to take control of a conversation, but to do so in a way that seemingly negated the control being exercised, was a competence that differentiated the skilled CSR from the less accomplished, who (like I did) struggled to keep up with the customer, the conversation, and the computer at one and the same time. These informally constituted knowledge hierarchies lay outside the purview of management and were viewed as a potential challenge to the carefully constructed architecture of team leadership and the control that was exercised through it. The new technology presented management with an opportunity to remove the advantage that an elite group of employees possessed. Scripting, prompts, and easy-to-follow algorithms would decrease the informal mentoring role that experienced workers had embraced. Management was definitely aware of this aspect of CMS and wanted to take advantage of it.[13]

CMS technology presented managers with an 'imagined' solution to the process and control issues they had identified as problems at the centre. For management, the new technology held out the hope of a 'trifecta win': reduced training costs, a smooth transition from a public-utility mindset, and an end to 'lax quality' standards associated with 'too much' agent autonomy. The switch to CMS was expected to resolve all these 'problems' in one swoop. To ensure this, though, it was necessary to retain Facom as a legacy system for data storage. CMS was designed and adopted to be 'wrapped around' the existing platform. This precaution guaranteed that, in the first instance, workers would have no alternative but to use the new system to progress each new call. This fundamentally altered the labour process.

Previously, workers had interacted directly with the database as *interpreters* for the public. Under the new system, agents would have to work through CMS, which was to be treated as 'the interpreter.' This change entailed more than simply abandoning an array of cluttered green screens for attractive and easy-to-read windows. CMS was premised on what was described by the technology-change manager as the 'say, do, ask' format.[14] This dictum refers to the prompts the system throws up with each new window. Agents were now *escorted* through the customer-service screens on their computers in a *preset order*. An end to dependence on agent memory in relation to codes was viewed as an important attribute of the new system. Even if more experienced CSRs did not follow the scripts verbatim – because 'you sound like an idiot – you sound like a robot' (FG2), they were required to follow a pre-defined order in their conversations with customers. Interactions with customers were now regulated by the automatic appearance of specific windows that required responses in order to advance the call. Agents could no longer trawl the system for the information and functions they required in order to provide quick resolutions to queries. Instead, set ordered algorithms walked the worker through procedures in a strictly linear fashion. This new format made it impossible for CSRs to move backwards and forwards across screens as required, and this seriously weakened their navigational role, which had once served as the link between the customer and the database. CSRs 'used' the system less than before; the emphasis now was on meeting its requirements. The new software had replaced the *lateral* logic of Facom with the *stem and branch* approach of CMS. One focus-group participant put it this way: 'The knowledge is still pretty much there because it's the processes that underlie it that's important … But just the way I see Facom, it's more work … You've got to know the codes and you've got to know how to use them, but with CMS I find that it's pretty much set by that IT logic of stem-and-branch and you've got to follow through, go through those options' (FG1).

New, technologically embedded operating procedures were meant to deliver the uniformity, standardization, and control that management yearned for in each call. This would put an end to the discretion and influence that CSRs had been relying on to carry out their work. New controls were lodged within the software. For example, strict limits were placed on the range of choices agents could now offer the public in the case of overdue accounts; CMS would only permit two repayment options, whereas previously CSRs had been issued with general guidelines for dealing with customer arrears. If the new options were unacceptable to the customer, the CSR had to escalate the call to the team leader for resolution. This limitation was yet one more of the 'building blocks' that inscribed the new technology with features that removed discretion from its intended users.

To summarize, management had various complementary intentions in introducing CMS at *Power*. The new system was an attempt to diminish training time and costs and to introduce greater levels of service standardization among agents; there is no question but that to the extent the new processes took hold, agent autonomy was restricted. Insofar as this was the case, skill levels would predictably decline. The new system required less navigational skill. It also entailed less decision making on the part of CSRs around such aspects of the job as setting up payment schedules for customers who were behind on their bills. There is no mistaking the intent to diminish job autonomy in the name of service rationalization. Moreover, this particular dynamic is not unique to this one case study. When we probe further into the history of the various call centres that have been included in this book, similar rationales on the part of management come to the fore.

At *Advisory Services*, for instance, service standardization was a founding principle of the new centre. As outlined by the centre's manager, before the facility was created in 1997 'the level of service and assistance that you received was dependent on the experience of the person you actually got at the time … People had a database that was not very user-friendly and so consequently they collected all their own information and they all had folders. The trouble was that every folder was different' (*Advisory Services*, call-centre manager).

Standardization of service is easier to control when training is centralized in one facility and when operating procedures are embedded in software as opposed to personal files or individual memories. A similar situation was described in other pre–call-centre service environments, including *Urban Space*, where the manager recounted that 'information was in people's heads, so if Di was on holidays the customer couldn't get an answer because no one knew until Di came back … They thought, "Well, okay, if we can document all the processes in a really clever information system and it's going to feed all those numbers into that one place, that would be our call centre"' (*Urban Space*, call-centre manager).

At *Power*, standardization through centralized control of information and its use meant less control by agents over how they used technology and what they relayed to customers. CMS had new controls embedded in it, and the intentions associated with its adoption clearly conform to the arguments of those researchers who point towards a Taylorisation of info-service work. To the extent that work of this sort can be Taylorized, something akin to this outcome was clearly envisaged by the managers who chose to adopt the new system. In short, the attractiveness of the new software for management was to be found in the greater levels of control it ceded to them, including both cost control and behavioural control.

This is normally where labour process theory leaves off, and it tends to confirm those analyses of the call centre that draw attention to technological control, limited autonomy, and diminished skill levels. However, this was really only the first chapter in what was to unfold at *Power*. To complete the analysis, having examined the originating intentions behind the adoption of CMS, we must now turn our attention to its use in practice.

5.4 Between the Cup and the Lip: The Adoption of CMS

The discourse that accompanied the introduction of CMS naturally enough did not emphasize the controlling features of the new system to which attention has been drawn. Instead, CMS was portrayed as a 'friendlier,' easier-to-use technology that would help CSRs to do their jobs better by providing higher levels of customer satisfaction. Happier, more pleasant customers would result in fewer callbacks and complaints, less congested call queues, and reduced levels of agent abuse. Cast in this light, the introduction of CMS was something to be celebrated rather than resisted, and so it was. One team leader recalled: 'The way it was promised in the early stages was this new system that would do all these fantastic things with no impact on the customer' (Focus Group 4, hereafter FG4). Right from the start of the roll-out, however, things did not go according to plan. Next we examine the effects of *using* the new technology on the originating intentions of management, beginning with the commercialization mandate.

As we saw in the introduction, the most immediate yet unanticipated impact that the new software system had on operations was a 'blowout' in customer-service levels as measured by the length of call queues and waits for service. Focus group members made these observations:

> The whole rationale with CMS was to reduce the call time ... [to] reduce the time that it takes to service the customer, so I think the underlying rationale there has been somewhat undermined or self-defeated ... We never used to have the queues that we do now, never. Fifteen in the queue, we've now got hundreds in the queue. (FG1)

> We have a GOS [grade of service] of consistently 70 to 80 [per cent], and they implement the new system and it drops to 20 – it's gotta make you wonder. (FG4, team leaders)

These problems were not a result of the inevitable familiarization period or other 'teething problems' associated with the adoption and use of a new technology. Rather, call-handling times increased because a new front-end system had been bolted on to – or more accurately, 'wrapped around' – the existing technological platform as a means of ensuring greater levels of process standardization (i.e., control). Each inbound call was now funnelled through the new software, while information was still stored in and entered back into the existing databases of the legacy system. If nothing else, this added time to information retrieval and job completion. In theory the CMS software would interact with the existing data archives in a seamless manner. However, as several focus-group participants explained, for many queries the agent still had to go back into the old system in order to progress the call:

> [Customers] may ask all these questions, but you can't really do them in

CMS and ... *Power* wants us to sound as though we know what we're talking about and if we're to do that, you have to use Facom because Facom can get you an answer ... So really we're actually using two systems at the same time and what's the point of doing that? (FG2)

We still have to go through CMS to get to the Facom screens that we want to get to, but that's because they [management] fiddled with them. If they hadn't fiddled with them, I would never use CMS [followed by general group assent]. (FG2)

Without probing, CSRs in the focus groups accurately traced these problems to the conflicting mandates of public-service provision versus the new logic of commercialization: 'CMS is not really power-company friendly, it's friendly for people who are silent faced, who design things' (FG3). Workers identified the old system with supplying power and the new technology with commodification, while in their minds the company was still principally a public-goods provider. Thus the new technology came to symbolize or stand in for a new definition of the organization and its mission – one that CSRs did not willingly embrace. The following statements provide evidence of this conflict over purpose and how it became integrated with disenchantment with and (eventually) conflicts over the new technology and the ways it was used:

Our bread and butter is still electricity and you can't service the customer properly when you can't even find where they live. (FG3)

It doesn't work because it's a premise-based system and they want it to be a customer-based system ... Power doesn't go to people, power goes to places, and that's what they should have looked at from the word go. (FG2)

As a result, even simple tasks, such as initial customer identification and matching customers to accounts, could be time consuming, inefficient, and – as the following vignette suggests, with more than a touch of irony – insensitive: 'When we get a deceased customer the system is not really right because we have to ID the dead person. So in theory, the person who is dead has to ring up to say "I am dead"' (FG4, team leaders).

CSRs were also acutely aware of how longer processing times, conversational lapses, and the redundant questions required by the new software made them appear in the eyes of the public:

> With CMS ... generally there'll be times where ... you'll be sitting there twiddling your thumbs, making small talk, because it's just sitting there doing nothing ... Now we have to wait on CMS ... Sometimes it makes you look stupid to the customers ... So it has slowed things down and it also kinda makes us look *not as empowered*. They might think this person doesn't know what they're doing, but it's not that, it's just that *we know where we're meant to go*, [but] *we can't go there* because CMS is having issues. (FG2; emphasis added)

This statement accurately identifies the disempowering effects that the new system was having on its users. In the focus-group narratives we also see some intriguing inversions of stereotypical labour/management relations. According to the CSRs, it was management rather than labour that had 'fiddled' with the system. This slowed down the pace of work and discredited the workforce in the eyes of the public. Quite clearly, the focus-group members were concerned about these outcomes.

Many of the informants viewed the degradation of service levels as a long-term phenomenon, and they railed against management's objective, which was to enhance commercialization at *Power* by presenting a more 'customer-friendly' face. In short, CMS was compromising existing customer-service levels. This degradation of service was directly attributable to the extra 'layer of control' that CMS represented and that was being brought into play every time a call was received. With the Facom system, workers could flip back and forth between screens and functions as required. Information could be carried over from one screen to the next, and CSRs could move directly to the screens they needed in order to complete a job. This freewheeling flexibility saved time and was part of what defined a skilled, experienced agent. With the new platform, workers were required to proceed in a specific linear order, screen by screen, regardless of each screen's relevance to the call at hand. Furthermore, it was impossible to backtrack in CMS; information displayed in previous screens could not be recovered if needed later in the call. This inflexibility slowed processes down, making for irate customers and frustrated workers. 'I hate this system,' declared one focus-group member. 'You've got a computer virtually arguing with you – you know, taking over what you're trying to do. What I hate about CMS is that *it does take over from you*' (FG3; my emphasis).

With respect to the second aim – reducing costs by shortening training times – long after CMS was introduced, training periods at *Power*

remained unaltered at eight weeks. The new system was more compat-
ible with on-the-job training and self-paced modularized learning, yet
the anticipated halving of training time did not materialize. There were
various reasons why. For one thing, agents still had to know enough
of the old system that they could go into it and retrieve information
if CMS couldn't or wouldn't do it for them. And besides having to be
competent with two systems, CSRs now also had to know how to overcome the problems that were generated by the new technology and its
problematic integration with the old system. Getting the two systems
to work together involved more than familiarity with two unique systems, and this extended training time in ways that management had
not foreseen. As one participant summed things up, it had been 'not
a very good idea to actually ... try and train people on something that
doesn't work' (FG2). Attempting to do so meant that the anticipated
reductions in training costs did not materialize. Moreover, CSRs found
the training regime associated with the new system to be inadequate
for the demands of the job:

> The training was too simplistic. You were sat down in front of a computer
> [and] told, 'This is how you find the ... information you are looking for.'
> You did a little self-training module ... that a twelve-year-old could do – it
> was fairly simple, you could memorize half of the answers – but it didn't
> teach you how to do it ... And then you get on the floor and you realize
> [that] the training was so simple you could only follow certain manoeu-
> vres but you didn't know how to get other information that you needed
> ... What you were told to do didn't work, and then you were constantly
> referring back to Facom because you couldn't get the information out of
> CMS that you needed. (FG2)

Most surprising, however, were the decidedly mixed results pertaining to the third objective, which was enhanced control through greater
process standardization. Plans to fully utilize the new software to limit
CSR discretion immediately had to be shelved. Management quickly
discovered that tying the hands of agents too tightly led to unsustain-
able increases in their own workloads, with intolerable numbers of customer disputes being passed up to team leaders for resolution. A team
leader described the collapse of the new protocols:

> The system was designed to control some decisions the CSRs made, but
> this had to be put aside in the beginning because it was totally unrealistic
> ... We ended up for the first three weeks with zillions of pieces of paper

with these freakin' arrangements on them. It's not realistic, you can't deal with people like that. If you had a bill for $185 and the customer said, 'Well, can I pay $90 today' ... the CSR would have to say, 'No, you have to pay $92.50 or my system won't take it.' You can't do that to people. You can't work with customers like that. (FG4, team leaders)

As recalled by this team leader, it quickly became apparent that the new work design was unworkable! Once the impracticalities of the new protocols became evident, management summarily removed the blocks on employee decision-making discretion that had been installed in the software. In other words, important elements of the CSR's job had to be reinstated shortly after they had been subsumed by the new system. This is an especially pertinent example of how efforts to introduce greater process standardization can actually work against the goal of better customer service.

Other adjustments followed quickly. With the enormous daily backlog of calls, the centre's manager decided to disengage the overhead neon boards that visibly display the grade-of-service statistics. These physical artefacts are a standard feature in many call centres and have been associated with 'management by stress' regimes. Turning them off was an admission the symbolism of which was hard to miss. More significantly, grade-of-service targets, which were built into individual employee-performance agreements, had to be recalibrated to reflect conformity with real *average* call-handling times as opposed to the *ideal* targets previously set by the resource planner. This had the effect of actually loosening performance targets. And to compensate for this, in a vain attempt to get the queues under control, management was forced to hire additional staff. This further undermined the cost-control initiatives associated with the project.

More generally, management's attempts to quarantine old skills were not realized. And all the while, new and still largely hidden skills were being created. It had been expected that CMS would require less skill to operate; this was one of the reasons why it had been adopted. The new system had been designed to reduce the worker's interpretive role in the relationship between the customer and the organization. CMS software was designed to communicate directly with the centralized database – a role previously performed by the CSR. The agent was supposed to become more of a relay operative, a *servant* rather than a *user* of the software. The loss of an active decision-taking role over such aspects of the job as negotiating repayment schedules was one manifestation of the new relationship between worker and technology. Knowledge of hundreds of codes and how to use them in the most efficient manner possible for the resolution of customer-service requests was to be replaced by 'point and click' operations, with the CSR simply following the prompts provided by computer-generated algorithms. An expectation of diminished skill levels was reflected in the condensed training periods that CMS software was thought likely to produce.

The problem was that conforming to the requirements of the new system was not always the most effective way of resolving a customer inquiry. Thus, offsetting the deskilling logic that was part of the designed system were new assimilating skills that were required in order to make CMS work. The *interpretative* skills of CSRs were not overridden; instead, new *integrative* skills were added to the mix. Agents were now responsible for knowing and maintaining a working relationship between the two operating systems. One agent summarized this point: 'You need *more* skill … You need to know not only how basically to serve the customer appropriately, you need to know how to put it in the system, cheat CMS, and also make sure everything is in Facom in the end, because it all has to end up in Facom … Basically kind of cheat the system, also … basically kind of pretty it up' (FG2).

As the above statement suggests, a number of new skill sets were created with the adoption of CMS, but these new skills were of a rather peculiar kind. First, CSRs had to develop new strategies for making the technology do what they required it to do. A new adeptness at manipulating the software and integrating its operations with the legacy system became part of the job. The first aspect of this type of work is commonly referred to in the IT literature as the invention of *workarounds* (Gasser 1986; Petrides, McClelland, and Nodine 2004; Suchman 1996). As the above quote illustrates, workers developed a colourful discourse to describe this activity and the skills attached to it. 'Lying to the computer,' 'cheating the system,' 'outsmarting the machine,' and 'prettying up' the work quickly became part of the call-centre's daily routines. Members of the focus groups described these new skills as necessary to getting the new technology to work. These new work attributes are worth investigating a little more closely.

Lying was practised when the new technology presented CSRs with inappropriate options, scripts, and screens. As an everyday work practice, agents lied in order to get around a technology that its users viewed as largely dysfunctional. For example, they could enter incorrect information to speed the system up and decrease call-handling times. 'We have to write the wrong way to do the right thing' (FG3).

Lying could also be engaged when the system was not responding in an appropriate fashion; or when the options it presented were inadequate to address a problem – that is, when the agent needed to author an alternative solution that the system would not otherwise allow. 'You've got to cheat it all the time, lie to it … You've got to lie' (FG3). 'With CMS you just have to lie to it the whole time, 'cause it will find you nothing' (FG2).

Workers would 'lie' to CMS to get past blocks that had been intentionally embedded in the new software in order to proceed with what they defined as their real job: 'Pick a path fork where you go a certain path, and if you pick the wrong one you're stuffed or you have to go right back to the very start. But the whole way it actually tries to structure you … if it's not the CMS way it doesn't care, it's not gonna let you do it. There are some situations where … like, for a loss of supply we might have a primary fuse blown … It doesn't give you the opportunity to explore that option, you have to lie to it' (FG2).

Work-arounds were expedient measures that agents developed for dealing with the contradictory requirements of using the new technology while fulfilling customer expectations. However, work-arounds could become more than an expedient practice. Successful ways around the system were quickly passed on from agent to agent through the informal knowledge networks that were still part of the call centre but outside the purview of management. Tricks for dealing with CMS could quickly attain the status of 'local wisdom' and folklore within the workplace, as suggested by the following anecdote: 'One of the guys upstairs said to me, "Hey, have you ever tried this? If you just put … 'cc' in the suburb it actually skips a screen and brings you to where you wanna be." Somebody just stumbled across it, and you think, "Hey, I am lying to this machine so well that I can even skip a screen that was absolutely useless anyway, to get to the screen that I wanna be in"' (FG2).

This worker's satisfaction at outwitting 'the machine' – that is, a redundant window – was both palpable and widespread. When asked how they had discovered their new tricks, CSRs replied in unison and with obvious pride that they were 'smarter than the system.' In other words, work-arounds could become empowering in their own right by validating CSR knowledge and skill in the face of perceived managerial intransigence and incompetence. This confirmation seems to have been an important part of the dynamics that defined technology change at *Power*, and front-line supervisors seemed willing to go along with the charades that CSRs were developing. As one team leader made clear in a very pragmatic fashion: 'I want you to go into CMS to start the call and come out of CMS to finish the call, but if you have to go into Facom after that to find out what you need to … so be it … If you have to answer an inquiry then you answer it the best way you can' (FG4).

In the end, it was such pragmatism rather than outright resistance that defeated management's original intentions. This is not to suggest that what we would commonly recognize as resistance to the changes was absent from this case study. We will deal in more detail with the topic of resistance in chapter 8, but it is worth pointing out here that the debacle of technology change did have other repercussions. While rumours of mass quits did not transpire, attrition rates at *Power* did spike upwards during these changes. 'Some people quit the day it came in … They did, they took about five calls and quit and walked out the door. By the end of the second day it was getting a bit sad. We had tears, we had tantrums, people crying … The frustration was enormous' (FG3).

Absenteeism also escalated after the CMS was introduced, with reported rates as high as 26 per cent on a daily basis. Such behaviour could be attributed to the added stress that was occasioned with using a technology that was not ready for release in a live environment. Failures associated with the project also served to delegitimize management's own knowledge claims. Workers were explicitly warned off ridiculing the situation after disparaging comments were posted on suggestion boards at the centre. One employee submitted a humorous short story about using the new system to the call centre's internal newsletter. This, too, provoked the ire of management: 'The word came back from management – "No, it's not funny." The point was that they don't like us making fun of the system that's going to cost more than we'll ever earn in our lifetimes. That was the feedback I got' (FG1).

In such situations one should not underestimate the corrosive effects of humour on authority-based legitimacy (see also Ackroyd and Thompson 1999; Collinson 2002). Finally, it could be suggested that workers' refusals to use the new system in the ways that had been intended represented a form of resistance. Workers were asserting through their actions that they knew more about their work and the best ways of doing it than anyone else.

5.5 Conclusions

The case study conducted at *Power* contains several important pointers for an analysis of the labour process in info-service work. It is obvious that the introduction of a new customer-service software system at *Power* had mixed, conflicting, and totally unanticipated outcomes on the call centre's operations. Whether we are considering the precipitous decline in customer service or the largely ad hoc adaptations that were made to the new situation, it is obvious that managers were ill prepared for many of these outcomes.

The extended materialist analysis that has been introduced into the analysis of this case study demonstrates that the goal of managerial control has lost none of its saliency in the information age. In the technological choices they made, managers were clearly attracted to the 'sausage factory'/'assembly line in the head' model of the call centre, with its deskilled work pools. Technologically engineered 'solutions,' or a 'technological fix,' clearly enjoyed a hegemonic status in management's thoughts and actions. The new technology of customer-management software had embedded in it both an implicit definition of the problems to be overcome – such as a lack of standardization in processes – and the controls needed to rectify the situation. Work standardization through greater levels of control trumped other concerns; or rather, it was considered self-evident that all else (e.g., better customer service) would follow automatically in the wake of greater managerial control. It was assumed that the new technology would deliver enhanced control over organizational aims, processes, and costs. These developments can be accounted for quite convincingly by those accounts of the call centre that emphasize the Tayloristic quality of work design and the centrality of control through technology. Quite simply put, there is no denying the 'Tayloristic impulse' displayed by management at this call centre.

An extended materialist analysis does not, however, end with managerial aims and actions. Such an approach also documents the challenges that arise when new technologies are implemented. Analyses of info-service work show that strategies based on technological control may be much more difficult to enact than in other work environments. Part of this can be accounted for by the very nature and purpose of call-centre work. Notwithstanding the dreams of at least some managers, it seems impossible to model human interactions, even in the highly commercialized context of the call centre. The parting comments of one focus group member that have remained fixed in my memory provide a fitting reminder on this score. With regard to worlds of work that are increasingly obsessed with the documented accountabilities of contemporary managerialism, including measurement, monitoring, and the achievement of kpi's – accountabilities that are supported by new information technologies such as CMS – she offers a powerful humanistic alternative that summarizes the nature of skill in call-centre work: 'It's not a perfect world and everybody is never the same. We're not computers, we're human beings, and we all deal with the customers differently. We all do our job properly, but we all do it differently and that's what it's all about' (FG3).

As this case study demonstrates, ICTs in the call centre are controlling and *also* are subject to inventive utilization in real-time interactions. This is where the skill comes in. CSRs are far from being highly skilled symbolic analysts in a knowledge economy (Reich 1991); that said, significant skill sets are attached to call-centre work, and this is likely to continue to be so, however strong the pressure to standardize, measure, and rationalize their work. While the simplest informational work can be fully automated with the adoption of such technologies as natural-speech recognition systems, other work will continue to require considerable levels of tacit knowledge and interpretive skill, as illustrated by the example of *Power*.

These findings dovetail with those of chapter 4 as well as with some of the larger themes introduced at the beginning of the book. With regard to the former, the argument has been advanced that info-service work conducted through contact centres entails the employment of midrange skill levels. This chapter has helped us understand why this is so by exploring in some detail the ways in which workers use ICTs in info-service work. Call centres employ technologies that rationalize work processes. CSRs have absolutely no opportunity to influence the adoption of the technologies they are assigned to use – this is a non-negotiable aspect of the job. The absence of any control over technological selection is one feature that distinguishes this work from highly skilled knowledge work, where selection of appropriate means is a major element in the exercise of skill (Alvesson 2004). On the other hand, as we have seen in both this chapter and the preceding one, workers do have some control over *how* they use these technologies, and this is why the work is far from being unskilled. In many call centres, workers continuously engage in interpretative labour – that is, they mediate between the needs of their publics and the organizational policies they are hired to represent in order to reach decision-based outcomes.

We are also reminded in this chapter of the conflicting tendencies in many work processes to which attention was drawn at the beginning of the book. The variability inherent in much info-service work – as was displayed at *Power* in the negotiation and mediation roles that

CSRs assumed in their relations with customers – inherently resists a strict Taylorization of work. Attempts to simplify work and workers' actions through the use of decision-making software ultimately proved unsuccessful at *Power*. This outcome did not, however, lead to a more trusting environment in which workers were extended greater levels of decision-making autonomy. Management's failure to fully realize its aims was a source of considerable frustration rather than a pointer towards a more humanistic work paradigm. As we will see in the next chapter, it is into this 'zone of indeterminacy' that managerialism enters in an attempt to influence final outcomes. Under this regime, workers are expected to account for their work activity in addition to executing it in ways that can be fully documented.

The focus group data presented above uncover a final noteworthy point: the importance workers attach to doing their jobs in a manner that they define as competent and that is validated by the public as such. In the first instance, it was the workforce that recognized the dangers posed by greater levels of computer-enforced standardization at *Power*. Workers resented managers precisely because they felt that the management project of introducing CMS to the call centre was undermining their ability to do their work in ways the public would perceive as competent. Implicit in their response was a critique of managerialism. Greater standardization of processes and outcomes through documented accountability is the goal of managerialism. Sadly, in this case management did not recognize the considerable levels of occupational commitment that were an everyday feature of the work being conducted at *Power*. Management's actions went some way towards undermining the high levels of accountability that already existed. More generally, a good deal of info-service work requires knowledgeable workers who are able to execute interpretative labour. Yet rather than trusting workers to get on with the job, new layers of control are added to it. When technical control proves to be inadequate, as was the case at *Power*, 'solutions' are looked for in other places. This dual movement of complexity and control is further developed in the next chapter, which introduces human resource management into the mix.

6 HRM and Call Centres: Culture and Identities

6.1 Introduction

First impressions matter in interactive service work generally and in call-centre info-service work in particular. For service users there is often little other than the first impression, along with a relatively brief, virtually mediated, encounter with a distant worker. Such situations invariably create an image – be it positive, negative, or indifferent – of the organization with which the individual is in contact. Satisfactory interactions diminish callbacks, complaints, and 'escalated calls.' They are vital to an organization's reputation, and this in turn may have implications for staff morale. In outbound telemarketing operations, first impressions may be even more ephemeral. In a matter of seconds an image is created that may result in a promising 'lead,' an eventual transaction, or a discontinued encounter. In other instances a negative impact may be created by the imposition of an outbound call in the first place. Then the worker has a very few precious seconds, if that, in which to counteract negative stereotypes and recoup the situation.

The significance of first impressions registered on me during my very first visit to a call centre, as well as later, when I compared this visit to site visits to heavy industry and in particular to underground and open-pit mines (Russell 1999). Visits to mine sites were always something of a sociological event in their own right and were certainly worthy of further reflection. Office operations on the surface were invariably the domain of management. Typically this was where the various forms of planning were carried out: engineering, geological analysis, future site development, financial administration, and human resource management (HRM). Blue collars, hard hats, and steel-capped boots were very seldom seen in these places. Production workers were usually present in these spaces only *if they had to be*.

At the sites of production it was a different story. Managers and their representatives were at best tolerated in these spaces and were expected not to get in the way of 'real work.' As soon as one stepped into the hoist, one was entering a different social world in which experienced miners called the shots.[1] In mining, then, two different social worlds co-existed in separate spatial realms. The world of the office was dominated by paper: blueprints, maps, geological surveys, plans, and employee files. Underground and in the smelting operations, experience and tacit knowledge were all-important. These impressions were reinforced by the simple fact that my fieldwork on changing employment relations in mining was conducted almost totally in the presence of workers alone: management was notable by its absence. The local union officials – who also worked regular shifts on the production and maintenance crews – would sign me in and then take me into the operations areas that I wanted to observe. Management, more often than not, was unaware that I was on-site conducting research.

Part of this scenario perhaps reflected two facts: that these sites were unionized and thus subject to union-shop rules, and that the unions were highly active at the local level. That said, my first visit to a call centre also occurred in the company of a union official, the regional vice-president of the Communications, Energy, and Paperworkers Union in Canada. The visit was to a large telco that was also fully unionized. As we entered this worksite I saw a marquee in the reception area, similar to the ones found in up-market hotel lobbies where announcements of the day's events and their venues are posted. Behind the glass display case with its gold lettering was signage welcoming us by name to the call centre! This little gesture provided a first inkling that the culture of such workplaces differs in significant ways from the mines I had been studying. Even though I had been invited at the behest of the union, the manager had incorporated the visit into the life of the call centre *as an event*. Besides welcoming us, the announcement alerted the workers who were commencing their morning shift that 'Professor Russell' would be on site that day as a guest of the centre. As a visible gesture, this was intended to convey a sense of bonhomie as well as to grant me recognition and status. While waiting for the manager to appear and swipe us through the security door and onto the operations floor, I could not help but think how different this reception was from arrivals at the mine sites, where far less care was devoted to the management of my presence.

No doubt it is possible to read other meanings into this situation. For our purposes, though, it is the care that went into *managing* a visit that stands out. The marquee board was there to convey, to both visitors and the workforce, meanings about the organization and what goes on within it. It was a physical artefact that played a role in the reproduction of an organizational culture. It was rich with sociological meaning in that it conveyed images of professionalism, respect, and care. No doubt it had the intended effect of creating a favourable first impression. In short, attention was being paid and precautions were being taken to manage a visit in ways that did not have a parallel in the mines I had visited.

The point of this vignette is to draw attention to the explicit effort that goes into the management and display of organizational culture in contemporary info-service work. A number of authors have pointed out the potential of using culture as a competitive resource (Bolman and Deal 2003; Deal and Kennedy 1982; Peters and Waterman 1988). In this vein, culture comes to be an object to be manufactured in new organizations, or rehabilitated in older ones, and is often identified with successful managerial leadership (Schein 1985). While much of this writing has been rightly criticized for its normative bent, its idealist underpinnings, its refusal to explicitly engage with the political dimensions of corporate culture, and its foundations in a functionalist sociology (Ogbonna 1992a; Schoenberger 1997), critical management theory has made the point that it must nonetheless be taken as a key attribute of contemporary managerial practice and thus deserving of further analysis (Alvesson 2002; Alvesson and Willmott 2002; Salaman 2001; Willmott 1993).

Besides the general upsurge in interest pertaining to organizational culture, there are other reasons why culture is especially salient in call-centre work. As with service labour more generally (Macdonald and Sirianni 1996; Leidner 1993), info-service work involves working *with* and *on* other people as part of the labour process. Apart from the interpretive labour, which was discussed earlier in terms of the info-service labour process, workers are expected to assume an ambassadorial role for the organizations they 'represent.' In this capacity, workers not only 'carry' an organizational culture forward to the public but also, by definition, play an essential role in reproducing it insofar as their work is all about establishing meanings and understandings on behalf of the organizations for which they act. Info-service work is, to a large degree, about the production of meaning through the use of information. Such work can be rich in symbolism. But in order for workers to undertake it in a systematic fashion, a symbolic and normative context must be established to which workers ascribe. Furthermore, management must be assured that workers are actively supporting the image the organization wishes to convey. This set of circumstances establishes the context for what we have termed managerialism – that is, the micromanagement of employees' selves. Managerialism provides workers with a template for carrying out the activities for which they are responsible, and it is accompanied by a host of safeguards that focus on documentation as a means of demonstrating accountability. As used here, managerialism provides a framework for fostering the creation of sanctioned meanings on behalf of the employer. In call centres, meanings are constantly being established, negotiated, and in some cases contested, and CSRs stand at the centre of these processes. Work in such environments is not necessarily or immediately mediated by a physical output that can be inspected for defects. Culture – that is, what the worker and the organization stand for – assumes a larger significance in the absence of physical flows, and managerialism presents itself as a check for controlling the production and presentation of information.

Apart from these considerations, it must be remembered that for the most part contact centres are relatively new workplaces; they haven't been around for that long (Russell 2008b; Bain and Taylor 2002a). Recall from the last chapter that when the centre at *Power* was initially set up it was largely staffed by workers who had transferred over from alternative modes of service delivery such as over-the-counter assistance. Within the first six months most of these workers were gone. They had migrated from one labour process replete with its own expectations and ways of doing things to a new and (for many) radically different environment. Management very quickly became attuned to the problem of 'misaligned expectations' and set about with new initiatives to redefine what it meant to be a call-centre employee. As we saw, the provision of 'wicked service' – that is, going beyond customer expectations as well as offering new products and services – was one way in which this ideal was articulated. The establishment of the call centre not only entailed replacing one workforce with another through attrition and growth, but also – and just as important – creating new staff with different expectations and behaviours. The point here is that all call centres have had to go through similar processes of (re)creating a workforce of CSRs.

Of course, in certain respects there is nothing novel about having to fashion a workforce with new capabilities and habits. The inurement of workers to new labour processes – technologies, ways of working, and changes in working pace and time – is part of the historical culture of capitalism (Marx 1971; Thompson 1967) and of every significant change to the way work has been conducted under it (see, for example, Meyer 1981; Rose 1990). As generations of sociologists have informed us, it is not possible to think about organizational life without considering culture (Gouldner 1954a; van Maanen and Kunda 1989; Kunda 1992), which, broadly speaking, can be defined as what an organization stands for. Organizational life has always involved traditions, folklore, and signifiers, which tell members and non-members alike where the organization comes from, what differentiates it from others, and what it expects of organizational members. However, such cultures have often developed organically; they have embodied reflection about the past more than conscious manipulation of the present. Furthermore, coexisting alongside 'official' cultures are workforce subcultures (Roy 1954, 1958; Mars 1994), the organic products of past working traditions, and current working conditions passed on through apprenticeships, initiation rites, and on-the-job learning.

To summarize these points, let us return to the comparison sketched out at the beginning of the chapter. During research visits to mine sites in the 1990s I was struck by the prominence with which mission and values statements were displayed at some of the companies. Nothing in previous reading about work or employment relations in mining had mentioned anything about missions and values. These were newly crafted documents, products of that decade when management began to re-engage with workplace culture in a deliberate and reflexive manner. Such texts were displayed prominently in visitor-reception areas and in managers' offices. They were, however, absent in the underground lunch rooms, the operational control rooms, the change rooms, the tool cribs, and more generally at any of the points of production. Though joint committees may have been involved in their production, one got the sense that such messages did not penetrate very deeply into the fabric of the activities that were being carried out. Workers certainly never referred to them in their accounts of their work. Success at imposing values statements through prescribed practices – perhaps with the exception of health and safety issues – was unremarkable to say the least.

The call centres that form the subject matter of this book are, at least superficially, different in this regard. Characteristically, at the sites included in this study, work areas are adorned with slogans, exhortations, and other physical traces of an officially sanctioned culture that are taken to embody what the organization stands for. In some centres, individual 'production' statistics are posted; in others, individual and team prizes for specific accomplishments are prominently displayed. In the mines one clearly had the impression that culture-building initiatives did not extend very deeply into worker subjectivities. Corporate culture had little to do with the ways in which workers defined themselves or their 'mission.' The generation of mission and values statements was something that *managers* engaged in; miners had more important things to get on with and appeared to take little note of such organizational discourses.[2] In the call centres that concern us here, the openness to managerial cultural initiatives is less certain, and that openness (or lack of it) is what is explored in this chapter. In these settings, inurement to work is not enough and workers are increasingly asked to put 'themselves' into 'their' work in ways that will make a difference. It is not simply a matter of getting the work done, or even – as in highly controlled environments – getting it done in a specific way so as to maximize production, but rather of fostering belief in organizational protocols as well as commitment to their pursuit in one's own work (Willmott 1993). As these objectives often fall under the remit of HRM, we next turn our attention to this set of practices.

6.2 HRM in Call Centres

Human resource management (HRM) is generally understood to encompass a range of activities that draw workers and the organizations that employ them together around a common set of objectives. This begins with the recruitment and selection of employees and goes on to cover training, employee development, performance evaluation, recognition and rewards, and, tangentially, some aspects of job design, including the role (if any) of work teams. Some researchers have gone on to distinguish between 'hard' and 'soft' variants of HRM, with the former emphasizing the employment of human *resources* and the latter emphasizing the development of *human capabilities* as a central plank of successful business strategy (Bolton and Houlihan 2007; Korczynski 2001; Storey 1991; Legge 1995). Several of these topics (e.g., recruitment and selection and training) were introduced in chapter 3 under an analysis of labour-market creation for call-centre employment. A focus on labour markets brings a macroscopic perspective to the employment relationship. An HRM approach, by contrast, focuses more exclusively on organizational practices and policies, taking as a given the external environment the organization operates in, including the labour market. In this chapter the main concern is the extent to which the internal organizational practice of HRM shapes identities in the workplace.

A number of previous analyses of the call centre have emphasized the importance of the cultural element in these work settings. There seems to be general agreement that managerial control via technology alone is insufficient, and our analyses in chapters 4 and 5 certainly support this conclusion. Different arguments have been advanced regarding why ICTs alone cannot guarantee outcomes that are necessarily satisfactory to management. Apart from the technological determinism that is inherent in such a position, control via technology alone does not recognize the indeterminacy that is inherent in all but the most routinized customer-service work encounters (Bain and Taylor 2000; Callaghan and Thompson 2001). If anything, these conditions are accentuated in the call centre, where physical co-presence between workers and customers/clients and the interactional cues this provides are absent, and where workers do exercise some control over the various phases of the interaction, including necessary pre- and post-call work as well as the duration and contents of the call (Russell 2002b, 2004; Wray-Bliss 2001). For this reason, some accounts from a labour-process perspective have begun to view HRM functions such as recruitment, selection, and training as necessary components in a complete analysis of info-service work (Callaghan and Thompson 2002). But it is necessary to extend the analysis of HRM as a mainstay of contemporary managerialism much further than this.

According to a number of researchers, the fact that it is *people* who are being worked with and on is what differentiates info-service work from other categories of labour. Bringing customers/clients directly into the labour process introduces new elements of variability and uncertainty, and this has required fundamental adjustments to the ways in which work is managed (Frenkel, Korczynski, et al. 1999). Human-service work introduces greater levels of ambiguity into work and perforce requires greater levels of employee discretion so that workers can cope with the complexities inherent in social interaction. In turn this raises the issue of how to control such discretion so that it is exercised in the best interests of the employer.

Some researchers argue that in these circumstances, bureaucratic systems of control are modified through the utilization of 'info-normative' controls in order to deal with the more customized demands of clientele

(Frenkel, Tam, et al. 1998). As suggested by the term, these are hybrid systems of managerial control that fuse features of bureaucratic compliance with the norms of professional behaviour (D'Cruz and Noronha 2006). Technology supplies a multitude of information on individual worker performance, which can be acted on by workers and their team leaders in accordance with organizational norms. The inculcation of such a normative outlook in employees is viewed as promoting self-regulation in the interests of the employing organization. The adoption of such an outlook on the part of the worker is abetted by facilitative styles of management, where performance data are used to 'coach,' develop, and reward (Frenkel, Korczynski, et al. 1999). Dependence on normative control implies a strong cultural component in the employment relationship. The development of such controls is helped along by the use of work teams (Ezzamel and Willmott 1998), which are a very common feature in the call-centre work environment.

While this analysis hints at the role of HRM, the concept of info-normative control remains theoretically underdeveloped and empirically untested, considering the explanatory weight it is intended to carry. For example, info-normative control is identified with facilitative management styles that are tied to team leadership positions, but little else is said about this strategy. Do workers' experiences of call-centre work teams and team leaders accord with the empowerment thesis conveyed in some accounts (Batt 2000, 2002; Frenkel, Korczynski, et al. 1999)? Certainly, other researchers have cast doubt on the benignant effects of work processes that remain tied to exacting quantitative targets (Taylor and Bain 2001; Taylor, Hyman, et al. 2002; Taylor, Baldry, et al. 2003). Meanwhile, it is also conceivable that systems of control that rely on measurement and documentation undermine those very aspects of professionalism that they are hoping to encourage.

More recent research (Korczinski 2002a, 2002b) has attempted to add further weight to the notion of info-normative control, with normative regulation issuing from workers being encouraged to imagine themselves as 'the customers' of their own practices. Training programs may bolster such creative use of the imagination (Sturdy 2000). More generally, some would argue that the advent of an entrepreneurial, consumption-oriented culture tied to late modernity (DuGay 1996; Salaman 2001) has rendered this mentality a natural *Weltanschauung* in service-oriented worksites. Again, certain managerial paradigms, such as the total quality management (TQM) movement, actively promote the notion of the all-important sovereign consumer, who is omnipresent both within the labour process ('internal customers') and out in the marketplace (Knights and McCabe 1997; Wilkinson et al. 1998). (Note that TQM, as such, was not applied explicitly in any of the operations considered in this book.) Viewing 'the self as customer' (Korczynski et al. 2000) or 'the customer as boss' (Fuller and Smith 1996; Korczinski 2002a) is hypothesized as leading to a certain level of self-regulation (Knights and Odhi 2002) or self-discipline (Edwards, Collinson, and Rees 1998; Rosenthal, Hill, and Peccei 1997). It implies that workers must be both empowered and willing to create and sustain customer 'enchantment' with the service that is being offered, though it is important not to overstate the levels of autonomy that front-line CSRs have attained (Korczynski 2002a).

Given this portrayal of working conditions, where relations between workers and customers are lent analytical priority over relationships between employees and managers/employers, workers (including CSRs) may have opportunities to create 'aesthetic projects' around their work – that is, to 'escape into the work' and to experience the pleasures and satisfactions of doing such work on behalf of their customers (Alferoff and Knights 2002; Korczinski 2002a; Wray-Bliss 2001). This suggestion follows from an analysis that places greater emphasis on the customer/employee relationship and on the possibility that front-line employees will find in that relationship a source of meaning and satisfaction (Russell, 2008b). Presumably, then, such an environment may prove auspicious for enhancing identification with the employing organization and with missions and goals that emphasize customer service – though, such being the case, one is left with this nagging problem: how to explain the penchant for managerialism, which emphasizes the micromanagement of people in such work environments.

In this chapter HRM is theorized as the operational face of managerialism. In settings where work has become more complex – as with info-service labour – job simplification may not be a readily available option. So instead, managerialism is brought to bear on the worker in relation to the job she does, rather than solely on the job. HRM aims to normalize the micromanagement of workers by utilizing 'objective' administrative practices such as performance management. Such normalization is a cultural accomplishment, which is to say that HRM both works *on* culture and works *through* the culture it seeks to develop. Developing explicit cultural initiatives that lend the workplace a certain 'feel' or 'buzz' is part of HRM's brief; in turn, organizational cultures are manifested and reproduced through the work undertaken and the sanctioned means by which it is accomplished.

HRM tries to influence how workers define themselves in relation to their work. As a set of practices, HRM attempts to obtain the worker's commitment by bringing organizational power to bear on the individual self. HRM seeks to develop accountable selves (Boltanski and Chiapello 2007). Yet actual practices such as performance management work against any serious level of trust being placed in employees. Instead, accountability is 'ensured' through continuous documentation, which is collected on workers – often by means of the ICTs they use – or which employees are required to supply as part of their normal job duties through regularized reflexive reporting and peer assessment. One notable description of the call centre that encapsulates the 'fun and surveillance' syndrome that is part of working life in many centres (Kinnie, Hutchinson, and Purcell 2000) captures this dynamic. This description suggests that call centres are strong on culture and that for this reason the cultural work of managers needs to be taken seriously. In this sense, culture embodies the creation of an image that the organization wishes to convey, such as a 'fun' place to work; but it also materializes a set of initiatives that seek to normalize the standard trappings of managerialism – such as ongoing surveillance and performance assessment – trappings that are probably just the opposite of 'fun' for the workers concerned.

HRM endeavours to *create* culture, often in fairly explicit ways; it also *expresses* a particular culture (managerialism and its associated practices) in its own right. To the extent that one can speak of call-centre culture, managerial initiatives that blend task fulfilment, documented accountability, and organized social events and activities into a form of 'manufactured sociability' capture the various dimensions of culture (Russell 2002b). Explicit cultural programming can take different forms. Social events may provide a respite from the ordinary productive routines of the call centre. Theme days with costumes, special foods, and other decorative accoutrements are a favourite means to provide a break from routine labour even as such occasions may require additional 'voluntary' staff labour that – it is assumed – the largely feminized workforces will unquestionably take up. More formally organized games may also be devised that involve competition among individual team members as well as contests among teams. These events are likely to revolve around meeting or surpassing specific metrics such as call-handling targets or sales objectives. Games and competitions are designed to make workers want to achieve corporate objectives; these often involve considerable imagination. The need for cultural inventiveness has actually spawned a consultancy business, with entrepreneurs promoting such practitioner-oriented titles as *The Fun Factor* and *Fun and Gains* (Greenwich 1997, 2001). One Singaporean call centre I visited had the aura of a television game-show set. Overachieving workers received opportunities to spin a large Wheel of Fortune, with prizes attached to specific points on the wheel. This wheel was centrally located on the call-centre floor and created a small spectacle every time it was used for both the 'worker/contestant' and the 'peers/audience.'

Competitive games and social events can be combined, as when teams or entire call centres compete for recognition in special achievement award ceremonies. In Australia the umbrella group for call centres, the Australian Teleservices Association (ATA), organizes yearly awards events at state and national levels. It is the call-centre managers who choose to enter these competitions – a decision that involves considerable strategic forethought. Receiving nominations in categories such as 'Greenfield Teleservices Centre of the Year,' 'Teleservices Centre of the Year [Under/Over Fifty Staff],' 'Teleprofessional [i.e., CSR] of the Year,' and 'Team Leader of the Year' fosters a sense of common purpose and encourages group affinity among employees. Such 'projects' invariably culminate in end-of-season galas, which are hosted by the ATA and are modelled after other awards ceremonies (i.e., that ones that feature sumptuous surroundings and formal attire). The manager of *Licensing* explained why he had taken his centre into the ATA competition: such events boost agent morale by creating a collective *nous* around a specific mobilizing project. As in the case of *Power* (see chapter 5), these undertakings may be used to construct a historical narrative of the centre, providing a sense of 'how far "we" have come together' since the start of operations; they can also help instil common goals.[3] In other words, participation in such culture-making events affords an opportunity to construct an 'imagined community' (Anderson 1991) at the workplace, in the process (perhaps) lending meaning to individuals' working lives (Alvesson 2004).

It goes without saying that the success of corporate cultural management should never be taken for granted. Cultural initiatives can sometimes go awry. One week after Australia went to war with Iraq in the Second Gulf War, an inventive manager at one call centre (not included in this study) devised a game called 'mini gulf weapons of mass destruction search game.'[4] After each successful sale, workers were 'invited' to putt a golf ball up a ramp and into a picture of a mosque in a mock bombing raid to destroy putative weapons of mass destruction. One woman refused to participate on the grounds that the game was culturally insensitive and a trivialization of war; she was summarily fired by her manager for refusing to accept that 'it was just a game.' It seems that other members of the worker's team were willing to go along with management's decision in favour of dismissal following a hastily convened team meeting to deal with the issue – a meeting from which the affected worker was excluded. The fired worker approached one of the unions participating in this project. Her case eventually reached the Federal Industrial Relations Commission, where her dismissal was ruled to be unfair. In the end, the worker was vindicated.

This world of manufactured culture is considerably removed from the rich ethnographical descriptions that have been left to us by previous generations of industrial sociologists. In these analyses, games – to the extent that they are mentioned – are the products of worker ingeniousness that are passed on as subcultural traditions. Such games may have a strategic element, as described in Burawoy's analysis of 'making out' in a piece-rate environment (Burawoy 1979; Roy 1952, 1954) as well as in other 'fiddles' and deceptions (Ackroyd and Thompson 1999; Mars 1994), or they may represent diversions from the daily grind of work routines, as in 'horseplay' (Roy 1958; Russell 1999). For the purposes of this discussion, the important thing to remember is that workers authored these activities of their own accord. Managers might have been complicit in such games, dimly aware of them, or completely ignorant of them, depending on their own location in the productive process.

We should not assume that subcultural forms of behaviour have been entirely banished from the newer workplaces of the information economy. A number of accounts have drawn attention to the variety of imaginative ways in which CSRs express their dissatisfactions (Bain and Taylor 2000; Knights and McCabe 1998; Mulholland 2004; Taylor and Bain 1999; see also chapter 8). The point here is that managers in the current environment actively contest for control of workplace culture through such initiatives as those previewed above (see also Willmott 1993). Organizational cultures are intended to forge specific identities. They do so by appealing to common cultural sensibilities, with management adopting aspects of popular culture and importing them into the workplace in an effort to normalize what may be a stressful setting. The game-show format mentioned above is a telling example of this practice. In this process, organizational culture is manufactured as games, spectacles, and 'good times.'

Organizational culture is also 'lived' through its infusion into training programs, performance evaluations, and other aspects of HRM that are intended to reflect and build the organizational culture (Alvesson and Willmott 2002). This is a more thoroughgoing and reflexive practice than previous attempts to influence employee behaviour through (for example) the extension of corporate welfare benefits (Edwards 1979; Meyer 1981; N. Rose 1990). In important ways, managerialism operates directly on the working self. In the contexts we are discussing in this book, work that is done on employee subjectivities occurs *within* the labour process proper as well as in preparation for it (e.g., role playing in training sessions and coaching by team leaders). In traditional bureaucratic organizations, we fill roles and we are recognized and rewarded according to how well we play our parts. In contemporary info-service work, we are expected to do something much deeper than this: we are expected to identify with the organization that employs us and to think, feel, and act accordingly (Alvesson 2004). Moreover, such behaviour is assessed frequently, in team meetings and via performance reviews, through the documentary processes of monitoring.

The outcomes of cultural programming are notoriously difficult to specify. Efforts at influencing identities at work may generate loyalty and commitment or they may provoke opportunism, cynicism, and dissent (Alvesson and Willmott 2002; Van Maanen and Kunda 1989; Kunda 1992). As the example of the Second Gulf War game demonstrates, management-initiated 'fun' in the workplace may be inherently fragile and can sometimes dramatically backfire (see also Houlihan 2002; Collinson 2002). Some researchers (Edwards, Collinson, and Rees 1998; Rosenthal, Hill, and Peccei 1997) have unearthed evidence that work cultures emphasizing quality or a greater HRM presence (Guest 1999) have had some resonance with workers in the form of greater self-discipline; others have expressed general scepticism regarding the depth of the roots sunk into employee subjectivities by contemporary HRM practices (Collinson 1992; Jenkins and Delbridge 2007; Knights and McCabe 2000; Ogbonna 1992b; Scott 1994; Thompson and McHugh 2002, ch. 13). With specific reference to call centres, some have questioned the efficacy of normative controls that are activated through identification with the organization's consumers (van den Broek 2004).

Along parallel lines, a number of researchers have attempted to show that where certain types of HRM, collectively labelled high-commitment management practices (Kinnie, Hutchinson, and Purcell 2000; Kinnie, Purcell, and Hutchinson 2000; Hutchinson, Purcell, and Kinnie 2000) or high-involvement/performance work systems (Batt 1999,

2000, 2002), are systematically put into practice, mutually beneficial results will obtain.[5] This is another way of drawing a connection between HRM and employee actions. Among the initiatives that are typically included are organized social activities of the sort discussed above, the use of work teams, selective recruitment, focused training, two-way communication (e.g., suggestion systems), performance-related pay, and employment security (Hutchinson et al, 2000). Batt (2000, 2002) – in line with previous studies that have focused on manufacturing industries (Arthur 1994; Appelbaum et al. 2000; Huselid 1995; Macduffie 1995) – emphasizes opportunities to engage in group problem-solving teamwork, participation in more highly skilled relational work, and the frequency of monitoring, with less surveillance being associated with better management practices. The focus of this genre of research is on organizational performance; the argument is that HPWSs, if they work right, benefit employers both directly through enhanced employee motivation and indirectly through lower attrition rates and reduced productivity losses of the sort that accompany lower staff turnover (Batt 2002).

The emphasis in this chapter is somewhat different. Casting back to the previous sections of the chapter, our main concern is the relationship between HRM and employee subjectivities. As an expression of managerialism, does HRM shape worker subjectivities in ways that enhance identification with management?

6.3 Identity in the Call Centre

The following sections take up two aspects of workplace culture and its effects on subjectivity. First, we examine levels of organizational identity – that is, worker identification with the aims and goals of the employer. Second, we explicate factors – including the HRM practices already alluded to in this chapter – that may help construct such subjectivities. In this way we seek to gain a better understanding of HRM's role in contemporary info-service work.

At the outset let us recognize that self-identity is a complex issue. It seeks to answer the question: 'Who am I?' This question can only be answered in a social context – that is, in terms of the social memberships that are important to individuals by virtue of the meanings they bestow (Castells 1997) and the roles those memberships assume in the construction of self-narratives (Giddens 1991). Individuals *anchor* their identities in particular collectives when the interpretative frameworks

Table 6.1
Organizational identity index (α = .727)

---

a) I strongly identify with the mission and values of this organization.
b) Working for this organization provides me with an important sense of who I am.

---

offered by those collectives resonate with a sense of 'who I am' and/ or 'who I want to become.' Organizational cultures provide such collective frameworks for 'making sense' of the world we live in. As such, social identities operate at a deeper level of being than role occupancy.

Alvesson (2004, 127) observes: 'Frequently identity talk involves messages and beliefs about the elite character of the firm, in terms either of claims to employ the "best people" or claims to have organizational conditions that facilitate high-quality work.' He is referring mainly to knowledge-intensive firms staffed by professional employees, which – as we have already established – most call centres, including the ones in this study, are not. Thus it is more likely to be the purpose and goals of the organization and the employment practices and policies that support its objectives that are most relevant when we examine identity in work settings such as call centres. Organizational identity can be defined as 'feelings of belonging to a community of people whose shared social identity follows from their being employed by a particular company' (ibid., 151). Such an association is a source of esteem for individuals who have developed a strong identity anchor in the organization. It provides a sense of purpose and meaning in life. It marks 'us' off from 'others.' 'Who I work for' and 'what I do' are matters of consequence when it comes to organizational identification with an employer.

For the purposes of our investigation, two questions on our survey seemed particularly apt for a discussion of organization identity (see Table 6.1). These two measures seem to capture the essence of what many researchers refer to as organizational identity – specifically, an attraction to the employing organization, a linkage between individual and organizational goals, solidarity with the organization, and feelings that the organization is an important constituent of self-conception (Parker 2000).

Additional measures could have been taken from the survey and added to this index, but only with an associated risk of validity loss. For instance, it is important not to conflate organizational identity with work identity. One can identify with one's work even while expressing cynicism towards the employer – the 'love the work, hate the job' syndrome. Other questions relate more to the concept of commitment than to identity, though there is a good deal of overlap between these two constructs (Edwards 2005). Organizational commitment is a touchstone for the discipline of HRM. Commitment refers not only to perceptions and attitudes towards the employer, but also to actions taken on its behalf, such as voluntary and discretionary measures that enhance the work-effort bargain. Organizational identity is a sociological precursor to commitment and performance. It is sociological in the sense that it is relational, and in more ways than one. Workers may identify with others by virtue of sharing a culture that is 'supplied' by the employing organization, though this is far from a certainty. Organizational identity may be stronger or weaker depending on the other attachments workers have both inside of work (e.g., occupational, work-group, and trade-union memberships) and external to work (e.g., gender, ethnic, political, community, religious, and familial identities). We could also say that organizational identity, while a necessary precondition, may not be sufficient for the display of commitment as we have defined it here. Even when one has strong identity attachments with the organization one works for, other things may get in the way of displaying commitment in observable ways. For example, I might wish to take advantage of opportunities to help the employer owing to the attachments that I feel, but other 'commitments' such as child-care responsibilities may prevent me from doing so in a regular manner.

Edwards (ibid.) has suggested that identity has more to do with image, whereas commitment is related to action. According to this line of reasoning, employees identify with organizations on the basis of the image they present, especially if an aura of prestige is attached to the entity. Thus employers may strive to present an 'employment brand' that they view as attractive in their search for desirable workers. Commitment, on the other hand, is related to what the organization does, and this includes its HRM policies and its treatment of employees. On closer inspection, it appears difficult to sustain a distinction between identity and commitment on these grounds. Surely the image of an employer, including the prestige associated with employment in the operation, is tied to what the organization does – with what it produces and how it goes about it. This would encompass its employment relations and the contribution of its HRM policies towards those relationships.

In this chapter we are mainly concerned with the subjective identities of call-centre workers and the effects of HRM practices on them. A focus on identity as opposed to commitment follows from the preceding comments and from two points in particular. First, if it seems reasonable to view identity as a theoretical precursor to commitment, it makes sense to begin with the former. Second, in terms of operationalization, identity covers less terrain than commitment – in other words, it is not as broad a concept. As previously suggested, while identity refers to attachments of the self, commitment extends this in that it also includes ensuing actions, which may themselves be determined by factors other than identity – factors that must remain extraneous to the analysis offered here.

Using the two questions cited above, we can create an index with possible values ranging from 2 (very low organizational identity) to 10 (very high identification with the organization). Computing means for the Australian sample as a whole, we obtain an overall estimate of 6.5. In Table 6.2, the mean rankings for each of the Australian call centres are compared.[6] The distribution of our data across this measure violates a key requirement for the use of a parametric test (i.e., Anova) when comparing means between and within the twenty case-study sites.[7] Owing to this, a non-parametric test is used to compare mean scores on organizational identity. For illustrative purposes only, the resultant scores can be divided into thirds and arrayed as high, medium, and low levels of identification with the employing organization. These are simply arithmetical cut-offs that do not have theoretical significance in their own right. The main concern at this point lies in comparing the call centres along this measurement of organizational identity.

The one thing that immediately stands out in the rankings in Table 6.2 is the predominance of public-sector and/or help lines at the upper ends of the organizational identity measure. Top-placed *Statewide* is one of the two new 'supercentres' (*Urban Space* being the other) that feature considerable job variety, and both these sites fall at the upper end of identification with the organization. Other centres of note in terms of manifested levels of organization identity include *Tender*, the help line for disabled people; *Advisory Services*, the publicly funded and managed legal-aid provider; *Delivery Services*; and *Government Pensions*. That the six highest-placed centres are all public-sector or not-for-profit operations is a rather stunning result. Meanwhile, the highest-ranking financial institution, *Bank1*, differentiates itself from the other centres in this sector by virtue of the fact that it is an occupationally based credit union serving a specific membership.

An insight into the culture of at least some not-for-profit info-service work is revealed in comments made by a supervisor at *Tender* in re-

Table 6.2
Organizational identity in Australian call centres*

	Organization	Mean rank
High	*Statewide*	777.40
	Tender	730.16
	Advisory Services	723.33
	Government Pensions	708.29
	Delivery Services	702.27
	Urban Space	694.07
	Bank1	685.47
	Insurer2	680.35
	Health Authority	672.08
	Bank2	647.25
Medium	*Telco2*	628.39
	Airline	584.75
	Collections	584.32
	Social Services	547.55
	Bus Company	545.81
	Health Premium	522.90
	Insurer1	514.21
Low	*Telco1*	471.51
	Licensing	420.97
	Telebet	348.25

*Kruskal Wallis test
Chi-square = 130.73, df = 19, p = .000

sponse to a question about the very low (7 per cent) attrition rates at this centre:

> Why people stay – I think it's the type of job that you do. You get something out of it, you can tell that you make a difference in peoples' lives. [In] a lot of call centres, to me, you don't – you're pushing products or you're … They're like white-collar factories, some of them, to me … We've had people who've worked in them and come here saying what a relief and what a big difference it is. I think in our organization people are still important in the relay service cause they're working for people. And so therefore it's like I am making a difference in people's lives … Not a lot of people today get that feel from their job. It doesn't matter what they do, sometimes it's just the processing job that they do. I think that holds some people here. (*Tender*, call-centre shift supervisor)

Comments such as these come very close to echoing sentiments that are reproduced in Sennett's (2006) discussion of why workers identify with the public health-care and education systems in the United States and Britain despite years of underfunding and political opprobrium. However, in addition to the social-recognition factor that Sennett connects to public service and that he associates with its perceptions of usefulness among members of the public, we would also direct the reader's attention in the preceding quotation to the references to job stress, 'white collar factories,' and the like. At this centre calls are not timed, agents are monitored comparatively infrequently, and service levels are a management rather than an employee performance measure.

The circumstances at *Tender* could not be more different from those prevailing at the lowest-ranked centre in terms of employee identification: *Telebet*, where it would be difficult to place a positive social value on the instrumentally transactional work that is associated with the gaming industry. That *Licensing* is at the bottom of the index may possibly be accounted for by the very adversarial industrial relations that were continuously being played out between unionized members of the workforce and the call-centre manager. As with *Telebet*, where workers do not place a high social value on the service they are providing, and *Licensing*, where highly conflictual employment relations are a regular part of the scene, these two factors may explain some of the other rankings in Table 6.2. For example, the comparatively low position of *Collections* could have something to do with the nature of the work at this centre. As a collection agency for fines and penalties that have been levied by the judicial system, workers at this centre may have to endure higher-than-average levels of abuse in their work. More contested industrial relations, especially at the federal level (see chapter 8), and the task of administering social policies that some might view as hostile towards their constituencies, may also have something to do with the placement of *Social Services* in Table 6.2, though admittedly this remains speculation.

Overall, the placement of organizations in Table 6.2 should give some pause for reflection. Specifically, the positioning of many of the public and not-for-profit operations in the top positions should serve as a caution to those who would urge greater emulation of private-sector practices through corporatization initiatives in the public sector. Such policies may come at a cost in employee goodwill in much the same manner as documented in chapter 5 with the commercialization of utilities distribution at *Power*. To advance this analysis a step further, we must now consider the effects of specific HRM practices on organizational identity.

6.4 Accounting for Organizational Identities

From the preceding review, a number of factors need to be considered in an analysis of the relationships between HRM and organizational affinities. First, attention must be paid to the *explicit* cultural initiatives that managers undertake – for example, the promotion of specific employee events that are intended to affect morale as well as employee perceptions of the employer. Second, we need to acknowledge that culture is also thoroughly embedded in how organizations go about producing what it is they are responsible for, including through their HRM practices. Thus, how work is organized, how technologies are used, and how workers are employed, trained, and paid, as well as the expectations that inhere to job performance, all indicate something about the nature of both the employer and the culture that permeates the organization. In short, it is possible to refer to both *explicit* and *embedded* aspects of organizational culture, both of which have potentially important effects on the extent to which workers identify with and relate to the employing organization. Some of these employment attributes fall squarely within the ambit of HRM as it has been constructed; other dimensions that are often associated with HPWSs, such as opportunities to use skills and the possession of manageable workloads, may extend beyond the reach of HRM policy proper.

Using the survey that was administered at the case-study sites, it is possible to construct indicators of employee perceptions of the various dimensions that enter into a notion of workplace culture and then examine how or to what extent they are related to the construction of organizational identities. For example, as we have seen, some researchers have drawn special attention to the consciously constructed managerial activities that are superimposed on call-centre work life (Kinnie, Hutchinson, and Purcell 2000). They suggest that such initiatives can relieve the hard edge of monitoring and target fulfilment, and they include this dimension of work in a notion of high-commitment management practices. Others are more sceptical of these claims (Russell 2002b) or have drawn attention to the 'dark side' of such activities (Taylor and Bain 2001; see also above). Conceivably, positive views of the workplace as a fun and convivial setting in which to work may increase identification with the employer and its objectives as workers come to

Table 6.3
Organizational culture index ($\alpha = .779$)

a) I usually participate in the organized social activities of the call centre.
b) I enjoy taking part in such social events as games and theme days at the centre.
c) The games and social events that are held at the call centre are an important aspect of the job for me.
d) I feel pressured into participating in call-centre social events. (reverse coded)
e) The performance competitions that management organizes at the centre make working here more enjoyable.
f) Performance competitions at the call centre cause conflict

appreciate the efforts managers make to improve the quality of working life. Alternatively, workers could view such initiatives as frivolous intrusions into the private domain of the self, or as corporate attempts at deliberate manipulation that breed cynicism rather than identification (Kunda 1992). To examine these claims and to analyse the effects more generally of working directly on culture, the questions in Table 6.3 have been used to develop a measure of workers' perceptions of explicit cultural endeavours.

This index is used to examine the effects of explicit managerially constructed cultural programs on workplace subjectivities and specifically organizational identities. The emphasis here is on explicit, conscious attempts to influence social action in the workplace. However, a notion of culture that includes only intentional efforts to manufacture immediate behavioural outcomes – such as one finds in the practitioner guides that advocate on behalf of 'strong cultures' (Peters and Waterman 1988) – is at best naive. Cultures are much more deeply embedded in the fabric of organizational life than such assumptions allow for. Decisions that managers take about how much to invest in training, what types of employment contracts to offer, and how to organize work flows also contribute to the (re)production of an organizational culture that may or may not be shared by employees, or may be shared to greater or lesser degrees. Such decisions by management denote deeply ingrained ways of thinking – convictions – that inform the 'feel' that every organization has. The notion of a social 'climate' is appropriate here. Others have suggested that it is appropriate to use the concept of a psychological contract in organizations as a way of probing the unwritten expectations, obligations, and promises that exist between workers and managers (Schein 1978; Rousseau 1995). Precisely because these are uncodified expectations, they suggest levels of trust and goodwill

Table 6.4
Trust/security index ($\alpha = .789$)

---

a) This organization recognizes and rewards employee loyalty.
b) Employees can trust this organization to do what's right by them.
c) Management has problems trusting its employees at this call centre. (reverse coded)
d) The likelihood of downsizing or retrenchment at this call centre is high. (reverse coded)
e) There tends to be an 'us' and 'them' relationship between employees and managers at this organization. (reverse coded)

---

that characterize an organization (Guest 1999). Presumably, where the extent of obligation is experienced as being greater, organizational identity will also be stronger.

Two further observations are in order. First, the concept of a psychological contract is theoretically contiguous with the HRM project. It is a state of mind that is held by individuals with respect to their employer. In other words, it refers to a relationship between individual employees and the employers they work for. As a set of practices, HRM is directed towards operating on the psychological contract and thereby influencing subjectivities and identities. The concept reflects the turn towards individualism in the employment relationship, a turn that is expressed in the discursive practices of HRM. It is more than likely not a coincidence that as social contracts/accords and collective bargaining have receded as a result of neoliberal economic and social policies, the notion of psychological contracts has become increasingly popular in the study of employment relations. Second, with its referents to trust and fairness, the idea of a psychological contract also covers the theme of security, which is one of the criteria applied in the designation of HPWSs.

Bearing these factors in mind, an attempt has been made to create, from the survey questions (see Table 6.4), a composite measure of employees' perceptions of trust/security in the organizations they work for. Presumably higher levels of trust and security will be reflected in greater levels of organizational identity.

Of course, trust is reinforced or broken by other undertakings in which management engages. A commitment on the part of the employer to invest resources in training and ongoing employee development conveys one set of messages to workers; organizational disregard of these matters sends a different set of signals. For this reason, respondents' evaluations of organizational training and development initiatives are important. We can conjecture that for a number of reasons, more positive assessments would be likely to promote stronger identity ties with the employer.

Workers may consider employer commitments to training and development to be an 'investment opportunity' undertaken by the employer that may also benefit the worker. Investments in training may be viewed as the presentation of opportunities for employees to advance within the organization through the operations of internal labour markets. Employer-based training may also be framed as a quid pro quo – that is, the employer has certain expectations as to work performance and provides workers with the necessary resources to fulfil those expectations in a realistic manner. Finally, we should not forget that training is an important means for workers to familiarize themselves with the organization's employment culture. Training, both as induction and as ongoing consolidation and learning, provides management with opportunities to reiterate its message over and over again with regard to standards, decorum, protocols, and expected levels of customer service. Meanwhile, workers are more likely to view the training they receive as adequate or better if the training is delivered in a pedagogically professional manner that covers all necessary facets of their work. In this regard, the ability to access additional training – again, to realize future opportunities for advancement – may also enter into evaluations of employer performance. We have tried to capture these aspects of training and development in ten items taken from the survey (see Table 6.5), which together constitute an organizational training index.

One feature of call-centre employment that is both unique and hypothetically important in establishing an organizational climate is the practice of work monitoring. Though call monitoring is practically a constant in the call centre, it can be conducted in different ways; as well, the frequency of occurrence may vary, and it may be used for different purposes. Monitoring may be done in an open side-by-side manner with employees, or it may be conducted covertly. Workers may or may not have a voice in determining how it is undertaken. Such observation may be used as part of training and development practices, for recognition and reward as part of contingent payment schemes (bonuses, etc.), or more directly as part of the technologies of control. Where monitoring is used in an open fashion as part of the training-and-development agenda, it may be construed as 'feedback,' which some workers may appreciate. On the other hand, if such surveillance is mainly associated with enforcing conformance to scripts, workers may view it mainly negatively. Monitoring is unlikely to induce greater identification with

Table 6.5
Training and development index ($\alpha = .857$)

a) The trainer(s) at this company do a good job.
b) The split between classroom and on-the-job training was about right.
c) The initial training that I received at this company was adequate for me to meet the expectations of my job.
d) The pace at which material was covered in my initial training was too fast. (reverse coded)
e) I feel that I should have received more training than I did before I went onto the phones. (reverse coded)
f) I am given adequate training when new products and services are introduced.
g) I receive adequate training on new processes (e.g. software or new ways of doing things) in my job.
h) I can access additional training if I don't think I am adequately responding to customer questions.
i) I am expected to learn new things too quickly in this job. (reverse coded)
j) The division between classroom and on-the-job training for new products and processes is about right.

Table 6.6
Monitoring index ($\alpha = .766$)

a) I receive useful feedback about the results of my monitored calls.
b) I am satisfied with the way in which call monitoring is used in this centre.

the employer; it may or may not diminish levels of identification. Two questions on the survey have immediate relevance for these issues (see Table 6.6).

Besides call monitoring, another common feature of the call centre is work teams. Cultural activity in call centres often assumes the presence of work teams, both as a structural backdrop and as a mobilizing feature as when team building/bonding activities are pursued. The importance of work teams varies from one centre to the next, but most centres have them: only three of the twenty Australian centres in this study had abandoned a team concept or had allowed work teams to whither. Yet as emphasized in preceding chapters, call centres are an anomalous setting for work teams. Info-service work is intensely individualized in the call centre, as is the work cycle. CSRs do not carry out fragments of tasks and then pass their work along to colleagues for the next step; rather, each individual agent is responsible for completing all steps in a client contact. In other work environments, researchers

Table 6.7
Work team index ($\alpha = .727$)

---

a) Team meetings give me an opportunity to have real input into the way things are run at this company.
b) My team leader tries hard to make this a good work environment.
c) I can always take a work-related problem to my team leader for consultation.

---

have drawn connections between the use of work teams and the mobilization of peer pressure to produce 'disciplined worker effects' (Ezzamel and Willmott 1998; Parker and Slaughter 1988; Rinehart, Huxley, and Robertson 1997; Sewell and Wilkinson 1992; Sewell 1998). However, in these studies there are generally serial work flows and high levels of task interdependency among workers. Call centres present us with what van den Broek, Callaghan, and Thompson ironically refer to as 'work teams without team work' (van den Broek, Callaghan, and Thompson 2004; van den Broek 2002; Wise et al. 2007). In these scenarios the existence of work teams is primarily about normative regulation. Individuals are selected for call-centre employment partly on the basis of their social and interpersonal skills (Callaghan and Thompson 2002), with work teams constituting primary socialization groups for new inductees (see also Mueller 1994; Procter and Mueller 2000).

The work-team index developed here attempts to measure two important aspects that have been attributed to this form of work design. First, it considers whether work teams provide employees with representational 'voice' in the call centre – that is, whether they are a source of empowerment for workers, giving them a sense of ownership over their work. Previous accounts of HPWSs (Batt 2000) have signalled the importance of work teams in skill development and utilization in info-service work. Second, it suggests the extent to which work teams promote the sort of facilitative management styles that have been associated with post-bureaucracy info-service work (Frenkel, Korczynski, et al. 1999). Where work teams are viewed as providing a mechanism for meaningful decision-making participation and where team leadership is perceived as facilitative rather than disciplinary in nature, we would expect the likelihood of identification with the employer to be greater. The work-team measure is composed of the three queries shown in Table 6.7.

To this point the measures that have been developed refer either to HRM activities explicitly directed towards cultural construction (i.e., that can be seen as directly working on the culture of the organization) or to aspects of HRM that include embedded cultural signifiers as part of their fulfilment, such as monitoring, training, and the utilization of work teams. To round off the analysis of potential factors affecting the extent of organizational-identity ties in the case-study sites, this analysis reintroduces the measures of skill and workload manageability that were developed in chapter 4. These items bring the labour process back into the discussion of identity. They reflect perceptions of fairness relating to the effort bargain as well as perceptions of the skill levels associated with info-service work (see Tables 4.1 and 4.3). Presumably, positive evaluations of these aspects of work would enhance identification with the employing organization.

Besides using these indexes to predict organizational identity, it is also important to consider the effects of four other factors that have the potential to affect organizational attachments. The employment status of workers, whether or not they are working full time or part time, and whether they are on permanent or casual contracts, could also have an important bearing on organizational identity. Generally the view is that non-standard or irregular employment contracts will create weaker organizational ties than those exhibited by full-time and permanent conditions (Batt 2002).

Little research has been conducted on trade-union membership and organizational identity, though various studies have reported that union members tend to be less satisfied with their work but also less likely to quit than non-union workers; at the same time, unionism is positively correlated with productivity through the opportunities it provides for the authentic exercise of employee voice (Freeman and Medoff 1984). In chapter 8 we will return to examine the effect of HRM on union membership. Here we are interested in the opposite relationship: the effect of union membership on workplace subjectivity. It could be argued that unions provide an alternative identity anchor for workers (Rose 2002). In a system of voluntary unionism such as now prevails in Australia, as well as in other countries (including Britain and New Zealand), where each individual decides whether or not to join a union and closed or union shops are prohibited by law, the act of joining a union does represent a commitment. One reason for joining a union is less-than-full confidence in the employer. In such cases union membership may come at the expense of identification with the employer. However, this argument makes certain assumptions about the reasons for joining a union. If other motives lay back of union membership, then the relationship need not be zero-sum, as implied by this argument. Extending this line of thinking further, some have suggested that HRM is likely to be *more* pronounced in unionized work settings (Guest and Hoque 1996; Sisson 1993); and though this does not speak to the issue of contested identities, it has also been reported that workers derive greater satisfaction from HRM policies than from trade-union representation (Guest and Conway 1999).

As for the fourth factor, the length of employee job tenure, again it seems reasonable to suggest that longevity in the job is positively related to organizational identity. If nothing else, greater seniority would present opportunities for the parties to become more familiar with each other and for the 'psychological contract' to mature. In the analysis that follows, job tenure is measured in months. The three remaining factors are represented by dummy variables that have been created to reflect union/non-union membership, full-time/part-time employment, and permanent/casual call-centre job positions.

To explore the relationship between workers' experiences of HRM and their identification with the employing organization, a step-wise regression analysis is conducted in which organizational identity is treated as the dependent variable and the factors outlined above are considered as potential determinants. This particular approach allows us to explore interaction effects among different variables as they are sequentially added to the analysis. Table 6.8 provides the results of this analysis.

The most important finding is that the evaluation of the skills associated with the work is the most powerful factor in statistically accounting for workers' identification with the organization that employs them. Perceived skill levels are the first variable that is entered in Model 1. The more skilled employees consider their work to be, the stronger the identification with the employing organization. But also significant at this stage are (in order of importance) trust, management's culture-building activities, satisfaction with training, approval of monitoring practices, team roles, and workload manageability. Skill alone accounts for more than one-third of the variation in organizational identity ($R^2 = .375$). Employment status (i.e., part-time or casual) has no noticeable effect on the strength of identity, nor does belonging or not belonging to a trade union. Job seniority at this stage has a very weak negative effect on organizational identity.

The next most salient variable, which is entered into Model 2, is employee trust in the organization. Recall that this covers the 'psychologi-

Table 6.8
Least squares regression for identification with employing organization, Australia call centres (Beta)

Independent Variables	Model 1	Model 2	Model 3	Model 4
Included				
Skill	.612***	Skill .477***	Skill .448***	Skill .412***
		Trust .252***	Trust .193***	Trust .172***
			Mgt Culture .154***	Mgt Culture .143***
				Monitoring .101**
Excluded				
Trust/security	.252***	Mgt Culture .154***	Monitoring .101**	Union .060
Mgt Culture	.217***	Monitoring .117**	Training .077	Training .058
Training	.181***	Training .101**	Union .058	Workload −.050
Monitoring	.170***	Work Teams .069	Work Teams .047	Work Teams .019
Work Teams	.150***	Union .045	Workload −.021	Permanent .016
Workload	.107**	Seniority −.025	Permanent .011	Full Time .007
Seniority	−.084*	Full Time .017	Full Time .005	Seniority .007
Union Membership	−.030	Workload .003	Seniority .003	
Permanent Employ	.020	Permanent .006		
Full Time	.005			
R^2	.375	.420	.438	.445
Adjusted R^2	.374	.418	.434	.441

cal contract' that workers have with their employers. In our usage of this concept, trust is operationalized to represent such things as the level of overall security that employees have – not just job security in the relatively narrow sense of not being made redundant, but overall confidence that the organization will continue to represent the terms and conditions that employees consider to be constitutive of the employment relationship they have with it. As Giddens (1991, 19) has observed, 'trust presumes a leap to commitment, a quality of "faith" which is irreducible,' and this seems to capture the dynamics we observe here. When trust/security is included in the analysis, other variables are rendered less important in accounting for identification with the organization. Specifically, workload manageability and satisfaction with the role afforded to work teams both lose their efficacy. It seems that workers who are satisfied that the job is making use of their abilities and who trust the employing organization to honour its side of the quid pro quo that constitutes an employment relationship take workload manageability in their stride. It may be that those who consider their jobs to be more skilled also see themselves as exercising greater control over their workloads and as able to limit the intensity of the effort bargain. This argument is lent a certain degree of possibility by virtue of the fact that skill and workload manageability exhibit a fairly strong bivariate correlation in the results ($r = .483$).

Meanwhile, the downgrading of work teams from Model 2, to statistical insignificance, should not come as a complete surprise. As suggested in other industry studies (Jackson, Sprigg, and Parker 2000), where work interdependency is low, teams are less likely to have the beneficial effects that HRM attributes to them. As previous chapters have emphasized, info-service work in call centres is essentially an individualistic labour process. Opportunities for joint problem solving and other forms of meaningful work-related collaboration are limited in the centres we have observed. There does not appear to be a great deal of skill development through the sort of team learning and problem solving that are used to define HPWSs (Batt 2000, 2002). Further to this point, when asked what they would do when confronted with a question they could not resolve, the largest percentage of respondents (44 per cent) indicated that their first stratagem would be to consult an operations manual or website, and only after that a team leader (29.4 per cent), and only third (23.6 per cent) their team peers. These results hold for most of the twenty centres considered in this study, where the main points of variation among operations are found in the use of individual problem-solving strategies as opposed to consultations with team leaders. Team-based problem solving was the favoured strategy of workers in only three of the centres examined here.[8] In short, then, the labour process of the call centre militates against meaningful team-work, as other analyses have previously suggested (van den Broek et al. 2004).

Besides being seen as venues for using and developing skills, work teams are often associated with other aspects of working life. This may include a governance role (i.e., work teams are expected to make decisions that affect how work is accomplished, for example, through work flow and roster planning). Across the sites, only a minority (40.5 per cent) were of the opinion that work teams provided an opportunity to make important decisions about how things were to be accomplished in the workplace; a larger percentage (57.1) shared a more cynical view – that team meetings were mainly opportunities for management to lobby for its agenda. In other words, there seemed to be greater agreement that work teams facilitate downwards rather than upwards communication. Also, almost half the sample (45.2 per cent) acknowledged that their team meetings were frequently cancelled because of the volume of call traffic. This again casts the importance of work teams in call centres in a critical light.

It has also been suggested that 'communities of coping' are an important dimension of call-centre life (Korczynski 2003), and it would seem that work teams are implicated in this. Overall, almost 60 per cent of the sample agreed that members of their work teams were an important source of social support, providing empathy in the wake of customer abuse. In this regard, though, work teams seemed to provide convenient, 'ready-made' as opposed to organic communities within the call centre. In response to more detailed questions on the importance of work teams to their experiences, almost 70 per cent of the respondents said they were as likely to socialize with members of other teams in the workplace as with fellow team members. That a higher proportion of the overall sample (45.2 per cent) attached greater importance to the roster they worked than to the team they worked on (35 per cent) is also instructive. This finding seems to indicate that workers did not see much difference between individual teams in their work environments, nor did they attach overwhelming importance to membership on a specific team. Relatively weak attachments to work teams would explain why this factor was of no great significance in accounting for the strength of organizational identity in the call centres. Moreover, these perceptions were shared almost equally between women and men in the study. While women were more likely to relate to team members as a source of social support in their work, this was the only point of significant difference with regard to how genders related to work teams.[9]

If work teams are of less importance in accounting for workplace identities, it is also the case that some of the negative features associated with work teams need to be scrutinized in greater detail. A number of researchers have identified work teams with surveillance, peer pressure, and Japanese-style 'management by stress' (Ezzamel and Willmott 1998; Parker and Slaughter 1988; Sewell 1998; Sewell and Wilkinson 1992). While these arguments have mainly been applied to research in manufacturing industries, they have also been extended to the call centre, where rewards for team performance have been observed to be part of a system of normative control that relies in part on peer pressure (van den Broek 2004; van den Broek, Callaghan, and Thompson 2004; Thompson, Callaghan, and van den Broek 2004). The participants of our study acknowledged few of these dynamics. For example, fewer than one in ten said that team peers had pressured them to take more calls, and just under one-third expressed concern about the effect their absence from work could have on team members. Once again, given the lack of task interdependency among CSRs in the labour process, comparatively weak team bonds seem to be characteristic of these workplaces; so is an absence of both positive and negative features attributed to work teams.

The final two models of Table 6.8 complete the analysis. Management-initiated cultural activities – the games, events, and competitions discussed earlier in this chapter – did go some way to strengthening organizational identity, but it was a relatively shallow effect. Workers – male and female in about equal proportions – generally said they participated in such undertakings and admitted to enjoying them. On the other hand, the largest proportions (43 per cent of men and 48 per cent of women) denied that such encounters were an important aspect of their job, and greater proportions of both women and men were less in favour as opposed to supportive of having more organization-sponsored events. When workers had positive experiences of management-sponsored social events, they were likely to express somewhat stronger affinities with the employer.

With regard to monitoring practices, workers largely agreed that they were needed, claimed to receive useful feedback from them, and expressed overall satisfaction with how call monitoring was being used in the workplace. Though the workers did not seem to feel threatened by monitoring, significantly greater proportions of female workers indicated that such surveillance was a stressor in their work. Once again, satisfaction with how monitoring was conducted bore a weak but significant relationship to identifying with one's employment.

When cultural initiatives and monitoring practices are considered, the importance of training loses its significance. Intuitively, this can be explained as follows. Training does have cultural messages embedded in it. However, as we saw in chapter 3, much of the training in call centres is dedicated to product and process knowledge. This is especially the case with ongoing training, where short product-life cycles, continuous marketing campaigns, new service options, and (in the case of public-sector centres) changing legislative requirements all dominate the training agenda. Training is not so much about acquiring new skill sets in order to take on more complex work as it is about constantly updating current information in order to perform essentially the same work. This aspect of training, which agents report as being central, is unlikely to enhance organizational identity over time. Rather, training in this work is routinized in much the same way as the labour process. As a result, training is not necessarily associated with internal career advancement, nor is it transferable across organizations to any significant degree.

Overall, the fully articulated model in Table 6.8 'explains' just under half (45 per cent) of the variation in organizational identity as we have defined it. Opportunities to use work skills and to develop them further are singularly the most important item in accounting for attachment to the employing organization; faith that organizations will honour commitments to their workers also adds to the robustness of the results. To put it another way, the labour process and its design as well as the state of employment relations are the two most important components affecting organization identity. Managerial efforts directed at winning over workers by making work environments 'fun places,' while significant, add relatively little additional power to the analysis; the same can be said of satisfaction with the monitoring practices that call centres utilize. To the extent that organizational socialization through training, reward and recognition programs, and other HRM initiatives is a major focus of management, we can conclude that 'strong cultural' intervention yields comparatively weak effects. Finally, we should note that this statistical model omits other potentially important factors that are likely to have a bearing on workplace subjectivities, but which were not measured in the workforce survey. In particular, as suggested in the last section, perceptions of engaging in socially useful work are likely to influence the extent of organizational identification.

6.5 Conclusions

Even if 'the prospect of constructing a *lifelong* identity on the founda-tion of work is, for the great majority of people ... dead and buried' (Bauman 1998, 27; my emphasis),[10] work still matters in terms of how we identify ourselves and give meaning to our lives. But the strength of employment as an 'identity anchor' can vary considerably, and this is mainly based on the nature of the work that is conducted in employ-ment. In this sample of call-centre information workers, considerable differences are encountered among those who derive an important sense of personal identity from the organization they work for, those who are neutrally inclined, and those who don't find organizational identification to be important to their definitions of self. Two factors are particularly salient in accounting for the strength of the employing organization as an identity anchor. The first is the labour process, or the way work is designed. Jobs that provide a sense of fulfilment through the demands they make and the purposes they serve are more likely to generate attachments than those that don't. The second key element that enters into the formation of organizational attachments is the trust factor, which is related to personal security. This aspect used to fall within the ambit of industrial-relations analysis, as in Fox's (1974) trea-tise on the importance of trust in the employment relationship. These findings pose a serious challenge for the future of info-service work.

As we have seen in the previous two chapters, generally info-service work has not been designed in a way that meets the criteria of produc-ing skilled, meaningful work. Workers view the work as semiskilled. If anything, the tendency is towards further standardizing jobs so that they may be more easily managed – a process that points to a distinct lack of trust. Workers respond to these conditions by 'putting the job in perspective.' Meaningful experience is often sought elsewhere.

As detailed in the next chapter, in a rapidly globalizing world the problem of trust becomes even thornier. In the globalized, 'anything goes' world of contemporary capitalism, personal employment securi-ty is increasingly seen as a luxury. Bauman (1998, 35) cautions: 'For the majority of people, other than the chosen few, in the present day flexible labour market, embracing one's work as a vocation carries enormous risks and is a recipe for psychological and emotional disaster.' Though Bauman is mainly concerned with the erosion of occupational identities in late modernity, the mobility that info-service providers have to set up and move work around the global economy with minimal opportunity costs acts as a powerful inhibitor to the formation of strong organizational attachments. The rise of HRM as the face of contemporary managerialism is best understood in terms of the labour process and the increasingly globalized nature of info-service work.

7 Globalizing Info-Service Work: Outsourcing to India[1]

CO-PRODUCED WITH MOHAN THITE

7.1 Introduction

Shortly after the beginning of the new millennium, when call-centre workers were being recognized as a separate occupational category in the employment-classification schemes of the wealthy countries, this labour process began to migrate to less developed countries, where it was quickly established as a *new industry*. The ability to source information and respond to queries from anywhere that digitized material can be received and transmitted is a powerful testament to the realities of globalization.[2] This chapter analyses a number of the implications attached to the globalization of information work. It is directed towards those changes besetting the world of work that were identified at the outset of the book – namely, changes in the social division of labour attached to the globalization of labour processes. Our attention is directed towards India, which as early as 2002 was attracting the lion's share (24 per cent) of global information outsourcing work (Thite and Russell 2007).

The phenomenon of outsourcing raises several intriguing questions for researchers. For instance, how similar or dissimilar is the work being conducted in countries such as India to that which is performed in the West? What implications does outsourcing hold for the economies that host these new activities? Does the outsourcing of info-service work portend a new division of labour in a more deeply integrated global economy or the reproduction of old asymmetries between wealthy and poor economies? While acknowledging that these are macroscopic questions, the intention here is merely to shed some light on these important issues by examining in detail the outsourcing of info-service work. A brief history of these activities will help us set the context for the study and dispel some myths.

In the early 1990s India's share of world trade amounted to less than 0.01 per cent and the country faced a severe balance-of-payments problem and an attendant foreign-exchange shortfall. This crisis resulted in abandonment of the Nehru model of state-led development and prompted a general opening up of the economy, complete with the usual neoliberal policy prescriptions for tariff reductions and deregulation (Chibber 2003; Das 2002; Srinivasan 2006). Unforeseen at the time, one of the first areas to experience growth in demand was the labour-subcontracting business. Usually, when subcontracting is considered, it conjures up images of the construction industry and unskilled labour. While labour export, especially to the Middle East, does involve this type of flow (Davis 2006), it is also necessary to factor into the picture the two million–plus university and college graduates who enter the labour market each year, many with degrees in engineering, mathematics, and the sciences (KPMG 2004; Raman, Budhwar, and Balasubramanian 2007; Srinivasan 2006). It is out of this field of graduates that a second labour flow, consisting of highly educated workers, was born during the 1990s.

The temporary emigration of skilled professional workers was also organized around the principle of labour hire, with Indian companies 'renting out' employees to work on the sites of their principal overseas clients. This form of skilled-labour hire became known as the *on-site* model of collaboration, and it represented the global take-off of the now famous Indian IT industry (Thite and Russell 2007). As a result of various conjunctural factors, including the Y2K panic and the dot. com boom, skilled Indian expatriates helped relieve the growing shortage of IT personnel in countries such as the United States. The on-site labour-hire strategy succeeded so well that by the close of the 1990s Indians accounted for almost half the H-1B work permits issued by the U.S. Department of Immigration for IT-related occupations (Mittal and Goel 2004).[3] This was the first in a series of 'happy' coincidences characterizing the growth of the Indian business-process outsourcing (BPO) services model.

Labour hire in the software industry received additional fillips during the 1990s, including the Euro-conversion projects that dominated economic integration in that part of the world at the dawn of the new century. As the reputation of the industry grew in the West, the demand for Indian IT workers continued to grow, in tandem with the profits of the agency companies that had arisen to organize the on-site model. It was only a matter of time before the next step was taken – the exportation of work to the Subcontinent. At first this involved mainly low-end work such as coding, but the real significance lay in the steam that was gathering for the next stage of global informationalism – namely, *outsourcing through offshoring*. In today's world it is faster and cheaper to move information than it is to move human bodies. Thus developments in ICT favoured the sending of work to people rather than bringing people to the source of the work. This relative shift from on-site to offshore models dramatically increased the amounts of work that could be outsourced.

Other events added impetus to the offshoring strategy. The dot.com crash centred in America pushed ahead a new round of corporate re-engineering and downsizing (Brenner 2003). Any activity that was not defined as core to business strategy/profit maximization, including IT support work, became a candidate for outsourcing. But the dot.com crash and the associated recession also had an impact on the nascent Indian computer-services industry. Generally the demand for IT personnel declined overall as IT companies cut back and reorganized their operations, and this slack was also experienced in India. However, the feasibility of offshoring did not stop with IT work alone. In their bid to cut costs, multinationals placed other processes such as back-office, corporate, and customer-support functions on the block. If such work could be done as efficiently overseas but at a cheaper cost than in-house, then suddenly it became eligible for export. Thus, when Indian companies began undertaking investments in what are termed information technology–enabled services (ITeS), this was partly in response to demands from overseas business clients for additional services.[4]

At the same time that Western MNCs were looking for ways to cut costs, Indian IT companies were looking for new investment arenas to move into in order to pick up the slack that the worldwide downturn in IT had created. An expansion in the full range of business services on offer, including both front- and back-office support, provided just such an opportunity for the Indian players. Another stroke of good fortune for aspirant Indian IT companies was the abundant and underutilized fibre-optic cable and broadband functionality that had been built during the heyday of the IT boom (Friedman 2006). Cable companies found themselves in a position akin to that of the railways at the end of the previous century: overextended, but also with large amounts of underutilized capacity. This infrastructure, which connected India to

Europe and North America, was waiting to be put to work. So, this confluence of rather fortuitous circumstances led to the third phase of global informationalism in which the largest Indian IT companies, including Wipro, Infosys, and Satyam, either established subsidiary arms or purchased existing Indian companies in order to provide a full suite of information services to overseas purchasers. In India this emergent industry is referred to as ITeS/BPO – information technology–enabled services in support of business-process outsourcing. These activities include 'back office' work such as data entry and processing; data analysis; corporate-support functions, including HRM administration (payroll, leave, and other forms of documentation); and, most relevant from our perspective, long-distance call-centre customer-service support and marketing (Srivastava and Theodore 2006). The largest Indian IteS/BPO subsidiaries were all established in the relatively short period between 1999 and 2002 in response to the aforementioned events and opportunities.

The rapidity of these developments and the growth that has been generated by them are, to say the least, stunning. Whereas the Indian IT export industry took roughly ten years to mature, and currently employs just over half a million workers, over the four-year period 2002–6 ITeS/BPO employment – much of it call-centre–related – has grown from 110,000 to an estimated 380,000 to 415,000 for 2005–6 (Government of India 2003; KPMG 2004).[5] More recent figures cite employment levels of over half a million in 2007 (Nasscom 2007) and an estimated 650,000 in 2008 (Callcentres.net 2008a). Meanwhile the provision of ITeS services is estimated to be worth about US$8.3 billion compared with $18.1 billion for IT services (2007) (Nasscom 2008). These data are noteworthy on two counts. First, the presumption of a linear movement from less-skilled, lower-value-added production in the information economy to higher-skilled, higher-value-added knowledge production does not accurately fit Indian developments. Rather, the economy appears to be moving all over the skill/value-adding chain, *from* comparatively high-value technical work (programming) *to* less-skilled customer-service and back-office work and more recently and contentiously to what some have termed knowledge-process outsourcing (KPO), which is postulated as the next phase in the outsourcing phenomenon (Raman, Budhwar, and Balasubramanian 2007). KPO would signal a move back up the skill/value ladder as professionals in such fields as medicine/health care, law, and accounting provide real-time service to overseas principals and their clients, in some cases via contact centres.

The reason for this serpentine pattern of growth is to be found in the logic and raison d'être of BPO. Theoretically, with the pools of human capital available, corporate strategy in India has rested on providing whatever services overseas principals need or can be interested in purchasing – a situation that Mirchandani (2009) has accurately characterized as 'globalization from above.' Though the BPO/offshoring model is said to overcome the constraints of distance and time, it actually rests squarely on those constraints. Clients derive two immediate and combined benefits. First, Indians work when workers in the West rest. Where outsourcing is possible it negates the need for work during unsociable hours (nights) in other parts of the world, as well as the wage premiums that have historically attended such labour. Second, wages and salaries in Indian IT/ITeS are generally about one-tenth what their Western counterparts receive (Srinivasan 2006).[6] Thus in terms of the economics of BPO, Western firms reap a double advantage: not only no overtime/penalty payments for operating on an around-the-clock basis, but an actual wage bill saving of up to 90 per cent for doing so! Indeed, so significant are the wage savings that the busiest time of the working 'day' for BPO workers is now the middle of the night, which corresponds to normal business operating hours in North America.

Estimates as to where these developments are leading need to be treated with caution. By 2002 India had close to a one-quarter share of the outsourced IT/ITeS global market, though this was still a drop in the bucket (0.8 per cent) in terms of global IT/ITeS value generated by the sector (Government of India 2003). Under one set of projections this could increase to a 4.4 per cent share of world production by 2012, with the employment of up to 2.7 million workers in ITeS and just under 1 million in IT (KPMG 2004). So by 2012, the information-outsourcing sector in all of its guises could employ some 3.7 million workers, but out of a workforce that currently numbers 500 million.[7] Cast in this comparative light, the information/BPO revolution in India is better represented and understood as an instance of highly uneven and combined development. Moreover, based on the employment numbers and projections attached to the industry, its potential contribution to the building of a middle-class society would seem to be distinctly limited (Focus on the Global South/Young Professionals Collective 2005). The limits of the export-led services-provision (ELSP) model of development that BPO represents (Thite and Russell 2007) follow from the basic point that, as a sector, IT/ITeS is chiefly articulated with foreign capital rather than the domestic economy. About 75 per cent of the value produced in IT services is directed to the export market, and an even higher 88 per cent of ITeS value is directed to exports – that is, to servicing overseas customers (Nasscom 2008).[8]

Such export dependence lends the outsourcing sector an insular quality – something that is graphically displayed by its spatial separation from the rest of urban India. Every first-tier Indian city now has its own vast high-technology park or district – often with an innocuous name such as 'IT City' or 'Technology City' – that houses the facilities of both Indian-headquartered and foreign service providers. Access to such facilities comes only with permission to pass through gates staffed by armed guards and always involves the production of a photo ID badge, bag checks, and possibly other security precautions – in other words, access is by prearranged invitation only. Inside the gates are beautifully tended gardens, opulent buildings with marble interiors, and Western-style food courts. Outside the gates are less pleasant realities (see Figure 7.1). This clash of two worlds is only one of the more obvious contradictions associated with this form of development. In this chapter we will focus on another contradiction that characterizes the employment relationship in Indian call centres. Our argument is that BPO accentuates the tensions between the informational and service aspects of info-service work over and beyond what we have already seen in the Australian call centres. This is giving rise to challenges on an order of magnitude that may be difficult to downplay. These issues are explored in greater detail in the following sections, beginning with an introduction to the case-study organizations where the research was carried out.

7.2 The BPO Case Studies

Among the more than four hundred ITeS/BPO providers in India, the trade literature usefully distinguishes between *captives* and *third-party providers* (Nasscom 2005; Srivastava and Theodore 2006). The former are the subsidiary operations of foreign multinationals. These are the operations that first drew public attention. Captive operations were created when companies such as GE-Finance, Dell, Hewlett Packard, IBM, American Express, Citigroup, and British Airways established call centres and data-processing centres in India. Essentially these facilities are 'in-house, offshore' operations, and they still constitute the largest share of employment in the ITeS/BPO sector. However, as highlighted in the previous section, national Indian companies are quickly entering

Figure 7.1: 'Dude, Where's My Childhood. Just a corner not very far away from the bits and bytes of Tech City.'

Photo by Murali Kumark, Bangalore, India, *The Hindu*, 11 October 2005.

the field in a major way. These indigenous companies are one component of the third-party segment.

Srivastava and Theodore (2006) provide a further breakdown of the ITeS outsourcing industry by distinguishing among multinational outsourcers, home shore–anchored outsourcers, offshore IT subsidiaries, and offshore non-IT subsidiaries. Multinational outsourcers are MNCs that specialize in providing outsourcing services. They include well-known firms such as IBM and Hewlett Packard, which serve their own corporate constituencies but also provide business services to other companies. Home shore–anchored companies are registered in the West but mainly operate from offshore locations such as India. Expatriates from countries such as India have often played an important role in starting them up. Offshore providers are constituted by indigenous firms founded and based in the country of offshore operation. Some of the largest of these are subsidiaries of indigenous IT companies, including Wipro, Infosys, and Satyam – names that readers are likely to become more familiar with in the future. Three of the four companies examined in this chapter have exactly this lineage, one dating back to 1999 and the other two to 2002, when they were founded in the immediate aftermath of the IT crash as a means to provide greater business diversification. The fourth organization also has IT parentage, but in this case an existing ITeS/BPO provider was purchased (again in 2002) and added to the existing IT company's portfolio. Each of the case studies presented in this chapter fits into the category of an offshore BPO provider. Finally, some of India's 'houses of industry' such as the Birla and Tata groups have gotten into the act by creating BPO entities of their own. These companies enter the field without any prior history in the information sector as offshore non-IT subsidiaries.

The rationale behind BPO helps account for some of the most immediate features of the organizations that undertake it. Without putting too fine a point on it, BPO providers exist solely to extend whatever services their clients demand. If these capabilities are not readily at hand, they are quickly acquired through strategic recruitment and hiring, often on a mind-boggling scale and followed up with intensive training. Thus the first feature of note about ITeS providers generally, including the four companies discussed here, is their size. At the time our study was being conducted (late 2005), employment in the case-study organizations ranged from 1,700 workers (referred to as 'process executives' in local industry argot), to 2,600 to 5,300 and finally up to 12,500. For convenience, the case studies can be referred to as *BPO1*, *BPO2*, *BPO3*, and

BPO4, with the attached number reflecting the increasing size of the organization's workforce. These are large companies by any standard, especially considering that they came into existence only after 1999. Average employment at the time of our study across the four companies was 5,525, compared to a mean of 161 across the twenty Australian organizations included here. In the Indian centres, agents are employed across multiple sites, which are often in different cities. For example, *BPO4*, the largest of the organizations discussed here, at the time of this study operated seven different facilities in five major cities.

The second notable characteristic of these organizations is their multifunctional character. The offshore indigenous providers do not exist to produce a single product such as insurance policies or reservations, nor do they serve single or even related markets. Rather, they are in the business of providing 'processes' to other, foreign businesses. Included under the ITeS/BPO acronym are both voice – inbound *and* outbound – and non-voice/back-office functions. Call centres provide services to the overseas customers of foreign firms. These services are sold to a variety of foreign principals, usually under multiyear contracts. Within the call centre domain, overseas principals cover a broad array of undertakings, including financial services, telecommunications, entertainment (e.g., cable television), health care, and IT support and services (e.g., help desk and Internet services). The sheer number of service-level agreements with a variety of foreign principals and product markets adds to the innate complexity of analysing this form of corporate organization.

This *industry* structure is reflected in the workforces we studied. At *BPO1* there was a 50:50 ratio between voice (i.e., call centre) and non–call-centre back-office work. *BPO4*, the largest firm, which employed 12,500 across seven locations, classified 60 per cent of its workforce as telephone-based 'process executives' (i.e., CSRs); the remainder were 'non-voice' workers. At *BPO2*, meanwhile, the labour force was divided on a 40:40:20 basis among inbound voice, outbound voice, and back-office operations respectively. Management at *BPO3* strove to emphasize to us that they were not a call centre as only 20 per cent of their employees were dedicated to voice-based customer-service delivery.

The business profiles associated with BPO have effects on how work is organized, and in this, too, Indian ITeS/call centres can be distinguished from their Western counterparts. Work teams are aligned with specific clients and the processes they require. This means there are no common metrics or kpi's across teams in any given centre. Instead, targets and kpi's are specified in service-level agreements between the client firm and the BPO provider and then applied to the relevant teams. In other words, work expectations are team/client specific. Though team sizes are similar to what is found in Western centres (i.e., around fifteen CSRs per team), the size of Indian operations makes for a huge number of teams. The number of client firms being served also adds to the complexity of the business structure. For example, *BPO2* had between 200 and 220 teams spread across twenty clients at three sites. At *BPO4* as many as sixty teams could be assigned to a single client. Sometimes, agents work across more than one client/process, which adds yet another dimension to the work. Other times, agents are dedicated to a single principal for the length of the service contract, which may involve participation in a variety of processes for that client (e.g., billing inquiries, password queries, and customer retention). This means that 'multiskilling' comes in a variety of forms – for example, working for two or more clients and/or performing different processes for each client. All of this seems to be variable and highly flexible, with plenty of morphing as determined by the volume of business – that is, number of clients – and those clients' individual needs.

BPO is a young industry in more ways than one. Entering a call centre in India is an experience somewhat akin to entering a fast-food restaurant in the West in terms of the first impressions one gains of the workforce. Apart from some middle-aged managers, the labour force is composed entirely of young workers. In our sample, taken from the four indigenous BPOs (n = 638), 92 per cent of the workforce was under thirty years of age. While very few workers were under twenty (1.6 per cent), only 7.4 per cent were in their thirties, and less than 1 per cent were over forty.

Workforces are also gender mixed to a far greater degree than is found in the Australian case studies or reported in other Western studies (Belt 2002a, Belt, Richardson, and Webster 2000; Durbin 2006; Mulholland 2002). Men constituted just over 60 per cent of the respondents and women just under 40 per cent. This gender ratio was not quite the mirror opposite of what was found in the Australian centres, where women constituted slightly more than three-quarters of the sample and men slightly less than one-quarter and where men made up no more than 44 per cent of the sample at any one location. A comparison of the Indian and Australian gender balances tells us much about how info-service work is socially constructed in the two societies in different ways. In Australia – as we saw in chapter 4 – the work is construed as semiskilled, and if anything, some of the skills associated with it are undervalued in terms of the recognition they receive in organizational training and development practices. In India, by contrast, info-service work has been branded as professional in nature and workers are officially referred to as 'process executives' (D'Cruz and Noronha 2006). Workers may or may not be quickly disabused of the notion that they are truly performing 'professional' roles; that said, men are more likely to be attracted to an 'executive' rather than a customer-service job title. In other words, info-service work is marketed in different ways in India as part of the creation of a specific labour force, and this has gender implications.

The creation of info-service labour markets interacts with differing societal assumptions regarding appropriate gender roles. Call-centre work has been regarded with some suspicion in India, partly because most of it is night work. Shift work, especially night-shift work, sits very uneasily with cultural norms regarding appropriate gender roles. Moreover, it is an expectation – especially relevant in certain regions of the country – that women will resign from salaried work after marriage. Resignations that come with marriage skew the gender balance in ways that are uncommon in Western societies, and this skewing is recorded in our sample returns as a BPO gender imbalance that favours men. Corresponding to these social mores, most workers (83 per cent) in our Indian sample were single, never having been married.

When we look beyond the youthful workforce demographics, the analogy between ITeS/BPO and the fast-food industry quickly collapses. It is not possible to obtain work in an Indian BPO at the basic process-executive level (i.e., entry level) with anything less than a university degree. Science graduates were being scooped up by the IT sector until 2002 and the global contraction. Meanwhile, ITeS serves as a mecca for general-arts graduates and for some science graduates awaiting IT opportunities. Prior to the BPO revolution, employment opportunities for graduates were scarce, with an impoverished state sector serving as the main employment mop. The opening up of thousands of positions in ITeS has been presented as a major coup, both for potential job seekers and for Western businesses in search of young, educated, and ambitious workers.

Labour markets for IT/ITeS/BPO are now well developed and stretch beyond the major tier-one cities (Mumbai, Delhi, Bangalore, Chennai), to smaller, tier-two cities such as Pune. In our sample the most common form of recruitment was through employment agencies. Thirty-two per cent of the sample obtained their current jobs in this fashion. Given the mushrooming growth of BPO, it should come as no surprise that external employment agencies play an important role in meeting the industry's recruitment needs. Employment agencies are followed by responses to newspaper/Internet ads (26 per cent), voluntary job applications (18 per cent), and employment referrals from friends or family (also 18 per cent) as the most important means by which labour is secured. Such is the need for labour that many companies now pay their employees bonuses (up to 30 per cent of their salary) for successfully referring friends to the organizations they work for. Campus recruitment and job fairs are also becoming commonplace, as are open houses, where the parents of prospective recruits can come and see first-hand what the working conditions are like – a strategy that is employed to help dispel cultural stigmas attached to women working at night. The actual screening of job applicants typically takes one week, with candidates being pigeonholed into 'employable,' 'trainable,' or 'non-hireable' categories. According to one of the managerial informants, for every hundred applicants only six to eleven can typically be placed in the employable group.[9]

Recruitment challenges in BPO are exacerbated by attrition rates (Bhatnagar 2007). In three of the four companies included in the study, voluntary exits were running at between 90 and 120 per cent per annum according to company HRM managers. At the fourth company, *BPO3*, the company that had the smallest amount of voice-based call-centre work, a voluntary turnover rate of 35 per cent per annum was still reported. With the employee base these companies are starting with and the growth trajectory they are on, attrition of this order quickly escalates into a major issue. For example, at *BPO2* three hundred new CSRs need to be hired each month just to remain on an even keel. Fifty per cent of this company's 100 per cent annual turnover occurs in the first three months of employment. The manager of human resources at this company spoke of new inductees showing up on the first day for the complementary breakfast, but no longer being in the employ of the organization by the noon lunch break! At *BPO3* the HRM department employs twenty staff whose sole job is selection and hiring.[10] Even though the department is held responsible for attrition within the first three months of an individual's employment, the unit is too busy to conduct an audit of its effectiveness.

In our sample, just over one-third (38 per cent) of respondents indicated an intention to stay with the organization they were currently working for; one-quarter (26 per cent) were definitely planning on leaving; the remaining 36 per cent were undecided. This yields a potential attrition level of 62 per cent, though it does vary significantly across the four firms. The reason most frequently cited for remaining with the current employer is satisfaction with wages (27 per cent); yet *dis*satisfaction with wages is also the most important factor behind decisions to quit. Wage dissatisfaction is listed by 39 per cent of those who intend to leave as the most significant factor in their decision, which lends weight to managers' contentions that job hopping and employee poaching (through the offer of better terms and conditions) are rife in the industry. Generally, captive centres (i.e., the in-house operations of foreign MNCs located in India) are viewed as offering better working conditions, but it is also the case that foreign owners are showing greater interest in selling their subsidiaries off to indigenous Indian BPO companies.

To sum up, there is much about info-service employment in India that distinguishes it from similar labour processes found in the West. The Indian industry uses a different business model and is structured in a completely different way. Relative to their counterparts in Australia, Indian call-centre workers exhibit very different age, gender, and education demographics. And finally, Indian BPO is confronting recruitment and attrition challenges of a different order of magnitude than is common in Australia.

These contrasts – especially the first one, which calls attention to the distinctive business model of BPO – make it tricky to compare Indian with Australian centres. The ITeS/BPO classification includes CSRs and call-centre work, but as we have just seen, it also includes significant amounts of other activities. Call centres in Australia and in other Western countries are predominantly in-house operations, internal to the organizations they serve and dealing in specific products. In India *an industry has arisen whose main product is the delivery of labour processes* to other overseas industries. Thus, the Indian sample could include both CSRs and other non–voiced-based employees. The potential 'apples and oranges' problem of comparing unlike with unlike has been minimized by precautions that were taken in the design of the study as well as by the research focus of this book.

First, HRM departments at the four participating BPOs undertook administration of the survey with instructions as to who was eligible to complete the questionnaire. These included the same parameters as were used in Australia – that is, workers who have three months of experience and who spend the bulk of their time providing inbound and/or outbound voice service. Second, the survey responses allowed us to identify CSRs as opposed to those who were engaged in non–call-centre work. The latter responses could then be treated as missing data and discarded from the cross-national comparative analysis. Fortunately, three-quarters of the submitted responses were from voice-based workers. At three of the sites over 90 per cent of the responses originated from call-centre employees. In the organization that had the lowest proportion of voice-based work, *BPO3*, 57 per cent of the responses were external to call-centre operations, so these returns could not be used in the comparative analysis that follows. While we need to be aware of these limitations, it is the case that they simply reflect the different organizing logics that have driven the development of call-centre work in India and in the West. In other words, methodological limitations that accompany comparative cross-national research simply reflect different organizational structures that are essential to heed.

The following sections take up themes that were canvassed at the Australian contact centres in earlier chapters, beginning with the question of employee skills in voice-based BPO work.

7.3 Skills and the Global Division of Labour

Prima facie, it is reasonable to entertain quite different hypotheses relating to the skill requirements associated with working in a BPO operation. Existing research is scant and offers conflicting insights. Taylor and Bain (2004, 2005, 2006) present a number of reasons why we might expect outsourced BPO work to be less skilled than that which is customarily located in in-house call-centre operations. As we have seen, Indian centres are very large and have been designed to process high volumes of information for multiple clients. As with other types of mass-production transactional work (Leidner 1993; Gutek 1995), the aim is to keep the work as simple as possible. Thus Taylor and Bain (2005, 269) associate BPO with a 'low value, low skill' model of the labour process: 'an extreme form of the mass production model ... The types of calls handled tend to be highly standardized, simple in content, tightly scripted and of short duration.'

Other researchers concur with this picture. Budhwar and Varma and their colleagues (2006) contend that high rates of attrition are associated with isolated, deskilled, and monotonous work, while Ofreneo, Ng, and Marasigan-Pasumbal (2007) suggest that objective working conditions in the BPO sector may provide conditions that are ripe for trade-union organizing. The management of cultural and linguistic differences has been seen to further promote what Mirchandani (2009) refers to as 'scripted Taylorism,' a model of highly standardized and repetitive work flows where the aim is to control for the possibility of slip-ups by keeping the work as straightforward as possible.

Yet many of these analyses also recognize – be it implicitly or (sometimes) explicitly – the potential for additional skills to enter into the BPO labour process. Workers must constantly negotiate the cultural and linguistic dualities that info-service provision to overseas customers entails. Hypothetically, this could be construed as requiring higher degrees of emotional labour and hence skill, as location and identity masking (Mirchandani 2009) and accent neutralization add to the demands for emotional self-management and inner control (Taylor, D'Cruz, et al. 2009).

Batt, Doellgast, and Kwon (2006) remind us of still other factors that come into play in the business dynamics of outsourcing. Invoking principal/agency theory (Eisenhardt 1989), outsourcing could be predicted to favour greater work simplification as one means by which a principal can maintain some control over the quality of the work that is done by off-premise agencies on its behalf. In other words, it is easier to validate the fulfilment of service-level agreements when the labour process is more transparent. If this is so, outsourcing may promote simpler transactional dealings as well as a plethora of performance measurements, which are imposed on the labour process as assurance for agreed-on service-delivery standards. As Batt, Doellgast, and Kwon (2006) suggest, one would expect that outsourced work such as what is taken on by BPOs would be less skilled than info-service work that is retained and conducted in-house by an organization: 'Companies are more likely to retain in-house services that are complex, that involve customer transactions that are nuanced or uncertain, and that provide services to highly valued customers' (ibid., 340).

Yet once again, there are mitigating factors that must be accounted for in the offshore outsourcing equation. As has already been noted, workers in the Indian BPO sector are more highly educated than their counterparts in Western info-service centres (see also Batt, Doellgast, et al. 2005). On entering employment, 'freshers' are imbued with an ethic of professional responsibility (D'Cruz and Noronha 2006). Efforts are made to attach professional identities to the work and to those who do it, beginning with the nomenclature attached to each position (e.g., 'process executive'). Additional material impetus is given to the discourse of professional middle-class occupational positions by HRM strategies that emphasize individual, performance-related pay packages and training-needs assessments (Budhwar, Luthar, and Bhatnagar 2006). As some have suggested with the notion of KPO, workforces of this calibre are better positioned to take on more demanding work rather than less skilled work (D'Cruz and Noronha 2007). Others (Srivastava and Theodore 2006) have observed that outsourcing may start with simple work, but as familiarity and confidence are gained, higher-end work is likely to follow if suitable workforces can be found (also see Sennett 2006, 87; Shah and Bandi 2003). In a similar vein, Huws (2003) reflects on a much more complex division of labour between wealthy and less developed countries that can no longer by analysed by assuming that the most highly skilled work is retained in the former.

In survey research with American and Indian managers, Batt and her colleagues turn up mixed results that encapsulate some of the conflicting arguments. Indian centres have a higher skill base (as measured by the educational attainment of workers), but Indian workers have less autonomy and discretion than their American counterparts who are working in American-based in-house or onshore outsourced operations. Control and monitoring are much tighter in the Indian centres, and this contributes to the high attrition rates in these workplaces. High turnover, in turn, reinforces greater levels of process standardization and monitoring for compliance, and this completes a suboptimal cycle of hiring, short job tenure, and quitting. In terms of a control/empowerment dichotomy, BPO is characterized by the employment relations of the former rather than the latter. Outsourcing places an even greater burden on the trust aspects of the employment relationship, and many actors (i.e., principals) respond with demands for high levels of documented accountability so as to minimize the element of trust. As Batt and her colleagues (2005, 2006) observe, BPO uses well-educated workers in suboptimal ways. Workers respond by quitting and job hopping.

The results from our survey support some of these findings but qualify others (refer to Table 7.1). In line with arguments made earlier to the effect that BPO is a more Taylorized version of info-service work, Indian workers are indeed more likely than Australian CSRs to concur that their interactions are too closely scripted (39 per cent of Indian CSRs versus 32 per cent of Australian); they are also *less likely* to agree that they have lots of discretion in their dealings with customers (36.4 per

Table 7.1
Indian/Australian responses to labour-process questions

Statement	Country	Strongly disagree	Mostly disagree	Neutral	Mostly agree	Strongly agree
Lots of discretion interacting with customers***	India	15.3	21.1	35.8	20.9	6.8
	Australia	7.5	17.5	22.5	36.2	16.3
Lots of variety in my work***	India	10.4	17.3	23.8	33.3	15.2
	Australia	23.5	31.8	15.3	21.7	7.8
Conversations too closely scripted***	India	7.8	18.4	34.6	27.9	11.3
	Australia	11.7	32.5	23.5	19.7	12.7
Need more flexibility to meet customer expectations***	India	4.5	9.8	31.3	34.7	19.7
	Australia	6.8	26.6	33.8	24.3	8.5

		Yes	No			
Participation in offline projects**	India	46.9	53.1			
	Australia	39.8	60.2			

		Several times a day	A few times a week	Seldom/ never		
Frequency of confronting difficult inquiries ***	India	11.3	47.3	41.3		
	Australia	24.0	44.7	31.2		

**p ≤ .01
***p ≤ .001

cent disagree/strongly disagree compared to 25 per cent of Australian CSRs). Following on from these results, BPO workers are also considerably more likely to agree that they need greater flexibility than they currently have in order to meet the expectations of their publics (54 versus 33 per cent of the Australian sample). Workers in BPO report dealing with difficult or challenging queries less than half as frequently as their Australian colleagues (11.3 per cent versus 24 per cent) and are more likely to consult with a team leader or trainer as opposed to a co-worker or Website (49.3 versus 32.4 per cent) when confronted with such a situation (not shown in Table 7.1). As indicated in the table, though the findings are robust (i.e., statistically significant), in some instances (e.g., work discretion and closeness of scripting) the differences between the BPO workers and Australian CSRs are not huge.

Offsetting these trends, however, Indian workers are also significantly more likely to agree that their work has lots of variety attached to it (49 versus 30 per cent). BPO workers also indicate that they are more likely than their Australian counterparts to be assigned to special offline projects (47 versus 40 per cent). Meanwhile, a higher proportion of Indian workers report using a greater number of software programs. On average, Indian employees utilize five software packages, as do their Australian opposites, but the modal figure at the Indian centres is four, while at the Australian centres it is only one. These latter results are best understood in the context of BPO, where, given the project-like nature of the work and the number of principals being served, there is greater likelihood of variety and change.

A mixed picture is also obtained if the knowledge content of the work performed is examined in greater detail. As to be expected, Indian CSRs are more likely to require a second language and to be familiar with economic variables. Australian workers more frequently require familiarity with government legislation as well as geographic/ locational knowledge. These demands are likely related to the industry make-up of our samples, with public-sector and transportation companies prominent among the Australian case studies and financial clients important in the case of BPO activities. Australian employees are more likely to use some form of mathematics in their work (83 versus 40 per cent of respondents), but of the workers that are required to use calculations, Indian agents are more likely to use more advanced operands (defined as more than simple, single-step arithmetical computations) than the Australian cohort.

Other evidence pertaining to work demands and skill is provided through an examination of training and familiarization patterns. On average the Indian respondents received approximately one week of additional training (India = 5.05 weeks; Australia = 4.28 weeks). This may be accounted for by the linguistic and cultural elements of training, which would be far more important in the Indian than in the Australian context. On the other hand, familiarization periods in India, defined as the length of time required for the agent to feel comfortable and proficient in her job, are almost half the Australian average (5.52 versus 9.92 weeks). Without further statistical analysis (see below), it is difficult to say whether such differences are attributable to work in

India being simpler, or whether workers who bring greater levels of human capital to the work find it easier to master.[11]

By controlling for the educational attainment of the respondents, it is possible to focus more specifically on the skill requirements of the work rather than on the human capital that workers bring to it. For practical purposes this involves comparing the responses of university-educated workers in the two countries. If we do this, it is still the case that Indian workers perceive themselves as having less discretion in their work (36.5 versus 30 per cent, p = .000), which, though still statistically significant, is half the differential exhibited by the whole sample. The implication here is that part of the previous results is the product of educational differences between the samples rather than differences in the skill demands of the work. More highly educated Indian workers may simply have higher expectations of job requirements and demands. Meanwhile, controlling for educational level makes little difference to previous results concerning the tightness of scripting (39 per cent of Indians versus 30 per cent of Australians dissatisfied), the perceived need for greater flexibility (54 per cent of Indians versus 29 per cent of Australians indicating a need for more flexibility in how they do their work), and encounters with difficult customer queries (11 per cent of Indian calls versus 29 per cent of Australian).[12] It is also still the case that familiarization times continue to average about twice as long in the Australian work settings for the subsample of university-educated employees.

By the same token, though, comparing workers with similar levels of educational attainment in the two countries makes little difference to the previous results pertaining to levels of job variety or software utilization in the job. If anything, differences in perceived job variety are somewhat enhanced, with 48 per cent of the Indian CSRs and 26.5 per cent of the university-educated Australians agreeing or strongly agreeing that their work exhibits a lot of variety. Greater numbers of Indian employees continue to report using more software programs than is the case at the Australian centres, while Indian workers continue to be seconded to special offline projects in greater numbers than their Australian colleagues (47.5 versus 43.5 per cent), though this represents a closing of the gap and is no longer statistically significant.

Summarizing the findings this far, we can say that though the info-service workforces in India and Australia are clearly different in terms of age, education, and gender composition, these factors do not account for all of the variation in the responses to questions pertaining to work skills. Not only are the job incumbents demographically different, but so also are the jobs. This point follows not so much from different labour processes, but rather from different business models and the implications of this for the organization of work. In the case of BPO, work is broader owing to the number of client partners, new contracts, and products that are constantly being taken on board. The complexity of this business model in turn gives rise to countermanding pressures, including further attempts to standardize, simplify, and document the work to the extent this is possible. We see both trends at work in these results. These data suggest the dual movement in work that previous chapters alluded to, where the greater inherent complexity of info-service work and the potential for enhanced worker autonomy are met head on by the realities of contemporary managerialism and the penchant for continuous documentation of worker activity and time. In Indian BPOs these contradictions appear to be notched up even further.

A more comprehensive overview of results dealing with skill factors may be obtained by employing the same nine-item index of skill that was used in chapter 4. Organizational rankings, which now include the four Indian case studies as well as the original twenty Australian entries, are profiled in Table 7.2. The addition of the Indian companies marginally *increases* the overall average skill level that is recorded. Just as important, the BPOs all fall within the upper 50 per cent of the table. BPOs are all present within the ten organizations that record the highest skill evaluations, and each exhibits a mean score that is higher than the overall average. Incidentally, the two highest-ranked BPOs conduct the highest proportion of call-centre work among the four Indian providers, with *BPO2* being 90 per cent phone-based employment and *BPO4* 60 per cent voice-based. Employing a one-way analysis-of-variance procedure confirms that the chief differences in Table 7.2 exist between the top two Indian companies (*BPO2* and *BPO4*) as well as *Delivery Services* and *Urban Space* on the one hand, and the Australian centres that have fewer skills attached to them on the other (e.g., *Telebet* and *Licensing*). Notably, the Indian centres do not differ significantly from one another on this measure of skill.

The work at the four BPO firms examined here is not evaluated as any less skilled than the jobs that have been designed in Western contact centres, but it does exhibit different structural features that help explain these results. For starters, each of the BPOs included in this study provided inbound, outbound, and blended services to a mix of overseas clients. *BPO2*, for example, had twenty such business users

Table 7.2
Skill rankings of participating Indian and Australian call centres (mean score on a scale from 9 to 45)

Skill level	Organization	Mean score on Skill Index	Significantly different (.05) from N other Organizations*
High skill			
33+	No entries		
Semiskilled			
32	No entries		
31	Delivery Services	31.7	4
	BPO2	31.6	10
	Gov't Pensions	31.0	–
30	Urban Space	30.8	5
	Bank 1	30.1	1
	Statewide	30.0	–
29	BPO4	29.9	4
	BPO1	29.5	2
	Telco2	29.3	3
28	BPO3	28.9	2
	Insurer2	28.3	1
	Health Authority	28.0	–
27	Social Services	27.9	2
	Health Premium	27.9	2
	Collections	27.9	–
	Bank2	27.8	2
	Telco1	27.6	2
	Bus Company	27.1	2
26	Advisory Services	26.7	–
25	Insurer1	25.9	2
	Airline	25.8	5
24	Tender	24.7	4
23	Licensing	23.7	7
	Telebet	23.1	14
22			
21			
Low skill			
9–20	No entries		
Average		28.3	

*Tukey's HSD

and was hoping to grow this by another four or five new contracts per year.[13] Also significant is the variety in foreign business customers, which needs to be taken into account. *BPO1*, for example, had contracts with firms ranging from an automotive company to a telco as was well as with its own IT parent company.[14] At each site different teams were assigned to different processes/clients, each with its own training program and metrics; however, depending on call volumes and complexity, workers might be assigned to two, three, or even four clients/processes, as we found at *BPO1*. Managers at this site remained certain that the work for which they had tendered was becoming more complex as the principals they worked with became more familiar with and confident in their workforce's capabilities. At other sites, such as *BPO4*, team members undertook a range of tasks – for example, billing services, customer retention work, and Internet connectivity. This added to the variety of work and increased the possibility of engaging in off-phone work (noted previously).

That the Indian CSRs independently rate their work in the same skill bands as the Australian respondents – albeit perhaps for different reasons – should not blind us to the overall nature of the labour process in the outsourcing of info-service work. As we saw in chapter 4, call-centre employment is the information economy's version of semiskilled work, and this holds equally well for the outsourcing encountered in the Indian case studies. This point is significant for two reasons. First, it indicates that labour processes are being truly globalized, with jobs of similar skill content being conducted at different nodal points across the world economy. But – and this is our second point – this new social division of labour, based as it is on the logic of competitive advantage, by no means suggests a flattening out or homogenization of socio-economic conditions and opportunities across the global economy, as has been argued by some (Das 2002; Friedman 2006; Kamdar 2007; Sheshabalaya 2005).

The work in India is both similar to and different from that which is conducted in Australia. The technologies of work are the same, with work teams connected to automated call-distribution systems and desktop computers. The social relations of work, however, differ in important ways. In India, info-service work is conducted as a separate industry that is connected to and serves the global economy in an immediate fashion. BPO has been inserted into a social context that differs significantly from that which prevails in Australia; this in turn affects how the work is socially constructed along gender and age lines. In

India a skilled workforce has been recruited to undertake semiskilled work. In the West, university students may work their way through school as call-centre temps (Arzbacher, Holtgrewe, and Kerst 2002; Bittner et al. 2002); in India, *university graduates* assume *permanent positions* in similar work environments. This creates special problems, such as high levels of attrition – levels that pose a formidable challenge to this new industry. As we will see in the next section, national context also has a bearing on work norms.

7.4 Work Intensity

Existing research on Indian call centres has not directly addressed the issue of work norms, focusing instead on questions of managerial control, job skill, and HRM policy. However, from these discussions it is possible to infer some general themes. For example, the adoption of Taylorized mass-production approaches that feature high levels of monitoring would seemingly correspond with comparatively intensive work regimes, though reference is more frequently made to the boring and monotonous aspects of routinized work flows (Budhwar, Varma, et al. 2006; Taylor and Bain 2006). One might also expect the dynamics of outsourcing to favour an intensification of work processes, given the expenses incurred by the presence of 'middlemen' (i.e., the BPO firms) and the associated transaction costs, which have to be recouped from somewhere. Large business clients constantly pressure contracting agencies to lower their costs, and these demands in turn are forced back onto the labour forces that actually do the work. Where there is competition for qualified labour, as there currently is in the ITeS/BPO labour market, wage reductions are not feasible. In their place, demands for greater work effort may be the only way of avoiding a profit squeeze that is constituted by declining revenues (i.e., expectations of falling costs on the part of the principal) and escalating wage bills (Thite and Russell 2007).

By some objective indicators, work in Indian BPOs is more arduous than in the Australian centres studied. Though CSRs in the two samples take almost identical numbers of calls per hour (an average of 13.7 across the Australian centres and 13.8 across the Indian locations), the Indian workers do so for longer periods of time. The normal working *night* in India is *nine hours*, which includes an hour of breaks (thirty minutes for lunch and two fifteen-minute breaks), or more than an hour longer than the regulated norm in Australia. While all four of the Indian centres in the study are 24/7 operations, only seven out of the twenty Australian sites featured night work. Moreover, in India the busiest period, when the greatest number of staff are rostered, falls between 5 p.m. and 7 a.m. local time. This coincides with the business day in America. Thus the 'graveyard shift,' which is customarily the least busy and often the least supervised roster in Western industry, is, in India, the period of greatest activity and associated stress. Night work is well and truly synonymous with BPO, even though it violates social mores with respect to women and work.

The working-time story in Indian BPO has other dimensions that generally do not figure into working conditions in Western call centres. Inadequate urban infrastructure (paved multilane roads and sufficient public transit) means that getting to and from work is a major logistical challenge in its own right. This can be exacerbated by the location of the technology parks that house many of India's call centres. For major companies, operations are often located in greenfield sites on the fringes of urban areas. Managing a call centre in India also means assuming responsibility for the logistics of getting the workforce to and from work. Larger companies subcontract this to specialized firms that own and operate large fleets of 'people movers.' In *BPO2*, for example, a fleet of two hundred vehicles logs an average of 250 kilometres per vehicle per day in ferrying its workforce to and from designated pick-up and drop-off points around the city of six million inhabitants.[15] This urban dynamic adds more hours to the working day, so that for many non-managerial staff, once commuting time is factored in, the working night stretches to eleven to thirteen hours.[16] The shortcomings of urban infrastructure also effectively remove one possible remedy to the pattern of long working hours – namely, voluntary part-time employment. The option of part-time work does not currently exist in India's BPO sector. In the companies considered here, a stunning 98.2 per cent of the respondents indicated that they were full-time employees, whereas among the Australian sample almost 40 per cent worked on a part-time basis. The realities of contemporary urban India severely restrict the option of voluntary part-time work, and this contributes to the particular gender profile of BPO that has already been discussed.

In chapter 4 a workload manageability/intensity index was introduced. In Table 7.3, the BPOs are entered into the calculations of work intensity in order to compare experiences among info-service workers in the two countries. The mean ranks for the Australian organizations differ from chapter 4 as the total number of responses is different with

Table 7.3
Work intensity at Indian and Australian call centres*

Workload management	Organization	Mean rank
High workload manageability (low intensity)		
Above 800	*Statewide*	847.31
	Gov't Pensions	801.63
	Bus Company	800.77
701 to 800	*Advisory Services*	771.08
	Collections	748.55
Medium workload manageability		
651 to 700	*Urban Space*	698.73
	Tender	674.42
	BPO2	656.14
	Telebet	655.88
	Telco2	652.02
601 to 650	*Licensing*	635.33
	Insurer2	634.12
	Bank1	631.96
	Bank2	602.63
551 to 600	BPO1	593.33
	Telco1	591.56
501 to 550	BPO3	542.49
	Airline	531.36
Low workload manageability (high intensity)		
451 to 500	BPO4	492.84
	Delivery Services	453.21
401 to 450	*Insurer1*	419.36
	Health Authority	400.67
Below 400	*Social Services*	388.95
	Health Premium	279.90

*Kruskal-Wallis test
Chi-square = 126.31, df = 23, p = .000

the addition of the Indian data, but the rank order of the Australian centres remains the same as previously. Significantly, the largest Indian firm in the study, *BPO4*, records one of the highest levels of work intensity; two others – *BPO1* and *BPO3* – also fall towards the lower end of presenting their workforces with manageable workloads. Overall, the workers at three of the Indian BPOs rate their workloads towards the lower end of being manageable.

One symptom of unmanageable workloads is job-related stress. Analysing the phenomenon of job stress more closely may provide additional clues as to why workloads in BPOs are experienced as comparatively intense. One-third of the Australian sample and just over one-third of the Indian sample (37.5 per cent) stated that work-induced stress was not a problem. While a higher proportion of Australian workers said they suffered from stress (60 per cent as opposed to 45 per cent of Indian CSRs), interesting differences emerged regarding which aspects of the work were related to stress. For the Indian cohort, meeting performance targets/kpi's was the most important stressor, followed by working unsociable hours (nights); call volumes were the third most frequently mentioned source of stress. Performance targets were seized upon by almost 30 per cent of those who reported stress; 21 per cent reported that night work was the greatest source of job stress. For the Australian workers, customer abuse featured as the most important factor associated with work-related stress (31 per cent of those who reported stress, compared to only 4 per cent of the Indian agents), followed by the repetitive nature of the work (21 per cent compared to 13 per cent for the BPO workers), and, finally, performance targets (19 per cent of stressed Australian workers and 29 per cent of Indians who reported stress).

These findings contain some surprises, as well as trends that lend support to the argument so far. Why a smaller proportion of Indian workers (45 per cent compared to 60 per cent) reported job stress is a matter for conjecture. Age and experience may have something to do with it. Young workers, who have little tenure as info-service employees, may still be experiencing the first flush of success in the labour market. Further examination reveals that age and job tenure are both positively, albeit modestly, associated with experiencing job stress (r = .104** and .127** respectively).[17] Younger workers, who have been in their jobs for shorter periods of time (such as tends to be the norm in the Indian companies), would experience less stress, all else being equal. The comparatively high ratio of Indian CSRs who are unsure whether they are experiencing stress (18 per cent of the Indian sample versus 7 per cent of the Australian) is also noteworthy. If the 'uncertain' category is aggregated with the 'yes' group, the differences between workers in the two countries become minimal.

The significance of kpi pressure in India and repetitive work stress in Australia is in line with what has been suggested earlier – that BPO offers greater opportunities for job variety, but also tighter control than is found in the Australian centres. For instance, monitoring in BPO call-centre work is omnipresent, enabled by the same means of production that agents use to perform their work. Instead of being periodic, the monitoring of work is constant in the outsourcing environment; and as we have seen, monitoring is given added impetus by the need to demonstrate conformance to service-level agreements (Batt, Doellgast, and Kwon 2006; Taylor and Bain 2005). Managers at the Indian companies, for example, indicated that it is usual to record all calls and that reviews of call performance are more likely to occur on a weekly rather than on a monthly basis, as is more common in the Australian centres. The Indian centres are also likely to make use of the latest monitoring technologies, such as 'screen capture' systems that allow managers to view the navigational processes agents use when responding to customers.

The greater influence of kpi's on Indian workers is also foretold when we examine how agents approach the performance targets that are part of call-centre work. While 32 per cent of the Australian sample indicated that their performance statistics are 'very important' to them, more than twice as many (71.6 per cent) Indian CSRs considered their personal performance to be 'very important' ($\Phi = .392^{***}$). The greater importance attached to personal work data may be conducive to stress, but this is by no means the only possible outcome. Work intensity is also associated with stress ($r = .389^{***}$), and as we have seen, three of the Indian centres are located in the upper ranges of work intensity.

That a greater proportion of Australian workers viewed customer abuse as a problem is also unexpected. Mirchandani (2009) contends that cross-national BPO work gives rise to a scrambling of global class boundaries. In globalized info-service work, highly educated middle-class Indians serve overseas publics that may include less educated and informed segments. Falling back on their education and skill, Indian CSRs may rationalize away the abusive behaviour of overseas customers simply as that of people who 'don't know any better.' This would have parallels where educated service workers in the West serve publics with fewer resources.

Overall, a variety of factors operating in diverse directions have an effect on job stress. Working conditions in BPOs, including insistence on tighter adherence to process protocols, more frequent monitoring, and work that is experienced as intensive, are likely to induce job-related stress. Additionally, the greater levels of individuation in the employment relationship at Indian firms, as signified by higher proportions attaching importance to both performance-related pay and personal job statistics, are more likely to provoke stress. On the other hand, youthful workers who have little job tenure but considerable levels of educational attainment may respond to such conditions in a variety of ways. Stress and consequent quitting constitute one outcome. Others may find the environment, at least in the beginning, challenging and hopeful. Often it is HRM's task to reconcile the contradictory features of the call centre, and to these issues we now turn.

7.5 HRM and Identity in BPO

HRM has a special significance in Indian BPOs. To HRM falls the task of 'moulding' customer service workers from the youthful, well educated, but largely inexperienced labour force that has presented itself to the burgeoning industry. Many workers enter BPOs directly from higher education. Many of the new recruits have distinctly limited experience in service work with foreign clients and products. This lends special importance to the training function in BPOs (Taylor and Bain 2004, 2006). In India it is more common to refer to human resource development (HRD) than to HRM, which testifies to the importance attached to this aspect of HR (Saini and Budhwar 2004). At Indian call centres, operations and process training, as well as language and cultural-awareness programs, feature heavily in HRD. This emphasis relates directly to the strategy of the industry and its political backers. Underresourced in terms of national infrastructure and physical capital, India pitches its competitive advantage to the world in terms of its human capital – that is, its workforce is skilled as well as willing to undertake any job that is a candidate for outsourcing. This emphasis on workforce quality lends HRD a predominant role in the marketing and operating practices of BPOs.

Other factors besides contribute to the prominent role of HRM in BPOs. As previously noted, outsourcing entails a loss of control over how work is done on the part of principals, which typically in this case are located thousands of kilometres away. To compensate for such vast distances, managers exhibit a heightened awareness of risk management and enact correspondingly tighter control systems. The BPO firms' penchant for accreditation is all about assuring foreign clients of their competence. It is no coincidence that Indian-based call centres strongly emphasize that they have gained international quality certifications and that they display those endorsements prominently (Thite and Russell 2007). Such endorsements are essential to winning legitimation in international business circles, and HRD plays a major part in this.

Finally, it should not be forgotten that HRM is the only (theoretical) outlet for employee representational 'voice' in the industry. For a variety of reasons (ibid.), BPOs remain almost entirely free of unionization. Opinions on the likelihood of unionization in this sector differ (Noronha and D'Cruz 2006; Taylor and Bain 2006; Taylor et al 2009; chapter 8 of this book). To this point HRM is the only outlet for employees to express their concerns; even then, HRM's ability to discharge this responsibility has been strongly questioned, given its unitarist underpinnings. Of course, as Hirschman (1970) pointed out some time ago, the other option to employee voice as well as organizational loyalty is exit, and as we have seen, this alternative is taken up in droves by BPO workforces. High levels of employee attrition then give rise to the other main order of business for HRM in BPOs – namely, recruitment and selection. Large amounts of time are poured into this activity by the HRM departments of BPOs – a consequence of to the 'burn and churn' dynamic that has come to characterize the industry (Budhwar, Varma, et al. 2006; Budhwar, Luthar, and Bhatnagar 2006; Budhwar, Malhotra, and Singh 2009). To a considerable extent the magnitude of the recruitment and selection challenge usurps resources that could be dedicated to training and development, and this in turn reinforces the attrition problem. Be that as it may, shaping workers and then replacing them when they leave are the core tasks of HRM in Indian BPOs.

To say the least, BPO presents a highly paradoxical employment-relations dynamic. The absence of competing identity anchors such as trade-union representation in the workplace gives large firms a comparatively free hand in their efforts to create cultures of dedication and commitment. As D'Cruz and Noronha (2006) point out, BPO providers are selling professionalism to their foreign clients, and they attempt to inculcate this ethic in their employees from the moment they are first interviewed. Having entered the industry with degree qualifications and undergone a rigorous culling process, workers are defined as skilled professionals – as 'executives' working for valued employers. They are expected to behave accordingly. This means adopting and living the organization's culture. In organizations with some longevity, HRM creates a historical narrative that inserts the individual into an organizational history (Bolman and Deal 2003). This is less feasible in BPOs because they are so new. In BPOs, HRM is not so much the guardian of the organizational culture; it *is* the culture, part of the professional image the industry tries to exude.

More concretely, enculturation entails imbibing the ethic of customer service, displaying a willingness to serve and all that goes with it, which includes speaking in a foreign voice, using a pseudonym, and shrugging off racist remarks from overseas customers. The aim, of course, is to forge a unique bond between individual and organization, one that will obviate the need for other parties/interlocutors. To the question 'Who are you?' the ideal response would be 'an employee of the "BPO Corporation."' This is what is meant by an identity anchor: doing what I do is a source of pride, part of who I am, and an integral element of the self. As Castells (1997) points out, identity extends beyond role occupancy: one doesn't have to 'play' a role if one is living an identity that provides meaning to one's actions in life. Ideally at least, identification with the organization translates into commitment to it and into performance on its behalf.

It is possible to entertain conflicting hypotheses when it comes to considering organizational identity in Indian call centres. In some ways, India takes on the appearance of a massive greenfield site – or more accurately, a series of greenfield sites contiguous with the tier-one and tier-two cities. BPOs have fashioned a labour market of their own making within these enclaves. Young and well educated but relatively inexperienced workers provide the human resources for this development. Before the advent of BPOs this stratum of society had comparatively sparse employment options. The advent of BPOs has been synonymous with new employment opportunities and with expectations that may fuel a sense of identification with these new developments. Large multinational and domestic operations have been branded as 'hip' entities, as part of a new India that is capable of taking on the world (Das 2002; Sheshabalaya 2005).

The 'hype and buzz' around the BPO sector is palpable. Seldom does a day go by without stories about BPOs (usually positive), and about new developments in the sector, appearing in the national press. A familiar refrain acknowledges that while India missed out on the benefits of the Industrial Revolution, the country is now getting a second opportunity in the form of the Information Revolution: this time, it is implied, it will be a different story. The outsourcing phenomenon has generated a sense of excitement, as indicated by a quick perusal of the industry association's, Nasscom's, publications. These factors and the fact that the industry plays on the resulting excitement may well enhance identification with the whole experience. The cultural trappings, including the 'spin' that is used to convey an appropriate meaning for BPO, are all part of the effort to win employee allegiance.

But ... another image of BPO emerges when one studies the tired faces making the trek homewards in the morning rush hour after a nine-hour night shift. It should not be forgotten that part of the identification with the BPO mission involves the partial denial of other aspects of the self, beginning with one's name (Mirchandani 2009). On this point it could be argued that BPOs represent a radical extension of corporate cultural initiatives. Employees do not work on the self, or try to incorporate the self into the organization's goals and objectives; indeed, BPOs require an *abandonment* of the self for the purpose of meeting alien expectations. Thus, unlike CSRs in the West, who are often urged to 'be themselves' in their interactions with the public, Indian workers are required to 'be someone else' – that is, to embrace an ideal that conforms to what management thinks 'the other' expects. Just how workers respond to these sorts of demands is a fascinating question. Conceivably, such requirements could be met with humour or confronted as part of a truly novel employment experience. Alternatively, such expectations could be seen as further emphasizing the servitude dimension of info-service work. Potentially, this could be a source of cynicism and resentment among BPO workers, or (as others have suggested) the basis for profound and disturbing levels of social alienation (Pradhan and Abraham 2009).[18]

To delve into these points further, the analysis in the previous chapter that examines levels of organizational identity is repeated here, this time including the four BPO case studies along with the twenty Australian worksites. Mean ranks for levels of identification with the employer, along with the Kruskal-Wallis test of variance, are displayed in Table 7.4. The results are strikingly unambiguous.

In terms of employee identification with the employing organization, the Indian BPOs take the three highest positions and four of the top five. Using our measure of organizational identification, there can be little doubt that identification with the employer is stronger in the Indian cases than, with one exception (*Statewide*), in the Australian ones. On individual items, Indian respondents are more likely to express agreement with the mission and values of the employer, while twice as many Indian employees hold that working for their current employer provides them with an important sense of self (64.7 versus 32.5 per cent). The Indian workers also express greater trust in the employing organization (50 versus 35 per cent agree that the employer recognizes and rewards employee loyalty) and are less likely to perceive an 'us'/'them' climate (37.2 versus 50.5 per cent) in the workplace. Consequently, In-

Table 7.4
Organizational identity at Indian and Australian call centres*

	Organization	Mean rank
High organizational identity	BPO2	1138.95
	BPO4	1071.57
	BPO3	1025.33
	Statewide	1014.50
	BPO1	984.88
	Advisory Services	980.70
	Tender	966.43
	Delivery Services	925.57
	Government Pensions	917.29
	Urban Space	901.94
Medium organizational identity	Bank1	894.57
	Insurer2	879.50
	Health Authority	867.76
	Bank2	835.82
	Telco2	812.21
	Airline	747.89
	Collections	740.82
	Social Services	700.51
	Bus Company	679.42
Low organizational identity	Insurer1	644.89
	Health Premium	642.80
	Telco1	591.02
	Licensing	520.89
	Telebet	421.34

*Kruskal Wallis test
Chi-square = 287.18, df = 23, p = .000

dian workers are more likely to agree that they look forward to going to work (62.6 versus 45 per cent).[19]

To a degree, these sentiments translate into behavioural intentions of the sort that signify organizational commitment. For example, while 51 per cent of the Australian cohort said that they did not mind staying late to finish up work, 63 per cent of the Indian sample concurred with this statement. In about equal proportions (53 per cent of the Australian CSRs, 51 per cent of the Indian), workers indicated a willingness to work extra hours *at ordinary rates of remuneration* in order to help the organization out; this, even though Indian workers toil at night and generally for an hour-and-a-half longer than their full-time Australian counterparts.[20] Finally, Australian workers were more likely to concur that they would attempt to avoid responding to a call just before break or end of shift periods than Indian CSRs (43 versus 30 per cent). Identity with the employing organization tends to be undeniably stronger among the Indian firms. Whether such goodwill is enough to compensate for other aspects of outsourced info-service work is another matter that beckons our attention.

7.6 The Contradictions of BPO

The results of the last section on the organizational identity of BPO workers beg one very large question: If Indian BPO workers express comparatively high levels of organizational identity, why is voluntary attrition such a large issue for the industry? In the literature on commitment, intention to stay with the employing organization is built into the very definition of the concept (Meyer and Allen 1991, 1997).[21] While this book has not explicitly examined the issue of commitment, preferring instead to focus on the problem of identity, it is still the case that there seems to be an inconsistency between the considerable levels of organizational identity exhibited by employees in BPOs and reported rates of staff turnover. Put simply, identification with the employer no longer seems to automatically translate into intentions to stay with the company. To investigate the paradox of *short-term commitment* further, measures that have been developed in previous chapters of this book can be brought back into the analysis.

As mentioned in Section 7.2, turnover rates at the four sites are considerable and echo what has now been recognized as a major challenge to the future of the ITeS outsourcing industry (Government of India 2003; KPMG 2004; Budhwar et al. 2009). The workforce survey used in this research contains one question that asks workers about their intentions to remain with their current employer and whether they plan to leave during the next three years. From this question a dummy variable that divides the respondents into those who definitely intend on staying and others can be constructed, with the object of identifying those factors that have a bearing on retention. Chapters 4 and 6 operationalized theoretical constructs that can be hypothesized as affecting organizational identity, such as satisfaction with the training and development regime offered by the employer, opportunities to use and develop skills, and satisfaction with various dimensions of HRM such as the conduct of monitoring, employer-led cultural initiatives, remuneration schemes, and the perceived trustworthiness of the employer.

This analysis was guided by the case that a number of authors (Huselid 1995; Macduffie 1995; Pfeffer 1998; Wood 1999) have made about so-called high-performance work systems (HPWSs). The HPWS concept designates bundles of complementary practices that are thought to lead to superior organizational performance, in part through better work experiences and in part through reductions in quit rates (Appelbaum et al. 2000; Batt 2000, 2002).

For present purposes, it is only necessary to examine the effects of these factors on intentions to remain with one's current employer. This is done in Table 7.5, which presents the results of a logistic regression analysis, taking the indicators that have previously been employed in the study of info-service labour processes and HRM and examining their relationship with workers' intentions to remain in their current BPO job.[22] All of the indexes, except for the one that measures trust and security, were found to be reliable for the Indian subsample, so they are taken over from the previous chapters. In the Indian sample it has, however, been necessary to disaggregate the elements of job security from the issue of trusting the employer. To measure job security, a single question from the survey can be employed: 'The likelihood of layoff or retrenchment at this call centre is high' (reverse coded). Trust is now measured by two items from the original scale: 'This organization recognizes and rewards employee loyalty'; and 'Employees can trust this organization to do what's right by them.'

Owing to the importance of external labour markets and the demand for 'employable' labour in the current BPO scene, another question that measures workers' perceptions of opportunities outside their current employment is included in the analysis. The overall state of the labour market that workers confront will likely have an effect on organizational retention. If workers face an advantageous labour market, quitting may escalate as individuals search for better terms and conditions. If the labour market is 'tight,' such job hopping becomes more difficult. As we have seen, given the steep trajectory of ITeS/BPO growth in India, a sellers' market characterizes the current labour scene. The issue here is the extent to which the opportunities presented by a buoyant labour market are moderated by HRM practices as well as by labour processes that are internal to organizations. To gage this, the following question is used in the analysis: 'If I were to lose my job here, it would be relatively easy for me to get as good a job at another call centre straight away.' This item is intended to measure CSRs' perceptions of the (un)favourableness of the local labour market in their occupational

Table 7.5
Logistic regression analysis of determinants of employee retention in Indian case studies

Variable	B	S.E.	Sig	Exp(B)
Work intensity	.019	.031	.547	1.019
Skill requirement	.189	.059	.001	1.208
Mgt Culture	−.022	.060	.707	.978
Work teams	−.040	.116	.728	.961
Trust	.046	.136	.738	1.047
Training	.039	.045	.378	1.040
Monitoring	−.327	.173	.059	.721
Job security	.088	.200	.659	1.09
Labour market	−.466	.209	.026	.628
Salary bonuses	.529	.276	.055	1.697
Employment seniority	−.064	.028	.024	.938

Nagelkerke R^2 = .312, p = .000

field and the effects of those perceptions on intentions to remain with the current employer.

Employers may alter remuneration schedules in a bid to retain labour. Variable pay related to individual performance is often included in HPWS practices and is common in BPOs. To gauge the importance of this element, the analysis also contains the following question: 'Any performance bonuses that I receive at this call centre are very important to me.' Presumably, where contingent pay is more important – that is, where workers have been more successful in accessing such income – intentions to leave the employment relationship will be diminished.

Finally, it is important to bear in mind that the state of the labour market may affect the seniority that workers have in their current positions. For one thing, the question of seniority introduces a temporal dimension to the analysis. Specifically, we want to know whether the effects of other factors are moderated when workers have spent more (or less) time in their current positions. For this reason, the number of months that employees have worked in their current positions is also considered in the analysis that follows.

From Table 7.5 it is apparent that two factors significantly enhance the likelihood that workers will remain with their present employer and that two other factors significantly diminish the same likelihood. These items are highlighted in Table 7.5. The longer a worker has been in his or her present position, the less likely that person is to remain, though the effect (ExpB) is not huge. More important in this regard are perceptions of external labour-market opportunities. If workers judge these to be good – and at the time of the study they were very good indeed – the odds of holding pat are reduced by about 37 per cent. The effects of these factors can, however, be undone at least theoretically by the internal policies that firms adopt. As suggested in Table 7.5, satisfaction with the skill requirements of the work considerably enhances the likelihood of employee retention (see also Bhatnagar 2007). That and incentivized remuneration systems that workers value are especially important in the bid to hold on to staff.

Incentivized salary schemes are widely practised across the BPO sector and, on average, are more important for the Indian respondents in the survey than for the Australian sample. Attaching importance to salary bonuses has the greatest positive effect on employee retention, according to these results. However, the ability of BPO firms to act on this point is another matter altogether. Given that the logic of outsourcing is premised on labour-cost savings, there are limits to the extent to which BPO companies can compete for labour on the basis of bonus payments. Meanwhile, satisfaction with the opportunities to use one's education and to take on more challenging work increases the probability of worker retention by about 20 per cent. However, as we have seen, workers from across the sample consider info-service work to be semiskilled in nature, and BPO employees on average rate their jobs as only slightly more skilled than do Australian CSRs. Generally, workers in the Indian sample do not view the work as highly skilled despite the recent publicity given to KPO. As long as highly educated workers remain underemployed – as we are suggesting they are – retention is likely to remain a major problem for corporate outsourcers in India, whatever HRM initiatives are put in place. Once again, the importance of the labour process that has been constructed around info-service work is highlighted in the study of employee retention in India's outsourcing sector.

7.7 Conclusions

The foregoing analysis has confirmed some of our conceptions of BPO outsourcing work while occasioning a rethink of others. Within the former category, the case-study results have corroborated arguments that point to both intensive work processes *and* considerable levels of employee identification with the organizations that offer them a place in this new export economy. Outsourcing is generally thought to ratchet up work effort. Currying favour with overseas principals, the project-like nature of much of the work, hustling for new business, and the importance of reputation and word of mouth in winning contracts all lead to a fast-paced, pressurized work environment. At the same time, though, this is packaged as a new opportunity that is not to be missed by employees with a taste for enterprise and sacrifice. Also important in this regard has been the absence of alternative work-based cultures that could compete with the BPO firms as a source of interpretative frameworks for lending meaning to work. Trade unions are almost completely absent from the BPO environment, while informal work collectives have had little time or space in which to congeal. The absence of alternative workplace identity anchors follows from both the newness of BPO industry, where virtually every site is a greenfield operation, and from the highly cloistered spaces (e.g., walled technology parks) in which such work is carried out.

Our results also point to the true globalization of a labour process. By this we mean that similar types of work are being carried out in very different locations – in this case, Australia and India. While BPO does create some variation in the ways that workers are assigned to work flows, major skill differences between the info-service work that is being conducted in the two countries do not emerge from the findings. Indeed, there is more variation among the Australian case studies than between the BPOs and some of the upper-end Australian centres. It can be suggested that these findings are part and parcel of the very fluid form of globalization that BPO represents. Why would we not expect the spatial mobility that characterizes much info-service work, with its 'here today, gone tomorrow' qualities, to have major effects on the social division of labour across the world economy?

In its current form, the type of globalization that is represented by the ITeS/BPO sector raises issues of longer-term employment sustainability – issues that we suggest express specific contradictions besetting these developments. As this chapter shows, the industry provides opportunities for gainful employment at nationally competitive salaries for young graduates, who reciprocate by bringing energy and commitment to their new-found employment. However, a perceived lack of career-building opportunities soon gives rise to employment hopping in search of short-term, marginal gains, even though general working conditions and career prospects remain similar from firm to firm. In the firms included in this study, it is not a question of low-skilled work being exported and taken up by BPOs, while high-level work remains in the West. Rather, the main differences are found in the workforces employed in info-service work. In India the employee asset base and the objective characteristics of the work are especially mismatched. This is a basic maladjustment, which is accentuated by the control dynamics built into third-party outsourcing. High turnover rates make it very difficult for firms to realize the investments they make in training and development. This dynamic has further consequences.

First, expectations of diminishing unit costs often accompany outsourcing over the life of a service contract. Firms that outsource expect unit costs to decline over time as the agent and its workers become more familiar and proficient with the processes involved. Productivity increases that are contingent on organizational learning are inherently more difficult to realize when there is constant staff turnover and low average levels of job tenure. Moreover, each contract is of limited duration. Uncertainty about the renewal of contracts, combined with high turnover, provides perverse incentives for underinvesting in training and career development and for keeping jobs as simple as work flows will allow. Meanwhile, an absence of career development and underutilization of existing skills fuels turnover in the industry, which in turn is used as justification for maintaining current structures and practices. In short, there is the making of a vicious cycle of 'burn and churn' associated with BPO on a very large scale. It is not at all clear that the forces impelling globalization will be able to overcome these problems; rather, just the opposite seems to be occurring. At present, much of the human capital in ITeS/BPO is underemployed. This dilemma is expressive of the logic of global labour markets, which are in – and are likely to remain trapped within – profound structural disequilibrium. In these conditions, ironically, employee capabilities are at one and the same time both the greatest asset and the largest challenge confronting the BPO sector.

Expanding on the theme of the sustainability of BPOs, we would be remiss if we did not also mention the environmental implications of this paradigm. BPO is an information industry par excellence, yet as we have seen, the logistical and environmental costs of getting this labour force to work on a daily basis are considerable. Comparatively low salaries currently make it feasible to subsidize the transportation of thousands of workers to and from the technology parks that dot urban India. Increasing energy costs, as well as escalating salaries, place the viability of this type of ad hoc logistic in question over the longer term.

As well, these arrangements, which are necessitated by the realties of urban life, place severe limits on offering more flexible employment alternatives, such as part-time work and work/study options that might otherwise alleviate current attrition problems.

Lastly, we should not mistake commitment on the part of young Indian BPO workers for complacency. For the moment a very dynamic labour market is propelling workers to exit rather than exercise voice through institutions of their own making. Should these conditions change, a movement from strongly unilateralist employment relations could quickly come about. In the next chapter we consider the role of unions in info-service work in greater detail, focusing mainly on Australia, but also returning briefly to India.

8 Discontent, Resistance, and Organizing in Info-Service Work[1]

8.1 Introduction: Work Relations in Call Centres

It is a truism that any sort of group work effort requires, at a minimum, a certain degree of coordination, which in turn relies on cooperation among members of the work unit. In call centres, managers generally oversee this coordination by constructing rosters and collecting and analysing performance data relating to schedule adherence, availability to take/place calls, time spent on the phones, and time spent in phone and non-phone activities. The immediate objectives are seamless service, with minimum call queues and waiting periods, and as much economic efficiency as possible (Houlihan 2006). Staffing can be a balancing act: managers want to avoid both overrostering (too many workers for the volume of call traffic) and underrostering (a degradation of service quality because of long queues or rushed responses to calls). Theoretically, work groups could self-manage these functions, yet rarely does one read about truly self-managed work teams in the literature about call centres, nor did we encounter them at this book's case-study sites. Instead, workers are presented with expectations and practices and are expected to comply with if not embrace both. As we have seen in previous chapters, call centres are rife with precise workload targets and monitoring practices. Workers are confronted with pre-designed jobs and established processes and are expected to accommodate themselves to systems of documented accountability.

In the real world of employment, performance expectations like these, which are embedded features of the labour process, may become targets of dispute. Previous studies have reported on a variety of non-compliant actions; some of these are specific to the call-centre labour process, while others would not be out of place in other work settings. Published examples of deviation from managerial expectations include remaining on the line after the interaction with the caller is complete in order to avoid taking the next call (Taylor and Bain 1999; Townsend 2005) and pretending to be on a call by mouthing words while in fact doing other work (Knights and McCabe 1998) – what could be termed 'faking it.' Not responding to callers in a timely fashion (Fernie and Metcalf 1998), delaying picking calls up (Knights and McCabe 1998), intentionally cutting callers off, and flicking calls to other departments or back into a general queue ('call bumping') are actions that have been documented in other ethnographic research conducted in call centres (van den Broek 2002; Townsend 2005).

There are more creative fiddles. Winiecki (2004) observed CSRs reflexively using computer-generated data to demonstrate compliance with call-centre targets while they were taking unscheduled breaks, and otherwise meeting kpi's on their own terms. Callaghan and Thompson (2001) and Knights and McCabe (1998) observed CSRs fiddling with the codes that register what the worker is actually doing, in ways that made it difficult for management to link workers to particular calls. Advances in technology have rendered some misbehaviours more difficult to carry out. For example, the adoption of 'drop down' call technology obviates the need to pick a call up, and likewise makes it less possible to evade the next one: once one interaction is completed, a fresh call automatically drops into the worker's headset. Clearly, workers at sites that do not yet have this feature are not keen to see its adoption, though even here, efficient utilization of the technology would still depend on agents actively signalling the end of the previous call.

Such forms of non-compliance often develop their own 'industrial' argot. Mulholland (2004) refers to the practice of 'slammin'' in an Irish call centre where she conducted research. This verb suggests hanging up on callers; actually, the practice refers to a scheme workers concocted to cheat a sales-bonus incentive plan. Manipulation of the data allowed employees to record more sales than they knowingly had made and thereby to earn higher bonuses than were intended.

Other acts shade off into more overt forms of resistance, which may involve group as well as individual dynamics. Such actions may explicitly target management and/or managerial goals. For example, resistance to the transition from a servicing to a sales role (with its associated scripts) has been observed in various call-centres that have been undergoing commercialization (Callaghan and Thompson 2001;

Russell 2007). The withholding of emotional labour and/or information through forms of 'emotional working to rule' that may sabotage managers' intentions has been noted in call centres (Knights and Mc-Cabe 1998) as well as in other service industries (Hochschild 1983).

Another form of non-participation may develop around cultural initiatives. Examples include declining to take part in games or theme days (Mulholland 2004) and ostracizing those (i.e., team leaders) who organize such events (Townsend 2005). Such conduct helps maintain the alternative cultures that develop organically in work teams and in informal work groups (van den Broek, Callaghan, and Thompson 2004; Townsend 2004) and that vie with officially sanctioned organizational cultures. In that sense, the conduct goes a step beyond mere withdrawal. The practice of 'smokin' – that is, slipping away for unscheduled group breaks (Mulholland 2004) – is one manifestation of active group cooperation in the pursuit of ends not sanctioned by management. Other forms of withdrawal behaviour include absenteeism ('scammin'; Mulholland 2004) and simply walking out or quitting (Callaghan and Thompson 2001). Again, it is important to recognize that though such actions are usually individual initiatives, sometimes they take on a collective dynamic. In Mulholland's study, workers as a group knew about and cooperated in 'slammin' – that is, in cheating the bonus scheme. Townsend (2005) documents how one team of CSRs organized a roster for taking sick days ('sickies') in protest against a new work schedule that saw job duties expanded. Chapter 5 of this book discussed the threat of group quits over dissatisfaction with a new customer-management software system.

Other forms of non-sanctioned behaviour are more difficult to theorize about. Several authors have described actions that can only be described as efforts to maintain self-identity or to protect the self. Often these behaviours are associated with maintaining one's dignity in the workplace. Under these notions, we could begin with the rejection of scripts in order to add the self to the act of communication (Alferoff and Knights 2001; Callaghan and Thompson 2001). One researcher (Barnes 2004) has flagged the significance of the personal work diaries that CSRs keep in some call centres. These personal entries are used to document unusually long calls, time spent in not-ready mode, and any other actions that management could define as anomalous to the regime of kpi's. While some workers keep a personal work diary to protect themselves against accusations of 'social loafing,' doing so could also be seen as an attempt to 'write' the self back into the labour process.

Other authors have observed employees identifying with customer rights at the expense of managerial prerogative (Korczynski 2001). Taken further, identification with the public can involve criticizing management for failing to fulfil organizational mandates on behalf of a public, or for acting to prevent workers from doing so (Alferoff and Knights 2001, 2002; Knights and McCabe 2000; Russell 2007; chapter 5 of this book). Such criticism may play out as disenchantment with management, which is released through irony, sarcasm, or uninvited jokes at management's expense (Collinson 2002). More serious still are 'whistle-blowing' activities that may expose organizational failures with serious social consequences (Bain and Taylor 2000). In at least some of these cases, identifying with one's work is not synonymous with assuming the corporate mantle. As has been suggested in some analyses from a critical management perspective (Knights and Odhi 2002; Knights and McCabe 2000), escape into one's work (Alferoff and Knights 2002) does not automatically translate into employee self-discipline in a way that is easily managed or is necessarily functional for management objectives.

The main focus of the research at hand has not been on what Scott (1990) terms the hidden transcripts of resistance – a subject that would not be particularly well suited to the survey analysis that has informed much of this book. That said, during our study we encountered (i.e., we could not help noticing) actions similar to those described above that clearly transgressed management's authorized proceedings. Some of these actions laid the groundwork for later employee grievances and led to contact with a union. To take just a few examples, starting at one of the first call centres I observed (Russell 2002b), the managers complained that CSRs were keeping their engaged codes active even after calls had been completed.[2] This was a means to exercise some control over the pace of work – specifically, the lapse of time between one call and the next – and not only in order to complete post-call wrap-up work. CSRs at this centre also fiddled with the codes in order to extend break times. In this way, workers could place themselves in not-ready mode, ostensibly doing post-call related work, when in fact they were on an 'unofficial' break.[3] This practice pushed call-handling times up while masking time taken for breaks. Showing greater ingenuity and cooperation, one employee at this centre had given his log-in identification number to other workers who were willing to log in and cover for him, again allowing for an extension of break time. This initiative seems to be the call-centre equivalent of workers punching in and out on time clocks for one another. Management at this centre was aware of the practice but at a loss as to how to document its existence so that they could take action against it.

At this same centre, each worker's telephone had a red button as part of the phone console. When call queues reached a certain length, the light was activated as a constant reminder of the need to keep call-handling times in check. Workers found this annoying and often covered the light with masking tape taken from office stores – a seemingly petty act of defiance but one that is nevertheless loaded with significance. Meanwhile, at the centre described in chapter 5 it seemed to be widely known that two workers had been fired at the same time, it was said for 'doctoring' their call-handling statistics by hanging up on callers.

Ackroyd and Thompson (1999) offer a theoretical template for making sense of such acts. They classify misbehaviour – a broader notion than resistance, and one that is not restricted to actions taken in response to managerial control strategies – into four categories: employee appropriation of work, time, product, and identity. All four are constitutive of acts of misbehaviour. They view the appropriation of *work* as fundamental to capitalist labour processes; in this category they include such acts as effort bargaining, output restriction ('soldiering'), and sabotage. These actions overlap with the appropriation of *time* and the appropriation of *product*. The former is taken to include time wasting, absences, and quitting; the latter refers to actions such as pilfering and theft. Finally, the appropriation of *identity* refers to participation in non-authorized activities that occur in the workplace but that may not be directly related to the job at hand, such as joking and initiation rituals, informal work-group and other subcultural activities, and explicit acts of group or class solidarity.

Some elements of this typology invite confusion, as the four categories are not mutually exclusive. Also, other forms of misbehaviour that have been observed with info-service work environments do not easily fit these classifications. For example, the appropriation of work includes both temporal aspects such as soldiering and physical aspects such as sabotage, even though these actions all seem quite far removed from one another. Readers would be hard pressed to distinguish between soldiering, which in Ackroyd and Thompson's template is an aspect of appropriating work, and time wasting, which is provided as an example of employee appropriation of time. It may simply be that by the appropriation of work the authors are referring to the misappropriation of time within the job cycle, whereas the appropriation of time by employees refers to 'theft of time' outside the immediate job cycle, though this is speculation on the author's part. In any case, for practical purposes such a distinction is difficult to retain in the work environment of a call centre. As we have seen, CSRs may soldier on the job by remaining in an occupied mode, while getting a precious breather from a relentless queue of calls; or they may use such fiddles in order to take non-rostered breaks away from the workstation. As well, in info-service work, where there may not be a physical output, it becomes more difficult to consider the appropriation of product as something separate from the appropriation of time. Indeed, many of the actions we have been considering boil down to the control of time and the stresses associated with the call-centre labour process. Likewise, in the absence of material outputs, sabotage may take on a different meaning in info-service work than that conveyed by Ackroyd and Thompson. For example, refusing to transition from a service to a marketing role by declining to actively engage with scripts and processes (i.e., by sabotaging managerial efforts to change the nature of the job) may have more to do with the protection of identity than with the appropriation of work.

Given the prominent role of HRM in many call centres, 'struggles' over identity seem to be taking on a new importance. This is perhaps to be expected when the self becomes an object of cultural colonization. Workers may refuse to participate in or fully lend themselves to such processes. For example, in the call centre described above (Russell 2002b), CSRs were reluctant to engage with a self-appraisal scheme that was one element in the bonus-recognition program that management had devised; one worker dismissed the program as 'good-sounding bullshit.'[4] Some workers did not wish to participate in the scheme even though, apparently, there was nothing to lose, and even though incentive awards were there for the taking. Perhaps this is because the scheme involved reflecting on the self in ways that workers found alien, unhelpful, or pointless. In rejecting this initiative, some workers were also (knowingly or otherwise) resisting a key plank of modern managerialism – namely, the purposeful self-documentation of accountability.

At the *Licensing* call centre, the shop steward reported receiving complaints about some of the social activities workers were expected to participate in. Some workers viewed such events as infantilizing and suggested that jobs should be rewarded for what they were worth, with no strings attached. Suggestions to engage in further team-building activities outside of normal working hours, such as weekend camps, were also met with scepticism by some employees at this centre; they insisted that their weekends belonged to themselves and not to the team.[5]

Chapter 6 discussed the worker who refused to participate in the 'bomb the mosque' game that the manager had constructed, finding this to be culturally insensitive and demeaning. In each of these instances, workers resisted managerially initiated cultural activities as a means to preserve their social space for alternative definitions of the self.

A variation on these withdrawal behaviours is also found in some cases. At *Licensing*, for instance, employees not only found the games to be childish but were resentful that resources could easily be found to support such activities while complaints about malfunctioning equipment went unattended. Rather than representing a form of withdrawal, actions such as these begin to shade into the exercise of voice. Nowhere is this more visible than in the case study that was taken up in chapter 5. Recall that in this instance, workers struggled with management over the best way to accomplish their work. This had numerous dimensions: refusals to follow prescribed operating procedures that were viewed as ill-serving the public; devising and sharing unauthorized 'work-arounds' to solve problems; the use of illicit humour that had management and the new customer-service software as its target; and a surge in individual quits, with persistent rumours of group quits. In an important sense these were struggles over identity – specifically, over the display of competence in interactions with a public.

Deviation from prescribed means of accomplishing work is definitely a form of misbehaviour. A refusal to go along with prescribed ways of doing things may be associated with taking shortcuts in order to free up or appropriate time. However, at the *Power* call centre (see chapter 5), conflict ran much deeper than this. Instead of shirking (a form of effort restriction), CSRs rejected management's operating procedures – an act that went to the heart of the job and what it meant to be a CSR. Rather than being manifestations of withdrawal, disputes over *the best way to do the work* have implications for greater involvement in work. Furthermore, such clashes may become attached to critiques of the ethos of managerialism and to the knowledge claims made on its behalf. Ways of knowing, different types of knowledge, and validity claims that substantiate what is known are integrally related to work identities. In info-service as in other types of work, experience and the tacit knowledge gained from it may clash with the culture of managerialism in ways that foster conflict over the best way to accomplish work tasks.

One suspects that a more systematic ethnographic analysis would have revealed more about misbehaviour than we have been able to touch on in this book. From the evidence we have, however, it seems that time and identity are touchpads of contestation in the call centre. Time, which includes the pace, intensity, and expectations around work, is the more immediate. But time can also invoke conflicts over identity. The work that is conducted, how it has been designed, and how time is passed in the workplace contribute to definitions of self – that is, they have an impact on who we are allowed to become. In other words, time spent in work both regulates and helps form identity. The organization of work carries powerful cultural messages. That said, contestations over identity and its appropriation involve more than the immediate activities of carrying work out. Broader cultural initiatives, including subcultural and countercultural activities, also enter the picture.

These theoretical reflections take us beyond a simple control/resistance dichotomy such as characterized early labour-process analyses. Control is a much richer and more complex concept than might appear at first sight. It has both temporal and cultural dimensions; it touches on the disposition of time even while influencing the cognitive perceptions that frame meaning. Misbehaviour does not necessarily consciously target control, though management strategies may certainly take aim at perceived misbehaviour. In other words, workplace misbehaviour expresses a certain degree of autonomy vis-à-vis managerial control. Meanwhile, misbehaviour may or may not shade off into a deliberate resistance to control. Resistance is not a simple mechanical reaction to control. As we have seen, resistance may not simply be an articulate expression of self-interest; it may also be an act of solidarity with other parties, such as users of organizational services. The relationship between control and resistance is much better portrayed as dialectical rather than as simply cause and effect; such an outlook is promoted by the type of extended materialist analysis that has been advocated elsewhere in this book.

Even seemingly individual acts of non-compliance with managerial dictates may have a collective component. Individual actions may foster collective sentiments and broader bonds of solidarity (Friedman 1977; Fantasia 1988). From the examples cited above, workers may turn a blind eye to or wink at such actions, refusing to 'daub in' co-workers, as Mulholland (2004) has illustrated in her discussion of management's unsuccessful attempts to document 'slammin' at a call centre. Also, co-workers may provide a ready audience for jokes or other subversive texts involving management. In other instances, workers may support or cooperate in the actions of others, as illustrated by the example of logging in and covering for a co-worker on an unrostered break. Finally, groups of workers may join in collective actions – for example, by conspiring to get rid of an unpopular team leader (Townsend 2004). Often this is where misbehaviour crosses the line and becomes resistance. Informally arranging 'sickies' with one another as a protest against job expansion (Townsend 2005), and sharing non-sanctioned 'workaround' processes with peers as a way of making work more efficient (Russell 2007; and chapter 5), are fine examples of group solidarity emerging from discontent over the way work is organized.

Another manifestation of such solidarity is encountered in the search for an independent collective voice at the workplace, or in union membership and participation. As pointed out long ago, there is no automatic identity between trade unions and resistance (Aronowitz 1973; Mills 1971; Hyman 1975, 1989). Yet the act of creating an independent form of representation, apart from and often in opposition to management wishes, does represent a significant degree of group solidarity. The issue of trade-union representation in call centres has special salience at the current moment. As previous chapters have laid out, call-centre managers have invested considerable energy into creating cultures that reflect current competitive priorities. Also, as is well known, the proportion of workers who are union members has declined precipitously in many countries. In Australia the fall in union density has been especially remarkable, declining from 49.5 per cent of the workforce in 1982 to just under 19 per cent in 2007 (Alexander and Lewer 2004; Bramble 2008; Peetz 1998). As detailed below, changes to the industrial relations framework in Australia have lent the act of joining a union – or even just maintaining membership – a significance that it might not have had under previous regimes. To appreciate this point, we must take a quick detour and explore the significant changes to the industrial-relations framework that have been registered in contemporary Australia. After that we will come back to the main theme of trade-union representation in info-service work.

8.2 From Partners to Pariahs: Unions in Australian Employment

At about the same time that call centres began to appear on the scene in Australia, the first tranche of labour-law reforms marking a radical departure from the almost century-old framework of regulated awards was delivered, courtesy of a newly elected conservative (Liberal/National coalition) government in 1996. The changes that have been heralded in have had profound implications for the meaning, functioning, and legitimacy of trade unions. Earlier than many Western economies, Australia first resolved the issue of trade-union recognition in industrial relations with the Commonwealth Conciliation and Arbitration Act of 1904. This measure, besides having the power to resolve disputes by rendering enforceable awards (i.e., compulsory and binding arbitration), also entailed the registration of trade unions. Only registered unions could petition the court to intervene in disputes and settle them through arbitration awards. Importantly, most such awards contained a union-preference clause – that is, a clause that favoured union members in hiring and employment. In brief, the new regime of compulsory arbitration provided for union registration and preference, protection from discrimination, and a monopoly over representational rights for registered unions.

Historians have argued that the arbitration act was a 'response not to an overwhelming need for a particular form of industrial dispute settlement, but rather ... a response to the need for trade union recognition' (Macintyre and Mitchell 1989, 18). Furthermore, as the authors go on to explain, 'through the process of registration, unions would be guaranteed more than recognition – they would also derive legal support for their systems of regulation. They could frame awards and be responsible for the policing of those awards against undercutting employers and non-conformist members of the workforce' (ibid., 16; see also Macintyre 2004, 61).

A founding objective of the 1904 act was 'to encourage the organisation of representative bodies of employers and employees and their registration' (quoted in Rimmer 2004). Historical data show that the act was highly successful in this respect. Trade-union densities, which after a series of recognition defeats in the 1890s had registered a puny 6 per cent of the workforce in 1901, stood at 25 per cent in 1914 and had shot up to a remarkable 51.6 per cent by 1921 (Markey 1989; Rimmer 2004). By comparison, union densities in Canada at this time stood at 16 per cent, declining to 12 per cent by mid-decade (Leacy 1983) and were only fractionally above this in America, at around 18 per cent (U.S. Department of Commerce 1975, calculated from series D 1-10 and D 952–69). It would be another fourteen years (1935) before the United States had statutory union-recognition laws, and it would be longer still (1944–8) before Canada legislatively addressed the issue of union recognition for the purposes of collective bargaining (Russell 1990).

Besides supporting comparatively very high levels of union membership at a time when unions in countries such as Canada and the United States were still struggling over the question of recognition, the Australian system generated other peculiarities. A hint of this is provided in the preceding quotation, where the authors refer to the role of unions in 'policing' awards. Indeed, applying for awards and overseeing their fulfilment became a major part of union activity. With the adoption of a basic national wage and quarterly indexation of it in the early 1920s, and with the Australian Council of Trade Unions (ACTU) assuming the lead role in national wage cases after 1931, individual union bargaining with employers became a distinctly secondary aspect of union functioning in Australia (Rimmer 2004; Hancock and Richardson 2004). The system that emerged gave rise to a form of territorial unionism in which the breadth of union coverage was impressive but union activity in the workplace often remained limited (Peetz 1998).

These patterns of employment regulation changed somewhat after the Second World War, when a three-tier system for fixing the terms and conditions of work operated. These protocols included the annual-national-wage case, spearheaded by the peak union body, the ACTU; industry award variations, also authored by the state; and, finally, over-award bargaining on the part of individual unions. Though there were oscillations in the relative importance of each of these mechanisms for altering the terms and conditions of employment, generally the Australian system remained highly centralized and collective bargaining assumed a distinctly adjunctive role – something to be controlled rather than promoted – right up until the early 1990s.[6] Once again, this is a major point of contrast with the highly decentralized systems of company- and establishment-level collective bargaining that have historically characterized the North American system of employment relations.

Renewed pressure for a decentralized system of enterprise bargaining as the chief means for setting the terms and conditions of labour emerged in the late 1980s, borne out of disillusionment on the part of both business and the labour movement with the economic outcomes associated with the Accord's incomes-policy experiment between the unions and the Labor Party government (Bramble 1989; Briggs 2001; Dabscheck 1995; Patmore 1992). Business interests in particular desired greater flexibility in determining specific terms and conditions, which would be tailored to the needs of individual employers; unions for their part grew increasingly restive with the material outcomes being generated by the various Accord agreements. Ironically (or perhaps not), it was the Labor Party that initiated the break with centralized award setting through the Industrial Relations Reform Act of 1993. This measure introduced the principle of enterprise bargaining as an alternative to award establishment; it also left the door open for non-union contracts through its Enterprise Flexibility Agreements.

These first tentative steps towards a new system of highly decentralized employment relations were locked into place with the Workplace Relations Act of 1996. This measure represented a major paradigm shift in Australian industrial relations (Lee and Peetz 1998). The terms used in the act are instructive in their own right. The act is about *workplace relations*, not *industrial relations*. While agreement making is set to displace award setting by the Industrial Relations Commission as the main means of establishing wages and working conditions, it is *enterprise bargaining* that is to take place, not necessarily *collective bargaining*. To give substantive meaning to these terms, the Workplace Relations Act replaced the principal of union preference in employment with that of 'freedom of association' – in other words, with a regime of voluntary unionism. Employers and unions were expressly prohibited from discriminating for or against union (non)members. That aside, requirements to bargain in good faith were also removed from Australian employment relations. Thus, even if a workforce was unionized, employers were under no obligation to bargain with the representatives who have been selected by the employees.

Again, these latter provisions stand in stark contrast to the protocols that became the bedrock foundation of North American industrial relations under the banner of Wagnerism (the American National Labor Relations Act of 1935, otherwise known as the Wagner Act, and Canada's PC 1003 and Industrial Relations and Disputes Investigation Act, of 1944 and 1948 respectively). These measures established a set of legal obligations that made the recognition of trade unions as well as a duty to bargain in good faith incumbent on employers, if a majority of the workers in the community of interest (most often the workplace, or firm) selected representation through unionization (Russell 1995). Subsequent arbitrational decisions went further in Canada, in the form of the *Rand* decision (1946), which made the payment of union dues rather than union membership compulsory if the majority of a workforce decided in favour of union representation (Russell 1990). Known in Australia as agency bargaining fees, these payments have been expressly prohibited, thus giving rise to the 'free rider' problem associated with collective mobilization that has historically bedevilled unions elsewhere. In short, during the 1990s Australia moved from a leader to a laggard position when it came to the recognition of collective voice in the workplace. A type of automatic trade unionism that was part of a highly centralized model of employment regulation gave way to a purely voluntary and completely decentralized system in which individual workers decided whether or not to belong to a trade union and individual employers decided whether or not to recognize and negotiate with unions. Overall, it would be difficult to imagine a more hostile set of conditions for unions to operate under.

Besides making union organizing and collective bargaining quite difficult, the Workplace Relations Act actively promoted non-union options, ostensibly under the pretext of introducing choice and flexibility to individual workplaces. Following New Zealand's lead of 1991, individual employment contracts, called Australian Workplace Agreements (AWAs), were introduced. Especially for new employees, these could be offered on a 'take it or leave it' basis as long as they did not present a 'net disadvantage' when measured against the standards of the relevant award (Macdermott 1997). Simultaneously, the act scaled back the contents of all future awards to a limited number (twenty) of 'allowable matters' that basically established minimum conditions of pay, leave entitlement, redundancy compensation, and pension contribution, among other things (Deery, Plowman, and Walsh 1997).[7] Apart from these allowable matters, all else had to be negotiated, including items that might have been in previous awards. Clearly, the intent was to pare awards back to residual documents of minimum conditions, while making it more difficult for unions to represent workers effectively in collective bargaining.

The 1996 changes to employment relations in Australia were particularly germane for first-time workers, for employees moving into new jobs, and for greenfield worksites – all conditions that have some relevance to the emergence of the call centre. So, just as the growth of call-centre employment was seen by some as a potential opportunity to organize afresh (ACTU 2002), the political/legal environment for doing so was becoming systematically more adverse as employment-relations law was recast in a neoliberal vein. Unions confronted a situation in which there were absolutely no guarantees that they would be recognized by employers and in which workers were being actively induced to enter into individual contracts that, at least initially, might offer better conditions than either the relevant industry award or a pre-existing collective agreement.

The industrial relations reforms of the 1990s were not the last, and we will pick up the thread again after analysing the dynamics of union membership among the call-centre sample under the conditions, as described above, that prevailed at the time of the research. Meanwhile, outside of Australia large-scale employment growth in customer-contact centres has sparked interest in whether such work might serve as a new frontier for union organizing (Arzbacher, Holtgrewe, and Kerst 2002; Bain and Taylor 2002b). This question is of concern both to researchers who are interested in issues of voice, representation, and recognition in new workplaces and to trade unions that hope to grow/replenish their shrinking memberships. In studying union organizing and membership in call centres, we are provided with another perspective on how workers view their employment and themselves. As argued in considerable detail in chapter 6, management invests significant effort through contemporary HRM measures in striving for 'oneness' in the workplace by working on subjectivities and identities through organizational culture. Examining trade unions in call centres provides a means for inspecting these initiatives from another angle. Before we do this, it will be helpful to critically summarize the existing research that has been conducted on unions and call centres.

8.3 From Resistance to Organizing, or Organizing as Resistance: Unions in Call Centres

The existing literature on call centres, with some important exceptions (Bain and Taylor 2002b; Rainnie and Drummond 2006; Rose 2002; Taylor and Bain 2001, 2003), sidesteps the issue of trade-union organization even when it dwells on the theme of resistance in info-service work (Knights and McCabe 1998; Knights and Odhi 2002). Conducive conditions for union organization are thought to include the existence of historical legacies that permit the extension of existing agreements to in-house contact-centre operations (i.e., in-house/captive units as opposed to outsourced centres) (Bain and Taylor 2002b). Also, a desire on the part of management for relations with a single union as opposed to relations with multiple unions in systems that permit this – as in Australia and Britain – may induce an employer to recognize a union that it would prefer to deal with. Public-sector, larger, and older brownfield sites are also considered more likely candidates for unionization, according to one study (Rose 2002).

Call-centre labour processes may provide fertile ground for union organizing, especially when they are driven by inflexible targets and backed up by intensive monitoring. Extreme working conditions, such as those uncovered by Taylor and Bain (2003) at one outsource provider, where workers were expected to field up to 900 calls per shift (!), offer an example of oppressive work processes generating discontent (also see Bain and Taylor 2002b; Taylor and Bain 2001; Fernie 2004). However, as the authors wisely note, grievances around the labour process may not provide sufficient encouragement to undertake union organization or to see it through to successful recognition. In this case study, organic leadership from within, and a widely shared sense that management had violated its 'psychological contract' with the workforce, were necessary precursors to a successful organizing campaign.

Some of the same factors, such as dissatisfaction with rostering and taken-for-granted expectations about arriving at work before the start of shifts (i.e., unpaid work), and a 'community unionism' orientation that was put into practice in a rural Australian community, figure in another case study of a successful call-centre union campaign studied by Rainnie and Drummond (2006). In other case studies, the protection/security afforded by union membership and a desire to improve on comparatively low pay packages are reported as figuring largely in decisions to join a union (Rose 2002; Bain and Taylor 2002b).

Militating against collective organization is the individualistic labour process associated with call-centre work, in that CSRs remain tied to solitary workstations and continuous one-on-one interactions with an external public. The 'time poverty' associated with the design of the jobs where efforts are made to occupy all available time with work or associated cultural activities (training and development, social events, etc.), as well as high levels of staff turnover, may also serve as obstacles to union organization (Bain and Taylor 2002b). Interestingly, some of the reported findings on the unionization of call centres tend to parallel contemporary macroscopic studies of union membership over a cross-section of occupational categories (Waddington and Whitston 1997).

The impact that HRM has on levels of unionization has not been directly considered in the literature on call centres; labour process theory tends to discount the role of HRM, and HRM analyses largely ignore the trade-union question (Russell 2008a,b). For example, one case study of a large banking centre suggests that the effects of HRM are limited; the workers in that study maintained a stronger commitment to the union than to the organization they worked for (Rose 2002). However, that study failed to consider whether the relationship between union membership and HRM is inverse, additive, or simply non-relational.

The more general literature on the relationship between contemporary HRM practices and unions' organizing success is mixed. Different studies present evidence that the unitarism of HRM has adverse effects on union organizing (Baird 2002; Bronfenbrenner and Juravich 1998; Buchanan and Hall 2002; Fiorito, Lowman, and Nelson 1987; Grenier 1988; Rundle 1998). Other research comes to different conclusions, suggesting the absence of a 'substitution effect' between HRM and union involvement (Fiorito and Young 1998; Harley 2002; Peetz 1998). British-based literature puts forward the case that HRM is more likely to be found (Sisson 1993), or to achieve its objectives (Scott 1994; Guest 2002), in unionized work environments. Alternatively, as argued in another study, union representation is more successful in delivering what workers want when HRM is present (Guest 1999).

Given that HRM has been identified with more unitary approaches to employment relations (Sisson and Storey 2000), it may have the effect – intentionally or otherwise – of disorganizing through marginalization autonomous or non-sanctioned work-group collectives. If HRM is theorized as both a discourse and a set of discursive practices that organize workers around employer objectives, it seems reasonable to suggest that overall, its effects will be negative when it comes to employees deciding whether or not to join and/or retain membership in a call-centre union. Such results could pertain regardless of whether a 'hard' form of HRM sets out to destroy initiatives to organize unions (Grenier 1988), or a 'soft' strategy intentionally attempts to win over hearts and minds (Scott 1994).

As we have seen, call centres attach a special importance to customer service, and this in turn evokes managerial expectations of workforce commitment (Korczinski 2001; Korczinski et al. 2000). Considerable resources are directed towards fostering commitment through HRM practices, and call centres may be considered something of a testing ground for much of the new HRM paradigm and the managerialism that stands back of it. As in chapter 6, we understand this paradigm to include the following: the utilization of work teams in all facets of the labour process (van den Broek 2002; Townsend 2005); a preoccupation with performance management based on the setting of precise targets and goals (Bain, Watson, et al. 2002); intensive, multiphase recruitment processes and continuous training and development programs (Belt et al. 2002; Callaghan and Thompson 2002); symbolic but highly visible recognition programs (Knights and McCabe 1997; Russell 2002b); and a cultural program that attempts to normalize all of this by importing popular culture into the workplace (Kinnie, Hutchinson, and Purcell 2000).

Less attention has been directed towards call-centre labour markets and their effects on unionization. Those who establish call centres not only attempt to leverage the advantages that different labour markets offer (e.g., wages, ground rents, skill pools) (Rainnie and Drummond 2006; Richardson, Belt, and Marshall 2000; Richardson and Belt 2001; Taylor and Bain 2004; Thite and Russell 2007) but also – as we saw in chapter 3 – *make* or *remake* local labour markets (Arzbacher, Holtgrewe, and Kerst 2002; Bittner et al. 2002; Russell 2002a). In exercising their preferences for specific types of employment contracts, managers fashion markets that may enhance or diminish opportunities for union membership (Benner 2002). For example, full-time permanent work is often viewed as more conducive to union-organizing efforts than part-time or casual employment.

Workers, too, have intentions in the labour market. These may include plans to exit early or to remain with the current employer. From labour's perspective, one could argue that soft labour markets, characterized by stiff competition for available jobs, exert a disciplining effect complete with a disinclination to become involved with a union. By the same token, a seller's labour market may be propitious for union joining when it reduces any perceived danger or fear factor associated with declaring oneself in favour of the union. Alternatively, one could suggest that insecure labour-market conditions may render current job attachment more valuable so that anything that defends workers against capricious managerial acts – for example, the protection offered by belonging to a union – is likely to be highly valued. Tight labour markets, on the other hand, could induce opportunistic behaviour, with workers continually shifting between employers and generally showing little interest in union participation. Suffice it to say at this point that the types of labour markets that are created and the state of any given labour market may have an impact on trade-union membership in call centres. This needs to be examined in greater detail.

The factors that have been hypothesized as affecting union-membership levels – including work design, the call centre's labour process, HRM, and labour-market characteristics – all come under the category of 'received conditions.' That is, they are circumstances that confront unions, each of which may be more or less propitious for union organizing activities. Such antecedents constitute both constraints and opportunities for unions. At the same time, unions do have some control over the mobilizing efforts and strategies they invest in organizing new members and (in a voluntary membership system) retaining old ones. This point acknowledges the dynamic dimension of union activity. It accepts that unions are not passive organizations that must await the right set of structural conditions before they can undertake their own initiatives (Bronfenbrenner and Juravich 1998). While an appreciation of workplace contexts is undoubtedly necessary, structural conditions are maintained and altered by the strategies that employers and unions adopt and by the decisions that workers take, for these are what ultimately determine the success of such initiatives (Turner, Katz, and Hurd 2001). Sensitivity to both agency and structure is required if the complexities of 'voice,' mobilization, and representation in the employment relationship are to be understood.

Taking this one step further, the potential role that unions assume in framing alternative interpretations of the social realities of work requires assessment. As suggested by social mobilization theory, workplace conditions can be framed as sources of legitimate discontent, generating alternative, commonly held interests that are distinct from managerial discourses (Tilly 1978; Fantasia 1988). Furthermore, such conditions can be posed in a manner that renders them susceptible to change through collective action (Kelly 1998; Milkman and Voss 2004). From this we can suggest that union membership is also a function of perceived union effectiveness. This begins with organizing, but then extends to effective representation of employee interests. These claims merely acknowledge that unions are important contributors to their own destinies by virtue of the strategies they adopt.

The next section analyses the importance of the factors identified above in accounting for call-centre union membership. This includes studying the effects of the labour process, call-centre HRM practices, and the labour market in which the worksites are located, as well as some aspects of union strategy in terms of employees' decisions to join a call-centre trade union. Some of these aspects have been given prominence in previous studies of call centres, but rarely have they been considered together in terms of their implications for trade-union organization. Earlier chapters of this book considered the call-centre labour process and HRM in detail; this material is now revisited in relation to the question of union membership. Use is made of the indexes that were constructed earlier. The purpose of doing so is to examine the effects on unionization of the following: workloads; job skills; work team functioning; organizational culture; and satisfaction with different aspects of HRM, including training and development as well as monitoring and performance review.

Before proceeding, it is necessary to reiterate that the recent legislative changes governing trade unions in Australia previewed above have made the task of analysing collective organization considerably more challenging. In the Canadian/American system, unions gear up for certification campaigns that have a finale; by contrast, in a voluntary regime such as the one that Australia has now adopted, acquiring and retaining members at individual worksites is a never-ending activity. Thus our task is twofold: not only to explain current levels of membership and non-membership at the research sites, but also to examine potential membership. This includes undertaking a study of non-union members who may hold different attitudes (favourable, neutral, hostile) to the prospect of joining a union should the opportunity present itself. In order to accommodate this aspect of the question, in the next section the sample is initially divided between existing union and non-union members for comparison. Then the latter group of non-unionists is further subdivided between those who are unsympathetic to union membership, those who are undecided, and those who would like to join a union. This strategy permits an analysis both of the existing situation and of possible future scenarios for call-centre unionization. Results are reported first for the sample as a whole, focusing on the determinants of employee union status; and then on the determinants of attitudes towards unions among current non-members.

8.4 Unionization in the Australian Case-Study Sites

Unionization among the survey respondents, broken down by industry sector, is displayed in Table 8.1. Clearly, there are wide variations among the different branches.

The transportation sector exhibits comparatively high levels of union membership among the survey respondents, including 65 per cent of the respondents at *Airline* and 61 per cent at *Bus Company*. Collective bargaining and the provisions of union-certified enterprise agreements regulate employment relations at both centres. Though the call-centre managers are not directly involved in determining the contents of such agreements, which extend to other departments besides the customer-service centres, managers at both worksites were more than happy to work within the framework of the collective agreement:

> I work with them. I would rather know what's going on 'cause I found in the past you work against them and it gets too hard, you get bogged down by red tape, politics ... They had a meeting with me yesterday ... It

Table 8.1
Union density among respondents by sector, Australia

Industry	%
Telecommunications	14.1
Transportation	63.7
Banking, insurance, and finance	17.1
Health care	49.4
Leisure	64.3
Public and social services	57.7
Total	41.0

was over and done with. I must say, it's made my job a lot easier, working with the union delegates. But ... enforcing this is the process we have to work with, and if you go outside these boundaries [union-management relations] I am not even going to listen. (*Bus Company*, call-centre manager)

Similar themes, along the lines of 'we've always had unions' and that it is best to work with them, pervaded employment relations at *Airline* as well. This site was currently on its seventh collective agreement. This is not to say that deunionization is not on the agenda in this sector, only that it is much more likely to take the form of outsourcing to offshore locations or the creation of new, non-union start-up ventures, which may indeed be 'spin-offs' from unionized parent companies. For the moment, though, the firms in the transportation sector exhibit many of the features that are commonly associated with mature union–management relations.

Above-average union densities were also reported at the leisure-services centre, *Telebet*; in one of the health-care insurers, the publicly operated *Health Authority*; and in the public and not-for-profit sectors more generally. Reported union densities in the two telecommunications companies and the four financial organizations that participated in the study were much lower. At some of these companies, managers revealed a distinct preference for 'individual' AWA employment contracts:

I think the major advantage [of AWAs] is that it's encouraging people sort of at all levels to work within the team and within the company ... It's actually just showing staff at all levels ... where they should report to if they have issues, or ... if they need assistance, what the chain of command is. (*Telco1*, call-centre manager)

Despite this outlook, 14 per cent of the respondents at *Telco1* said they belonged to a union. At *Telco2* there was a 60:40 ratio between those who were on individualized contracts and those who were covered by the union-negotiated collective agreement. Only those workers who had signed AWAs were eligible to participate in the centre's bonus scheme, which effectively gave them higher take-home pay than their unionized counterparts. Though the federal government has attempted to legitimate AWAs on the grounds that they are a more flexible instrument in terms of meeting both individual and business needs, according to the manager at *Telco2* they have been

> designed, obviously, in consultation with the employee advocate.[8] It's a set of conditions that is exactly the same for every single consultant, so there's no individual negotiation [sic], they've been designed for the sales-consultant role across the organization and they agree to that for a three-year period. (*Telco2*, call-centre manager)

Though there were union members at *Telco2* (17 per cent of the sample claimed union membership), there was no shop steward in the call centre, nor could the current manager recall any recent grievances or disputes involving the union. This manager knew which union was present, but obviously, remuneration structures (e.g., the bonus scheme) were geared towards marginalizing potential union influence.

The financial sector is well known for having lower-than-average union densities, and according to the results of the survey, this sample was no exception. Among the respondents who were employed as CSRs in the financial-services sector, 17 per cent indicated that they currently belonged to a trade union. However, this did not take into account the considerable variation among the sites. The largest organization in this sector, *Bank2*, had fended off an organizing drive several years earlier. An in-house staff association was substituted as the main venue for employee voice. Consequently, only 13 per cent of the respondents at *Bank2* indicated that they belonged to a union. Union membership and influence at *Insurer2* was also minimal, at 9 per cent of the sample; while 19 per cent of the respondents at *Bank1* said they were union members. According to the call-centre manager at *Bank1*,

> I don't see how they [the union] could make any difference to what we are trying to achieve … I don't think they have that much strength in the financial-services industry, it's not like some of the other industries where there's probably a need for it … But that all said, I don't see that the un-

ion's being proactive in … trying to make a presence in some of the financial services industries either. I mean … I haven't seen a union rep walk
through the door in more than two years. (*Bank1*, call-centre manager)

At *Insurer1*, on the other hand, the manager estimated unionization
rates in the call centre to be in the neighbourhood of 30 per cent, while
36 per cent of the sample from this centre indicated they were union
members. At this firm, the Financial Services Union is seen very much
as a partner rather than as a marginal entity. As recounted by the manager,

I think it's a good balance we've got, so we've very rarely had an issue in
IR and I put it down to if we have an issue with the union then it tends to
be that I've done something wrong and, you know, we're both trying to
get the same thing – making sure that we're looking after people. They're
looking after people that are union, that are part of their group, and we're
looking after people who work for us. (*Insurer1*, call-centre manager)

In the data analysis that follows, the factors that have been identified as potentially important in accounting for union membership are
considered in greater detail. These factors include labour-market variables, labour process and HRM factors, and union actions and influences. This is exploratory research insofar as the object is to identify
important items – positive *or* negative – that have a bearing on existing
and potential call-centre union membership. Since the dependent factor is a categorical variable (i.e., each respondent either was or was not
a trade-union member at the time of completing the survey), a logistical
regression procedure is the most appropriate analysis to conduct.

We begin with the labour markets that are created when new operations such as call centres come on-stream. As argued in chapter
3, employers create labour markets through the recruitment and hiring practices they engage in. Certain types of workers are preferred
whether it is with regard to age, gender, educational attainment, or other designated criteria. Employers categorize workers into potentially
ideal groups based on past experiences or what they believe to be the
case. Of course, the employer may have greater or lesser discretion in
these matters. Greenfield sites in areas of high unemployment may offer greater leeway to employers in shaping the labour market (Bristow,
Munday, and Gripaios 2000; Rainnie and Drummond 2006; Richardson and Belt 2001; Richardson, Belt, and Marshall 2000; Russell 2002a),

whereas managers will have less discretion if workers are transferred to brownfield call-centre sites from other areas of an existing organization. This scenario may occur when previous forms of service delivery are replaced with a customer-contact centre and existing employees are given the first opportunities to apply for the new positions, as occurred at *Power* (chapter 5) and in several of the other case-study sites in the transportation and public sectors. Also potentially important is the permanency attached to the job – that is, whether it is designated as a casual or permanent contract, and whether it is a voluntarily full-time or part-time position. Such conditions, which are attached to employment, send signals to workers, who in turn develop varying levels of attachment to the jobs they occupy. Thus, employee intentions to remain in or exit the employment relationship represent the other side of the labour-market coin.

Included among our labour market factors are eight variables that relate to whom employers hire (age and gender of worker, educational attainment), the employment status they are hired into (full-time or part-time, permanent or casual), the length of time the respondent has occupied the current job (in years), whether that person intends to remain in the current job, and, finally, the respondents' perceptions of the labour market they sell their labour power in. This last variable is measured by the question, 'If I were to lose my job here, it would be relatively easy for me to get as good a job at another centre straight away' – agree, disagree, etc. The educational-attainment variable is a dummy variable for university attendance/graduation; the measures of full-time and permanent employment and intention to remain in current employment are also dummy variables.

The relevant aspects of the labour process are captured by the two indexes introduced in chapter 4, which measure the perceived skills associated with the work and reported workload manageability. However, it is also the case that contemporary HRM practices have a direct bearing on the labour process. HRM represents elements of a system of control that includes monitoring and performance evaluation as well as aspects of work design such as the presence of work teams. HRM, as it has been operationalized here, also includes employee perceptions of organizational culture, security, and trust. Recall that organizational culture refers to explicit managerial interventions in daily work routines aimed at creating a normative culture – interventions such as the promotion of sanctioned social activities – while perceptions of trust, cooperation, and relations between workers and managers are measured by a trust/security index (see chapter 6). Also, for the purposes of analysing the effects of HRM on union membership, a specific question from the survey that asks respondents whether the employer is unreceptive to unionization is considered. This question gets to the point of whether management at an organization is anti-union; whether this is conveyed to workers; and whether this attitude on management's part has an impact on a voluntary system of union membership. Workers' perceptions of HRM – perceptions relating to work teams' roles, monitoring practices, cultural initiatives undertaken by management, satisfaction with training and development programs, and the trustworthiness of management – are all taken from chapter 6 and the measures that were introduced there.

Lastly, the impact of union actions on reported membership is examined. The factors in play here may be of two types: less direct ones that have an effect on individuals; and conscious union strategies directed towards attracting and retaining members. Whether there is a history of trade-union membership in a respondent's family and whether a culture of unionism is being passed along intergenerationally are examples of points that fall outside the control of any union but that may nonetheless influence the decisions taken by workers. Conscious union strategies include developing an effective presence in the worksite by supporting an active shop-steward/union-delegate structure and by providing services that members value. The union variables employed here include the following: whether the union has shop-steward representation in the workplace; if it does, whether those reps are perceived as effective;[9] whether there is a family history of union membership; whether one's co-workers are union members; and whether the union provides services defined as valuable. The first four of these items have been constructed as dummy variables; the last is a Likert scale question.

The results of this analysis are presented in Table 8.2. The Exp(B) statistic measures the effect that each independent variable has on union membership. If it is greater than 1, the odds of union membership are increased by virtue of the independent variable; if it is less than 1, the independent variable works to decrease the likelihood of union membership. Only those items that exert a statistically significant effect, or that come close to doing so, are included in Table 8.2. In order of importance are peer influences, valuing the services the union provides, and satisfaction/dissatisfaction with work teams and workplace monitoring practices. Additionally, the age of the respondents, their gender (female), and their intentions to remain in the job approach a level of statistical significance that is worthy of note.

It is evident from Table 8.2 (ExpB) that peer influence is the single most important factor in accounting for voluntary union membership. In the absence of compulsory mechanisms such as the union or closed shop, peer influence (and perhaps pressure) is critical both for building membership and for retaining it. Knowing that one's co-workers are union members increases the odds of joining a union to a considerable degree. Whether the strength of peer influence is an outcome of past union-organizing efforts or of inherited historical conditions, or simply an expression of group solidarity, is a matter of some conjecture. Given that call centres are comparatively new ventures, most of them having been established in the aftermath of the 1996 industrial relations reforms, I seriously doubt whether union membership is some kind of historical residue from an earlier system that favoured union preference. Meanwhile, the singular importance of peer influence illustrates some of the dilemmas that confront unions in a voluntary system of industrial relations. The key question confronting organizing efforts in a system of voluntary membership is how to get up to that level of critical density in any workplace where peer influence can become a significant factor, where union membership takes on a momentum of its own in a path-dependent manner. Further complicating things is that this level of support must be generated not only for a specific event – such as in a Canadian-style union-certification campaign – but also in a day in and day out manner as new employees come on board. If nothing else, this reminds us of the essentially social dimension that pertains to individual decisions whether to join a union.

Also important in contributing to current union levels are an understanding on the part of workers of what unions do and the assigning of value to these functions. Workers who believe that the services unions provide are beneficial are more than three times as likely to be in a union as workers who don't. What benefits in particular do workers associate with union membership and value? When our respondents were asked to rank the three most important reasons why they had joined a union, the largest proportion (41.5 per cent) nominated as their number-one reason the job and employment security they associated with membership. This vastly outweighed the role of unions in gaining better wages and conditions and a general belief that unions are important representatives of workers, which were put forward by 18.9 per cent and 18.7 per cent of existing members as the most important reasons for belonging to a union. Initially at least, workers identify unions with providing services and in particular with protection against arbitrary authority – the so-called 'insurance' model of unionism. This does not mean that workers are not interested in empowerment. That unions provide voice into how things are done in the workplace and that unions are an effective way to attain representation are two of the second-most-important reasons provided for union membership. This suggests that in the current climate, juxtaposing servicing with organizing strategies may not be the most effective way to pose the problem. Initially, most people voluntarily join a union for the services they offer, having recognized that these services can best be provided on a collective basis. Workers become empowered when they begin to learn that such services are better provided when they are involved in their co-production rather than simply their consumption.

Given the stated importance of job protection as a reason for taking out union membership, it is not surprising that older workers are more likely to be unionists. This remains an area of concern for the labour movement, especially as the age profile in some industry sectors that are heavy users of call centres is skewed towards youth (e.g., financial services and telcos, where 60 and 50 per cent respectively of the sample is under thirty). Will younger workers be more likely to join unions as they acquire more experience and seniority, or is a new generation of low-tenure non-union labour forming? Meanwhile, the greater proclivity on the part of women to join unions in call centres once again puts the lie to old stereotypes. It is the case that women in our study are about 10 per cent more likely to indicate an intention to stay in their current job for the foreseeable future and that women are overrepresented among workers over forty, who, as we have seen, are more likely to be union members, as are workers who intend to remain in their jobs.

The results of Table 8.2 also suggest that workers who express greater satisfaction with the functioning of work teams and with the manner in which call monitoring is being conducted are less likely to be union members. These findings suggest that when teams are perceived as providing effective voice in the workplace and when bureaucratic forms of supervision are replaced with coaching, development, and approachable management, the demand for union representation declines. Likewise, as illustrated in Table 8.2, those who are satisfied with monitoring practices and the purposes to which they are put are 22 per cent (.785 – 1) less likely to be in a union. Conversely, those who hold concerns about monitoring are more likely to seek out union membership. This suggests that monitoring may have traction as an issue for call-centre unions, again depending on what management does with it. Notably, other labour-process and HRM factors do not exert important influences on union density among respondents. Perceived skill levels, managerially inspired cultural activities, employer hostility towards unions, and the overall employment climate are not significant. Neither is work intensity on its own a determining factor. Rather, in line with the main tenets of social mobilization theory (Kelly 1998; Tilly 1978), it is only when employment practices are framed as 'issues' that resonate with workers that they may become catalysts for organizing. In this respect the monitoring of work appears to bear special attention. It may also be the case that for union members, labour-process issues are less important precisely *because* a union is present in the workplace.

One of our case studies, *Bus Company*, provides an instructive example of these dynamics at work. The labour force at this call centre was divided among full-time, permanent part-time, and casual staff on a 55:27:18 per cent basis. Prior to 2000 there was very little union membership or activity at the site. As of May 2004, when research at the centre commenced, union density as reported by the manager was 70 per cent, with 61 per cent of the survey respondents indicating that they belonged to the union. This increase in membership cuts completely against the grain of general trends in Australian trade unionism since at least the early 1990s, thereby making this an instructive case study of union success. What factors were responsible for the turnaround in union fortunes at this one company?

Shortly into the new decade, *Bus Company* acquired the Australian division of a large international carrier. That division had already established two customer-contact centres to service its market. Both these centres were urban based, whereas the smaller *Bus Company* centre was located in a regional town where the company had its origins. It was feared that with the merger, the *Bus Company* centre would be closed in a community where workers would find it difficult to replace such jobs. An effective union organizer was able to tap into these concerns, and workers migrated en masse to the union. The retention of this call centre and the mothballing of the other two facilities added greatly to the union's legitimacy in the workplace. Workers viewed their union membership as an important aspect of their employment. Meanwhile, management took a pragmatic approach to this new reality. 'They're here, I am going to have to work with them,' summed up the manager's view of the situation.[10] In an era of low-cost budget carriers, wages and conditions at the company have been retained, including Sunday penalty rates of double time-and-a-half in the call centre. Despite a comparatively young workforce divided between full- and part-time,

Table 8.2
Logistic regression of determinants of trade-union membership and pro-union attitudes of non-union members, Australia

Variables included in the model	Determinants of union membership		Determinants of pro-union attitude among non-members	
	ExpB	Sig	ExpB	Sig
Co-workers in union	6.417	.000	14.214	.003
Services union provides are beneficial	3.427	.000		
Satisfaction with work teams	.825	.04		
Satisfaction with monitoring practices	.827	.09	.816	.07
Satisfaction with training and development			.771	.04
Job skill			6.83	.01
Satisfaction with OH & S			2.36	.14
Age	1.30	.16	16.04	.06
Gender (female)	1.86	.14	13.83	.13
Intending to stay in job	1.81	.16	70.47	.08
Full-time work			.001	.07
Permanent work			.404	.04
Job tenure (years)			3.56	.15
Ease of replacing current job			56.20	.05
Mother a union member			.706	
Nagelkerke R^2	.598			

permanent and casual, a campaign to keep the call centre open mobilized workers into joining the union and becoming active members.

Among non-union members in the survey, 48 per cent expressed antipathy towards unions and said they would never join one; 14.5 per cent expressed pro-union sentiments; and 37 per cent were undecided about the question of joining a union. The third column of Table 8.2 focuses on those non-union members who expressed a pro-union attitude. In other words, the subsample of non-unionists has been further subdivided into those who indicated a willingness to join a union and others who were hostile towards or undecided about membership. As shown in Table 8.2, with regard to those aspects that are under a union's control, attaching a value to what unions do is the most important factor in accounting for pro-union expressions by current non-members. This increases the odds of expressing positive union perceptions by non-members.

Other factors that enhance pro-union sentiments include full-time work, gender (women), and family influences, especially if the respondent's mother was a union member. This most likely reflects the gender mix of the sample and the fact that most CSRs are women. Satisfaction with the state of occupational health and safety in the workplace increases the odds of expressing pro-union views, perhaps because unions receive credit for improvements in this sphere, while satisfaction with the skill demands of the work and with HRM training and development lowers the odds of being in the 'union favourable' camp. As these items may enter into an overall evaluation of the work, satisfaction with what organizations offer on this score could be expected to diminish interest in union membership. On the other hand, the longer non-union members have been in their jobs, the less likely they are to express an interest in union membership, perhaps becoming confirmed in their views over time. The age of respondents and their labour-market plans also approach statistical significance, with older workers and those who intend to remain more likely to be willing to consider joining a union. Finally, perceptions of external labour-market conditions also approach significance. If the respondent considers her labour-market position to be favourable – that is, if she believes that she could replace her current job with an equivalent position with little difficulty – the odds are that she will be more favourably disposed to joining a union.

When non-union members were asked directly why they didn't join the union, the largest proportion nominated the expense of union dues as the most important reason (31.5 per cent). Significantly, the second-largest group (19 per cent) said that never having been approached by the union to become a member was the most important reason for not belonging. This factor provides additional evidence that in some of our workplaces the union presence is a shallow one. In such cases unions have failed to make the shift from automatic coverage and representing workers in wage tribunals through the awards system to an organizing model, which is a requirement for survival under the new regime. In the first instance, organizing is premised on convincing potential members that unions have valuable services they can provide constituents. In this sense, organizing and providing services, far from being opposing strategies, can be part of a single bid to increase union membership. And just as organizing does not cease under a voluntary system, extending the range of services to include education and collective empowerment according to group needs can be part of a long-term strategy to maintain activism and membership in the workplace.

8.5 A Postscript from Australia: Work Choices and Beyond

During the 2004 federal election the coalition of conservative parties succeeded in capturing control of the Australian Senate, which had up until then been the last barrier to further neoliberal labour-law reform. Within months the government's ten-year-long wish list for completing the transition to a radically decentralized and individualized employment-relations system was under way. It is important to realize, however, that from 1996 onwards, organizing had been made more difficult for unions. This is reflected in our survey results, which indicate that the greatest proportion of non-unionists cite receipt of the same or better conditions as union members as the second-most-important reason for not joining a union. This situation has been created by decisions that have been handed down since the passage of the 1996 Workplace Relations Act (e.g., *Electrolux Home Products Pty Ltd v. AWU*, 2004) – decisions that in effect have barred unions from assigning bargaining fees to non-members who receive the same benefits as a result of union efforts. In other words, 'free riding' is rewarded. In addition, some employers, notably in the mining sector (Bowden and Russell 2000), but also in some of the sectors considered in this book, have offered substantial increases to workers who are willing to abandon collective agreements in favour of individual AWA contracts. For instance, as recounted above, only workers who have signed the company-authored AWAs at *Telco2* are eligible to participate in the organization's call-

Table 8.3
Union member participation rates, Australia

Union activity	% of union members
Vote in union-leadership elections	49
Vote for new EBAs	74
Vote in disputes (e.g., strike votes)	37
Attend union meetings	48
Run/campaign for union position	4
Negotiation of new EBAs	12
Attend union training schools	9
Participate in joint union/mgt committees	8
Serve as union delegate	9
Recruit new members	13
Distribute union information	14
Attend union OH&S training	11

centre bonus incentive scheme. Effectively, this means that for doing exactly the same work, non-union workers in the company's employ are likely to receive greater net remuneration than those who stick with the union. Without any obligation to bargain in good faith, or to bargain at all, unionized workers may be thrown back onto lower award rates, while those who have been willing to abandon the union, or who have not joined in the first place, receive increases at above-award rates on individual agreements.

For current union members, our survey results show a range of involvement in union-related activities (see Table 8.3). Attendance at union meetings is impressive, as is participation in the ratification of new agreements. On the other hand, more active involvement such as participation in union education and training seminars, which might lead to serving as a shop steward, or participating in organizing and/or bargaining, remains exceptional for most union members.

The Work Choices legislation of 2005 has rendered the organization of such participation even more difficult by setting forth new types of legal employment agreements and by introducing prohibited-content regulations for union-certified agreements. Thus, despite the title of the legislation, employee choice is restricted, not enhanced, by the legislation (Hall 2006). Organizing is made more difficult as a result of the prohibition of payroll deductions of union dues by an employer (i.e., the automatic dues check-off), even if the employee desires this. Any terms that refer to the use of labour-hire workers through employment agents (i.e., curbs on the use of temporary workers), or their terms of employment, have also been proscribed as prohibited content from future collective agreements. Employer greenfield agreements are an entirely new labour-contract category that may also have relevance to call centres. Under these provisos, employers commencing 'a new business, project or undertaking' (Nankervis, Compton, and Baird 2005) may unilaterally establish the terms and conditions of employment for a period of one year. That is, employers can make agreements with themselves (Riley and Sarina 2006), while presenting workers with a 'take it or leave it' proposition.

Worse, union organizing has been made more difficult by the prohibition on any language in collective agreements that would allow for a number of legitimate trade-union activities. Various provisions now bar from these agreements such things as union training leave, paid attendance at union meetings, and the encouragement of union membership. Under Work Choices, activities that are likely to increase union participation – from taking up union membership through to the encouragement of active participation in the affairs of the union – can no longer legally be included in collective agreements. Additionally, Work Choices limits unions' capacity to service their members by, among other things, excluding clauses that refer to mandatory union participation in dispute resolution such as grievance handling, or that set terms allowing for legal industrial action. At the same time, union rights of entry into workplaces have been greatly circumscribed, and so has been the legal right to strike (Nankervis et al. 2005; Riley and Sarina 2006).[11]

Work Choices is probably the most repressive set of trade-union laws to have been enacted in the post-1945 era in any developed democratic nation. Its passage has privileged the corporations power of the state, which relates to the rights and duties of corporations and those who deal with them in relation to the traditional constitutional basis of labour legislation in Australia – namely, the power to legislate on matters pertaining to conciliation and arbitration in the framing of labour law (McCallum 2006). The Work Choices legislation was intended to gut trade unions, to so hobble them as to make them irrelevant to most participants in the labour force.

Unlike previous neoliberal attempts at industrial-relations reform such as those carried out under Thatcher in Britain, the Howard government, when it had the opportunity, went for a 'big bang,' all-or-nothing approach. The Work Choices legislation had not been mooted during the election campaign of 2004. Its scope came as a shock to the Australian public, who remained distrustful of the new laws and their consequences for the remainder of the government's mandate. At the first opportunity to pass judgment, in late 2007, the electorate ended the governing party's eleven-year run in office, electing in its place a new Labor government. This followed a three-year 'Your Rights at Work – Worth Fighting and Voting For' campaign, run by the ACTU, which featured electoral mobilization in key marginal seats, a sophisticated advertising campaign, and several one-day protest rallies. The new government immediately moved to outlaw Australian Workplace Agreements and to introduce a new set of rules, which will be rolled out over the term of its first mandate, which ends in 2010. There is, however, little likelihood that union-preference protocols will be reintroduced to workplaces, while union rights of entry, the challenges posed by free riding, and the assessment of bargaining fees will no doubt continue to be hotly contested issues in the years ahead. In other words, though there will be modifications, the regulatory regime will almost certainly continue to be anchored on an ethos of individual voluntarism. This means that many of the existing challenges of organizing new occupational groups such as info-service workers will continue to confront contemporary trade unions.[12]

8.6 Resistance and Organization in Indian BPOs

Indian call centres are not simply the efficient, high-performance, problem-free outsourcing solutions as advertised in the trade literature by industry bodies such as Nasscom. If one cares to look, signs of worker discontent and resistance are readily apparent, though sometimes manifested in different ways than in Australia. For example, simply getting workers to work on a daily basis is a huge logistical undertaking for BPOs. In contrast to the employment situation in countries like Australia, where transportation to and from work is the employee's responsibility, in Indian BPOs it is part of the cost of doing business and thus is something that must be managed by the employer. The HRM manager at *BPO2* commented on the challenges he faced in just ensuring that workers turn up when they are rostered for work. Absenteeism is a growing problem at this operation, and management has adopted some rather novel incentives to diminish it, including the presentation of red roses to female workers when they board the company transportation vehicles at their designated pick-up stations.[13] Another form of employee withdrawal – attrition – was discussed at length in chapter 7. Quit rates in excess of 100 per cent per year and corresponding complaints of a 'culture of job hopping' and labour poaching on the part of competitors are common in the sheltered technology parks of modern India. This level of attrition points to an absence of attachment on the part of workers to their employment, which translates at best into a short-term and highly conditional commitment. Clearly, not all is well.

Patterns of employee discontent are evident as well in the withholding of effort during the labour process itself. Workers putting irate customers on mute, deliberately withholding information in order to shorten call-handling times and enhance personal performance statistics, providing a *talla* (false solution) to provocative customers, walking customers through redundant processes to get some breathing time, and 'flicking' calls so that the agent can go back to the end of the call-receiving queue, have all been reported by different researchers (D'Cruz and Noronha 2006; Taylor and Bain 2005). On a more playful note are reports of agents 'taking the piss' out of customers in training sessions and with one another (Mirchandani 2009) and, more creatively, doctoring customer-satisfaction surveys to provide good feedback on themselves. Some have been known to provide virtuoso performances after deducing the call-monitoring schedule (Noronha and D'Cruz 2006).

Some of these responses to the call-centre labour process are similar to what has been reported in Australian and other Western-based operations. That said, the offshoring, BPO element undoubtedly raises novel issues such as responses to racist encounters. The aforementioned bodies of research focus on individual or peer-group forms of resistance within the labour process for one principal reason: at the time the research was carried out, mobilizing around collective resistance – specifically, around trade-union organization – was unknown. In some cases this is explicitly acknowledged, while in others the very omission of any reference to unions is an indication that they are a missing presence in the employment relations of BPOs.

Thus, it was with some surprise that during an interview with an astute and forthcoming vice-president of operations at *BPO2* we were informed quite matter-of-factly that 'it's not a question of if, but a question of when' a trade-union presence in BPOs will begin to register.[14] Even more noteworthy, this comment was entirely unsolicited: the manager had raised the subject of unionization voluntarily, without any prompting whatsoever. Like our co-researchers, we had assumed that there would be little point in even raising the question of unions in the BPO context – that unions were simply not part of the employment equation. Further elaboration on the manager's part assured us that this was not a 'throwaway' comment, nor had he any intention of being alarmist or sensational. Indeed, *BPO2* had already confronted two organizing efforts. According to the manager, ITeS/BPO is well on the way to becoming a mainstream industry in India, and as a consequence, unionization has become much more probable. It is also likely that unionization will rise up from within the industry as opposed to being the result of external organizing campaigns by labour organizations that do not have their roots in BPOs.

These observations made during a 2005 interview have turned out to be prescient. At approximately the same moment, the Union of Information Technology Enabled Services Professionals (UNITES) was holding its founding convention. UNITES is the Indian affiliate of UNI, an ILO-accredited network of service-sector unions. The organization focuses on mobilizing workers in the ITeS/BPO sector. In this task the new union faces formidable challenges. The sequestration of workforces in gated, well-guarded technology parks to which union officials have no right of entry is an immediate barrier to organizing; so is the exemption of the ITeS/BPO sector from domestic labour-law provisions that regulate employment standards (Focus on the Global South/YPC 2005; Thite and Russell 2007). A youthful, well-educated middleclass labour pool whose members are unlikely to regard their current employment as permanent, and correspondingly high rates of attrition and mobility, add to the challenges of creating an effective collective voice in BPOs (Noronha and D'Cruz 2006). Further contributing to this gestalt is the labelling of call-centre jobs as 'executive' positions and the fostering of professional identities that go with them (ibid. 2006). In India, trade-union organization is something that blue-collar workers undertake, not something engaged in by middle-class employees working in white-collar jobs for large global corporations.

Yet despite the odds, UNITE has made progress. Confronting the rhetoric surrounding ITeS/BPO is the reality of the work and the employment relations that govern the industry. In a little under two years (as of early 2007), UNITE has reported upwards of seven thousand new recruits, though not all of these are full financial members (Taylor et al. 2009). The union has made some headway in bargaining, having signed agreements with four large firms, and has drawn significant national publicity for its organizing campaigns around safe transportation to and from work and the employer's duty of care following two

270 Smiling Down the Line

separate murders of BPO workers on their way home from work.[15] Still, the road ahead for UNITES will not be easy. The union's international director has described organizing India's BPO sector as the 'ultimate challenge' in his career of organizing in developing nations.[16] UNITES is up against determined and recalcitrant transnational and domestic employers and is having to develop strategies that will not alienate its primary constituency, which is young middle-class workers. It needs to find ways to gain an independent and effective employee voice regarding the worrying issues that have developed around India's BPO industry. Undoubtedly – and as UNITES officials are certainly aware – this will mean combining pragmatic unionism with militancy in strategically novel ways. While the further organization of the industry will be no mean feat, it can no longer be said that BPO is an entirely union-free zone.

9 Concluding Reflections

When research about call centres first commenced, many of the terms referred to in these pages still did not exist. Designations such as ITeS/ BPO and 'supercentre,' as well as natural-speech-recognition and screen-capture technologies, would have produced only shrugs a decade ago. Such have been the changes in the ways information is produced and conveyed that the task of analysing the subject matter in this book has been rendered all the more challenging. Info-service work is not something that is easily pinned down for inspection; there have been ongoing changes and new developments in the ways it is carried out. For that reason our focus throughout the book has remained on the call centre. Within its walls a new labour process for producing and disseminating information has led to shifts in work design – or what is frequently referred to as the technical division of labour – as well as to changes in the social division of labour and the ways in which such work is managed. This book is an effort to chart, analyse, and ultimately understand the meaning of these changes. Such transformations are constituted by both material and social developments that strictly speaking make it inaccurate to wedge these two concepts apart. The new ICTs, described in previous chapters, have made the information economy a possibility. Business decisions to invest in certain technologies and not others and to use those technologies in certain organizational ways have made the social relations of production in these work processes a contemporary reality.

I have been careful in this book to refer to an information economy and info-service work rather than to the now more fashionable 'knowledge economy.' More accurately still, we should be referring to the economics of information production through the conduct of info-service labour. Though the exploitation of knowledge has made this possible, info-service work should not be conflated with the organized pursuit of knowledge. Rather, as argued throughout the book, info-service work is best seen as the current era's equivalent to the semiskilled labour of yesteryear. This analogy should not be taken in a literal sense; it is a relative claim. What is definitely *not* being said is that contemporary info-service work is of the same nature as the production systems that characterized the industrial period of high Fordism. To my mind, there is no question that today's positions in contact-centre-based customer-service work entail greater education, training, and skill utilization than the assembly-line jobs of the industrial economy. In this respect, the post-industrial sociologists of the last century were correct in their predictions that work upgrading would accompany informationalism (Bell 1973; Block 1990; Castells 1996; Herzenberg, Alic, and Wial 1998; Hirschhorn 1984; Zuboff 1988). But they were also only partly correct.

For it is also the case that we have seen little evidence of information work morphing into knowledge work. Rather, info-service work uses the outputs of knowledge – its technologies, business tools, and management theories – to produce and distribute information. At the moment there is considerable debate over the whole theme of knowledge management and whether such a practice is feasible, let alone desirable. Within the realms of knowledge creation, despite the best efforts of current academic and political managers, scientific and artistic effort may at best be *indirectly directed* through the allocation of resources or other inducements, rather than *managed* in any strict sense of the term. This follows from the fact that the outputs of such endeavours cannot be known with any degree of certitude before their creation, which renders attempts at detailed management rather futile. With info-service work, on the other hand, as we have seen throughout this book, attention and practice are directed towards the management of information and of the workers who are responsible for disseminating it. Here the main contention revolves around whether there are or should be alternatives to the dominant management paradigms that have characterized capitalist industrial production.

I have mentioned the economics of information. With this term the practice of management in a strict sense is introduced into the analysis. This entails the calculative use of human and non-human resources to produce designated outputs in the amounts and of the types desired. We have seen this mindset at work in the preceding chapters. The pressures underlying the quest for rationalization move the labour process and its management in a very different direction from what has been enumerated in post-industrial theory, which is why prognoses that are derived from this paradigm are at best only partly accurate. Critics of contemporary management have argued persuasively that because info-service work is subject to the same rationalizing pressures as characterize capitalist production in general, such work reproduces mass-production systems of types that are all too familiar. Tayloristic systems, or hybrid systems that involve a large dose of Taylorism (e.g., 'team Taylorism'), are reborn in the information economy. I do not doubt the motivations and intentionality of moving in this direction; I do, however, doubt whether such projects will succeed in info-service work. The tension between intent and results is what we have attempted to capture throughout the book with theoretical devices such as charting relations between the three changes in the world of work in chapter 1 and introducing an extended materialist analysis in chapter 5.

Some labour process theorists have suggested that call centres are more aptly described as 'Taylorism plus' organizations, while others have argued on behalf of alternatives, which they capture in such terms as 'high-performance work systems' or 'mass-customized bureaucracies.' Each diagnosis towards enhancing our understanding of what goes on in info-service work raises additional queries. For example, our research has found little empirical evidence of HPWSs in the contact centres examined in this book. This is not to imply that such a paradigm might not become more influential in the future, which as always is 'up for grabs' (see below). Additionally, there is little support for the use of indicators that have been used for identifying HPWS in older industries but that currently seem to have little applicability to info-service work as it is currently undertaken. Meanwhile, from a labour-process perspective, if we acknowledge that info-service work entails more than or differs from classical Taylorism, an obligation remains to specify the distinctiveness of these workflows.

I have, indeed, tried to specify that distinctiveness in my analysis of the changes I see besetting much contemporary work – namely, the unscrambling of existing technical and social divisions of labour and the compensatory employment of the practices of modern managerialism. As the informational component of production increases and information assumes the status of a productive output in its own right, work becomes more complex and at the same time is subject to greater decentralization. Managerialism, the micromanagement of people, or simply 'people management,' is one response. Human resource management is the discursive expression of managerialism in the contemporary work-place. It sets out to obtain employee 'buy in' – that is, identification with the aims and objectives of the employer. Ideally, workers are to become self-disciplining agents, but in info-service work this is not borne out of autonomy or freedom at work or even necessarily commitment to organizational practices. In common with Taylorism, benchmarks, pro-tocols, and kpi's are laid out in great detail, though this has not had the effect of simplifying or deskilling work. Part of contemporary work experience is about continuously documenting conformance with such metrics, and this is taken to demonstrate accountability – indeed, it *constitutes* accountability. Contemporary managerialism, defined as such, arises out of the inadequacies of Taylorism in informational work set-tings. Taylorism has traditionally been associated with work simplifi-cation. While this approach may be of use in some information work settings, in others the nature of product and service markets renders it inadequate if not counterproductive. Many jobs are now simply too large and too varied to be subject to the strictures of classical scien-tific management and a highly detailed division of labour. This does not mean that they have been replaced by jobs that feature self-man-agement in the true sense of the term, or by (semi)-autonomous work groups, socio-technical teams, or HPWSs. Rather, managerialism is the new credo, packaged and marketed as human resource management.

This book has expressed serious doubts about the success of the managerialist project, whereby management lays out what it wants and how it wants it achieved, and workers respond by striving to meet such objectives, while continuously documenting their efforts or hav-ing those efforts documented for them. Such a project is a highly one-sided affair indeed, and many will see it as such. It denies labour all rights except the 'right' to display conformity with preset means and goals. These are not the ideal precursors for the realization of commit-ment on the part of people.

The managerialist project is challenged by yet another theme ex-plored in this book – the realities of globalization. Though this is quite possibly the most overworked term in the social-scientific lexicon of the past decade, any serious political economy must pay special atten-tion to deepening our understanding of this phenomenon. I have used the term in conjunction with work that is undertaken for global mar-kets using like labour processes located at different hubs around the world. This has rendered such ideas as production for the home mar-ket and the need for proximity between production and consumption

– even in many branches of service work, and especially those with a large informational component – increasingly irrelevant. Still, there is much debate about what the globalization of supply chains stands for. I have suggested that globalization can be understood as a new type of economic integration in which *competitive advantage* organized around the exploitation of wage arbitrage trumps *comparative advantage*. The analysis of BPOs in this book argues that similar types of work, or jobs requiring comparable skills, are being conducted at the behest of transnational organizations in locations of convenience. In other words, what is most notable are the similarities, rather than the differences, in info-service work that is carried on in both the global North and the global South for vastly different real wages. I realize that at the current moment this position is contentious, just as its implications for both developed and less developed economies are highly problematic, but the possibilities for further debate are enticing and should be taken up with gusto by critical researchers.

If, for argument's sake, the reader finds somewhat credible the portrayal of globalization presented in this book, the implications for managerialism are noteworthy. They foretell the sort of insecurity and risk that other researchers (Beck 2000; Boltanski and Chiapello 2007; Glyn 2007; Standing 1999) have associated with the new era. This being the case, we need to ask ourselves why identity ties to organizations that may be here today but somewhere else tomorrow should be stronger than in the past. Why would the majority of employees, whether in investment-exporting or outsource-receiving economies, deeply commit themselves to the employment arrangements that have been heralded by globalization?

The dynamics of globalization lend additional impetus to managerialism even while undercutting its results. This occurs through the outsourcing and subcontracting relationships that underpin global economic ties. The uncertainties and potential risks associated with such transactional arrangements place a premium on managerial oversight as well as on documentation, assurance, and accreditation. In this way the practices of managerialism are also globalized. HRM, for example, is now a global phenomenon employing similar discourses and techniques regardless of location. As suggested above, however, the relationship between globalization and managerialism is also a contradictory one. Globalization promotes the use and extension of managerialist practices even while it undermines the objectives of those practices. This observation raises intriguing questions. Can workforces become inured to the continuous chop and change that is implied by globalization? Are there limits to the toleration of human-made insecurities?

As for the future of info-service work, it will probably itself be subject to the contradictory developments that have been sketched out here. There will be ongoing attempts to simplify work that is not defined as adding value – or at least enough value (i.e., that does not return profit to companies at a requisite rate) – and these will be hastened as a result of the crisis that capitalism is facing in the early twenty-first century. Further work rationalization may take various forms. The public may be encouraged to self-service through the imposition of user fees on transactions that require service staff. Already we see some private-sector firms heading down this road. Customer self-service is being actualized through more extensive use of Web-based delivery, whereby the public navigates to and through organizational sites to acquire e-services online.

More interesting from our perspective is the future of informational work that does *not* easily adapt itself to self-service. In this book we have seen that more and more fields of business and public service are coming under the ambit of voice-based info-service provision. Up until now this has mainly but not entirely involved transactional work. I say 'not entirely' because numerous operations in this study are involved in more than simple transactional work – providing advice, discussing options, and creating plans for people. Every indication is that these trends will continue and likely deepen. Already, certain fields of professional labour are coming under the format of the labour processes discussed in this book. The author has visited call centres where registered nurses dispense medical guidance through tele-health lines. At another centre, certified urban planners provide advice on zoning and urban-development applications. It seems that even trade unions have discovered the benefits of member-contact centres; some organizations are utilizing this format to provide industrial/legal assistance to members and potential members who solicit advice. Knowledge process outsourcing (KPO), as it has come to be known in India, is yet another example of these trends. At present this approach is being applied to such diverse labours as legal work (contract drafting, document analysis, patent research), health-care and pharmaceutical research (patient-imaging diagnostics, pre-clinical studies, clinical data management), and financial analysis.

These latest developments may entail the professionalizing of info-service work, or they may be harbingers for bringing professional work into the modes of information production and distribution analysed in this book. Will the twin dynamics of managerialism and globalization result in ongoing efforts to rationalize such labour in the ways discussed here? Or will the professional ethoses and histories associated with such work at last provide a basis for the construction of better, more dignified organizational designs than we have observed in this study? What types of relationships will develop between professional and in many cases long-standing occupational cultures and new work designs that employ the call-centre format? Where will such work be carried out, and with what effects on host societies? Surely questions such as these are an invitation to further study that, we can hope, will attract the attention of the present as well as future cohorts of researchers.

Notes

Chapter 1

1 Hockschild's original theory of emotional labour was based on an analysis of the work of airline flight attendants.
2 IT employment refers to work in such occupations as programming and software design and development.
3 Budde (2004) reports that the use of integrated voice recognition practically doubled from 5.2 to 9.2 per cent of all transactions conducted through contact centres between 2003 and 2005 in Australia. On the other hand, the use of more sophisticated natural-speech-recognition technologies remains in its infancy, though of interest to many call-centre managers.
4 Clearly, teams have been used with the goal of forging stronger ties with the overriding goals of the organization (Parker and Slaughter 1988; Sewell 1998; Procter and Mueller 2000, Pt I; Thompson and McHugh 2002, ch. 20).
5 Not all of the authors cited include all of the HR practices referred to in the text. Only such items on which there appears to be overlap at least among some of the authors are included in our treatment of contemporary HR practice.
6 A long line of sociological and social-psychological research has also noted the importance of informal work groups as incubators of alternative meaning structures (Burawoy 1979; Gouldner 1954a, 1954b; Mayo 1977; Mars 1994; Roy 1952, 1954; Scott 1994).

Chapter 2

1 Interview, call-centre manager, 17 November 2004.
2 A very preliminary paper emerged from this fieldwork and was published

in the Federal Government Task Force's final communication, *The Final Report of the National Forum on the Information Highway and Workplace Issues: Challenges and Opportunities* (Russell 1997).

3 A final report titled 'Voice, Representation, and Recognition: Unions and Call Centres' (2006a) was prepared by the author. As implied by the subtitle, this text focused on factors that are conducive to or that pose obstructions to union organization in call centres.

4 Research of the type undertaken in this study has not been encouraged by changes to Australian industrial-relations legislation enacted in 1996 and again in 2006. Refer to chapter 8 for further details.

5 It is likely the case that the interviews with management at two of the companies helped gain agreement on participating in the workforce survey.

6 In Australia the Australian Teleservices Association (ATA) is the peak body that serves as a network for call-centre managers. It is organized on both a state and national level and is tasked with organizing seminars, conferences, and contact-centre competitions.

7 These sociologically instructive adjectives that are used to designate different value markets for essentially the same product are the company's, not mine.

8 These are actual examples of the types of calls that were received while the author was 'double jacking' alongside CSRs at this call centre.

Chapter 3

1 As Edward Thompson (1966) offers in accounting for the title of his magnus opus *The Making of the English Working Class*: 'Making because it is a study in an active process, which owes as much to agency as to conditioning' (9).

2 For the most part the role of the call-centre manager has been neglected in studies of this work process. For an important exception see Houlihan (2006).

3 Interview, *Insurer1*, call-centre manager, 4 August 2004.

4 Callaghan and Thompson (2002) also draw attention to the paradox that exists between meticulous recruitment and selection processes and high levels of attrition in call centres, but fail to offer a convincing explanation as to why organizations persist in sticking with such recruitment procedures.

5 This is sometimes referred to as 'relationship management' – a term that is avoided in this text on account of the implicit assumptions it contains regarding positions of superordination that often don't apply in CSR interactions with the public.

6 Interview, *Urban Space,* call-centre manager, 21 October 2004.

7 Interview, *Insurer 1,* call-centre manager, 4 August 2004.

8 This centre prides itself on how far it has taken e-work. It was, for example, the only centre in the study to request a paperless version of our survey. As a result, the questionnaire at this site was administered completely online during working time.

Chapter 4

1 Workers from the call centre of an electrical-appliances manufacture that attended a call-centre shop-stewards seminar that the author organized vividly reinforced this point.

2 See Mulholland (2004) and van den Broek (2004) for sceptical views of these claims.

3 An Alpha coefficient of .70 or higher is customarily taken as evidence that the index is a reliable measure – that is, that its various components are all measuring/referring to the same thing.

4 The Anova procedure requires homogeneity of variance for the variables that are used.

5 Interview, *Insurer2,* call-centre manager, 12 December 2004.

6 Herzenberg, Alic, and Wial (1998) distinguish between semi-autonomous jobs and tightly constrained jobs. Though they place customer-service work in the former category (67), they also note that computer monitoring is leading in the direction of more constrained labour processes.

7 As Batt (2000, 547) comments, even low-value customer streams should not be associated with low-skilled work: 'Even at this level, employees must be skilled in several software packages and have negotiating skill to deal with tough customers ... Residential service reps must be quite sophisticated in their knowledge of information systems and manipulation of databases to retrieve the necessary information.'

8 It is most likely the case that one or two other centres (e.g. *Health Premium, Bank1*) would also have exhibited significant differences from a number of other centres had we received a greater number of responses from them.

9 Interview, *Telebet,* call-centre manager, 17 November 2004.

10 Field notes, 31 March 2004.

11 The questions read as follows: 'I have to become emotionally detached from callers when I am responding to them'; 'I have to mask my true feelings when I am dealing with callers'; and 'I can be my true self when I am on the phone with callers' (reverse coded). The higher the score, the greater the emotional effort that is put in the job ($\alpha = .700$).

12 Each of these variables is measured by a single question on the survey. The question on depression reads: 'This job leaves me feeling depressed.' The question pertaining to work pressure reads: 'I feel as though I am under a great deal of pressure in my job.'

13 *** = significant at .000 level.

14 Whereas the centre used to process between five and six thousand bookings per day, current figures (2005) stand between five and six hundred per day. Online bookings have made up the difference. The centre has lost about thirty agent positions as a result of these changes (interview, *Airline*, call-centre manager, 29 July and 2 August 2005).

Chapter 5

1 Parts of this chapter first appeared in Russell, '"You Gotta Lie to It": Software Applications and the Management of Technological Change in a Call Centre,' *New Technology, Work, and Employment* 22, no. 2 (2007): 132–45.

2 *Power* is a fictitious name.

3 Interview, call-centre manager, 24 August 2001, and induction session for new employees, 9 January 2002.

4 *Power* is the only call centre where I can recall seeing a TV in the work area. While having a TV in a staff lounge or a break room is common practice, it was highly unusual to see a TV out in the operations area.

5 This was previous research to the workforce surveys that are the subject matter of this book. It included the administration of an earlier and less developed survey instrument at four contact centres, the results of which are reported in Russell (2002a, b; 2004; 2006b).

6 Interview, *Power* call-centre manager, 24 August 2001.

7 Fieldwork observation, 31 August 2001.

8 Training session, 10 January 2002.

9 There have been exceptions to the tendency to treat ICTs in call centres in the manner I have described. See, for example, Mulholland (2002) for an interesting analysis of tech change and negative impacts on productivity in a call centre she studies; and Collin-Jacques (2004) for an analysis of varying software-design choices and the effects they have on the work of nurses delivering telehealth services.

10 As at other call centres (Bain, Watson, et al. 2002), workers at *Power* have definite targets they are expected to meet. Talk times that average between 108 and 126 seconds and a 90-second post-call wrap-up period are among the most commonly articulated targets.

11 Such possibilities have been explored in a series of call-centre articles by Batt (1999, 2000, 2002) and Batt and Moynihan (2004).
12 Interview, *Power* call-centre manager, 5 September 2001.
13 Interview, *Power* technology-integration manager, 24 January 2002.
14 Ibid.

Chapter 6

1 Managers going underground would sometimes be given an intentionally rough ride down the shaft by the hoist operators.
2 See Russell (1999,103) for examples of workers dismissing new workplace cultural initiatives.
3 Interview, *Licensing* call-centre manager, 16 May 2001.
4 L. Yallamas, 'Woman Fights Sacking for Refusing to Play War Game', *Courier Mail*, 8 April 2003, p. 5.
5 Useful critiques of the HPWS approach can be found in Fleetwood (2007); Godard and Delaney (2000); and Legge (2004).
6 Mean rankings are derived by the sum of ranks for each organization divided by the number of responses from each organization.
7 The scores in each organization do not exhibit homogeneous variation and thereby violate the homogeneity assumption.
8 Consultation with co-workers as the most common strategy for resolving difficult queries is in evidence only at *Advisory Services*, *Health Authority*, and the smallest of the financial call centres, *Bank1*.
9 The correlation between gender and perceptions that team members are an important source of social support in the workplace (Φ) is a modest .097 (p < .05)
10 Similar points are registered in Standing (1999); Beck (2000); and Boltanski and Chiapello (2007).

Chapter 7

1 Sections of this chapter dealing with the skills associated with BPO work first appeared in Russell and Thite (2008).
2 Ulrich Beck marvels at the fact that arrival and departure announcements at Berlin's international airport now emanate in real time from California, thereby cancelling the need for evening and night-time work at the German airport and the penalty rates associated with these shifts. The instantantaneity and cheapness of long-distance communications has in

Beck's words allowed for 'globalized labour cooperation or production' (2000).

3   These are employer-sponsored – or in this case, client sponsored – non-permanent immigrant visas for temporary workers.

4   Interview, ITeS associate vice-president, HR, *BPO3*, 17 October 2005 (Bangalore).

5   The lower estimates are taken from Government of India (2003), but growth appears to have been faster than projected by the government in 2003, by some 35,000 employees. These estimates also fall within the range that was cited to us in an interview with the vice-president of operations for *BPO2* (13 October 2005, Bangalore).

6   The figures quoted in Srinivasan (2006, 28, Table 2) are generally in line with what HR call-centre managers reported to us during interviews. For example, at one major BPO, starting CSR salaries were pegged at R130,000 per year or $A4062, exactly 10 per cent of the average $A40,000 salary earned in Australia. Our data are for the fourth quarter of 2005.

7   These figures refer to the total labour force, which is divided into 'organized' and 'unorganized' categories. In the 2001 census, only 10 per cent of India's total labour force was employed or worked in the 'organized' sector of the economy – that is, the sector that pays wages, maintains accounts, and is subject to federal and state regulations. Almost 60 per cent of the labour force remained on the land, either as cultivators or as agricultural labourers, (Census of India 2001).

8   Calculated by authors from Nasscom (2008), estimates for fiscal year 2007.

9   Interview, chief people officer, *BPO2*, 13 October 2005, Bangalore.

10 Other authors such as Budhwar, Varma, and colleagues (2006) have noted that HRM in Indian call centres is of necessity preoccupied with recruitment and selection.

11 This refers to the two dimensions of skill that Spenner has (1983) has distinguished between – the skill of the job and the skill of the job holder.

12 All results are statistically significant at the .001 level using the Chi-square statistic.

13 Interview, vice-president of operations, *BPO2*, 13 October 2005, Bangalore.

14 Interview, operations manager, *BPO1*, 18 October 2005, Hyderabad.

15 This equates to 50 000 km per day. Interview, chief people officer, *BPO2*, 13 October 2005, Bangalore.

16 Managerial staff would generally work even longer hours. For further details on BPO working time, see Noronha and D'Cruz (2006).

17 Significant at the .01 level.

18 It has been suggested by Pradhan and Abraham (2005) that this form of identity denial and replacement could lead to the formation of multiple personality disorders in certain workers.

19 Trust is not something that Indian workers consider is reciprocated on management's part, with Indian employees agreeing in equal proportions with their Australian counterparts that management has trouble trusting its staff. This easily fits in with the high emphasis on control that BPO exudes. All reported differences are significant at the .000 level.

20 Indian workers were less likely to disagree that they would be willing to work extra hours than their Australian counterparts, whereas a greater proportion of Indian agents were undecided on this question. This may have something to do with the more complex logistical issues of getting home from work after a shift in India.

21 'The most widely studied behavioural correlate of commitment has been tenure in the organisation, or its obverse, turnover' (Meyer and Allen 1991, 73). See also Meyer and Allen (1997); Cohen (1993); DeCotiis and Summers (1987); Iverson and Buttigieg (1999); Jaros (1997); and Whitener and Waltz (1993).

22 A logistic regression analysis is used here as the dependent variable; intention to stay with employer is a binary variable.

Chapter 8

1 An earlier version of some sections of this chapter first appeared in Russell (2008a).

2 Results from this centre have not been used in this study. A previous version of the survey instrument that is used in this book was piloted at this centre. The observations reported on here are derived from interviews that were conducted with centre managers and team leaders in June 2000.

3 Interview, acting call-centre manager, 23 August 2000.

4 Team meeting, 5 July 2000.

5 *Licensing*, team meeting, 22 May 2001.

6 Policy makers tended to associate collective bargaining with 'wage breakouts' and inflation.

7 Under the 2006 'Work Choices legislation, this has been reduced to five allowable matters, which must be contained in all awards.

8 AWAs were introduced in 1996 under the new Howard government's Workplaces Reform legislation. The employee advocate was a new position created by the legislation. The purpose of this office was to ensure that the conditions contained in an AWA did not offer any 'net' disadvantage to

the employee. Conditions in AWAs could differ from the relevant industry award, or from the contents of an existing collective agreement, but overall, there was to be no net disadvantage.

9 Prior to the onset of enterprise bargaining and even afterwards, it was not unheard of for unions representing workers to have no shop-steward structure at the point of production. AWIRS reports in its 1995 review of Australian industrial relations that 30 per cent of workplaces with union members did not have a shop steward; this figure increased to almost 40 per cent in the private sector (Morehead et al. 1997, p. 140; see also Peetz 1998). This distinguishes the Australian system in an important way from North American industrial relations in unionized workplaces.

10 Interview, *Bus Company* call-centre manager, 21 May 2004.

11 This list of prohibited content is not exhaustive. I have only drawn attention to those clauses that have particular relevance to the discussion of union organizing in call centres.

12 For an enlightening comparison that analyses the challenges confronting unions under Britain's 'New Labour' industrial relations legislation, see G. Gall (2006).

13 Interview, chief people officer, *BPO2*, 13 October 2005, Bangalore.

14 Interview, vice-president of operations, *BPO2*, 13 October 2005, Bangalore.

15 Details of these tragic events and other information are contained in a compilation of press clippings that the union supplied to the author under the title of Unite@One.

16 Interview, Unite Regional Secretary Asia-Pacific, 22 April 2007, New Delhi.

References

ABS (Australian Bureau of Statistics). 2006. 'Australian and New Zealand Standard Classification of Occupations (ANZSCO).' Cat. No. 1220.0. http://www.abs.gov.au

– 1997. *Australian Standard Classification of Occupations,* 2nd ed. Canberra: Commonwealth of Australia.

ACTU. 2002. (Australian Council of Trade Unions). 'On the Line: The Future of Australia's Call Centre Industry.' http://www.actu.asn.au/Archive/Papers/OnTheLineTheFutureOfAustraliasCallCentreIndustry.aspx

Ackroyd, S., and P. Thompson. 1999. *Organizational Misbehaviour*. London: Sage.

Adler, P. 1986. 'New Technologies, New Skills.' *California Management Review* 29, no. 1: 9–28.

Alexander, R., and J. Lewer. 2004. *Understanding Australian Industrial Relations*. Melbourne: Thompson.

Alferoff, C., and D. Knights. 2002. 'Quality Time and the Beautiful Call.' In *Reorganizing Service Work: Call Centres in Germany and Britain*, ed. U. Holtgrewe, C. Kerst, and K. Shire. 183–203. Aldershot: Ashgate.

– 2001. 'We're All Partying Here: Target and Games, or Target as Games in Call Centre Management.' Second Critical Management Studies Conference.

Alvesson, M. 2004. *Knowledge Work and Knowledge-Intensive Firms*. Oxford: Oxford University Press.

– 2002. *Understanding Organizational Culture*. London: Sage.

Alvesson, M., and H. Willmott. 2002. 'Identity Regulation as Organizational Control: Producing the Appropriate Individual.' *Journal of Management Studies* 39, no. 5: 619–44.

Anderson, B. 1991. *Imagined Communities*. London: Verso.

Appelbaum, E., T. Bailey, P. Berg, and A. Kalleberg. 2000. *Manufacturing Ad-*

vantage: Why High Performance Work Systems Pay Off. Ithaca: Cornell University Press.

Armstrong, P., and H. Armstrong. 1994. *The Double Ghetto,* 3rd ed. Toronto: McClelland and Stewart.

Aronowitz, S. 1973. *False Promises: The Shaping of American Working Class Consciousness.* New York: McGraw-Hill.

Arthur, J. 1994. 'Effects of Human Resource Systems on Manufacturing Performance and Turnover.' *Academy of Management Journal* 37, no. 3: 670–87.

Arzbacher, S., U. Holtgrewe, and C. Kerst. 2002. 'Call Centres: Constructing Flexibility.' In *Reorganizing Service Work: Call Centres in Germany and Britain,* ed. U. Holtgrewe, C. Kerst, and K. Shire. 19–41. Aldershot: Ashgate.

Australian Qualifications Framework Advisory Board. 1996. 'Introduction to the AQF.' Car Hon: Curriculum Corporation.

Badham, R. 2005. 'Technology and the Transformation of Work.' In *The Oxford Handbook of Work and Organization,* ed. S. Ackroyd, R. Batt, P. Thompson, and P. Tolbert. 115–37. Oxford: Oxford University Press.

Bain, P., and P. Taylor. 2002a. 'Consolidation, "Cowboys," and the Developing Employment Relationship in British, Dutch, and US Call Centres.' In *Re-Organizing Service Work: Call Centres in Germany and Britain,* ed. U. Holtgrewe, C. Kerst, and K. Shire. 42–62. Aldershot: Ashgate.

– 2002b. 'Ringing the Changes? Union Recognition and Organization in Call Centres in the UK Finance Sector.' *Industrial Relations Journal* 33, no. 3: 246–61.

– 2000. 'Entrapped by the "Electronic Panopticon"? Worker Resistance in the Call Centre.' *New Technology, Work, and Employment* 15, no. 1: 2–18.

Bain, P., A. Watson, G. Mulvey, P. Taylor, and G. Gall. 2002. 'Taylorism, Targets, and the Pursuit of Quantity and Quality by Call Centre Management.' *New Technology, Work, and Employment* 17, no. 3: 170–85.

Baird, M. 2002. 'Changes, Dangers, Choice, and Voice: Understanding What High-Commitment Management Means for Employees and Unions.' *Journal of Industrial Relations* 44, no. 3: 359–75.

Baldry, C., P. Bain, and P. Taylor. 1998. '"Bright Satanic Offices": Intensification, Control, and Team Taylorism.' In *Workplaces of the Future,* ed. P. Thompson and C. Warhurst. 163–83. Houndmills: Palgrave Macmillan.

Baran, B., and S. Teegarden. 1987. 'Women's Labor in the Office of the Future: A Case Study of the Insurance Industry.' In *Women, Households, and the Economy,* ed. L. Beneria and C. Stimpson. 201–44. New Brunswick: Rutgers University Press.

Barley, S. 1990. 'The Alignment of Technology and Structure through Roles and Networks.' *Administrative Science Quarterly* 35, no. 1: 61–103.

– 1986. 'Technology as an Occasion for Structuring: Evidence from Obser-

vations of CT Scanners and the Social Order of Radiology Departments.'
Administrative Science Quarterly 31, no. 1: 78–108.

Barnes, A. 2004. 'Diaries, Dunnies, and Discipline: Resistance and Accommo-
dation to Monitoring in Call Centres.' *Labour and Industry* 14, no. 3: 127–37.

Batt, R. 2002. 'Managing Customer Services: Human Resource Practices, Quit
Rates, and Sales Growth.' *Academy of Management Journal* 45, no. 3: 587–97.

– 2000. 'Strategic Segmentation in Front-Line Services: Matching Customers,
Employees, and Human Resource Systems.' *International Journal of Human
Resource Management* 11, no. 3: 540–61.

– 1999. 'Work Organization, Technology, and Performance in Customer Service and Sales.' *Industrial and Labor Relations Review* 52, no. 4: 539–64.

Batt, R., V. Doellgast, and H. Kwon. 2006. 'Service Management and Employment Systems in U.S. and Indian Call Centres.' In *Offshoring White-Collar
Work*, ed. S. Collins and L. Brainard. 335–72. Washington: Brookings Institution.

Batt, R., V. Doellgast, H. Kwon, M. Nopany, P. Nopany, and A. da Costa. 2005.
'The Indian Call Centre Industry: National Benchmarking Report.' Ithaca:
Cornell University, Global Call Centre Industry Project.

Batt, R., and L. Moynihan. 2004. 'The Viability of Alternative Call Centre
Production Models.' In *Call Centres and Human Resource Management: A
Cross-National Perspective*, ed. S. Deery and N. Kinnie. 25–53. Houndmills:
Palgrave Macmillan.

– 2002. 'The Viability of Alternative Call Centre Production Models.' *Human
Resource Management Journal* 12, no. 4: 14–34.

Bauman, Z. 1998. *Work, Consumerism, and the New Poor.* Buckingham: Open
University Press.

Beck, U. 2000. *What Is Globalization?* Cambridge: Polity.

– 1992. *Risk Society: Towards a New Modernity.* London: Sage.

Bell, D. 1973. *The Coming of Post-Industrial Society.* New York: Basic.

Belt, V. 2002a. 'Capitalising on Femininity: Gender and the Utilisation of Social
Skills in Telephone Call Centres.' In *Re-Organizing Service Work: Call Centres
in Germany and Britain*, ed. U. Holtgrewe, C. Kerst, and K. Shire. 123–45.
Aldershot: Ashgate.

– 2002b. 'A Female Ghetto? Women's Careers in Call Centres.' *Human Resource Management Journal* 12, no. 4: 51–66.

Belt, V., R. Richardson, and J. Webster. 2002. 'Women, Social Skill, and Interactive Service Work in Telephone Call Centres.' *New Technology, Work, and
Employment* 17, no. 1: 20–34.

– 2000. 'Women's Work in the Information Economy: The Case of Telephone
Call Centres.' *Information, Communication, and Society* 3, no. 3: 366–85.

Bendix, R. 1974. *Work and Authority in Industry: Ideologies of Management in the Course of Industrialization*. Berkeley: University of California Press.

Benner, C. 2005. '"South Africa On-Call": Information Technology and Labour Market Restructuring in South African Call Centres.' *Regional Studies* 40, no. 9: 1025–40.

– 2002. *Work in the New Economy: Flexible Labor Markets in Silicon Valley*. Oxford: Blackwell.

Berggren, C. 1992. *Alternatives to Lean Production: Work Organization in the Swedish Auto Industry*. Ithaca: Cornell University Press.

Betcherman, G. 1991. *Employment in the Service Economy: A Research Report Prepared for the Economic Council of Canada*. Ottawa: Minister of Supply and Services.

Beynon, H. 1973. *Working for Ford*. London: Penguin.

Bhatnagar, J. 2007. 'Talent Management Strategy of Employee Engagement in Indian ITES Employees: Key to Retention.' *Employee Relations* 29, no. 6: 640–63.

Bittner, S., M. Schietinger, J. Schroth, and C. Weinkopf. 2002. 'Call Centres in Germany: Employment, Training, and Job Design.' In *Re-Organizing Service Work: Call Centres in Germany and Britain*, ed. U. Holtgrewe, C. Kerst, and K. Shire. 63–85. Aldershot: Ashgate.

Blauner, R. 1964. *Alienation and Freedom: The Factory Worker and His Industry*. Chicago: University of Chicago Press.

Block, F. 1990. *Postindustrial Possibilities*. Berkeley: University of California Press.

Bloomfield, B., and A. Danieli. 1995. 'The Role of Management Consultants in the Development of Information Technology: The Indissoluble Nature of Socio-Political and Technical Skills.' *Journal of Management Studies* 32, no. 1: 23–46

Bolman, L., and T. Deal. 2003. *Reframing Organizations: Artistry, Choice, and Leadership*. San Francisco: Jossey-Bass.

Boltanski, L. and E. Chiapello. 2007. *The New Spirit of Capitalism*. London: Verso.

Bolton, S., and C. Boyd. 2003. 'Trolley Dolly or Skilled Emotion Manager? Moving on from Hochschild's Managed Heart.' *Work, Employment and Society* 17, no. 2: 289–308.

Bolton, S., and M. Houlihan. 2007. 'Risky Business: Rethinking the Human in Interactive Service Work.' In *Searching for the Human in Human Resource Management*, ed. S. Bolton and M. Houlihan. 245–62. Houndmills: Palgrave.

Bowden, B., and B. Russell. 2000. 'Benchmarking, Global Best Practice, and

Production Renorming in the Australian Coal Industry.' In *Globalization and Its Discontents*, ed. S. McBride and J. Wiseman. 97–110. Basingstoke: Macmillan.

Bramble, T. 2008. *Trade Unionism in Australia: A History from Flood to Ebb Tide*. Cambridge: Cambridge University Press.

– 1989. 'Award Restructuring and the Australian Trade Union Movement: A Critique.' *Labour and Industry* 2, no. 3: 372–98.

Braverman, H. 1974. *Labor and Monopoly Capital: The Degradation of Work in the Twentieth Century*. New York: Monthly Review.

Brenner, R. 2003. *The Boom and the Bubble: The U.S. in the World Economy*. London: Verso.

Briggs, C. 2001. 'Australian Exceptionalism: The Role of Trade Unions in the Emergence of Enterprise Bargaining.' *Journal of Industrial Relations* 43, no. 1: 27–43.

Bristow, G., M. Munday, and P. Gripaios. 2000. 'Call Centre Growth and Location: Corporate Strategy and the Spatial Division of Labour.' *Environment and Planning A* 32, no. 3: 519–38.

Bronfenbrenner, K., and T. Juravich. 1998. 'It Takes More Than House Calls: Organizing to Win with a Comprehensive Union-Building Strategy.' In *Organizing to Win: New Research on Union Strategies*, ed. K. Bronfenbrenner, S. Friedman, R. Hurd, R. Oswald, and R. Seeber. 19–36. Ithaca: Cornell University Press, 1998.

Brown, A. 1995. 'Managing Understandings: Politics, Symbolism, Niche Marketing, and the Quest for Legitimacy in IT Implementation.' *Organization Studies* 16, no. 6: 951–69.

Buchanan, J., and R. Hall. 2002. 'Teams and Control on the Job.' *Journal of Industrial Relations* 44, no. 3: 397–417.

Buchanan, R., and S. Koch-Schulte. 2000. 'Gender on the Line: Technology, Restructuring, and the Reorganization of Work in the Call Centre Industry.' Ottawa: Research Directorate, Status of Women Canada.

Budde, P. 2004. *Australia – Call Centres.doc*. Paul Budde Communication Pty. Ltd. http://www.budde.com.au/buddereports/1104/Australia_Call_centres.aspx?related=y

Budhwar, P., H. Luthar, and J. Bhatnagar. 2006. 'The Dynamics of HRM Systems in Indian BPO Firms.' *Journal of Labor Research* 27, no. 3: 339–60.

Budhwar, P., N. Malhotra, and V. Singh. 2009. 'Work Processes and Emerging Problems in Indian Call Centres.' In *The Next Available Operator: Managing Human Resources in Indian Business Process Outsourcing Industry*, ed. M. Thite and B. Russell. 58–82. New Delhi: Sage.

Budhwar, P., A. Varma, V. Singh, and R. Dhar. 2006. 'HRM Systems of Indian Call Centres: An Exploratory Study.' *International Journal of Human Resource Management* 17, no. 5: 881–97.

Burawoy, M. 1979. *Manufacturing Consent: Changes in the Labor Process under Monopoly Capitalism.* Chicago: University of Chicago Press.

Burchell, B., J. Elliott, J. Rubery, and F. Wilkinson. 1994. 'Management and Employee Perceptions of Skill.' In *Skill and Occupational Change,* ed. R. Penn, M. Rose, and J. Rubery. 159–88. Oxford: Oxford University Press.

Burgess, J., and J. Connell. 2006. *Developments in the Call Centre Industry: Analysis, Changes, and Challenges.* London: Routledge.

– 2004. 'Emerging Developments in Call Centre Research.' *Labour and Industry* 14, no. 3: 1–13.

Callaghan, G., and P. Thompson. 2002. '"We Recruit Attitude": The Selection and Shaping of Routine Call Centre Labour.' *Journal of Management Studies* 39, no. 2: 233–54.

– 2001. 'Edwards Revisited: Technical Control and Call Centres.' *Economic and Industrial Democracy* 22, no. 1: 13–37.

Callcentres.net. 2008a. 'Asian Contact Center Industry Benchmarking Report.'

– 2008b. 'Australian Outsourcing and Contact Centre Industry Presentation.' Centre for Work, Organisation, and Well-being, Griffith University, research symposium on call centre research, August.

Campbell, I. 2004. 'Casual Work and Casualisation.' *Labour and Industry* 15, no. 2: 85–111.

Cappelli, P. 1993. 'Are Skill Requirements Rising? Evidence from Production and Clerical Jobs.' *Industrial and Labour Relations Review* 46, no. 3: 515–30.

Castells, M. 1997. *The Power of Identity.* Malden: Blackwell.

– 1996. *The Rise of the Network Society.* Oxford: Blackwell.

Castilla, E. 2005. 'Social Networks and Employee Performance in a Call Centre.' *American Journal of Sociology* 110, no. 5: 1243–83.

Census of India. 2001. Office of the Registrar General and Census Commissioner, India. http://www.censusindia.net

Chibber, V. 2003. *Locked in Place: State-Building and Late Industrialization in India.* Princeton: Princeton University Press.

Chinoy, E. 1992. *Automobile Workers and the American Dream,* 2nd ed. Urbana: University of Illinois Press.

Clement, W., and J. Myles. 1994. *Relations of Ruling: Class and Gender in Post-Industrial Societies.* Montreal and Kingston: McGill–Queen's University Press, 1994.

Cohen, A. 1993. 'Organisational Commitment and Turnover: A Meta-Analysis.' *Academy of Management Journal* 36, no. 5: 1140–57.

Cohen, L., A. El-Sawad, and J. Arnold. 2009. 'Western Theories in an Indian Context.' In *The Next Available Operator: Managing Human Resources in Indian Business Process Outsourcing Industry*, ed. M. Thite and B. Russell. 182–214. Delhi: Sage.

Collin-Jacques, C. 2004. 'Professionals at Work: A Study of Autonomy and Skill Utilization in Nurse Call Centres in England and Canada.' In *Call Centres and Human Resource Management: A Cross-National Perspective*, ed. S. Deery and N. Kinnie. 153–73. Houndmills: Palgrave Macmillan.

Collinson, D. 2002. 'Managing Humour.' *Journal of Management Studies* 39, no. 3: 269–88.

– 1992. *Managing the Shopfloor: Subjectivity, Masculinity, and Workplace Culture*. Berlin and New York: W. de Gruyter.

Cooley, M. 1980. *Architect or Bee? The Human/Technology Relationship*. Boston: South End.

Dabscheck, B. 1995. *The Struggle of Australian Industrial Relations*. Melbourne: Oxford University Press.

D'Alessio, N., and H. Oberbeck. 2002. 'Call Centres as Organisational Crystallisation of New Labour Relations, Working Conditions, and a New Service Culture?' In *Reorganizing Service Work: Call Centres in Germany and Britain*, ed. U. Holtgrewe, C. Kerst, and K. Shire. 86–101. Aldershot: Ashgate.

Das, G. 2002. *India Unbound: From Independence to the Global Information Age*. New Delhi: Penguin.

Davis, M. 2006. 'Fear and Money in Dubai.' *New Left Review* 41: 47-68.

Dawson, P. 2000. 'Technology, Work Restructuring, and the Orchestration of a Rational Narrative in the Pursuit of "Management Objectives": The Political Process of Plant-Level Change.' *Technology Analysis and Strategic Management* 12, no. 1: 39–58.

D'Cruz, P., and E. Noronha. 2007. 'Technical Call Centres: Beyond "Electronic Sweatshops" and "Assembly Lines in the Head."' *Global Business Review* 8, no. 1: 53–67.

– 2006. 'Being Professional: Organizational Control in Indian Call Centres.' *Social Science Computer Review* 24, no. 3: 342–61.

Deal, T., and A. Kennedy. 1982. *Corporate Cultures*. Reading: Addison-Wesley.

DeCotiis, T., and T. Summers. 1987. 'A Path Analysis of a Model of the Antecedents and Consequences of Organisational Commitment.' *Human Relations* 40, no. 7: 445–70.

Deery, S., R. Iverson and J. Walsh. 2004. 'The Effect of Customer Service Encounters on Job Satisfaction and Emotional Exhaustion.' In *Call Centres and Human Resource Management: A Cross-National Perspective*, ed. S. Deery and N. Kinnie. 201–22. Houndmills: Palgrave.

– 2002. 'Work Relationships in Telephone Call Centres: Understanding Emotional Exhaustion and Employee Withdrawal.' *Journal of Management Studies* 39, no. 4: 471–96.

Deery, S., D. Plowman, and J. Walsh. 1997. *Industrial Relations: A Contemporary Analysis*. Sydney: McGraw-Hill.

Denzin, N. 1970. *The Research Act: A Theoretical Introduction to Sociological Methods*. Chicago: Aldine.

Department of Human Resources and Social Development Canada. 1992. *National Occupational Classification*.

Dicken, P. 2007. *Global Shift: Mapping the Changing Contours of the World Economy*. London: Sage.

Dose, C. 2002. 'Call Centres and the Contradictions of the Flexible Bureaucracy.' In *Re-Organising Service Work: Call Centres in Germany and Britain*, ed. U. Holtgrewe, C. Kerst, and K. Shire. 146–60. Aldershot: Ashgate.

Drucker, P. 1954. *The Practice of Management*. New York: Harper.

Dudley, K. 1994. *The End of the Line: Lost Jobs, New Lives in Postindustrial America*. Chicago: University of Chicago Press.

Duffy, A., N. Pupo, and D. Glenday, eds. 1997. *Good Jobs, Bad Jobs, No Jobs: The Transformation of Work in the 21st Century*. Toronto: Harcourt Brace.

Du Gay, P. 2007. *Organizing Identity*. London: Sage.

– 1996. *Consumption and Identity at Work*. London: Sage.

Durbin, S. 2006. 'Gender, Skills, and Careers in UK Call Centres.' In *Developments in the Call Centre Industry: Analysis, Changes and Challenges*, ed. J. Burgess and J. Connell. 117–35. London: Routledge.

Edwards, M. 2005. 'Organization Identification: A Conceptual and Operational Review.' *International Journal of Management Reviews* 7, no. 4: 207–30.

Edwards, P., M. Collinson, and C. Rees. 1998. 'The Determinants of Employee Responses to Total Quality Management: Six Case Studies.' *Organization Studies* 19, no. 3: 449–75.

Edwards, R. 1979. *Contested Terrain: The Transformation of the Workplace in the Twentieth Century*. New York: Basic.

Ehrlich, L., and B. Russell. 2003. 'Employment Security and Job Loss: Lessons From Canada's National Railways.' *Labour/Le Travail* 51: 115–52.

Eisenhardt, K. 1989. 'Agency Theory: An Assessment and Review.' *Academy of Management Review* 14, no. 1: 57–74.

Ellis, V., and P. Taylor. 2006. '"You Don't Know What You've Got Till It's Gone": Recontextualising the Origins, Development, and Impact of the Call Centre.' *New Technology, Work, and Employment* 21, no. 2: 107–22.

Ezzamel, M., and H. Willmott. 1998. 'Accounting for Teamwork: A Critical Study of Group Based Systems of Organizational Control.' *Administrative Science Quarterly* 43, no. 2: 358–96.

Fantasia, R. 1988. *Cultures of Solidarity: Consciousness, Action, and Contemporary American Workers*. Berkeley: University of California Press.

Felstead, A., D. Gallie, and F. Green. 2004. 'Job Complexity and Task Discretion: Tracking the Direction of Skills at Work in Britain.' In *The Skills that Matter*, ed. C. Warhurst, I. Grugulis, and E. Keep. 148–69. Houndmills: Palgrave.

Fernie, S. 2004. 'Call Centre HRM and Performance Outcomes: Does Workplace Governance Matter?' In *Call Centres and Human Resource Management: A Cross-National Perspective*, ed. S. Deery and N. Kinnie. 54–74. Houndmills: Palgrave.

Fernie, S., and D. Metcalf. 1998. '(Not) Hanging on the Telephone: Payment Systems in the New Sweatshops.' London: Centre of Economic Performance, London School of Economics.

Fiorito, J., C. Lowman, and F. Nelson. 1987. 'The Impact of Human Resource Policies on Union Organizing.' *Industrial Relations* 26, no. 2: 113–26.

Fiorito, J., and A. Young. 1998. 'Union Voting Intentions: Human Resource Policies, Organizational Characteristics, and Attitudes.' In *Organizing to Win: New Research on Union Strategies*, ed. K. Bronfenbrenner, S. Friedman, R. Hurd, R. Oswald, and R. Seeber. 232–46. Ithaca: Cornell University Press.

Fleetwood, S. 2007. 'Searching for the Human in Empirical Research on the HRM-Organisational Performance Link: A Meta-Theoretical Approach.' In *Searching for the Human in Human Resource Management*, ed. S. Bolton and M. Houlihan. 41–60. Basingstoke: Palgrave Macmillan.

Focus on the Global South and Young Professionals Collective. 2005. *When the Wind Blows: An Overview of Business Process Outsourcing (BPO) in India*. Mumbai.

Fox, A. 1974. *Beyond Contract: Work, Power, and Trust Relations*. London: Faber.

Freeman, R., and J. Medoff. 1984. *What Do Unions Do?* New York: Basic.

Frenkel, S., M. Tam, M. Korczynski, and K. Shire. 1998. 'Beyond Bureaucracy? Work Organization in Call Centres.' *International Journal of Human Resource Management* 9, no. 6: 957–79.

Frenkel, S., M. Korczynski, K. Shire, and M. Tam. 1999. *On the Front Line: Organization of Work in the Information Economy*. Ithaca: Cornell University Press.

Friedman, A. 1977. *Industry and Labour*. London: Macmillan.

Friedman, T. 2006. *The World Is Flat: A Brief History of the Twenty-First Century*. New York: Farrar Straus Giroux.

Fuller, L., and V. Smith. 1996. 'Consumers' Reports: Management by Customers in a Changing Economy.' In *Working in the Service Society*, ed. C. Macdonald and C. Sirianni. 74–90. Philadelphia: Temple University Press.

Gall, G., ed. 2006. *Union Recognition: Organising and Bargaining Outcomes*. London: Routledge.

Gallie, D. 1991. 'Patterns of Skill Change: Upskilling, Deskilling, or the Polarization of Skills.' *Work, Employment, and Society* 5, no. 3: 319–51.

Gasser, L. 1986. 'The Integration of Computing and Routine Work.' *ACM Transactions on Office Information Systems* 4, no. 3: 205–25.

Gereffi, G. 1994. 'The Organization of Buyer-Driven Global Commodity Chains: How US Retailers Shape Overseas Production Networks.' In *Commodity Chains and Global Capitalism*, ed. G. Gereffi and M. Korzeniewicz. 95–122. Westport: Praeger.

Giddens, A. 1991. *Modernity and Self-Identity: Self and Society in the Late Modern Age*. Cambridge: Polity.

Glucksmann, M. 2004. 'Call Configurations: Varieties of Call Centre and Divisions of Labour.' *Work, Employment, and Society* 18, no. 4: 795–811.

Glyn, A. 2007. *Capitalism Unleashed: Finance, Globalization, and Welfare*. Oxford: Oxford University Press.

Godard, J., and J. Delaney. 2000. 'Reflections on the "High Performance" Paradigm's Implications for Industrial Relations as a Field.' *Industrial and Labor Relations Review* 53, no. 3: 482–502.

Goffman, E. 1959. *The Presentation of Self in Everyday Life*. Garden City: Doubleday.

Good, T., and J. McFarland. 2005. 'Call Centres: A New Solution to an Old Problem.' In *From the Net to the Net: Atlantic Canada and the Global Economy*, ed. J. Sacouman and H. Veltmeyer. 99–113. Toronto: Garamond.

Gouldner, A. 1954a. *Patterns of Industrial Bureaucracy*. New York: Free Press.

– 1954b. *Wildcat Strike*. Yellow Springs: Antioch.

Government of India. 2003. 'Task Force on Meeting the Human Resources Challenge for IT and IT Enabled Services.' New Delhi: Ministry of Communications and Information Technology, Department of Information Technology.

Gramsci, A. 1971. *Selections from the Prison Notebooks of Antonio Gramsci*. New York: International.

Greenbaum, J. 1995. *Windows on the Workplace: Computers, Jobs, and the Organization of Office Work in the Late Twentieth Century*. New York: Monthly Review.

Greenwich, C. 2000. *Fun and Gains*. Sydney: McGraw-Hill.

– 1997. *The Fun Factor*. Sydney: McGraw-Hill.

Grenier, G. 1988. *Inhuman Relations: Quality Circles and Anti-Unionism in American Industry*. Philadelphia: Temple University Press.

Grey, C. 1999. '"We Are All Managers Now."' *Journal of Management Studies* 36, no. 5: 561–85.

Grint, K., and S. Woolgar. 1997. *The Machine at Work: Technology, Work, and Organization*. Cambridge: Polity.

Guest, D. 2002. 'Human Resource Management, Corporate Performance, and Employee Wellbeing.' *Journal of Industrial Relations* 44, no. 3: 335–58.

– 1999. 'Human Resource Management: The Workers' Verdict.' *Human Resource Management Journal* 9, no. 3: 5–25.

– 1990. 'Human Resource Management and the American Dream.' *Journal of Management Studies* 27, no. 4: 387–97.

– 1987. 'Human Resource Management and Industrial Relations.' *Journal of Management Studies* 24, no. 5: 503–21.

Guest, D., and N. Conway. 1999. 'Peering into the Black Hole: The Downside of the New Employment Relations in the UK.' *British Journal of Industrial Relations* 37, no. 3: 367–89.

Guest, D., and K. Hoque. 1996. 'Human Resource Management and the New Industrial Relations.' In *Contemporary Industrial Relations: A Critical Analysis*, ed. I. Beardwell. 11–36. Oxford: Oxford University Press.

Gutek, B. 1995. *The Dynamics of Service*. San Francisco: Jossey-Bass.

Hall, R. 2006. 'Australian Industrial Relations in 2005 – the Workchoices Revolution.' *Journal of Industrial Relations* 48, no. 3: 291–303.

Hancock, K., and S. Richardson. 2004. 'Economic and Social Effects.' In *The New Province for Law and Order: 100 Years of Australian Industrial Conciliation and Arbitration*, ed. J. Isaac and S. Macintyre. 139–206. Cambridge: Cambridge University Press.

Harley, B. 2002. 'Employee Responses to High Performance Work System Practices.' *Journal of Industrial Relations* 44, no. 3: 418–34.

Harley, B., C. Wright, R. Hall, and K. Dery. 2006. 'Management Reactions to Technological Change: The Example of Enterprise Resource Planning.' *Journal of Applied Behavioral Science* 42, no. 1: 58–75.

Harvey, D. 1989. *The Condition of Postmodernity*. Oxford: Basil Blackwell.

Herzenberg, S., J. Alic, and H. Wial. 1998. *New Rules for a New Economy: Employment and Opportunity in Postindustrial America*. Ithaca: Cornell University Press.

Hill, S. 1991. 'How Do You Manage a Flexible Firm? The Total Quality Model.' *Work, Employment, and Society* 5, no. 3: 397–415.

Hirschman, A. 1970. *Exit, Voice, and Loyalty: Responses to Decline in Firms*. Cambridge, MA: Harvard University Press.

Hirshhorn, L. 1984. *Beyond Mechanization: Work and Technology in a Post-Industrial Age*. Cambridge, MA: MIT Press.

Hirst, P., and J. Zeitlin. 1991. 'Flexible Specialization versus Post-Fordism: Theory, Evidence, and Policy Implications.' *Economy and Society* 20, no. 1: 1–56.

Hochschild, A. 1983. *The Managed Heart*. Berkeley: University of California Press.

Holman, D. 2002. 'Employee Wellbeing in Call Centres.' *Human Resource Management Journal* 12, no. 4: 35–50.

Holman, D., R. Batt, and U. Holtgrewe. 2007. 'The Global Call Centre Report: International Perspectives on Management and Employment.' http://www.globalcallcenter.org

Houlihan, M. 2006. 'Agency and Constraint: Call Centre Managers Talk about Their Work.' In *Developments in the Call Centre Industry: Analysis, Changes, and Challenges*, ed. J. Burgess and J. Connell. 152–69. London: Routledge.

– 2002. 'Tensions and Variations in Call Centre Management Strategies.' *Human Resource Management Journal* 12, no. 4: 67–85.

– 2000. 'Eyes Wide Shut? Querying the Depth of Call Centre Learning.' *Journal of European Industrial Training* 24, nos. 2–4: 228–40.

Human Resources and Skills Development Canada. 2006. *National Occupational Classification*. http://www.hrsdc.gc.ca

– 1992. 'National Occupational Classification.' http://www.hrsdc.gc.ca

Huselid, M. 1995. 'The Impact of Human Resource Management Practices on Turnover, Productivity, and Corporate Financial Performance.' *Academy of Management Journal* 38, no. 3: 635–72.

Hutchinson, S., J. Purcell, and N. Kinnie. 2000. 'Evolving High Commitment Management and the Experience of the RAC Call Centre.' *Human Resource Management Journal* 10, no. 1: 63–78.

Huws, U. 2003. *The Making of a Cybertariate: Virtual Work in a Real World*. New York: Monthly Review.

Hyman, R. 1989. *The Political Economy of Industrial Relations: Theory and Practice in a Cold Climate*. Houndmills: Macmillan.

– 1975. *Industrial Relations: A Marxist Introduction*. London: Macmillan.

Iles, P. 2001. 'Employee Resourcing.' In *Human Resource Management: A Critical Text*, ed. J. Storey. 133–64. London: Thompson.

Iverson, R., and D. Buttigieg. 1999. 'Affective, Normative, and Continuance Commitment: Can the "Right Kind" of Commitment Be Managed?' *Journal of Management Studies* 36, no. 3: 307–33.

Jackson, P., C. Sprigg, and S. Parker. 2000. 'Interdependence as a Key Requirement for the Successful Introduction of Teamworking: A Case Study.' In *Teamworking*, ed. S. Procter and F. Mueller. 83–102. Basingstoke: Macmillan.

Jaros, S. 1997. 'An Assessment of Meyer and Allen's (1991) Three-Component Model of Organizational Commitment and Turnover Intentions.' *Journal of Vocational Behavior* 51, no. 3: 319–37.

Jenkins, S., and R. Delbridge. 2007. 'Disconnected Workplaces: Interests and Identities in the 'High Performance Factory.' In *Searching for the Human in Human Resource Management*, ed. S. Bolton and M. Houlihan. 195–218. Basingstoke: Palgrave Macmillan.

Kamdar, M. 2007. *Planet India*. New York: Scribner.

Kelly, J. 1998. *Rethinking Industrial Relations: Mobilization, Collectivism, and Long Waves*. London: Routledge.

Kenney, M., and R. Florida. 1993. *Beyond Mass Production*. New York: Oxford University Press.

Kinnie, N., S. Hutchinson, and J. Purcell. 2000. '"Fun and Surveillance": The Paradox of High Commitment Management in Call Centres.' *International Journal of Human Resource Management* 11, no. 5: 967–85.

Kinnie, N., J. Purcell, and S. Hutchinson. 2000. 'Managing the Employment Relationship in Telephone Call Centres.' In *Changing Boundaries in Employment*, ed. K. Purcell. 133–59. Bristol: Bristol Academic Press.

Knights, D. 1990. 'Subjectivity, Power, and the Labour Process.' In *Labour Process Theory*, ed. D. Knights and H. Willmott. 297–335. Basingstoke: Macmillan.

Knights, D., and D. McCabe. 2000. '"Ain't Misbehaving"? Opportunities for Resistance under New Forms of "Quality" Management.' *Sociology* 34, no.3: 421–36.

– 1998. '"What Happens When the Phone Goes Wild?": Staff, Stress and Spaces for Escape in a BPR Telephone Banking Work Regime.' *Journal of Management Studies* 35, no. 2: 163–94.

– 1997. '"How Would You Measure Something Like That?" Quality in a Retail Bank.' *Journal of Management Studies* 34, no. 3: 371–88.

Knights, D., and F. Murray. 1994. *Managers Divided: Organisation Politics and Information Technology Management*. Chichester: Wiley.

Knights, D., and P. Odhi. 2002. '"Big Brother Is Watching You!" Call Centre Surveillance and the Time-Disciplined Subject.' In *Social Conceptions of Time*, ed. G. Crow and S. Heath. 144–61. Basingstoke: Palgrave.

Korczynski, M. 2003. 'Communities of Coping: Collective Emotional Labour in Service Work.' *Organization* 10, no. 1: 55–79.

– 2002a. *Human Resource Management in Service Work*. Houndmills: Palgrave.

– 2002b. 'Call Centre Consumption and the Enchanting Myth of Customer Sovereignty.' In *Reorganizing Service Work: Call Centres in Germany and Britain*, ed. U. Holtgrewe, C. Kerst, and K. Shire. 163–82. Aldershot: Ashgate.

– 2001. 'The Contradictions of Service Work: Call Centre as Customer-Oriented Bureaucracy'. In *Customer Service: Empowerment and Entrapment*, ed. A. Sturdy, I. Grugulis, and H. Wilmott. 79–102. Houndmills: Palgrave.

Korczinski, M., K. Shire, S. Frenkel, and M. Tam. 2000. 'Service Work in Consumer Capitalism: Customers, Control and Contradictions.' *Work, Employment, and Society* 14, no. 4: 669–87.

KPMG. 2004. *Strengthening the Human Resource Foundation of the Indian IT Enabled Services/IT Industry*. Delhi: Nasscom.

Kunda, G. 1992. *Engineering Culture: Control and Commitment in a High-Tech Corporation*. Philadelphia: Temple University Press.

Laurila, J. 1997. 'The Thin Line between Advanced and Conventional New Technology.' *Journal of Management Studies* 34, no. 2: 219–39.

Leacy, F. ed. 1983. *Historical Statistics of Canada*, 2nd ed. Ottawa: Statistics Canada.

Lee, B., and H. Kang. 2006. 'A National Survey of Korean Call Centres.' In *Developments in the Call Centre Industry: Analysis, Changes, and Challenges*, ed. J. Burgess and J. Connell. 75–91. London: Routledge.

Lee, M., and D. Peetz. 1998. 'Trade Unions and the Workplace Relations Act.' *Labour and Industry* 9, no. 2: 5–22.

Legge, K. 2004. 'Silver Bullet or Spent Round? Assessing the Meaning of the "High Commitment Management"/Performance Relationship.' In *Human Resource Management: A Critical Text*, ed. J. Storey. 21–36. London: Thompson.

– 1995. *Human Resource Management: Rhetorics and Realities*. London: Macmillan Business.

Leidner, R. 1996. 'Rethinking Questions of Control: Lessons from McDonald's.' In *Working in the Service Society*, ed. C. Macdonald and C. Sirianni. 29–49. Philadelphia: Temple University Press.

– 1993. *Fast Food, Fast Talk: Service Work and the Routinization of Everyday Life*. Berkeley: University of California Press.

Lipietz, A. 1987. *Mirages and Miracles*. London: Verso.

– 1985. *The Enchanted World*. London: Verso.

Littler, C. 1982. *The Development of the Labour Process in Capitalist Societies*. London: Heinemann.

Livingstone, D. 1999. *The Education–Jobs Gap*, Toronto: Garamond.

Macdermott, T. 1997. 'Industrial Legislation in 1996: The Reform Agenda.' *Journal of Industrial Relations* 39, no. 1: 52–76.

Macdonald, C.L., and C.J. Sirianni, eds. 1996. *Working in the Service Society*. Philadelphia: Temple University Press.

MacDuffie, J. 1995. 'Human Resource Bundles and Manufacturing Performance: Flexible Production Systems in the World Auto Industry.' *Industrial Relations and Labor Review* 48, no. 2: 197–221.

Macintyre, S. 2004. 'Arbitration in Action.' In *The New Province for Law and Order: 100 Years of Australian Industrial Conciliation and Arbitration*, ed. J. Isaac and S. Macintyre. 55–97. Cambridge: Cambridge University Press.

Macintyre, S., and R. Mitchell. 1989. 'Introduction.' In *Foundations of Arbitration: The Origins and Effects of State Compulsory Arbitration 1890–1914*, ed. S. Macintyre and R. Mitchell. 1–21. Oxford: Oxford University Press.

Markey, R. 1989. 'Trade Unions, the Labor Party, and the Introduction of Arbitration in New South Wales and the Commonwealth.' In *Foundations of Arbitration: The Origins and Effects of State Compulsory Arbitration 1890-1914*, ed. S. Macintyre and R. Mitchell. 156–77. Oxford: Oxford University Press.

Mars, G. 1994. *Cheats at Work: An Anthropology of Workplace Crime*. Aldershot: Dartmouth.

Marx, K. 1971. *Capital, Volume I*. Moscow: Progress.

Mayo, E. 1977. *The Human Problems of an Industrial Civilization*. New York: Arno.

McBride, S. 2005. *Paradigm Shift: Globalization and the Canadian State*. Halifax: Fernwood.

McCallum, R. 2006. 'Justice at Work: Industrial Citizenship and the Corporatisation of Australian Labour Law.' *Journal of Industrial Relations* 48, no. 2: 131–53.

McLoughlin, I., R. Badham, and P. Couchman. 2000. 'Rethinking Political Process in Technological Change.' *Technology Analysis and Strategic Management* 12, no. 1: 17–37.

Menzies, H. 1996. *Whose Brave New World? The Information Highway and the New Economy*. Toronto: Between the Lines.

Meyer, S. 1981. *The Five Dollar Day: Labor Management and Social Control in the Ford Motor Company, 1908–1921*. Albany: SUNY Press.

Meyer, J., and N. Allen. 1997. *Commitment in the Workplace: Theory, Research, and Application*. Thousand Oaks: Sage.

– 1991. 'A Three-Component Conceptualisation of Organisational Commitment.' *Human Resource Management Review* 1, no. 1: 61–89.

Milkman, R. 1997. *Farewell to the Factory: Auto Workers in the Late Twentieth Century*. Berkeley: University of California Press.

Milkman, R., and K. Voss, eds. 2004. *Rebuilding Labor: Organizing and Organizers in the New Union Movement*. Ithaca: Cornell University Press.

Mills, C. 1971. *The New Men of Power: America's Labor Leaders*. New York: Kelley.

Mirchandani, K. 2009. 'Transnationalism in Indian Call Centres.' In *The Next Available Operator: Managing Human Resources in Indian Business Process Outsourcing Industry*, ed. M. Thite and B. Russell. 83–111. New Delhi: Sage.

Mittal, A., and S. Goel. 2004. 'Globalization and Indian IT Industry: A Strategic Perspective.' In *Information Technology: Issues and Challenges of Globalization*. 4–11. New Delhi: Indian Institute of Foreign Trade.

Morehead, A., M. Steele, M. Alexander, K. Stephen, and L. Duffin. 1997. *Changes at Work: The 1995 Australian Workplace Industrial Relations Survey.* South Melbourne: Longman.

Mueller, F. 1994. 'Teams between Hierarchy and Commitment: Change Strategies and the "International Environment."' *Journal of Management Studies* 31, no. 3: 383–403.

Mulholland, K. 2004. 'Workplace Resistance in an Irish Call Centre: Slammin', Scammin', Smokin' an' Leavin'.' *Work, Employment, and Society* 18, no. 4: 709–24.

– 2002. 'Gender, Emotional Labour, and Teamworking in a Call Centre.' *Personnel Review* 31, no. 3: 283–303.

Nankervis, A., R. Compton, and M. Baird. 2005. *Human Resource Management: Strategies and Processes,* 5th ed. Melbourne: Thomson.

Nasscom. 2008. 'IT-BPO Sector Overview.' http://www. nasscom.in/ Nasscom/templates/normal_page.aspx?id+54612

– 2005. 'NASSCOM's Ranking of Third Party Players.' http://www.nasscom. in/Nasscom/templates/normal_page.aspx?id+2577

Nasscom Analysis. 2007. 'Indian BPO ITeS Industry Factsheet.' http://www. scribd.com/doc/6925928/Indian-ITESBPO-Industry-NASSCOM-Analysis-Aug07

Nelson, D. 1980. *Frederick W. Taylor and the Rise of Scientific Management.* Madison: University of Wisconsin Press.

Nelson, M., and J. Smith. 1999. *Working Hard and Making Do: Surviving in Small Town America.* Berkeley: University of California Press.

Neuman, L. 2006. *Social Research Methods: Qualitative and Quantitative Approaches.* Boston: Pearson.

Noble, D. 1984. *Forces of Production: A Social History of Industrial Automation.* New York: Oxford University Press.

Noon, M. 1994. 'From Apathy to Alacrity: Managers and New Technology in Provincial Newspapers.' *Journal of Management Studies* 31, no. 1: 19–31.

Noronha, E., and P. D'Cruz. 2006. 'Organising Call Centre Agents: Emerging Issues.' *Economic and Political Weekly,* 27 May: 2115–21.

OECD (Organisation for Economic Co-operation and Development). 2001. *Employment Outlook.* Paris.

Ofreneo, R., C. Ng, and L. Marasigan-Pasumbal. 2007. 'Voice for the Voice Workers: Addressing the IR Concerns in the Call Center/BPO Industry of Asia.' *Indian Journal of Industrial Relations* 42, no. 4: 534–57.

Ogbonna, E. 1992a. 'Managing Organisational Culture: Fantasy or Reality?' *Human Resource Management Journal* 3, no. 2: 45–54.

– 1992b. 'Organization Culture and Human Resource Management: Dilemmas and Contradictions.' In *Reassessing Human Resource Management*, ed. P. Blyton and P. Turnbull. 74–96. London: Sage.

Orlikowski, W. 1996. 'Improvising Organization Transformation Over Time: A Situated Change Perspective.' *Information Systems Research* 7, no. 1: 63–92.

Orlikowski, W., and J. Yates. 2006. 'ICT and Organizational Change: A Commentary.' *Journal of Applied Behavioural Science* 42, no. 1: 127–34.

Parker, M. 2000. *Organizational Culture and Identity*. London: Sage.

Parker, M., and J. Slaughter. 1988. *Choosing Sides: Unions and the Team Concept*. Boston: South End.

Patmore, G. 1992. 'The Future of Trade Unionism – an Australian Perspective.' *International Journal of Human Resource Management* 3, no. 2: 225–45.

Peetz, D. 1998. *Unions in a Contrary World: The Future of the Australian Trade Union Movement*. Cambridge: Cambridge University Press.

Peters, T., and R. Waterman. 1988. *In Search of Excellence*. Sydney: Harper and Row.

Petrides, L., S. McClelland, and T. Nodine. 2004. 'Costs and Benefits of the Workaround: Inventive Solution or Costly Alternative.' *International Journal of Educational Management* 18, no. 2: 100–8.

Pfeffer, J. 1998. 'Seven Practices of Successful Organizations.' *California Management Review* 40, no. 2: 96–124.

Pfeffer, J., and J. Veiga. 1999. 'Putting People First for Organizational Success.' *Academy of Management Executive* 13, no. 2: 37–48.

Picot, G., J. Myles, and T. Wannell. 1990. *Good Jobs/Bad Jobs and the Declining Middle: 1967–1986*. Ottawa: Business and Labour Market Analysis Group, Analytical Studies Branch, Statistics Canada, no. 28.

Piore, M., and C. Sabel. 1984. *The Second Industrial Divide*. New York: Basic.

Polanyi, K. 1965. *The Great Transformation*. Boston: Beacon.

Porter, M. 1985. *Competitive Advantage: Creating and Sustaining Superior Performance*. New York: Free Press.

Pradhan, J., and V. Abraham. 2005. 'Social and Cultural Impact of Outsourcing: Emerging Issues from Indian Call Centres.' *Harvard Asia Quarterly* 9, no. 3.

Procter, S., and F. Mueller, eds. 2000. *Teamworking*. Basingstoke: Macmillan.

Rainnie, A., and G. Drummond. 2006. 'Community Unionism in a Regional Call Centre: The Organiser's Perspective.' In *Developments in the Call Centre Industry*, ed. J. Burgess and J. Connell. 136–51. London: Routledge.

Raman, S., P. Budhwar, and G. Balasubramanian. 2007. 'People Management Issues in Indian KPOs.' *Employee Relations* 29, no. 6: 696–710.

Raz, A., and E. Blank. 2007. 'Ambiguous Professionalism: Managing Efficiency and Service Quality in an Israeli Call Centre.' *New Technology, Work, and Employment* 22, no. 1: 83–96.

Reich, R. 1991. *The Work of Nations*. New York: Vintage.

Reiter, E. 1991. *Making Fast Food*. Montreal and Kingston: McGill–Queen's University Press.

Richardson, R., and V. Belt. 2001. 'Saved by the Bell? Call Centres and Economic Development in Less Favoured Regions.' *Economic and Industrial Democracy* 22, no. 1: 67–98.

Richardson, R., V. Belt, and N. Marshall. 2000. 'Talking Calls to Newcastle: The Regional Implications of the Growth in Call Centres.' *Regional Studies* 34, no. 4: 357–69.

Riley, J., and T. Sarina. 2006. 'Industrial Legislation in 2005.' *Journal of Industrial Relations* 48, no. 3: 341–55.

Rimmer, M. 2004. 'Unions and Arbitration.' In *The New Province For Law and Order: 100 Years of Australian Industrial Conciliation and Arbitration*, ed. J. Isaac and S. Macintyre. 275–315. Cambridge: Cambridge University Press.

Rinehart, J., C. Huxley, and D. Robertson. 1997. *Just Another Car Factory*. Ithaca: Cornell University Press.

Ritzer, G. 2004. *The McDonaldization of Society*. Thousand Oaks: Pine Forge.

Rose, E. 2002. 'The Labour Process and Union Commitment within a Banking Services Call Centre.' *Journal of Industrial Relations* 44, no. 1: 40–61.

Rose, E., and G. Wright. 2005. 'Satisfaction and Dimensions of Control among Call Centre Customer Service Representatives.' *International Journal of Human Resource Management* 16, no. 1: 136–60.

Rose, M. 1994. 'Job Satisfaction, Job Skills, and Personal Skills.' In *Skill and Occupational Change*, ed. R. Penn, M. Rose and J. Rubery. 244–80. Oxford: Oxford University Press.

Rose, M., R. Penn, and J. Rubery. 1994. 'Introduction: The SCELI Skill Findings.' In *Skill and Occupational Change*, ed. R. Penn, M. Rose, and J. Rubery. 1–37. Oxford: Oxford University Press.

Rose, N. 1990. *Governing the Soul: The Shaping of the Private Self*. London: Routledge.

Rosenthal, P., S. Hill, and R. Peccei. 1997. 'Checking Out Service: Evaluating Excellence, HRM, and TQM in Retailing.' *Work, Employment, and Society* 11, no. 3: 481–503.

Rousseau, D. 1995. *Psychological Contracts in Organizations: Understanding Written and Unwritten Agreements*. Thousand Oaks: Sage.

Roy, D. 1958. '"Banana Time": Job Satisfaction and Informal Interaction.' *Human Organization* 18, no. 4: 158–68.

– 1954. 'Efficiency and "The Fix": Informal Intergroup Relations in a Piecework Machine Shop.' *American Journal of Sociology* 60, no. 3: 255–66.

– 1952. 'Quota Restriction and Goldbricking in a Machine Shop.' *American Journal of Sociology* 57, no. 5: 427–42.

Rundle, J. 1998. 'Winning Hearts and Minds in the Era of Employee-Involve-
ment Programs.' In *Organizing to Win: New Research on Union Strategies*, ed.
K. Bronfenbrenner, S. Friedman, R. Hurd, R. Oswald, and R. Seeber. 213–31.
Ithaca: Cornell University Press.

Russell, B. 2008a.'Unions in the Information Economy: Info-Service Work and
Organizing in Australian Call Centres.' *Journal of Industrial Relations* 50, no.
2: 285–303.

– 2008b. 'Call Centres: A Decade of Research.' *International Journal of Management Reviews* 10, no. 3: 195–219.

– 2007. '"You Gotta Lie to It": Software Applications and the Management of
Technological Change in a Call Centre.' *New Technology, Work, and Employment* 22, no. 2: 132–45.

– 2006a. 'Voice, Representation, and Recognition: Unions and Call Centres.'
Report submitted to the Queensland Council of Unions.

– 2006b. 'Skill in Info-Service Work: Australian Call Centres.' In *Developments
in the Call Centre Industry: Analysis, Policy, and Challenges*, ed. J. Burgess and
J. Connell. 92–116. London: Routedge.

– 2004. 'Are All Call Centres the Same?' *Labour and Industry* 14, no. 3: 91–109.

– 2002a. 'Making, Remaking, Managing, and Controlling Customer Service
Agents: Brownfield and Greenfield Call Centre Sites.' *Research and Practice in
Human Resource Management* 10, no. 1: 35–52.

– 2002b. 'The Talk Shop and Shop Talk: Employment and Work in a Call Centre.' *Journal of Industrial Relations* 44, no. 4: 467–90.

– 1999. *More for Less: Work Reorganization in the Canadian Mining Industry*.
Toronto: University of Toronto Press.

– 1997. 'Some Thoughts on the Socially Desirable Workplace.' In *Final Re-
port of the National Forum on the Information Highway and Workplace Issues:
Challenges and Opportunities*. Ottawa: Human Resources Development
Canada.

– 1995. 'Labour's *Magna Carta*? Wagnerism in Canada at Fifty.' In *Labour
Gains, Labour Pains: 50 Years of PC 1003*, ed. C. Gonick, P. Phillips, and J.
Vorst. 177–92. Halifax: Fernwood.

– 1990. *Back to Work? Labour, State, and Industrial Relations in Canada*. Scarbor-
ough: Nelson.

Russell, B., and M. Thite. 2008. 'The Next Division of Labour: Work Skills in
Australian and Indian Call Centres.' In *Work, Employment, and Society* 22, no.
4: 615–34.

Saini, D., and P. Budhwar. 2004. 'HRM in India.' In *Managing Human Resources
in Asia–Pacific*, ed. P. Budhwar. London: Routledge.

Salaman, G. 2001. 'The Management of Corporate Culture Change.' In *Human
Resource Management: A Critical Text*, ed. J. Storey. 190–205. London: Thomson.

Schein, E. 1985. *Organizational Culture and Leadership*. San Francisco: Jossey-Bass.

– 1978. 'How Culture Forms, Develops, and Changes.' In *Gaining Control of the Corporate Culture*, ed. R. Kilmann, M. Saxton, and R. Serpa. 17–43. San Francisco: Jossey-Bass.

Schoenberger, E. 1997. *The Cultural Crisis of the Firm*. Oxford: Blackwell.

Scott, A. 1994. *Willing Slaves? British Workers under Human Resource Management*. Cambridge: Cambridge University Press.

Scott, J. 1990. *Domination and the Arts of Resistance: Hidden Transcripts*. New Haven: Yale University Press.

Sennett, R. 2006. *The Culture of the New Capitalism.* New Haven: Yale University Press.

– 1998. *The Corrosion of Character*. New York: Norton.

Sewell, G. 1998. 'The Discipline of Teams: The Control of Team-Based Industrial Work through Electronic and Peer Surveillance.' *Administrative Science Quarterly* 43, no. 2: 397–428.

Sewell, G., and B. Wilkinson. 1992. '"Someone to Watch Over Me": Surveillance, Discipline, and the Just-in-Time Labour Process.' *Sociology* 26, no. 2: 271–89.

Shah, V., and R. Bandi. 2003. 'Capability Development in Knowledge Intensive IT Enabled Services.' *European Journal of Work and Organizational Psychology* 12, no. 4: 418–27.

Shaiken, H. 1984. *Work Transformed: Automation and Labor in the Computer Age*. New York: Rinehart and Winston.

Sheshabalaya, A. 2005. *Rising Elephant*. Delhi: Macmillan.

Silver, B. 2003. *Forces of Labour: Workers' Movements and Globalization since 1870*. Cambridge: Cambridge University Press.

Sisson, K. 1993. 'In Search of HRM.' *British Journal of Industrial Relations* 31, no. 2: 201–10.

Sisson, K., and J. Storey. 2000. *The Realities of Human Resource Management*. Maidenhead: Open University.

Smith, C., R. Valsecchi, F. Mueller, and J. Gabe. 2008. 'Knowledge and the Discourse of Labour Process Transformation: Nurses and the Case of NHS Direct for England.' *Work, Employment, and Society* 22, no. 4: 581–99.

Smith, V. 2001. *Crossing the Great Divide: Worker Risk and Opportunity in the New Economy*. Ithaca: Cornell University Press.

Spenner, K. 1990. 'Skill: Meanings, Methods, and Measures.' *Work and Occupations* 17, no. 4: 399–421.

– 1983. 'Deciphering Prometheus: Temporal Change in the Skill Level of Work.' *American Sociological Review* 48, no. 6: 824–37.

Srinivasan, T. 2006. 'Information Technology Enabled Services and India's Growth Prospects.' In *Offshoring White Collar Work*, ed. S. Collins and L. Brainard. 203–31. Washington: Brookings Institution.

Srivastava, S., and N. Theodore. 2006. 'Offshoring Call Centres: The View from Wall Street.' In *Developments in the Call Centre Industry: Analysis, Changes, and Challenges*, ed. J. Burgess and J. Connell. 19–35. London: Routledge.

Standing, G. 1999. *Global Labour Flexibility: Seeking Distributive Justice*. Basingstoke: Macmillan.

Storey, J. 2001. 'Human Resource Management Today: An Assessment.' In *Human Resource Management: A Critical Text*, ed. J. Storey. 3–20. Padstow: Thompson.

– 1992. *Developments in the Management of Human Resources*. Oxford: Blackwell.

– 1991. 'Introduction: From Personnel Management to Human Resource Management.' In *New Perspectives on Human Resource Management*, ed. J. Storey. 1–18. London: Routledge.

Strange, S. 1998. *The Retreat of the State: The Diffusion of Power in the World Economy*. Cambridge: Cambridge University Press.

Sturdy, A. 2000. 'Training in Service – Importing and Imparting Customer Service Culture as an Interactive Process.' *International Journal of Human Resource Management* 11, no. 6: 1082–103.

Suchman, L. 1996. 'Supporting Articulation Work.' In *Computerization and Controversy: Value Conflicts and Social Choices*, ed. R. Kling. 407–23. San Diego: Academic.

Taylor, F.W. 1967. *The Principles of Scientific Management*. New York: Norton.

Taylor, P., and P. Bain. 2007. 'Reflections on the Call Centre: A Reply to Glucksmann.' *Work, Employment, and Society* 21, no. 2: 349–62.

– 2006. 'Work Organisation and Employee Relations in Indian Call Centres.' In *Developments in the Call Centre Industry: Analysis, Changes, and Challenges*, ed. J. Burgess and J. Connell. 36–57. London: Routledge.

– 2005.'"India Calling to the Far Away Towns": The Call Centre Labour Process and Globalisation.' *Work, Employment, and Society* 19, no. 2: 261–82.

– 2004. 'Call Centre Offshoring to India: The Revenge of History?' *Labour and Industry* 14, no. 3: 15–38.

– 2003. 'Call Centre Organizing in Adversity.' In *Union Organizing: Campaigning for Trade Union Recognition*, ed. G. Gall. 153–72. London: Routledge.

– 2001. 'Trade Unions, Workers' Rights, and the Frontier of Control in UK Call Centres.' *Economic and Industrial Democracy* 22, no. 1: 39–66.

– 1999. '"An Assembly Line in the Head": Work and Employee Relations in the Call Centre.' *Industrial Relations Journal* 30, no. 2: 101–17.

Taylor, P., C. Baldry, P. Bain, and V. Ellis. 2003. '"A Unique Working Environ-

ment": Health, Sickness, and Absence Management in UK Call Centres.'
Work, Employment, and Society 17, no. 3: 435–58.

Taylor, P., P. D'Cruz, E. Noronha, and D. Scholarios. 2009. 'Union Formation
in Indian Call Centres.' In *The Next Available Operator: Managing Human
Resources in Indian Business Process Outsourcing Industry*, ed. M. Thite and B.
Russell. 145–81. New Delhi: Sage.

Taylor, P., J. Hyman, G. Mulvey, and P. Bain. 2002. 'Work Organization, Control, and the Experience of Work in Call Centres.' *Work, Employment, and
Society* 16, no. 1: 133–50.

Taylor, S., and M. Tyler. 2000. 'Emotional Labour and Sexual Difference in the
Airline Industry.' *Work, Employment, and Society* 14, no. 1: 77–95.

Thite, M., and B. Russell. 2007. 'India and Business Process Outsourcing.' In
Globalisation and Work in Asia, ed. J. Burgess and J. Connell. 67–92. Oxford:
Chandos.

Thomas, R. 1994. *What Machines Can't Do: Politics and Technology in the Industrial Enterprise*. Berkeley: University of California Press.

Thompson, E. 1967. 'Time, Work-Discipline, and Industrial Capitalism.' *Past
and Present* 38: 56–97.

– 1966. *The Making of the English Working Class*. New York: Vintage.

Thompson, P., and G. Callaghan. 2002. 'Skill Formation in Call Centres.' In
Re-Organizing Service Work: Call Centres in Germany and Britain., ed. U. Holtgrewe, C. Kerst, and K. Shire. 105–22. Aldershot: Ashgate.

Thompson, P., G. Callaghan, and D. van den Broek. 2004. 'Keeping Up Ap-
pearances: Recruitment, Skills, and Normative Control in Call Centres.' In
Call Centres and Human Resource Management: A Cross-National Perspective,
ed. S. Deery and N. Kinnie. 129–52. Houndmills: Palgrave.

Thompson, P., and D. McHugh. 2002. *Work Organisations*. Basingstoke: Palgrave.

Tilly, C. 1978. *From Mobilization to Revolution*. Reading: Addison-Wesley.

Torrington, D. 1989. 'Human Resource Management and the Personnel Function.' In *New Perspectives in Human Resource Management*, ed. J. Storey. 56–66.
London: Routledge.

Townsend, K. 2005. 'Teams, Control, Cooperation, and Resistance in New
Workplaces.' Ph.D. diss., Department of Industrial Relations, Griffith University.

– 2004. 'When the LOST Found Teams: A Consideration of Teams within the
Individualised Call Centre Environment.' *Labour and Industry* 14, no. 3:
111–26.

Tuckman, A. 1995. 'Ideology, Quality, and TQM.' In *Making Quality Critical:
New Perspectives on Organizational Change*, ed. A. Wilkinson and H. Willmott. 54–81. London: Routledge.

Turner, L., H. Katz, and R. Hurd. 2001. *Rekindling the Movement: Labor's Quest for Relevance in the 21st Century*. Ithaca: Cornell University Press.

U.S. Department of Commerce. 1975. *Historical Statistics of the United States: Colonial Times to 1970*. Washington: Bureau of the Census.

U.S. Department of Labor. 2006. *Occupational Outlook Handbook*. Bureau for Labor Statistics. http://www.bls.gov

Van den Broek, D. 2008. '"Doing Things Right" or "Doing the Right Things"? Call Centre Migrations and Dimensions of Knowledge.' *Work, Employment, and Society* 22, no. 4: 601–13.

– 2004. '"We Have the Values": Customers, Control, and Corporate Ideology in Call Centre Operations.' *New Technology, Work, and Employment* 19, no. 1: 2–13.

– 2002. 'Monitoring and Surveillance in Call Centres: Some Responses from Australian Workers.' *Labour and Industry* 12, no. 3: 43–58.

Van den Broek, D., G. Callaghan, and P. Thompson. 2004. 'Teams without Teamwork? Explaining the Call Centre Paradox.' *Economic and Industrial Democracy* 25, no. 2: 197–218.

Van Jaarsveld, D., A. Frost, and D. Walker. 2007. 'The Canadian Contact Centre Industry: Strategy, Work Organization, and Human Resource Management.' Global Call Centre Industry Project.

Van Maanen, J., and G. Kunda. 1989. '"Real Feelings": Emotional Expression and Organization Culture.' In *Research in Organizational Behaviour, Vol. 11*, ed. L. Cummings and B. Staw. 43–103. Greenwich: JAI.

Waddington, J., and C. Whitston. 1997. 'Why Do People Join Unions in a Period of Membership Decline?' *British Journal of Industrial Relations* 35, no. 4: 515–46.

Wagner, E., and S. Newell. 2006. 'Repairing ERP: Producing Social Order to Create a Working Information System.' *Journal of Applied Behaviour Science* 42, no. 1: 40–57.

Wallace, C., G. Eagleson, and R. Waldersee. 2000. 'The Sacrificial HR Strategy in Call Centres.' *International Journal of Service Industry Management* 11, no. 2: 174–84.

Warhurst, C., and P. Thompson. 1998. *Workplaces of the Future*. Hampshire: Macmillan Business.

Weiss, L. 1998. *The Myth of the Powerless State*. Ithaca: Cornell University Press.

Wharton, A. 1996. 'Service with a Smile: Understanding the Consequences of Emotional Labor.' In *Working in the Service Society*, ed. C. Macdonald and C. Sirianni. 91–112. Philadelphia: Temple University Press.

Whitener, E., and P. Walz. 1993. 'Exchange Theory Determinants of Affective and Continuance Commitment and Turnover.' *Journal of Vocational Behavior* 42, no. 3: 265–82.

Wilkinson, A., T. Redman, E. Snape, and M. Marchington, eds. 1998. *Managing with Total Quality Management: Theory and Practice*. Basingstoke: Macmillan.

Williams, K., C. Haslam, and J. Williams. 1992. 'Ford versus Fordism: The Beginning of Mass Production.' *Economy and Society* 6, no. 4: 517–55.

Willmott, H. 1993. 'Strength Is Ignorance; Slavery Is Freedom: Managing Culture in Modern Organizations.' *Journal of Management Studies* 39, no. 4: 515–52.

Willmott, H., and T. Bridgman. 2006. 'Institutions and Technology: Frameworks for Understanding Organizational Change – the Case of a Major ICT Outsourcing Contract.' *Journal of Applied Behavioral Science* 42, no. 1: 110–26.

Winiecki, D. 2004. 'Shadowboxing with Data: Production of the Subject in Contemporary Call Centre Organisations.' *New Technology, Work, and Employment* 19, no. 2: 78–95.

Wise, S., C. Smith, R. Valsecchi, F. Mueller, and J. Gabe. 2007. 'Controlling Working Time in the Ward and on the Line.' *Employee Relations* 29, no. 4: 352–66.

Womack, J., D. Jones, and D. Roos. 1990. *The Machine That Changed the World*. New York: Rawson Associates.

Wood, S. 1999. 'Getting the Measure of the Transformed High-Performance Organization.' *British Journal of Industrial Relations* 37, no. 3: 391–417.

Wray-Bliss, E. 2001. 'Representing Customer Service: Telephones and Texts.' In *Customer Service: Empowerment and Entrapment*, ed. A. Sturdy, I. Grugulis, and H. Willmott. 38–59. Houndmills: Palgrave.

Zapf, D., A. Isic, M. Bechtoldt, and P. Blau. 2003. 'What Is Typical for Call Centre Jobs? Job Characteristics and Service Interactions in Different Call Centres.' *European Journal of Work and Organizational Psychology* 12, no. 4: 311–40.

Zuboff, S. 1988. *In the Age of the Smart Machine*. New York: Basic.

Index

absenteeism, 13, 158, 237; in BPO, 267

abuse, of CSRs, 43, 124, 151, 180, 191, 222. *See also* emotional labour

accent neutralization. *See* training in Indian BPO

accreditation, in BPO, 20, 223–4

Ackroyd, S., 239

aesthetic labour, 16, 170

algorithms, 13, 135, 147, 148, 156. *See also* customer management software

alienation, 226

Alvesson, M., 176

America. *See* United States

apathy, 13

arbitrage. *See* employment arbitrage

archives. *See* data file management

attrition, 13; and commitment in BPO, 228; and emotional labour, 125; and employee resistance in BPO, 268; and gender, 83–4; and HPWS, 175, 229; and HRM in BPO, 224; in Indian BPO, 43, 47; in Indian case studies, 207–8; and labour markets, 63, 83; manager's responses to, 86–7; mass quitting, 158; in not-for-profits, 178–9; reasons for quitting, 84–5, 129; – in BPO, 209, 211, 230–1, 232–4; in relation to recruitment, 69, 72, 86, 280n4; and skill, 110–11, 119; – in BPO, 218; and stress in BPO, 223; and tech change, 139; among transferees, 132

Australian Council of Trade Unions (ACTU), 245; in success of anti–Work Choices campaign, 267

Australian Services Union (ASU), 39

Australian Teleservices Association (ATA), 25, 49, 133, 172, 280n6

Australian Workplace Agreements (AWAs), 247, 264, 268, 285n8; in case of study organizations, 254–5; outlawing of, 267. *See also* employment relations

automatic debit, 131, 144

automated call distribution (ACD), 8, 9, 36, 91, 136

automotive industry, 89

autonomy: example of, 123; and ICTs, 10; in Indian BPO, 211–13, 214; and labour force survey, 32; limits to, 107, 111, 128–9, 138, 150,

Studies in Comparative Political Economy and Public Policy